INTRODUCTORY READINGS IN
POLITICAL BEHAVIOR

INTRODUCTORY READINGS IN
POLITICAL BEHAVIOR

Edited by

S. SIDNEY ULMER, MICHIGAN STATE UNIVERSITY

RAND McNALLY & COMPANY

Chicago

RAND McNALLY POLITICAL SCIENCE SERIES

Morton Grodzins, *Advisory Editor*

PREFACE

OF the many approaches to the study of government and politics, none has received greater attention in recent times than the behavioral approach. This emphasis is not reflected, however, in the standard textbooks of political science, and one who would keep his students abreast of such developments is forced to retail the product through class lectures. It is a principal assumption of this volume that students of government should be exposed firsthand to the work being done by those who study and observe political life from a behavioral perspective.

The selections are chosen to illustrate the organization of theory and research around particular concepts, revealing in turn the marked diversity in inferential and concrete research findings which flow from conceptual variation. Continuity among the subdivisions is furnished through introductory notes which suggest the possibility of relating all concepts, in varying degrees, to that of socio-political system. Thus, a group may be seen as a particular type of system, decision-making as occurring within a system and as a response to system demands, communications as a form of the interaction common to all systems, power as the influence of system participants over the allocation of system resources, role as a coterie of behavioral expectations associated with a certain status, and elites as system members possessing disproportionate power or other values.

Although the readings were selected primarily for the reason stated above, several additional considerations were brought to bear on the choice. The first of these was comprehension at the undergraduate level. Under the leadership of Professor Joseph LaPalombara, the Department of Political Science at Michigan State University has for some time been concerned with upgrading and broadening the traditional introductory work in the discipline. As co-ordinator of the Department's introductory course, I have had a personal concern with that goal, and my interest in it has carried over to this volume. It is not suggested that every selection in this book is easily understood by all beginning freshmen; in a few cases, the material may be of use only at the graduate level. However, most of the readings (judging from experimental use with Michigan State students) are believed to be comprehensible to the alert undergraduate whether freshman or senior. While materials were chosen primarily to exemplify concepts, where alternatives were available substantive variation was promoted. Thus the illustrative pieces are drawn from all the major fields of political science.

By combining the goals of conceptual illustration, improved comprehension, and substantive variation, the resulting volume is thought to be particularly flexible. It may be used in a survey course in political behavior, whether at the graduate or undergraduate level, and as a supplement in introductory courses in political science or American government thereby broadening the traditional offering. Finally, in any substantive area those selections drawn from that particular field may serve to illustrate the behavioral focus in the field.

The editor wishes to extend his appreciation to the various authors whose work appears in these pages. In particular I should like to thank the following publishers for permission to quote from their materials in my article, "Homeostatic Tendencies in the United States Supreme Court." Felix Frankfurter, "Mr. Justice Roberts," 104 *University of Pennsylvania Law Review,* 311, 1955; John P. Frank, *Marble Palace,* Alfred A. Knopf, 1958; John W. Thibaut and Harold H. Kelley, *The Social Psychology of Groups,* John Wiley and Sons, Incorporated, 1959; and Talcott Parsons, Robert F. Bales, Edward A. Shils, *Working Papers in the Theory of Action,* The Free Press of Glencoe, Illinois, 1953.

TABLE OF CONTENTS

Preface

Introduction

Chapter TEN   Elites

INTRODUCTORY READINGS IN
POLITICAL BEHAVIOR

INTRODUCTION

TO a lesser degree than the physical sciences, the social sciences at any point in time are characterized not by what they have been but by what they are becoming. The continually enlarging focus of attention which has characterized political science since 1880 is an excellent illustration of this point. To our preoccupation with political doctrine, public law, and comparative government, we have added a concern for political parties, pressure groups, and administrative agencies. This has enabled us to define what have become the traditional areas of political science as political theory, political parties, international relations, and political institutions. Study in each of these four general fields has had its particular features. In political theory we have focused on the relations between man and state and devoted our time to analyzing the writings of the past. The field of political institutions has given greatest attention to the framework of rules (written and unwritten) by which the business of politics is conducted. In parties we have been concerned primarily with the role of the party in a democracy and how that role relates to success at the polls. Finally, in international relations the greater proportion of time has been allocated to international law and to international issues viewed within the formal structure of world and regional organizations.

While each area of study has been unique in its way, a common deficiency has characterized each of them. That deficiency is basically one of degree, but it involves, in general, failure to give adequate recognition and emphasis to the human factor in political affairs. Politics—no matter how defined—is, or involves, people, what they do, and why. It is just such a recognition that gives point to the study of political behavior. The political behavior orientation is not a substitute for other perspectives, but supplements the approaches to knowledge which have been and continue to be the hallmark of more traditional workways. All research into politics and government in the final analysis shares a common goal, i.e., to give meaning to the political phenomena which we experience. This is no less true of the traditional approaches with their focus on events, ideologies, institutions, and structures than of the behavioral orientation which features the analysis of personal and group behavior in a political context.

1

While theory building must begin with the establishment of existing fact, political facts may be significant only insofar as they are connected with other facts to form laws or generalizations. A major purpose of political research is to find such connections. When we have accumulated an adequate number of laws and significant concepts, it is generally useful to arrange this material into an axiomatic system or theory. This involves the construction of a set of axioms (laws temporarily taken for granted), definitions, and the theorems that follow from them. It is toward the development of a body of theory formally rationalizing experienced political phenomena that many political scientists are now working.

It is only when viewed in this light that some of the fundamental differences between those working from the traditional and behavioral perspectives are revealed. This is not to say that important differences of focus, emphasis, and method are nonexistent. The political behavior approach *does,* after all, *focus* on behavior and the psychological and sociological variables which affect it; the behavioral orientation *is interdisciplinary* and it *does stress* the inextricable relationship of theory and research. But, most important, the behavioral approach involves certain assumptions which may be said to characterize it. These assumptions can be grouped together and expressed as the belief that laws of human behavior exist and are subject to discovery. Now, what does this mean? It does not in any way imply that a science of politics or political behavior can produce results comparable to those yielded by the study of matter. Social scientists are not privileged to work with materials which behave consistently in terms of universal physical principles. For the political or social scientist, time and place are more crucial. Evidence to date suggests few universal laws; and the great role of environment in shaping human behavior is now established.

Moreover the political or social scientist is, on the whole, deprived of the experimental setting used so fruitfully by the physicist. The large number of social and psychological variables with which the social scientist must deal make control difficult and findings tentative. Finally, social scientists have yet to reach the agreement on methods and procedures which is generally found in the physical sciences. Thus it is seen that the basic assumptions underlying the political behavior approach must, of necessity, be less extreme than might be imagined and must incorporate a conscious recognition of the difficulties and limitations inherent in any attempt to develop a science of man or human behavior. But short of the relative certitudes of the physical sciences, the behavioral sciences reflect a belief that some advance from the present state of the social disciplines may be made. Such progress does not require that we emulate the absolute character of Galileo's law of falling bodies which states that the distance a released body falls varies directly with the square of its time $(d = 16t^2)$. We may seek to identify and express uniformities in political behavior and the conditions and requisites associated with such uniformities on a probability basis.

Such a probabilistic approach, when applied to social data, is not free from limitations of time, place, and circumstance. But even so, such expressions may be useful as well as informative. There is advantage in knowing, for example, the probability that Catholics will vote democratic or the probability that democratic judges will support civil liberty claims. The nature of our goal is responsible for two of the major characteristics of the political behavior approach. Our search for probabilistic laws of human behavior requires a large number of observations. Indeed, confidence in such laws is directly related to the number of times we have experienced or observed the phenomena in question. Probability theory cannot be as fruitfully applied to institutions such as legislative bodies, courts, or executive agencies since the number of such institutions at any one time is relatively small. The behavioral focus is in essence a focus on action or the acts of individuals or groups in various social settings. The immediate increase in our observational universe which is gained by shifting attention from institutions to behavior increases the relevance of probability theory for the analysis of political data.

The second major feature of the political behavior approach is the marked predilection for quantification. This tendency is motivated by the necessity of dealing with great quantities of action or behavior and concern for the requirements of scientific method. The former requires no further comment; the latter reflects the nature of the knowledge which the behavioral scientist is trying to produce. Scientific method supplies knowledge that can be transmitted from person to person *qua* knowledge. Arnold Brecht calls this "intersubjectively transmissible knowledge." In simple language this means knowledge that can be communicated from any person to another as long as the recipient comprehends the meaning of the words and signs used and is able to perform the operations described in the transmission. This does not imply that the recipient of such a communication must accept what is transmitted either as to the exactness of observation or validity of conclusions. For what is communicated is evidence—not conclusions. A major function of scientific method is to exclude nontransmissible evidence such as intuition, religious revelations, or private knowledge.

The behavioral sciences, as a result, stress the value of developing and utilizing more precise techniques for observing, classifying, and measuring data. For it is by the development of such techniques that the possibilities of communication to and replication by other interested scholars are maximized. It is precisely this requirement of scientific method that is largely responsible for the widespread use of quantitative techniques by those who analyze behavior. Statistical theory and associated procedures introduce precision into discussions of evidence and inference and improve the chances of replication. Since these tools are applicable primarily to quantified materials, the behavioral sciences lean heavily to the use of such data. As the readings in this volume well illustrate, those working from the behavioral perspective have done much to stimulate our thinking in new directions. And in so doing they have been instrumental in increasing the amount of effort being devoted to the production and transmission of scientific knowledge within the discipline.

PART I

Behavior and its Determinants

CHAPTER ONE

INTRODUCTION
TO
POLITICAL BEHAVIOR

RECENTLY, a group of political scientists published a collection of essays under the title: "Approaches to the Study of Politics." Such a title suggests that there are many paths to political knowledge. The various approaches are commonly differentiated in terms of the basic unit of analysis and the methods applicable to the unit chosen. The unit selected for analysis may be an institution such as a court, a legislative body, or an adminstrative agency or it may be a text such as the writings of Plato, Hobbes, and other political philosophers. The behavioral approach identifies the behavior of individuals or groups of individuals in political situations as the primary unit of analysis. In so doing it rejects political institutions and other more traditional foci of analysis as primary units for research. It should not be thought, however, that the behavioral scientist has no interest in institutions; a behavioral study may have implications for institutional development and function maintenance. Thus the institution is often a secondary consideration of the analyst.

In the selections which follow, Samuel Eldersveld and his colleagues enumerate in more detail what those who describe themselves as political behavioralists are attempting. In addition, David Truman discusses briefly the consequences of the recent vigorous activity in the behavioral sciences for political science.

Research in Political Behavior

SAMUEL J. ELDERSVELD, ALEXANDER HEARD,
SAMUEL P. HUNTINGTON, MORRIS JANOWITZ,
AVERY LEISERSON, DAYTON D. McKEAN,
DAVID B. TRUMAN

POLITICAL BEHAVIOR AND POLITICAL SCIENCE

Political behavior is not a field of political science. Rather, political behavior research is one way of studying most of the customary subject matter of political science. The political behavior approach is distinguished by its attempt to describe government as a process made up of the actions and interactions of men and groups of men. It is concerned, at the minimum—as is all political science—with the activities of governments, political parties, interest groups, and voters. The study of political behavior attempts to discover the extent and nature of uniformities in the actual behavior of men and groups of men in the political process.

This approach involves two basic requirements. In the first place, it calls for the formulation of concepts, hypotheses, and explanations in systematic terms, borrowing wherever appropriate from other social sciences. Secondly, it depends upon empirical methods of research, whether adapted from other social sciences or developed distinctively, since the actions of men and groups cannot be known except through direct observation or through inference from other behavioral data.

The inquiry into how men *ought* to act is a separate concern of political science and is not a concern of political behavior research. Similarly, the studies of law, constitutions, and formal organization *per se,* all parts of established political science research, are not the focal point for the study of political behavior. Values, laws, and formal structure, however, are important in determining the behavior of men, and as such they are part of the data with which political behavior research is concerned. The political behavior approach implies no denial of values in the political process. It suggests, in fact, that the systematic observation of behavior is an especially useful way of understanding the character of values that operate in the political system. Likewise, the concern of political behavior research with the process of government involves no neglect of legal and constitutional structure. On the contrary, the political behavior approach seeks to go beyond the data supplied by constitutions, statutes, administrative decrees, or judicial decisions—themselves evidence, directly or indirectly, of political behavior—to a more complete description of governmental structure-in-action. It seeks to disclose sets of recurring patterns in the way people behave, involving relationships of leadership and subordination, functional specialization, and the like, which are in varying degrees changeable even though relatively persistent. Laws, after all, are always normative—they express standards or goals—and are only sometimes descriptive of actual behavior. The statement of the conditions under which they are descriptive, and when they are not, is one of the tasks of political behavior research.

The political behavior approach is not a completely new way of studying government. It is rather an orientation which can be traced back many years and which deserves renewed emphasis. Work has been done in the study of political parties and pressure groups which utilizes this approach, and there is a sensitivity to it in the study of public administration and other governmental areas. The path of political behavior research was, indeed, staked out by Charles E. Merriam in his presidential address to the American Political Science Association in 1925. At that time he prophesied:

Some day we may take another angle of approach than the formal, as other sciences tend to do, and begin to look at political behavior as one of the essential objects of inquiry. Government, after all, is not made up merely of documents, containing laws and rules, or of structures of a particular form, but is fundamentally based upon patterns of action in types of situations.

POLITICAL BEHAVIOR AND SOCIAL SCIENCE

A principal reason for the emphasis upon political behavior research at this time is the use which can be made of new theories, concepts, and research techniques developed in other fields of social science. Although the study of political behavior is concerned with the actions of men and groups of men in politics, there are basic similarities between the actions of men and groups of men in politics and the actions of men and groups of men in other social institutions and situations. Consequently, many of the techniques and concepts developed, particularly by psychology, social psychology, and sociology, for the study of human behavior in general are applicable to the study of human behavior in politics.

As new techniques and concepts are evolved in related disciplines, they afford new opportunities to the student of political behavior to reappraise his own problems, theories, and methods. This does not mean that the procedures of other social sciences can be incorporated in their entirety into political behavior research. Many of the concerns of these other sciences are not relevant to the study of the political process. This is especially true of those which deal with experimental laboratory situations after the manner of the natural sciences. The interest of the student of political behavior is more in being systematic about political realities than in being systematic in experimental situations from which to reason by analogy about politics. But this does not alter the fact that political behavior research in political science can benefit immensely from a selective use of the theories, concepts, and techniques of the other social sciences. Nor are the benefits of such adaptation likely to accrue only to the study of politics. A genuinely behavioral science of politics is essential to the full development of general social science.

The political behavior approach requires important use of historical knowledge. As a matter of convenience and in the interest of completeness of data, research in current and immediately observable political behavior is necessarily emphasized. Some types of basic data may never be collected unless they are collected by contemporary observation. Over the years, data on past behavior patterns, preserved unsystematically and by chance, may become lost or difficult to interpret. Some kinds of data on political behavior, however, will not become available to researchers until some time after the behaviors occur. Moreover, an adequate description of current behavior may require an understanding of those continuities, social habits, and traditions which are reflected in contemporary attitudes and actions.

POLITICAL BEHAVIOR AND RESEARCH METHODS

The view that the actions and interactions of men make up the process of governing requires primary focus upon systematic research and necessitates the use of empirical methods. Such interactions cannot be known except through observation of them or at least through other observations from which they can be more or less directly inferred. In other words, the units of the data must always be reducible to terms of the observed behavior and relationships of men.

In its use of the empirical method, political behavior research attempts to reduce its assumptions to explicit propositions and concepts and always to increase the generality of its explanations. The accomplishment of this aim requires a systematic statement of assumptions and hypotheses—as attempted in the research plans in this report—and a rigorous ordering of evidence. The general objective presupposes empiricism, but not crude and indiscriminate empiricism. Rather its requires a systematic statement of hypotheses and a rigorous ordering of evidence which will permit: (1) the effective identification of behavioral uniformities and the conditions under which they are to be expected; (2) ease of replication and validation in successive researches; and (3) an accretion of systematic knowledge of the institutions upon which attention is focused.

The political behavior approach thus has as its basic objectives the identification of the recurring uniformities of political activity and the development of generalizations about political action. To this end it requires the formulation of concepts that can be tested by successive researches and that will facilitate the building of a body of systematic knowledge about various phases of the political process. These aspirations do not necessarily imply that it is possible to reduce all political behavior to known causal relations and thereby achieve complete predictability and control in the political process. They do imply, however, that it is possible to achieve a deeper understanding of political institutions and processes by tracing, to a greater extent than has been done in the past, the uniformities of political behavior and the conditions under which they may be expected to appear.

Because the political behavior orientation implies a major emphasis upon systematic research and upon empirical method, it aims at being quantitative wherever possible. But it cannot be limited by such possibilities. The political scientist cannot escape the obligation and must not deny himself the opportunity to ask important questions, important in the description of the political process, simply because his answers must be more or less qualitative. He deals with the political institution and he must systematically reckon with that assignment, whether in qualitative or in quantitative terms.

The Impact on Political Science of the Revolution in the Behavioral Sciences

DAVID B. TRUMAN

The term "behavioral sciences" is one of recent currency, and its variable meanings may, without a word or two of explanation, cause some confusion. It is sometimes used as an equivalent for the social sciences, a loose usage that is probably inevitable as long as the term is fashionable and is thought to provide a key to foundation cash boxes. More narrowly, and perhaps more accurately, the phrase refers to those bodies of knowledge, in whatever academic department they may be found, that provide or aspire to provide "verified principles" of human behavior through the use of methods of inquiry similar to those of the natural sciences. In conventional university organization, such knowledge and such aspirations may be found in a vari-

Reprinted from *Research Frontiers in Politics and Government: Brookings Lectures 1955,* pp. 202–31 by permission of The Brookings Institution. Copyright 1955 by The Brookings Institution.

ety of places, from schools of public health to departments of linguistics, but their incidence is normally greatest in departments of psychology, sociology, and anthropology, and the term most commonly serves as a shorthand expression for the concerns typical of these three fields. This restricted meaning is the one that I shall use.

DEVELOPMENTS IN THE BEHAVIORAL SCIENCES

Whether or not they merit glorifying by the word "revolution," the developments in the behavioral sciences in the past three decades have been numerous and impressive. . . .

For present purposes it is appropriate to examine these developments under two headings: developments in the realm of research technique and those in the realm of expanded theory and verified propositions. The first of these is, significantly, far easier and less treacherous to evaluate than the second, partly because development of the tools of data collection and analysis has been rapid and unmistakable.

IN RESEARCH TECHNIQUE.   The techniques of the sample survey can claim a place at the top of any list of such developments, not only because they constitute a basic instrument of social research in their own right, but also because their refinement has stimulated a series of achievements, primarily in the invention of ancillary techniques but also to some extent in the construction of explanatory theory. The roots of this technique are fairly old, indeed ancient if one traces them back to the unsystematic efforts of politicians and journalists to estimate the intentions of a mass electorate. The core of the skill, however, is the design and administration of the population sample, and this is comparatively modern. Stimulated by the commercial utility of even fairly crude estimates of intentions and susceptibilities of consumers, rudimentary techniques of population sampling became a commonplace device in the business world by the 1920's. The potentialities of population sampling for non-commercial, social, and political research, however, were not widely recognized until the 1930's. Partly as a means of promoting the acceptance of these techniques in market analysis and partly as an opportunity for testing them against the official results of elections, polling of samples of prospective voters developed in the middle of the 1930's. What began as a by-product extended into fairly continuous surveys of popular opinion on various issues of the day, until "Gallup poll" became a generic term familiar over the globe. . . .

Both the state of the art and the character of existing obstacles are suggested in the following comment in the essay on "statistical practice" in the *Encyclopaedia of the Social Sciences:* "It is so difficult to insure representativeness of the sample that in most inquiries relative to population complete enumeration is preferred."

"Representativeness" was a problem in practical sampling rather than in general theory. Experience with the quota sample, on which opinion surveyors relied in the 1930's, and the development of probability sampling by the Bureau of the Census and the Bureau of Agricultural Economics in the early 1940's reduced this problem to manageable proportions.

Paralleling and, in part, flowing from the growth of skill in sampling a number of techniques, both for the collection and for the analysis of data have been invented or significantly improved. Thus as the crudity of samples has been reduced, attention has been turned to the inadequacies in interviewing. The sources of unreliability have been explored and their bearing on the validity of results has been examined in systematic fashion, so that the dangers in this phase have been identified even though the means of controlling them have not been fully provided.

At the same time, criticism and experimentation have contributed materially to increasing sophistication in the design of survey questions and questionnaires and in the substantive aspects of interviews generally. Drawing on and adapting experience in counseling and psychotherapy, the design and administration of questions have come a long way from the intuitive, rather hit-or-miss techniques used in early opinion and community surveys. The merits of the open-ended question as compared with the fixed-alternative or "poll-type" question and of the focused or "depth" interview have been explored and developed to the point where the investigator's range of choice among interviewing tools has markedly widened.

In slightly different fashion the maturing of sample-survey methods has been stimulated by and has contributed to advances in techniques of measurement, notably the analysis of attitudes through the use of scales. The early work of Bogardus, Thurstone, and Likert was largely independent of the techniques of the sample survey. As the later devices have begun, however, to produce data of greater reliability, warranting the use of more precise techniques of analysis than the early polls justified and inviting more complicated sorts of inferences than they could support, the two research tendencies have come together. Significant steps have been taken, notably in the work of Guttman, Lazarsfeld, and others, to adapt and extend the earlier measurement devices, thereby stimulating significantly more penetrating analysis of survey data. Similarly, the survey device has been extended to approximate some of the power and efficiency of experimentation through the use of the so-called panel technique. By successive re-interviews of a population sample—the panel—it is possible to get at changes, and at some of the causes of changes, in attitudes and behavior.

The past two decades have also seen a considerable development and extension of experimentation, both in the controlled laboratory setting and in the natural situation. This has taken various forms. Among them are the numerous techniques for observing, recording, and analyzing behavior in small groups which, especially since the work of Elton Mayo and Kurt Lewin, have become the identifying equipment for specialists in the new "field" of group dynamics. Among these, reference should also be made to the techniques collectively known as sociometry, devised by J. L. Moreno for the analysis of interaction and influence structure in small groups. These and related developments, whether employed in the laboratory or in the "field," not only have contributed a considerable body of information on face-to-face groups of various sorts but also have provided stimulus to greater sophistication in observational field work generally.

Finally, it may be appropriate to mention the elaboration and expansion of the techniques for analyzing communications content. Although their beginnings run back considerably more than twenty-five years, the skills of the content analyst, especially with respect to the devices for systematic classification and for quantitative analysis, have received a marked degree of extension and refinement within the past two decades.

This cursory and necessarily superficial glance at some recent developments in the behavioral sciences is sufficient at least to suggest that within the realm of technique it is reasonable to speak of major developments. One may legitimately think of this as a technological revolution, even if one concludes that, unlike other such changes, its consequences are limited.

IN THEORY.   When one turns to the realm of theory, especially theory resting on some measure of empirical verification, the task of evaluation becomes considerably more formidable. Not only are theories in the behavioral sciences numerous, but the possible implications of these formulations for the work of the political scientist have scarcely been explored. Any comment on this point, therefore, is likely to be superficial and subject to serious challenge.

At the risk of indulging in severe oversimplification, I should like to venture the observation that in the realm of theory the behavioral sciences have produced two quite different bodies of propositions, one rather narrowly concerned with individual behavior or with action in small, face-to-face groups and the other aimed at an inclusive explanation of a wide range of action not specifically relevant to any particular institutional context. Although it is doubtful that in either of these there is much in the way of revolutionary content, both have some value for the student of political processes and institutions. At the same time, however, neither more than approaches a solution to the most troublesome problems in such study. The difficulty of estimating the existing or the probable impact of behavioral science theory on political science lies precisely in the gap between these two statements. Behavioral science theory has implications of value to the student of politics, but it goes no more than part of the way toward the solution of his intellectual problems.

So sweeping a characterization cannot, certainly within the limits of a single lecture, be proved, but it clearly calls at least for illustration and for argument. I should assert that a sizable fraction of behavioral science theory, whether in psychology, sociology, or anthropology, is non-institutional. That is, it is principally concerned with explaining the effects of a given institutional pattern on the behavior of an individual or an aggregate of individuals and not with explaining or even describing the operation of the institution itself. Thus, of course, all or almost all of psychology is individual. The preoccupations of psychology are with categories and processes of individual behavior—learning, conditioning, motivation, perception, discrimination, and so on. Again, despite the existence of competing doctrines, a major preoccupation remains the characteristics and development of individual personality under the influence of physiological and, more recently, social factors.

The growth of social psychology has increased the number and kinds of factors considered in the whole gamut of psychological analysis, but it has not changed the emphasis. Concerned with the behavior of men in groups, the social psychologist is nevertheless characteristically interested in the effects of group environments on the behavior of individuals, in the individual psychology of interpersonal influence.

For understandable reasons the environments most closely studied by the social psychologist have been those of small, face-to-face groups, whether in experimental or natural situations—family, club, classroom, gang, clique, and neighborhood. These groupings are more amenable to the requirements of scientific procedure than are more inclusive formations. It seems probable, moreover, that if one is concerned principally with effects on individual behavior, such groups are primary, in the sense of degree of importance, and therefore peculiarly basic to the discipline.

Not all concerns with the small group have been exclusively psychological, of course. As the curiosities and theories of the investigator become more characteristically sociological, they are less concerned with effects on individuals than with the structure of groups and with the effects on group performance resulting from differences in intragroup communication, from variations in the performance of specialized roles within the group, and from variations in the tasks undertaken by it.

This borderland of psychology, sociology, and anthropology, which has come to be known most commonly as group dynamics, has produced a respectable body of theory, both basic and applied, notably on the subject of leadership. Its preoccupations, however, are only slightly less microcosmic than those of the psychologist and are only slightly less non-institutional. . . .

Although the sociological and anthropological concern with small groups, which considerably antedates the more psychologically oriented research in group dynamics, has been more likely to place the group in a larger institutional context and to investigate changes stemming from such contexts, its focus has remained the small unit. The broadest reach in empirical terms within these fields, moreover, has been the small city or community, although perhaps exception should be made of some kinds of broad, aggregative research concerned with social class and demography. The formulation of theory of a more inclusive sweep has not been, strictly speaking, the objective or the product of the efforts of the behavioral scientist. That function has been left to the more historically and philosophically inclined sociologist or anthropologist, concerned with reflections about the state of society, in the tradition of Max Weber and Mannheim, or to speculative synthesizing like that of Talcott Parsons.

By way of . . . summary, the developments in the behavioral sciences over the past quarter century, thus cursorily and perhaps somewhat unfairly reviewed, appear a good deal more revolutionary in the realm of technique than in that of validated and expanded theory. Both the characteristic techniques, moreover, and the tested propositions of which the number is considerable, typically have been microcosmic. Both have concentrated on the individual or on the restricted group to the virtual exclusion of larger organizations and more inclusive institutions.

Though this concentration has occurred, one should not assume that in either respect the behavioral sciences have no relevance for the political scientist. But it should not be astonishing that their area of greatest impact to date has been in connection with the study of voting behavior, the most individualized, in a sense most uncomplicated, and perhaps least important element in the political process. The theory that has emerged, largely through the use of the sample survey technique, is exclusively a social psychological theory of electoral choice, with only the barest suggestions of implications for other features of the electoral or political process.

A further word should be said, however, concerning theoretical developments in behavioral science. Whatever the limits on its scope and on its applicability to the problems of the political scientist, theory in the behavioral sciences has become far more completely fused with empirical research and theorizing has become more self-consciously central to the concerns of investigators than was the case shortly after World War I. One has the distinct impression that the volume of taxonomic description of concrete phenomena has declined and that there has occurred an increased and general commitment to the discovery of uniformities, to the use of observation for the verification of hypotheses, and to the search for empirically supported generalizations.

The traces of this can be seen in several areas not far from the concerns of the political scientist. As Herbert Simon has pointed out . . . significant beginnings have been made on an organizational theory, although it cannot yet help us much in dealing with large and complicated structures. From various sources in the behavioral sciences the suggestive concept of role has been developed, through which a number of significant propositions of potentially broad relevance have been formulated. Some preliminary elements of a theory of communications are beginning to appear. Along somewhat different lines, there has been an increasing interest in the creation and exploitation of formal models, of which the theory of games . . . is a major example. Whatever one may think of the utility of any such models, and in my opinion skepticism is in order, experimenting with them at least represents a serious theoretical preoccupation. Much the same thing may be said of the efforts of Parsons and his associates to develop a general theory of action. This inclusive effort at a high level of abstraction admittedly seems to promise to be valid immediately only for relatively simple features of a social system. Whether or not one shares the implied faith that the treatment of more complex characteristics is almost within reach, one must acknowledge that this effort, along with less ambitious theoretical endeavors, nevertheless represents a considerable degree of ferment—a renewed commitment to theory and to the discovery and statement of behavioral uniformities.

CHAPTER TWO

PSYCHOLOGICAL BASES
OF
POLITICAL BEHAVIOR

THIS section and the one following focus on the question: "How do we account for differences in political behavior?" An attempted answer may start from the premise that man is a unique creation of the forces of nature. One cannot proceed very far, however, without considering the nature of man or more specifically the psychological make-up of the person. For while the influence of environment on human behavior may be accepted, the particular form in which its consequences are manifest cannot always be explained by analyses of the social environment. Thus, an understanding of political behavior may require an understanding of the psychology of the person, as well as the environment to which the personality is exposed.

The personality of the individual may, therefore, be considered the result of two basic factors. There is first the organic foundation of personality reflected in such things as physical make-up, reflexes, drives, intelligence, temperament, and mass movement. These elements, of course, operate as a limitation on the types of attitudes, habits, and ideas which develop in group life. But more importantly they provide a vast range of potential behavior patterns which may be called forth by culture, the second basic factor in personality development. Within the limitations imposed by original nature, therefore, the individual will develop a personality reflecting the behavior and attitudes of his particular subgroup in society. This view of

18

man's nature as being essentially plastic differs drastically from that represented by Thomas Hobbes who believed that in a state of nature man's natural personality was free to express itself and did so through conflict, war, and other hostile behavior. Modern psychology replaces the static concept of Hobbes with one which recognizes personality as resulting from the interaction of original nature and social environment.

Since political behavior may be influenced by personality, psychological knowledge of the individual cannot be safely ignored. The following selections focus on the role of personality in political life. John McConaughy's study suggests that certain distinct personality types seem drawn to legislative institutions as a framework for need-satisfying behavior. Robert Lane shows that variations in psychological needs relate significantly to the acceptance or rejection of politically espoused goals. The idea that general dispositions and concrete political attitudes are intimately associated is argued by Harold Lasswell in a nonstatistical piece and by Herbert McClosky in a paper utilizing the tools of modern social research. Leon Kamin supports this contention with his finding that a voting decision may turn on such things as the ethnic connotation of a candidate's name.

In none of this, however, is it necessary to assume that personality is always a prime factor in explaining political behavior. As Edward Shils points out, attitudes must be distinguished from behavior. The authoritarian personality (even if we can identify him) does not necessarily engage in authoritarian behavior. Thus, some situations afford considerable scope for personality to affect behavior, while in other situations behavior is so structured as to be relatively immune from personality influences. The second type of situation will be considered in Chapter Three.

Psychology Looks at Morals and Politics

HAROLD D. LASSWELL

In common with any branch of social and political science psychology bears an instrumental relationship to morals and politics. Our moral values are acquired from the interplay of original nature with the culture into which we are born; our values are derived from that part of culture that includes the basic postulates of metaphysics and theology; our values are implemented by the part of culture called science and practice (including psychology and politics).

If there is any universal human experience it is this one: Moral inten-

Reprinted from *Ethics* (April 1941), pp. 325–36 by permission of The University of Chicago Press. Copyright 1941 by The University of Chicago.

tions are often frustrated by weaknesses of which the individual is aware, yet feels incapable of removing. The relationship of psychological knowledge to many such cases of moral frustration is benign, for by the timely application of this knowledge the moral intention may be properly implemented. Soldiers who want to fight for their country are often prevented from doing so by sudden seizures of panic, by sudden attacks of blindness, by partial paralysis of arms and legs. These are the shell-shock cases that appear in any war, especially in wars where nonprofessional soldiers are recruited to the armed forces and exposed to danger. The sufferers may be individuals who sincerely desire to fulfil their patriotic duty; yet they are prevented by crippling weakness. Patient psychological observation has disclosed many of the causes that contribute to these traumatic seizures and has devised methods of relief. Often the sufferer has struggled to keep out of his mind both the fear of death and the feeling of self-contempt for experiencing fear. By his struggle against these disrupting and embarrassing thoughts and feelings, the soldier intensified his level of anxiety to an unbearable degree, and found partial relief in self-crippling reactions—the symptoms of shell shock—panic, blindness, paralysis. His personality was divided against itself. Such personalities can be assisted by appropriate psychological methods to achieve integration, hence to free themselves from the dominance of impulses that frustrate moral purpose.

The spectacle of frustrated moral intention is familiar in the ordinary experiences of civilian life. One is reminded in this connection of the history of a successful young lawyer who became inspired with the determination to rid his city of graft and corruption. He put his dynamic energy and professional skill at the service of a citizens' organization that began to make a genuine impression on local politics. But there was a serious flaw in the program; the intentions of the young lawyer were continually running into difficulties because of his alcoholic excesses. From time to time he was seized by an insatiable thirst and went on a debauch that lasted several days. He was no silent, morose, retiring drinker who gloomily contemplated suicide in splendid isolation as his conscience slowly dissolved in alcohol; he belonged, rather, to the irritable variety whose sensitiveness to insult becomes progressively more acute as his perceptions of reality grow dim. He frequently held doormen, waiters, and even casual pedestrians responsible for alleged indignities heaped upon him. Hence the crusader for civic virtue occasionally figured in a public brawl, casting himself and his cause into disrepute. Fortunately something is known about a few of the many varieties of excessive alcoholism. This civic leader belonged to one of the more benign and better understood varieties, the proper psychological measures relieved him of his illness, thus removing an almost fatal barrier to his good intentions.

Less spectacular are the problems of those administrators who struggle against a conspicuous defect in their handling of others. One administrator, otherwise impeccable, was continually subject to angry outbursts against colleagues and subordinates. He struggled manfully against his "failing," this internal check on the achievement of his intention to set a praiseworthy pattern of administrative conduct. For a while he tried to gain self-control by will power. He tried all the standard remedies of folklore—he "counted to ten," but even when he counted to ten times ten, he still took the hide off his subordinates when the arithmetic was over. Often such rudimentary expedients work; but the personality structure of this man contained so many incompatible tendencies that he had need of less ritualistic and more insightful methods.

All these men frustrated their best intentions. Psychological study showed that they defeated themselves by turning destructive impulses against themselves. More than that, the root of their destructiveness was found in some lack of respect for themselves. The "terrible tempered Mr. Bang," the administrator with the irascible temper, was a man who was struggling against certain tendencies to treat himself with contempt. It was found that his eruptions were connected with situations in which he was thrown with persons of more commanding physique than his own. By patient self-observation, he obtained insight into the degree to which his adjustments to life had been determined by his feelings of helplessness, and of compensating rage, at his diminutive body build. Such negative valuations of the self were not part of his conscious waking life. On the contrary, he automatically deflected his attention from his slightness of stature and failed to see the full intensity of his self-contempt, and to free himself from its destructive results.

There is no doubt that the young lawyer and civic crusader who disgraced himself and his cause was acting destructively. Here, again, the significant source of his destructive impulses was severe anxiety about the status of the self. His drunken orgies came just after crises in which he was excessively tense, excessively intent upon the persuasion of others. The moment the ordeal was over, he relapsed into a state of weak self-indulgence. Through it all he was screening from himself the contempt that he felt for himself as one who was so excessively dependent upon the favorable emotional responses of other people. His concern about being unmanly was one of the most embarrassing threats to his self-respect.

The disciplined study of human personality has confirmed the ancient saying that the enemy of man is man, is man's own destructiveness. And more: the causes of destructive impulses have been painstakingly explored, and the upshot is to emphasize anew the pathogenic importance of insufficient self-respect. We can recognize these basic relations the most readily in the lives of children. We are familiar with the child who bullies weaker playmates, and we know how often this is connected with deep concern about the status of the self and represents an overcompensation against ridicule for a weak and flabby appearance. We know, too, the timid and "beaten" child, wholly withdrawn into itself, hopeless of affection. Destructive impulses spring in no slight degree from deficient self-respect; these impulses may be discharged, in part, against other persons, as with the bully, or against the self, as with the "beaten" child.

These basic relations, so easy to grasp with reference to children, we often fail to extend to the whole of life, where they apply with equal truth. Part of the difficulty here is the complex interrelationship of destructive impulses and destructive practices. Even though we are in control of our own destructive tendencies, we may act destructively upon others. Despite our good intentions, even when we have been emancipated from self-crippling reactions, we may still have destructive effects upon other people. A great barrier to moral achievement, in addition to insufficient self-knowledge, is insufficient knowledge of the institutional routines of society and their effect upon others.

A typical problem of this kind confronts the administrator who sincerely desires to contribute to the welfare of others, yet finds it difficult to obtain the needed facts about the lives of other people and the way they are affected by official acts. The head of a huge department of government may earnestly seek to contribute to the realization of a democratic society. He may understand that such a society is a commonwealth of mutual deference, a community in which there is opportunity for the maturing of talent into socially useful skill. Assume that this administrator is put in charge of many local communities, such as those of a resettlement administration. How is he to find out the facts about the impact of his administrative decisions upon the quality of living in these villages?

Moral intentions, we repeat, call for more than self-knowledge. They must be implemented by reliable knowledge of the attitudes of other people through time and of the factors that affect them. This is a realm to which modern psychological observation has made steady contribution. It is no longer necessary for the administrator to rely exclusively upon the hasty impressions of a busy field trip, or upon occasional petitions and protests. Competent participating observers can record their experience with fidelity and make it available to decision-makers. Sometimes the results show that democratic processes lack vitality because the local manager of the community has failed to maintain genuine consultation. It is obvious that democracy requires that people shall participate in the decisions that most concern them; but many community managers grow slack, and the frequency of democratic consultation dwindles toward zero. The observer can assemble the facts that are needed to portray the fluctuating volume of democratic processes of consultation. Fewer and fewer citizens may take part in community meetings. More and more citizens, when interviewed under conditions that encourage candor, may express scepticism about "what good it does" to take a hand in collective activities. The complaint may be that the local manager has no real influence and that the central administration at Washington does what it pleases. Washington seems far away and capricious in its decisions. A checkup over a period of several months may reveal that the central administrators have taken many decisions without clarifying— much less consulting—the local community. Busy administrators, despite all of their sincerity, often fail to clarify—and one way to defer to the personality of another is to make clear to him what is going on. A checkup may also show that the government appears most often in a deprivational role—as a tax collector, a rent collector, an evictor, and the like. Seldom if ever does the government express appreciation for a job well done. And expressions of appreciation are among the most rudimentary, yet important, ways of contributing to the self-respect of deserving people.

In a democratic society, then, we are concerned about the flow of appreciation, of clarification, of consultation—for these are the specifics of deference. When men and women are deferred to, they are appreciated, clarified, consulted. Whatever practices interfere with the flow of mutual respect, and arouse destructive impulses, endanger the fulfilment of a democratic order.

Manifestly the enemy of a democratic society is human destructiveness in all its forms—destructive impulses, destructive practices. If our moral intention is to realize a democratic society, we need a science of democracy to implement the goal. Such a science will draw heavily upon the findings and the observational methods of psychology, especially since psychological methods are the means especially appropriate to the discovery of the human consequences of living under any social order. Some of the methods of psychology are appropriate to the cultivation of self-knowledge by candid self-observation, in this way reducing the frustration of moral intentions by incompatible tendencies within the personality itself. And by the proper correlation of psychological methods with other scientific procedures we may gain the knowledge needed to identify and to control destructive practices no less than destructive impulses.

Institutional practices are destructive when they arouse great concentrations of destructive impulse. It is evident that profound crises of destructiveness are fostered by irregularity in the tempo of social change and by lack of balance in social structure. Whatever contributes to such irregularities and unbalance is dangerously destructive.

Irregularity of social change places too great a burden upon the capacity of men to adjust to their environment. Those who increase abruptly in influence are prone to act destructively—to behave with arrogant lack of consideration toward their fellows. Those who are made suddenly weak are also provoked to destructiveness—and take out their hostilities against themselves or others.

Our modern world has conspicuously suffered from the destructive crises nourished by irregularities that we can attribute to lack of control over the machine. Thanks to the rapid introduction of machine methods of production, the carriers of Western European civilization imposed their will upon peoples throughout the world—upsetting established patterns of life, precipitating colossal problems of immediate adaptation. The humiliations to which non-European peoples were subjected led to those vindictive movements of revenge against European hegemony that we witness today.

The abrupt change in the comparative strength of European states intensified the difficulties of harmonious adjustment among the bearers of European civilization itself. Rival arrogances—made more lethal by the gadgets of a machine society—doomed the citizens of every modern power to increasing insecurity of life and limb.

In addition to the crises among European and non-European peoples, and to the clashes of European peoples with one another, our world has witnessed the crises generated in the process of modifying the internal structure of every modern society. The rapid emergence of the specialist on market manipulation—on bargaining, the businessman—put in positions of influence in society men who were not specialists upon the harmonious adjustment of men in society.

The insecurities that were generated by irregular social development were intensified by the imbalances that were accentuated in the structure of a given society. By social structure we mean the basic practices that prevail at a given time and place in the distribution of values among the members of a community. The influence of any group is measured by its control over values—by its share in the deference, income, and safety of the community. When values are highly concentrated in a few hands, the rule of balance is broken, and lack of balance in social structure contributes to insecurity. The destructive impulses of the predominant few are expressed in arrogant disregard of others; while the destructive impulses of the subordinated many are provoked into internalized or externalized forms of expression. An enemy of democracy is unbalanced social structure; and whatever practices undermine social balance are in need of exposure and revision.

What does it mean to achieve the rule of balance in society? A balanced social order achieves a commonwealth of mutual deference. To be deferred to is to be taken into consideration—to be consulted, appreciated, and clarified. In a democratic commonwealth there is a relatively general share in power, respect, and insight. To share in power is to be consulted on important decisions; decisions are the choices that are backed by the most deprivational sanctions at the disposal of society (usually violence). The function of government in any community is to make the most influential decisions. (The most influential communities in world-affairs are states.) The *function* of government is not, of course, to be confused with the *institution* of government; the institution of government is what happens to be called government in a given time and place. We know that the function of government may be but partly exercised by what is locally known as the institution of government. Indeed, as in the case of monopoly business corporations, the institution that exercises one of the important functions of government may be called "business."

To democratize power, then, is to maintain the practice of general participation in the making of influential decisions. Closely associated with the democratization of power is the democratization of respect; respect is another part of deference. To be respected is to be appreciated, and society is stratified into respect classes as well as into power classes or income classes. We can speak of power classes in the community, dividing the population into policy-makers, managers, and rank and file. (In a democracy, of course, the recruitment of policy-makers is on the basis of skill and popular responsibility.) When we speak of respect classes, we divide people according to degrees of reciprocal intimacy, according to intermarriage, mutual participation in clubs and social life. (Where the respect—or "social"—classes are immobile from one generation to another, we speak of them as "castes.")

Our own civilization has been conspicuously deficient in the practice of mutual respect. No more flagrant example could be found than the attitude taken up in nominally democratic societies toward those who were thrown out of work in the late collapse. It is true that not many of those who were squeezed out of the processes of production starved to death. Most of them were given enough to keep breath in their bodies. But we were not sensitive to the fact that men who are thrown out of employment are also thrown out of respect. We added insult to injury by stigmatizing these millions as "unemployed," by treating them as a burden on their fellow-men, a dead weight on the taxpayer, a mass of humanity for whom there was no longer a respected place in society. We kept them from dying, it is true, but we gave them no reason to live. We forgot that men want not only a job; they want security and opportunity on a respected job.

Some of the dictators have been more canny than some of the leaders of states aspiring toward democracy. Instead of a shovel and a job in a make-work program—open to vaudeville jokes and neighborhood insult— some of these dictators have given millions of young people a shovel and a job and a gun in the building of a new social order. It is impossible to exaggerate the loathing with which any friend of democracy looks upon many of the measures of totalitarian depotism, but it is unwise to forget that the partial success achieved by these despotisms is that they have appealed to the craving for respect that is a powerful characteristic of human personality.

To democratize the distribution of deference is to share power, respect, and insight. There is insight when there is a sense of common purpose—and an understanding of common methods—throughout the community. There is insight when men and women are equipped with the skill of observation that enables them to discover and to regulate their own destructive impulses. There is insight when there is a division of labor that specializes human energy upon the disciplined scrutiny of the established practices of society for the purpose of discovering those whose consequences are destructive.

The psychological sciences put squarely in the forefront of attention the human consequences of all the laws and customs of a given society. By appropriate methods of observation it is possible to discern the degree to which any set of established practices operates destructively upon human nature by stimulating destructive impulses. At the root of destructive impulses lies deficient self-respect. Sufficient self-respect is largely dependent upon a continual inflow of respect from the personal environment—an inflow that enables the child to develop without the warping that arises from an unstable emotional environment and the adult (mature or senescent) to count upon security and opportunity in a respected place in society.

That we face colossal crises of self-destruction in our historical period is a tragic fact from which no man can escape. And yet there are positive features in the life of our time. There is a blind mass groping for security in a respected place in society, a blind groping for deference that lends itself momentarily to the exploitation of despotic demagogues, but that can gain clarity and vitality if given insight and direction.

It is the province of psychological science to contribute to the development of an applied as well as a general science of politics, an applied science that bears much the same relation to the general science of politics that medical science bears to general physiology. The general science of politics is concerned with the factors affecting the magnitude and the distribution of values—of influence, with specific reference to the distribution of deference. The science of democracy is concerned with the factors affecting the achievement and the perpetuation of a democratic distribution of influence—with special reference to the distribution of deference—of power, respect, and insight.

From the past we are equipped with many sagacious insights into the causes and preventives of human destructiveness. In the literary remains of eminent teachers of classical Egypt, classical China, classical Greece, and classical Rome we find brilliant definitions and characterizations of human nature in society. The distinctive contribution of our generation, as of many future generations, will not be in the field of general definition—for the basic definitions of morality have been given long ago. The task that is urgent in the life of mankind is to take these terms of ambiguous reference —these inspiring, penetrating, impressionistic remarks—and give them an operational meaning in the world of our time. To this end we cultivate the needed skills of patient observation, of careful record-making, of cautious analysis. We deplore only that those who gave us brilliant definitions in the past did not enrich our social inheritance by data of observation. They did not supply us with precise criteria of the promising civil servant, conciliatory judge, benevolent leader; they did not leave a disciplined record of their own experience in observing the acts of men. And our social inheritance is rich in suggestive remarks and poor in recorded data. Centuries of human experience have been irretrievably lost because our predecessors did not apply themselves to the task of making reliable records of what they saw. We must make up that gap in the legacy that we leave to future generations.

For our task is not to add new general definitions of moral ideas. It is not even to improve upon the sentences that have been used in the past in deriving moral definitions from the key propositions of theology and metaphysics. In this sense our aim in the cultivation of science is modest. Yet in another sense our aim is enormously high; it is nothing less than to give hands and feet to morality, to discern with ever increasing accuracy the causes and controls of human destructiveness. Moral values are *acquired* from the experience of human nature in contact with culture; they are *derived* from a specialized branch of culture, metaphysics and theology; they are *implemented* by other specialized branches of culture, psychological, social, and political science, and psychological, social and political practice.

Authoritarianism "Right" and "Left"

EDWARD A. SHILS

The authors of *The Authoritarian Personality* have demonstrated in a more plausible manner than any previous investigators that there is a determinate relationship between particular attitudes towards public objects and symbols

Reprinted from *Studies in the Scope and Method of 'The Authoritarian Personality'*, edited by Richard Christie and Marie Jahoda (1954), pp. 42–49, by permission of the publisher. Copyright 1954 by The Free Press of Glencoe, Illinois.

and "deeper" cognitive and emotional attitudes or dispositions. There are many technical scientific questions concerning the adequacy of the canons of precise interpretation of the interview data, and earlier sections of this paper have criticized the conceptual scheme used in the analysis of political orientations. Nonetheless the consistency of the results as well as the statistical significance of many of the more important differences provide grounds for accepting their claim that general disposition and particular concrete political attitudes are intimately related.

The authors are not however content with this conclusion. Their interest is to estimate the probability of Fascism in the United States. By their analysis of personality structures, they seek to predict which types of persons will accept Fascist propaganda and become Fascists. They assume except for a few passages where the Marxist heritage reasserts itself that political behavior is a function of deeper personality characteristics. Social structure only plays the role of setting off the chain of personality-impelled actions. Once these are started, political activity and the political system take their form directly from the content of the impulses and beliefs of those participating in them. The entire discussion is very remote from the actual working of institutions—the interviewers did not seek to obtain information about how the subjects actually behaved in their workshops or offices, in their churches and voluntary associations, in their trade union meetings, etc. The authors tell us nothing of the *actual* roles of their subjects and for this reason, they encounter no obstacles to their view that political conduct follows from personality traits.

Yet it is obvious that this is so only within very broad limits and under rather special circumstances. The expectations of our fellow men are certainly of very great weight in the determination of our conduct—to varying degrees, of course, depending on our responsive capacities or our social sensitivity. Persons of quite different dispositions, as long as they have some reasonable measure of responsiveness to the expectations of others will behave in a more or less uniform manner, when expectations are relatively uniform. Naturally not all of them will be equally zealous or enthusiastic about the action which they perform in accordance with the expectations of particular colleagues, superiors and inferiors who are present and in accordance with the expectations symbolized in abstract rules, traditions and material objects. To a large extent, large enough indeed to enable great organizations to operate in a quite predictable manner, they will conform despite the possibly conflicting urges of their personalities. The foreign policy of a country is not ordinarily a direct and primary resultant of the personality of the Foreign Minister even though aspects of his personality will enter into his policy. The traditions of his country, the realistic perception of the international situation and of the situation with which he is presented by his civil servants, the expectations of his colleagues in the Government, the demands of the leaders of his party who wish to be re-elected as well as his own conceptions of justice, of the national interest, of superior and inferior nations, etc.—all weigh in the balance in which policy is decided. The position of a civil servant or a business executive in the middle ranks of the hierarchy of this organization is even more restrictive of the range of freedom enjoyed by the personality qualities of the individual than is that of a leader or high official.

Now it is certainly true that these actions are not completely divorced from the personality of the actor. He must have sufficient sensitivity to the expectations of others, he must be capable of understanding the symbols in his situation. He must be oriented towards the approval of his colleagues and of his constituency and he must have some degree of reality-orientation which enables him to persist in a course once undertaken. Other qualities are necessary too for this capacity to act in a diversity of situations but they are all compatible with a fairly wide range of variation in such categories as tolerance of ambiguity, distrust and suspicion, preoccupation with sexual concerns, aggressiveness towards outgroups, and others of the sort dealt with by the Berkeley group. The Berkeley group has no realization of the extent and importance for the proper functioning of any kind of society of this kind of adaptiveness to institutional roles. For them conformity is only compulsive conformity, adherence to conventions is rigid conventionalism, both of which are obviously more closely related to the substantive content of the dispositional system of the ordinary run of conformity and respect for conventions which enables any society to run peacefully and with some satisfaction to its members.

Their belief that personality traits dominate public behavior has more truth when we turn to situations which have no prior organization, where there is, in other words, no framework of action set for the newcomer by the expectations of those already on the scene. A new political party, a newly formed religious sect will thus be more amenable to the expressive behavior of the personalities of those who make them up than an ongoing government or private business office or university department with its traditions of scientific work. Personality will play a greater part in positions of leadership than in positions in the lower levels of an organization, because by the nature of the organization the higher positions have a greater freedom from elaborate expectations of fixed content. Personality structure will also be more determinant of political activities when the impulses and the defenses of the actors are extremely intense, e. g., when the compulsive elements are powerful and rigid or when the aggressiveness is very strong.

However, even when we have made these qualifications, the fact remains that it takes more than one set of personality characteristics to make a political movement,—even one which has the more favorable conditions we have just stated. The Middle West and Southern California are well strewn with small scale nativist-fundamentalist agitators of the type which might be called Fascist. Yet they have never had any success in the United States despite their numbers and despite the existence in the Middle and Far Western population of a vein of xenophobia, populist, anti-urban and anti-plutocratic sentiment, distrust of politicians and intellectuals—in fact very much of what the Berkeley group would regard as the ingredients of Fascism. Since an *Ethos* or general value system are not the same as differentiated behavior in a system of roles, these people have never been able to constitute a significant movement.

The failure of American nativism to organize its potential followers in the United States has been a consequence of a lack of organization skill in its aspirants to leadership, by the unstable and fluctuating relationships of the anti-authoritarian and the authoritarian components in the personalities of their followers and their consequent inability to sustain loyalty. They have had the necessary orientation or *Ethos* but they have lacked the minimum capacities to act in the roles necessary for a movement or an institution.

The internal organization of the various nativist groups in the United States has always been extremely loose, while the interconnections among the groups have despite repeated efforts to establish some degree of unity, been perhaps even more tenuous. The nativist leaders have almost without exception been characterized by their inability to organize an administrative apparatus for their movements, or to hire or attract others to do the work for them. The organization of an administrative apparatus involves a minimum of the capacity to trust other individuals and to evoke their trust and affection to an extent sufficient for them to pursue the goals set by the organization or its leaders. American nativistic-fundamentalistic agitators have lacked this minimum of trust even in those who share their views.

In the main, nativist leaders have been personalities who were driven into their "vocation" by strong paranoid tendencies or what is now called an authoritarian personality. Their paranoid tendencies have, however, been so diffuse in their objects, that even their own fellow nativists have been looked upon as potential agents of deprivation. Where the leader has been either so distrustful of others or, in order to overcome his fear of his own impotence, maintains in himself certain illusions of omnipotence, he seeks to do everything in the organization. It is usually too much for him. Especially since his aggressiveness keeps intruding into his efforts to do the routine work of his group. Demanding affection and loyalty, and fearing it when it is given, the aspirants to nativist leadership in the United States have had a hard row to hoe.

Their intense and self-inhibiting demands for affection and their interpretation of any failure as a deliberately inflicted deprivation are exacerbated because the normal modes of social ascent are closed to them. In the United States, the person with diffuse aggressiveness is likely to fail in his efforts to enter any of the occupations demanding persistent routine effort or offering high rewards of creativity in the exercise of authority. Hence, the paranoid tendencies of the nativist agitators which must have been generated quite early in their careers are accentuated by failures suffered during their adult years. Practically none of the nativist leaders could be called a reasonably successful individual in the conventional sense except perhaps for one who despite his external vocational success is alleged to have suffered for a long time from his social rejection at Harvard on account of his negroid appearance.

The impulsiveness which has driven these men into extremely aggressive behavior and speech has likewise prevented them from developing the flexible self-control required to build the administrative machinery in their organizations. They have been people who are driven by their immediately pressing impulses to take instantaneous action: their defenses, although strong on one side are completely open on the flank. They hate authority, for example, sufficiently for them to build up by reaction-formation a belief that the best society is one in which there is a great concentration of authority— but they cannot control their anti-authoritarianism in actual situations. Hence the movements remain small because they cannot tolerate leaders and any effort to unify the fragments is attacked as the gesture of a menacing authority. Their poor reality-orientation led them to think that they were constantly on the verge of success and therefore to underemphasize those techniques necessary to consolidate their position for a long slow movement.

An examination of the physical state of their offices and files, even among the more successful ones, has revealed extreme disorder, and they themselves in their offices show impatience and irrationality in the use of their equipment. The manner in which they transacted business, as revealed both by observation and from their correspondence has indicated inability to conduct coherent, continuous discourse. The frequent quarrels among the leaders within a group have testified to their undisciplined, unchanneled aggressiveness. Their local followership and indeed even their more remote followership have been based largely on a direct unilaterial personal relationship between the leader and the group. There is no hierarchical structure of the sort which is absolutely necessary if the actions of large numbers of people are to be coordinated. The leaders and their lieutenants who come and go seem to be incapable of the sustained continuous work of the "ward-heeler" who also uses direct personal contact as a means of control.

Public meetings were often conducted in an informal unplanned manner—more like a religious revival in a storefront church—without any of the highly organized arrangements employed so successfully by the Nazis in calling forth the awe and devotion among their followers. At a meeting in Chicago organized by G. L. K. Smith, for example, the speakers strolled in individually, stopping to chat with the audience; during the speeches there was a constant movement to and from the platform. The speakers were too informal to inspire discipline among their followers, and the movement gave the appearance of being limited in size by the number of people with whom the leaders could personally be acquainted while the difficulties in personal relationships of these persons imbued with the authoritarian ethos meant there had to be a constant turnover in membership.

The hostilities of the nativists flow out against all groups who appear distinguishable from themselves. The symbols "national" and "Christian" seem hardly adequate to bind such random aggressiveness which by its very diffuseness prevents unification and solidarity.

Despite the intensity of their animosities against those who diverge from the standards of nativist Americanism, the nativists have not on the whole appeared to be persons who have been capable of separating their love and hate componets, and to attach them to objects in a persisting manner. The amount of attachment to objects, to say nothing of affection or congeniality of which they have been capable, has not offered the possibilities of sustaining a continuously ongoing organization. Furthermore, inasmuch as there has been no formal authority to articulate their actions, and to tie them to the organization, their spontaneous affection for their fellow members has had to carry a burden far too heavy for its meager supply. It is entirely possible that these same people with their prickly anti-authoritarianism and their universally diffused distrust, could not have sustained the structure of a more formal hierarchical body even as well as they do the present internal organizational disorder of the nativist sects.

This brief summary of certain features of American nativist organization and personality structure hardly support the Berkeley Group's views that a large number of authoritarian personalities as such could produce an effective authoritarian movement. Movements and institutions, even if they are authoritarian, require both more and less than authoritarian personality structures. On the other hand, a liberal democratic society itself could probably not function satisfactorily with only "democratic liberal personalities" to fill all its roles.

The tasks of a liberal democratic society are many and many different kinds of personality structures are compatible with and necessary for its well being. Even authoritarian personalities are especially useful in some roles in democratic societies and in many other roles where they are not indispensable, they are at least harmless.

The fact that there is no point to point correspondence of personality and social role does not however mean that they have no approximate relationship to one another. The task of social research in this field is to clarify and make more determinate the scope of this relationship. *The Authoritarian Personality* both by its very solid achievement and its very significant deficiencies has contributed towards our progress in the solution of this task.

Conservatism and Personality

HERBERT McCLOSKY

If justification were needed for taking notice once again of the liberal-conservative distinction, it would be sufficient, I suppose, merely to observe that this division has been injected into the politics of Western nations for at least two centuries and, depending on the nature of one's criteria, perhaps longer.

INTRODUCTION

The distinction between the two camps has not always been sharply drawn, of course, for both have been compelled, as a condition for survival, to hold important beliefs in common. Moreover, each has reversed itself on certain issues, such as government regulation of the economy, casting off old views in favor of beliefs previously cherished by the other. Competing for popular support in elections, and succeeding one another in office, the two camps have, of necessity, taken on many values in common, tempering their programs and adjusting their courses to the practical requirements of political contest. In a system like ours, where the parties have functioned less as ideological movements than as brokerage organizations hoping to attract majority support from almost every segment of the electorate, the distinction has tended to be dulled even further, until, at the actual scenes of daily political struggle, it has often faded entirely. . . .

[But] the political writings of Russell Kirk, Clinton Rossiter, John Hallowell, or Richard Weaver, of the refurbished Southern Agrarians like Donald Davidson, the poets of nostalgia like T. S. Eliot, or of magazines like *Measure,* the *National Review,* the *American Mercury,* and *Modern Age*—express with varying degrees of intensity and spiritual violence the principles and doctrines which have enjoyed currency among self-styled conservatives

Reprinted from *The American Political Science Review,* vol. 52 (1958), pp. 27-45 by permission of the publisher. Copyright 1958 The American Political Science Association.

for generations. Thus, despite modifications imposed by political exigency and despite even the sharp reversals that have occasionally developed on specific issues, the outlook of conservatism has, like liberalism, remained fairly firm through recent centuries. This suggests that both conservatism and liberalism may be "natural" or polar positions around which individuals of certain habitual outlooks, temperaments, and sensibilities can comfortably come to rest and be united with others of like disposition. . . .

THE CONSERVATISM MEASURE: DEFINITION AND VALIDITY

Because it is a key term in the language of political conflict, choked with emotive connotations, "conservatism" has naturally evoked controversy over its meaning. The problem of defining it has, furthermore, been confused in recent decades by the already mentioned switch in the economic attitudes of both conservatives and liberals, and by the rise of movements of the "radical right" of which the fascist parties are the most extreme example but which are also represented in somewhat milder form by such groups as the Conservative Citizens' Committees. Some prefer to reserve the "conservative" label for the advocates of laissez-faire capitalism, for critics of the New Deal, or for Republicans of whatever ideological persuasion; for some it mainly signifies intemperate right-wing values of the McCarthy or *Chicago Tribune* type; while for others, it recalls the somewhat romanticized image of a Boston Brahmin—genteel, cultivated, practical, a gentleman of exquisite sensibilities and manners, a critic of the vulgarities of mass society, saddened by, though resigned to, the heavy price of equalitarian democracy. . . .

In the face of these diverse opinions, we cannot hope that the definition employed in our research, and the measure or "scale" that we constructed from this definition, will satisfy everyone. We have made an earnest effort, however, to extract from the tradition of self-styled conservative thought, and especially from the writings of Edmund Burke, a set of principles representing that tradition as fairly as possible. We have concentrated upon those attitudes and values that continually recur among acknowledged conservative thinkers and that appear to comprise the invariant elements of the conservative outlook. By the same token, we have tried to avoid attitudes or opinions that seemed to us situationally determined and which, for that reason, appear to be secondary and unstable correlates of liberal or conservative tendencies. Many attitudes that arise mainly from party or class affiliation fall into this category, *e.g.*, attitudes toward free enterprise, toward trade unions, toward expansion of government functions, toward the New Deal and its welfare measures, toward tariffs, farm supports, and a number of similar issues that have featured prominently in political campaigns.

In spite of the differences, there is astonishing agreement among the disciples, and among disinterested scholars as well, that the following are characteristic, if not quintessential elements of the conservative outlook.

(1) Man is a creature of appetite and will, "governed more by emotion than by reason" (Kirk), in whom "wickedness, unreason, and the urge to violence lurk always behind the curtain of civilized behavior" (Rossiter). He is a fallen creature, doomed to imperfection, and inclined to license and anarchy.

(2) Society is ruled by "divine intent" (Kirk) and made legitimate by Providence and prescription. Religion "is the foundation of civil society" (Huntington) and is man's ultimate defense against his own evil impulses.

(3) Society is organic, plural, inordinately complex, the product of a long and painful evolution, embodying the accumulated wisdom of previous historical ages. There is a presumption in favor of whatever has survived the ordeal of history, and of any institution that has been tried and found to work.

(4) Man's traditional inheritance is rich, grand, endlessly proliferated and mysterious, deserving of veneration, and not to be cast away lightly in favor of the narrow uniformity preached by "sophisters and calculators" (Burke). Theory is to be distrusted since reason, which gives rise to theory, is a deceptive, shallow, and limited instrument.

(5) Change must therefore be resisted and the injunction heeded that "Unless it is necessary to change it is necessary not to change" (Hearnshaw). Innovation "is a devouring conflagration more often than it is a torch of progress" (Kirk).

(6) Men are naturally unequal, and society requires "orders and classes" for the good of all. All efforts at levelling are futile and lead to despair (Kirk and Rossiter), for they violate the natural hierarchy and frustrate man's "longing for leadership." The superior classes must be allowed to differentiate themselves and to have a hand in the direction of the state, balancing the numerical superiority of the inferior classes.

(7) Order, authority, and community are the primary defense against the impulse to violence and anarchy. The superiority of duties over rights and the need to strengthen the stabilizing institutions of society, especially the church, the family, and, above all, private property.

Some of the points in the conservative creed are, unfortunately, distinguished more for their rhetoric than for the clarity and crispness of their content. Nevertheless, owing to the fact that they comprise an integrated outlook, we were able to construct a scale that makes it possible to measure the strength of conservative belief in individuals and groups, and thus to classify persons according to the degree of conservatism they exhibit.

In constructing this scale, we began with an initial pool of 43 items, the majority of which were fairly straightforward statements of the various conservative beliefs just discussed. Here, for example, are some typical items from the original set of 43:

If something grows up over a long time there is bound to be much wisdom in it.

If you start trying to change things very much, you usually make them worse.

It's not really undemocratic to recognize that the world is divided into superior and inferior people.

All groups can live in harmony in this country without changing the system in any way.

You can usually depend more on a man if he owns property than if he does not.

Our society is so complicated that if you try to reform parts of it you're likely to upset the whole system.

I prefer the practical man anytime to the man of ideas.

A man doesn't really get to have much wisdom until he's well along in years.

I'd want to know that something would really work before I'd be willing to take a chance on it.

No matter how we like to talk about it, political authority comes not from us but from some higher power.

Private ownership of property is necessary if we are to have a strong nation.

It is never wise to introduce changes rapidly, in government or in the economic system.

It's better to stick by what you have than to be trying new things you don't really know about.

Together with the items from a number of other scales we were simultaneously trying to build, the 43 items in the conservatism pool were submitted, through survey methods, to a large general sample of persons in the vicinity of the Twin Cities who were asked to state, in relation to each item, whether they agreed or disagreed. The patterns of their responses were then analyzed, with a three-fold purpose in mind: 1) to select from each pool those items which, by reproducibility and other statistical tests, clustered sufficiently to convince us that they belonged to the same universe; 2) to reduce the number of items in each scale to manageable proportions (we began with more than 2300 items, and over 80 pools of scale items); and 3) to ensure that every item selected for a given scale was in fact measuring some degree of the same attitude dimension or, in other words, that all the items in the final scale were consistent with each other.

Altogether, the responses of over 1200 persons were sampled and analyzed in this preliminary scale-construction stage, a procedure that took more than two years to complete. Some 539 items, comprising an inventory of 53 separate scales, survived this stage. The remaining thirty item pools failed to meet our scale standards and were dropped. Conservatism emerged as a twelve-item scale, tighter, more refined, and with greater internal consistency than was found in the original 43-item pool, with which, however, it correlated +.83. Although the twelve-item scale did not encompass as wide a range of values as were contained in the initial item pool, its ranking of people from extreme conservatism on the one end to liberalism on the other was very close to the rank order yielded by the original 43 items, as the high correlation attests. Empirically, then, the shorter scale may be taken as an adequate, if not actually a superior and more refined substitute for the initial set of "conservative" items. (The scale has subsequently been refined further in a succeeding study, and the items reduced in number to nine.)

The validation of a scale, *i.e.*, determining the degree to which it in fact measures the thing it purports to measure, is at best a difficult and frustrating affair. Although we have not yet exhausted all the validation procedures planned for this scale, several considerations bearing on its validity can be offered. For one thing, the scale possesses a certain amount of "face validity," which is to say that the items it includes express on their face the values which most knowledgeable people would designate as conservative. In one validation procedure employed, we submitted subsets of items from the twelve-item conservatism scale to an advanced senior-graduate class in political theory, whose members had no prior knowledge of the study or its purposes. Each student was asked to supply a name or label for the group of statements and to write a paragraph explaining or justifying the label he had chosen. Of 48 students participating, 39 volunteered the word *conservatism* as best describing the sentiments expressed in the statements, five offered names that were virtually synonymous with conservatism *(e.g., traditionalism),* while two supplied other names and two did not answer.

Thus, over 90 per cent of an informed group recognized that the items expressed values characteristic of conservatism, and were able to supply explanations consistent with the labels they chose.

The conservatism scale also correlated highly, and in the predicted direction, with several related measures that were being tested at the same time. For example, persons who scored as strongly conservative in the preliminary runs also proved, by comparison with the low scorers, to hold extremely conventional social attitudes, to be more responsive to nationalistic symbols, and to place greater emphasis upon duty, conformity, and discipline.

We also checked a number of individual statements that were not included as part of the conservatism scale but which, nevertheless, express sentiments or opinions that would be widely recognized as related to conservatism. In all but a few instances, the persons who score as extreme conservatives agree with these statements far more frequently than do those who score as liberals. The following are a few examples:

	PER CENT AGREE	
	Liberals (N = 258)	*Extreme Conservatives* (N = 282)
Duties are more important than rights.	32%	63%
The world is too complicated to be understood by anyone but experts.	26%	51%
You can't change human nature.	30%	73%
People are getting soft and weak from so much coddling and babying.	31%	68%
The heart is as good a guide as the head.	22%	58%
We have to teach children that all men are created equal, but almost everyone knows that some are better than others.	35%	73%
No matter what people think, a few people will always run things anyway.	33%	63%
Few people really know what is in their best interest in the long run.	43%	77%

By reason of such criteria, we believe that the conservatism scale possesses the properties of a valid measure, and that it can be used with confidence in group studies or in research involving large samples. . . .

RESULTS

In turning now to some of the outcomes of the research, I will confine myself in the main to the data that bear most immediately on personality and related attributes, omitting, for reasons of space, the material on political and social attitudes with which both studies have been greatly concerned.

INTELLIGENCE.   One of the clearest findings in both studies is that, contrary to claim, conservatism is not the preferred doctrine of the intellectual elite or of the more intelligent segments of the population, but the reverse. By every measure available to us, conservative beliefs are found most frequently among the uninformed, the poorly educated, and so far as we can determine, the less intelligent. The following table sets out a few of these relationships:

TABLE I. COMPARISON OF CONSERVATIVES AND LIBERALS BY EDUCATION AND
KNOWLEDGE, MINNESOTA SAMPLE*

	Liberals	Moderate Liberals	Moderate Conservatives	Extreme Conservatives
	(N = 190)	(N = 316)	(N = 331)	(N = 245)
Education				
% with grade school education	9	14	29	49
% with some college education	47	33	21	12
Awareness				
% scoring low	9	25	45	66
% scoring high	54	32	21	9
Intellectuality				
% scoring low	7	20	34	56
% scoring high	62	43	26	11

* In this and the following tables *high* always means a score in the upper third of the scale named; *low* always means a score in the lower third of the scale named. The middle third is omitted from these tables. The table should thus be read across, as follows: Whereas 54 per cent of the Liberals score among the upper (or "high") third of the distribution on the Awareness scale, 32 per cent of the Moderate Liberals, 21 per cent of the Moderate Conservatives and only 9 per cent of the Extreme Conservatives have "high" scores on Awareness. It should also be noted that the differences between the extreme groups in this table, and in all the subsequent data reported, are statistically significant beyond the 1 per cent level of significance, which is to say that the probability is less than one in 100 that differences of these magnitudes could be occurring by chance, given the size of our samples.

The Awareness scale, referred to in the table, is a test not only of actual knowledge but also of the clarity of one's grasp of the social process, past and present. It serves, to some extent, as a crude intelligence test. The same can be said, though less authoritatively, for the Intellectuality scale, which assesses the degree to which intellectual habits have been formed and are perceived as attractive. The findings on these measures make plain that there is a sharp decline in the level of information and intellectual grasp as one moves from the more liberal to the more conservative sections of the population. Similarly, an increase in the level of knowledge is usually accompanied by a corresponding decrease in the incidence of conservatism. Individual items correlated with intelligence bear out the same general tendency. Thus, the item "I was a slow learner in school" is answered yes by 34 per cent of the Extreme Conservatives but by only 14 per cent of the Liberals. These differences on Awareness and Intellectuality remain large and statistically significant even when education and other status factors are controlled.

Of course, not all conservatives are uninformed, not all liberals are knowledgeable, and not all the unlearned are conservative. The data show clearly, nevertheless, that the most articulate and informed classes in our society are preponderantly liberal in their outlook. Procedures carried out with a special sample of civic and political leaders in [another] study bear this out even further, regardless of party preference or of other affiliations that might ordinarily be expected to have an influence upon liberal-conservative tendencies.

SOCIAL-PSYCHOLOGICAL ATTRIBUTES. Related to status and intelligence are a set of traits that reflect the interrelation of personality and life-style, and especially the degree to which people feel themselves to be the masters or

TABLE II. COMPARISON OF CONSERVATIVES AND LIBERALS BY
PERSONALITY TRAITS — SOCIAL

	Liberals (N = 190)	Moderate Liberals (N = 316)	Moderate Conservatives (N = 331)	Extreme Conservatives (N = 245)
Dominance				
% low	9	19	37	51
% high	72	50	29	14
Anomie				
% low	71	48	32	10
% high	4	16	30	59
Alienation				
% low	57	47	35	18
% high	11	20	27	45
Bewilderment				
% low	61	40	33	10
% high	9	20	34	57
Pessimism				
% low	44	35	31	19
% high	25	35	42	53
Social Responsibility				
% low	12	25	36	62
% high	47	31	23	8
Self-Confidence				
% low	18	23	32	35
% high	46	38	24	20
Guilt				
% low	62	42	36	18
% high	16	18	28	47

victims of their immediate environment and of themselves. These traits have to do with one's sense of security, with the sense of belonging, isolation, and social support, with feelings of worthlessness, submissiveness, inferiority, timidity, self-assurance, personal strength, and the like. In the preceding table are some of the scales we developed to assess this universe of feelings and attitudes, together with the scores registered by liberals and conservatives for each of these traits.

As these figures make plain, the Conservatives tend to score at the more "undesirable" end of the distributions on every one of the above traits. Uniformly, every increase in the degree of conservatism shows a corresponding increase in submissiveness, anomie, sense of alienation, bewilderment, etc. To some extent, the vast differences appearing in this table are a function of the somewhat higher status and education of the liberals in the sample. But the differences remain almost as large even when we control for these factors. Conservatism, in our society at least, appears to be far more characteristic of social isolates, of people who think poorly of themselves, who suffer personal disgruntlement and frustration, who are submissive, timid, and wanting in confidence, who lack a clear sense of direction and purpose, who are uncertain about their values, and who are generally bewildered by the alarming task of having to thread their way through a society which seems to them too complex to fathom.

Readers of Eric Hoffer will recognize in these findings support for his brilliant, intuitive characterization of the conservative and of the conditions which give rise to him. Far from being the elite or the masters or the prime movers, conservatives tend on the whole to come from the more backward and frightened elements of the population, including the classes that are socially and psychologically depressed. The significance of this, and of other findings reported in this section, will be considered in the evaluation section shortly to follow.

CLINICAL-PERSONALITY VARIABLES.   Turning now to a set of traits that are more straightforwardly clinical and psychological, conservatives and liberals are found to be sharply distinguished from each other in many of these characteristics as well. The differences, furthermore, are consistent with those cited in the personality-life style group. Scores on the more important of the clinical variables are shown in the following table.

The figures demonstrate with overpowering effect that conservatives tend once more to score on the more "undesirable," poorly adapted side of these personality variables. Of the four liberal-conservative classifications, the extreme conservatives are easily the most hostile and suspicious, the most rigid and compulsive, the quickest to condemn others for their imperfections or weaknesses, the most intolerant, the most easily moved to scorn and disappointment in others, the most inflexible and unyielding in their perceptions and judgments. Although aggressively critical of the shortcomings of others,

TABLE III. COMPARISON OF CONSERVATIVES AND LIBERALS
BY PERSONALITY TRAITS — CLINICAL

	Liberals (N = 190)	Moderate Liberals (N = 316)	Moderate Conservatives (N = 331)	Extreme Conservatives (N = 245)
Hostility				
% low	59	38	26	9
% high	18	37	46	71
Paranoid Tendencies				
% low	56	42	28	13
% high	16	27	37	62
Contempt for Weakness				
% low	61	33	21	5
% high	8	18	29	55
Need Inviolacy (Ego Defense)				
% low	68	58	36	17
% high	11	20	38	60
Rigidity				
% low	58	43	29	14
% high	18	32	41	60
Obsessive Traits				
% low	47	40	29	22
% high	24	31	43	55
Intolerance of Human Frailty				
% low	52	30	17	6
% high	8	16	23	54

they are unusually defensive and armored in the protection of their own ego needs. Poorly integrated psychologically, anxious, often perceiving themselves as inadequate, and subject to excessive feelings of guilt, they seem inclined to project onto others the traits they most dislike or fear in themselves. . . .

V. CAUTIONS AND QUALIFICATIONS

Impressive though the conservatism data may be, we must take note of several important qualifications and problems bearing upon their interpretation, to which fuller attention will eventually have to be given. Here, for reasons of space, I can only comment briefly upon a few of these points.

1. The findings refer to aggregates, not to specific individuals. Doubtless, many of us know individual conservatives whose personalities differ in key ways from the prototypic pattern described here. In our research, some conservatives have been turned up who, in personality and other attributes, essentially resemble liberals. These, however, are exceptions, since the prob-

abilities are strong that a conservative selected at random from the general population will resemble the conservative profile that emerges from the preceding data.

2. A question might also be raised about the propriety of classifying highly informed, upper status conservatives in the same category with un-educated conservatives of low status. Conceivably, the "elite" and the "mass" conservatives are motivated by very dissimilar influences and could be scoring high on conservatism for quite different reasons. This possibility cannot be dismissed lightly, especially when one considers that status and education factors account, by themselves, for a significant share of the total variance found in our data. Subsequent analyses will make it possible, we hope, to settle this matter conclusively; but for the present, at least one important consideration can be noted: when education and other status factors are controlled, we find that informed, upper status conservatives differ from informed, upper status liberals in precisely the same ways that conservatives in general differ from liberals in general; or, for that matter, in the same ways that "mass" conservatives differ from "mass" liberals. While the *range* of the scores varies as occupation, education, or knowledge varies the *direction* and *magnitude* of the differences between liberals and conservatives remain very much the same for all status and education levels. In short, personality factors seem to exercise a fairly uniform influence on the formation of conservative or liberal outlooks at all social levels.

3. The association between conservatism and the traits outlined exists in the form of correlations, which only tell us that the two go together. *How* they go together, and which is antecedent to which, is a more difficult and more elusive problem. Conservative doctrines appear, in some measure, to arise from personality needs, but it is conceivable, at least, that both are the product of some third set of factors. Both, for example, may have been learned or acquired simultaneously, through family indoctrination, in which case the connection between the two would be more epiphenomenal than causal. I do not think that this explanation can account for more of our results, but it will need to be checked out further.

4. The terms employed in the description of traits must be seen as relative and as having been mainly defined by the items in the scales themselves. Satisfactory external validation has not always been available. Also, although clinical terms have been employed that might be used in the diagnosis of psychotics, we have used the terms only as terms of tendency within the normal population. None of them is intended to signify the presence of a pathological mental state.

5. One must be careful to avoid the reductivist fallacy of assigning all significance in the problems considered to personality factors. Equally, one

must avoid the temptation to "psychologize" problems to such an extent as to strip them of their significance as genuine political or philosophical problems.

6. The term liberalism has been inadequately defined in our study so far. We have tended to call someone liberal if he rejected the values of conservatism. While our findings suggest that most of these people would in fact meet the definition of a liberal, our present classification of liberals is crude and needs to be refined. All persons who reject conservatism may not be liberals, for, as in the case of the "authoritarian-democratic" dimension, liberalism-conservatism may not be variables, paired in such a way that a high score on one necessarily signifies a low score on the other.

7. The connections between classical conservatism (or liberalism) and such factors as party affiliation, attitude on economic issues, and liberal-conservative self-designation have been extensively explored in our research, but could not be reported in the present paper. The correlation between them tends, however, to be fairly low, suggesting that for the present, at least, many Americans divide in their party preferences, their support of candidates, their economic views, their stands on public issues, or their political self-identifications without reference to their beliefs in liberalism or conservatism. The latter have influence, of course, especially among some of the more articulate groups; for the general population, however, political divisions of the sort named appear to be more affected by group membership factors than by personality.

8. Some readers may be inclined to identify our "conservatives" with "right-wing authoritarians," in the belief that we are measuring the latter rather more than the former. This view would be difficult to support, however, for not only have we defined conservatism by reference to its most frequently articulated values (which are by no means identical with right-wing values), but we have also found that while right-wing authoritarians are in some respects a more extreme version of our conservatives, there are also significant differences between the two.

9. Finally, our findings have so far been drawn entirely from Minnesota samples, and the degree to which the conclusions can be generalized to conservatives everywhere and at all times is open to debate. We shall soon have comparable data on a national cross-section sample, which I have reason to think will bear out the present results. In fact, I am inclined to believe that the connections between conservatism and the personality configurations presented in the foregoing would very likely prevail wherever, and whenever, the members of a society are free to choose between conservatism and alternative, liberal systems of belief. But this is a subject for future research.

Certain Personality Factors of State
Legislators in South Carolina

JOHN B. McCONAUGHY

Some twenty years ago Harold D. Lasswell, in his *Psychopathology and Politics,* attempted to show by case histories some of the motivations and personality characteristics of certain political types. This book was a pioneer in its field because it applied the psychoanalytic "free fantasy" technique to the field of political science. The case histories were chosen from those in selected hospitals and from the official files of certain psychiatrists. From these case histories, Lasswell was able to obtain information which threw new light on the actions of such political types as the agitator and the administrator. He then developed the formula $p\}d\}r=P;$ where p equals private motives, d equals displacement onto public objects, r equals rationalization in terms of public interest, $\}$ means "transformed into," and P signifies the political man.

Lasswell's techniques are invaluable for the study of political personalities and motives. It is unfortunate that others have not utilized them more fully and thereby added to the store of knowledge concerning the personalities of politicians; but a partial explanation lies in the fact that the techniques themselves present obstacles to their ready use by political scientists. In the first place, the case histories are usually confidential and difficult to obtain. In the second place, in order to evaluate them validly the political scientist needs training as a psychiatrist as well as a political scientist. Finally, most of the case histories deal with either neurotic or psychotic individuals who came to the hospital or the psychiatrist only because they were somewhat abnormal. Although the study of the abnormal helps one to understand the normal, it would be a contradiction of terms to consider the abnormal typical of the normal. And while it is true that abnormality is a matter of degree rather than *non sui generis,* still the degree of difference can be so great as to be the difference between the reactions of politicians in a democratic United States and a nazi Germany or a communist Russia. There is no question about the validity of Lasswell's analysis concerning the individuals whom he studied; but because of the nature of his data and their selection, it is difficult for others to corroborate his findings

Reprinted from *The American Political Science Review,* vol. 44 (1950), pp. 894–903 by permission of the publisher. Copyright 1950 by The American Political Science Association.

and to determine whether or not his individuals are typical or representative of the average politician.

The Political Science Department at the University of South Carolina, in cooperation with the Psychology Department, has been interested in developing new techniques which could be applied more widely to politicians at present active in politics. These techniques have the advantage of studying the normal rather than the abnormal; they are more objective than subjective, and are capable of being checked by other political scientists with a minimum amount of training in psychology, rather than in psychiatry. The principal disadvantage of these techniques is that they are extensive rather than intensive. A political scientist using Lasswell's methods could probe deeper into individual cases than the researcher using the new techniques.

The procedure followed consisted of giving a battery of personality and opinion tests to eighteen legislators, state senators and representatives of South Carolina. The majority of the tests were administered at the State House during the regular session of the General Assembly; a few, however, were given to the men in their home offices. The legislators were promised absolute anonymity in order to encourage truthful answers. One control group for two of the tests, the Unlabelled Fascist Attitude Test and the Lentz C-R Opinionaire, was composed of a South Carolina service club of 28 members. A second control group for the C-R Opinionaire was composed of 21 adult men who had finished four years of college work and had received their A.B. degrees. A graduate student, with training in both political science and psychology administered the tests and did the statistical research.

In general the legislators were quite cooperative in taking the tests, once they were assured that their identity would not be disclosed. The principal difficulty in administering the tests to them was the fact that they were extremely busy most of the time while the legislature was in session; consequently, each individual had to be given one test at a time. This operation required a high degree of patience. On the other hand, the fact that the legislators were meeting in Columbia, where the University is located, offered some compensating advantages.

Some explanation should be made of the statistical methods used in this research, since political scientists may not be as familiar with them as are psychologists. Whenever equivalents were available, the raw scores of the tests given were converted into percentiles before comparisons were made, so that as many as possible of the scores would be given in the same unit of measurement. There were eleven factors tested by this particular battery of tests, and for each factor the following seven statistical values were found:

1. The frequency distribution, a tabular presentation showing how many cases are found in each step interval of the entire distribution.

2. The average, as found by the formula $\Sigma(F \cdot M)/N$, in which sigma (Σ) denotes "the sum of," F denotes frequency, M denotes the midpoints, and N denotes the number of cases.

3. The median, that point in a series above which 50% of the cases are located and below which 50% of them are located. This is found by merely counting one-half of N and using the score found at that point.

4. The standard deviation, the measure that sets the approximate limits of the middle two-thirds of a distribution when marked off above and below the average. It is found by the formula $\sqrt{\Sigma(FD^2/N}$ in which sigma (Σ) denotes "the sum of," F the frequency, D^2 the square of the deviation of each score from the average, and N the number of cases.

5. The correlation of scores of the legislators with their ages by the rank-difference method. In order to use this method, each politician was given a rank number according to his age, the oldest having number one and the youngest number eighteen. Each legislator was also given a number for each factor analyzed according to his scores, one denoting the highest score and eighteen the lowest. The correlation between the two was found by the formula $p = 6\Sigma D^2/N(N^2 - 1)$, in which p denotes *rho* or the coefficient of correlation, Σ denotes "the sum of," D^2 denotes the square of the difference between the ranks of age and score for each man, and N denotes the number of cases. The coefficient of correlation is found by squaring the differences between the rank orders of ages and scores, adding these and multiplying the sum by six. This is the dividend of the final fraction. The number of cases is then squared, one is subtracted from this figure and the result is multiplied by the number of cases. The product is then divided into the dividend. A positive coefficient would indicate a correlation between high scores and age; a negative coefficient would indicate a correlation between high scores and youth. A coefficient is considered significant only when it is at least $\pm .30$.

6. A comparison of the averages of the scores of the older men with those of the younger. The ages of the men tested were 29-32-35-37-39-46-46-48-49-50-50-56-57-64-64-70. Therefore the youngest quarter, or quartile, of the men would be those from 29 to 38 years of age and the oldest would be from 59 to 70 years of age. The average of each of the extreme quartiles was found by the formula Σ scores/N. These averages were used to substantiate the coefficients of correlation.

7. Scattergrams were utilized to give a graphic picture of different correlations. The scores of the different men were plotted on the Y, or vertical, axis, and the variable factor (urbanity, education, or sales) was plotted on the X, or horizontal, axis. Each legislator, represented by a line, is placed

in the correct position on the graph according to his score and the variable factor. A freehand line is drawn to show the general trend of the correlation. A positive correlation on such a scattergram would be shown by a line proceeding from the lower left-hand corner of the graph to the upper right-hand corner. A perfect negative correlation would be shown by a line proceeding from the upper left-hand corner to the lower right-hand corner at a 45 degree angle. A line proceeding from the upper middle of the graph to the bottom middle of the graph shows no correlation. The freehand line is drawn in such a manner that there is an equal number of short lines, representing the scores and the variable factor, on each side of the major line.

The tests given in this survey were the Bernreuter Personality Inventory, the Guilford-Martin Inventory of Factors G-A-M-I-N, the Edwards Unlabeled Fascist Attitude Test and the Lentz C-R Opinionaire. All have the advantage that the traits being measured are not discernible by the person taking the test, thereby increasing the validity of the test.

The outstanding feature of the Bernreuter and the Guilford-Martin tests is that they measure several different factors of personality at one time, saving much time in administration. The following traits are measured by the Bernreuter Personality Inventory:

(1) B1-N. A measure of neurotic tendency. Persons scoring high on this scale tend to be emotionally unstable. . . . Those scoring low tend to be well-balanced emotionally.

(2) B2-S. A measure of self-sufficiency. Persons scoring high on this scale prefer to be alone, rarely ask for sympathy and encouragement, and tend to ignore the advice of others. Those scoring low dislike solitude and often seek advice and encouragement.

(3) B3-I. A measure of introversion-extroversion. Persons scoring high on this scale tend to be introverted; that is, they are imaginative and tend to live within themselves. . . . Those scoring low are extroverted; that is, they rarely worry, seldom suffer emotional upsets, and rarely substitute daydreaming for action.

(4) B4-D. A measure of dominance-submission. Persons scoring high on this scale tend to dominate others in face-to-face situations. Those scoring low tend to be submissive.

Norms have been compiled for male and female high school students, college students and adults, with which the scores of examinees may be compared. The Bernreuter Test has been criticized because of the fact that it shows a positive correlation between introversion and neurosis, which may be an artifact due to the use of some identical items in the two scales B1-N and B3-I. A test which could have been used in place of the Bernreuter would have been the Guilford-Martin S-T-R-D-C test, but the Bernreuter test was adopted because it is the most widely used test and therefore affords the best basis for comparison.

TABLE I. BERNREUTER PERSONALITY INVENTORY

	Average P.R.	*Median P.R.*	*S.D.*	*Rho-Correlation with Age*
B1-N	32.83%	28.33%	24.19	—.04
B2-S	65.89%	72.50%	21.99	—.08
B3-I	28.78%	26.00%	20.93	—.02
B4-D	58.33%	62.50%	22.26	—.02

In interpreting the above table, the average adult male would score 50 per cent. The table indicates that the South Carolina political leaders are far less neurotic than the average male adult, far less introverted, more self-sufficient, and slightly more dominant. Indeed, the political leaders seem to be better adjusted to life and more stable than the average male voter. The results would seem to throw serious doubt on the theory sometimes advanced by psychoanalysts that politicians go into politics because of feelings of insufficiency or an inferiority complex. The politician is no dreamer; apparently he is a realist who enjoys meeting people and going on parties.

The traits measured by the Guilford-Martin Inventory of Factors G-A-M-I-N are:

(1) G. General pressure for overt activity.
(2) A. Ascendency in social situations as opposed to submissiveness.
(3) M. Masculinity of attitudes and interests as opposed to femininity.
(4) I. Lack of inferiority feelings; self-confidence.
(5) N. Lack of nervous tenseness and irritability.

TABLE II. GUILFORD-MARTIN INVENTORY OF FACTORS G-A-M-I-N

	Average P.R.	*Median P.R.*	*S.D.*	*Rho-Coefficient with Age*
G	54%	59%	25.68	—.30
A	67.17%	72%	21.61	—.30
M	69.72%	67%	19.09	.35
I	76.83%	83%	23.15	.06
N	60.19%	61.67%	26.50	.41

As Table II shows, the politicians tested were only slightly more energetic than the average male population, but they were much higher than average in respect to ascendancy in social situations, masculinity and lack of nervous tenseness and irritability. The political leaders were highest in lack of inferiority feelings. Only 23.17 per cent of the total adult male population ranks higher in lack of inferiority feelings than the average South Carolina political leader tested. The findings on lack of inferiority feelings also agree with B2-S on the Bernreuter Personality Inventory.

The Edwards Unlabelled Fascist Attitudes Test is based on a similar test, composed by Stagner, which arrived at the conclusion that while subjects may reject any statements labelled "fascist," they may accept the same statements if they are not so labelled. Stagner's pioneer work in the field measures such phases of fascism as militarism, nationalism, anti-radicalism, contempt for the lower classes and opposition to labor unions. Edwards' purpose was to include attitudes toward birth control, education, status of women, status toward religion, etc., for these phases can be a more delicate and less recognizable test of a fascist tendency.

The lowest possible score obtainable on the Edwards Test is 20; the highest possible score is 100. In order to be sure of the meaning of the Edwards Test in South Carolina a control group composed of 28 adult members of a service club in South Carolina was used to provide a comparison with the legislators. This control group consisted of persons of varying ages.

TABLE III.   EDWARDS UNLABELLED FASCIST ATTITUDES TEST

	Midpoint	*Average*	*Median*	*S.D.*	*Rho-Age and Score*
Legislators	60	58.72	55.33	11.96	.38
Control Group	60	59.33	57.00	10.98	

	Rho County Sales and Score	*Rho H.S. Graduates and Score*	*Rho Urban Percentage and Score*
Legislators	—.31	—.42	—.38

It can be seen from Table III that the South Carolina political leaders averaged below the control group in fascist tendencies. (The political leaders also averaged from 1.3 points to 6.6 points, according to age, below the average made by the students who took the tests under Edwards.) In addition, this table shows that fascist tendencies increase with age but are inversely proportional to county sales, high school education and urban percentage of the voters who elect the South Carolina political leaders.

TABLE IV. LENTZ C-R OPINIONAIRE

	Conservatism Av. P.R.	Median P.R.	S.D.	Rho with Age
S.C. Legislators	64.78%	67.50%	26.58	.41
Control Group #1	60.00%	68.50%	21.74	
Control Group #2	54.26%	59.50%	20.37	

	Rho with Sales	Rho Education	Rho Urbanity
S.C. Legislators	−.45	−.03	−.13

The Lentz C-R Opinionaire, which tests conservatism-radicalism, is based on the assumption that the conservatism-radicalism difference among persons is dependent upon the degree of their opposition or favor toward change.

Although the South Carolina political leaders are among the top 36.22 per cent of the most conservative male adults in the United States, they average only slightly more conservative than the two South Carolina control groups. As indicated in the table, conservatism increases heavily with age and decreases quickly when legislators are from counties with high retail sales, which is an index of prosperity. The effects of education and urbanity of the electorate upon the political ideas of their representatives are too small to be statistically significant.

In conclusion, the Bernreuter Inventory given to eighteen of 170 South Carolina legislators indicated that the political leaders were decidedly less neurotic than the general male population; that they were more self-sufficient; that they were decidedly more extroverted; but that they were only slightly more dominant. The Guilford-Martin Inventory of Factors G-A-M-I-N indicated that South Carolina political leaders have, to an insignificant degree, more general pressure for overt activity than the average person; that they are decidedly more masculine than the general male population; that they are, to a large degree, more self-confident than the average person and have fewer feelings of inferiority; and that they are less irritable and tense than the average person. The South Carolina leaders, according to the Edwards Unlabelled Fascist Attitude Test, are less fascist than those treated by Edwards. The acceptance of fascist ideas by the leaders decreases with the prosperity, education and urbanity of the county which they represent. The C-R Opinionaire indicates that South Carolina political leaders are, to a significant degree, more conservative than the general college population, but not much more conservative than the samples of South Caro-

lina population used as control groups. The counties in South Carolina
with the largest retail sales send more liberal political leaders to the state
capitol than counties with low retail sales.

In conclusion, it must be stressed that the results reported are highly
tentative and should be used with extreme caution. The sample of eighteen
political leaders is too small to be conclusive for the country as a whole.
The eighteen leaders came from only one state, and personality traits might
differ in other areas. It is to be hoped, consequently, that political scientists using similar techniques in other parts of the country may be able to
add information which either corroborates or refutes the results obtained
in South Carolina.

The Fear of Equality

ROBERT E. LANE

We move in equalitarian directions; the distribution of income flattens out;
the floor beneath the poorest paid and least secure is raised and made more
substantial. Since the demise of Newport and Tuxedo Park, the very rich
have shunned ostentatious display. The equality of opportunity, the chance
to rise in the world is at least as great today as it was thirty years ago. The
likelihood of declining status is less. Where does the energy for this movement come from? Who is behind it?

Since 1848, it has been assumed that the drive for a more equalitarian
society, its effective social force, would come from the stratum of society
with the most to gain, the working classes. This was thought to be the revolutionary force in the world—the demand of workers for a classless society
sparked by their hostility to the owning classes. It was to be the elite among
the workers, not the *lumpenproletariat,* not the "scum," who were to advance this movement. Just as "liberty" was the central slogan of the bour-
geois revolution, so "equality" was the central concept in the working class
movement. Hence it was natural to assume that whatever gains have been
made in equalizing the income and status of men in our society came about
largely from working class pressure.

But on closer investigation the demands for greater liberty or "freedom"
turn out to have been of an ambiguous nature. The middle classes sought
freedom of speech and action in large part for the economic gains that this

Reprinted from *The American Political Science Review,* vol. 53 (March 1959),
pp. 35–51 by permission of the author and the publisher. Copyright 1959 by The
American Political Science Association.

would give them, and moralized their action with the theology of freedom. But the freedom that they gained was frightening, for it deprived them of the solidary social relationships and the ideological certainty which often gave order and meaning to their lives. On occasion, then, they sought to "escape from freedom." The older unfree order had a value which the earlier social commentators did not appreciate.

There is a parallel here with the movement toward a more equalitarian society. The upper working class, and the lower middle class, support specific measures embraced in the formula "welfare state," which have equalitarian consequences. But, so I shall argue, many members of the working classes do not want equality. They are afraid of it. In some ways they already seek to escape from it. Equality for the working classes, like freedom for the middle classes, is a worrisome, partially rejected, by-product of the demand for more specific measures. Inequality has values to them which have been overlooked. It is these attitudes on status and equality that I shall explore here.

I. EXTENDED INTERVIEWS WITH FIFTEEN MEN

This discussion is based upon extended interviews of from ten to fifteen hours each (in from four to seven sessions) with a sample of American urban male voters. The sample is a random selection from the white members on a list of 220 registered voters in a moderate income (not low income) housing development where income is permitted to range between $4,000 and $6,500, according to the number of dependents in the family. Out of fifteen asked to participate, fifteen agreed, for a modest cash consideration. The characteristics of the sample, then, are as follows:

They are all men, white, married, fathers, urban, Eastern seaboard.

Their incomes range from $2,400 to $6,300 (except for one who had just moved from the project. His income was $10,000 in 1957.)

Ten had working class (blue collar) occupations such as painter, plumber, oiler, railroad fireman, policeman, machine operator.

Five had white collar occupations such as salesman, bookkeeper, supply clerk.

Their ages ranged from 25 to 54; most are in their thirties.

Twelve are Catholic, two are Protestants, one is Jewish.

All are native born; their nationality backgrounds are: six Italian, five Irish, one Polish, one Swedish, one Russian, one Yankee. Most are second or third generation Americans.

All were employed at the time of the interviews.

Their educational distribution was: three had only grammar school

*education; eight had some high school; two finished high school; one had
some college; one completed graduate training.*

The interviews with these men were taped, with the permission of the
interviewees, and transcribed. They were conducted by means of a schedule
of questions and topics followed by conversational improvised probes to discover the underlying meanings of the answers given. The kinds of questions
employed to uncover the material to be reported are illustrated by the following: "What do you think the phrase 'All men are created equal' means?"
"How would you feel if everyone received the same income no matter what
his job?" "Sometimes one hears the term 'social class'—as in working class
or middle class. What do you think this term 'social class' means?" "What
class do you belong to?" "How do you feel about it?" There were also a
number of questions dealing with status, private utopias, feelings of privilege
or lack of privilege, and other topics, throughout the interview schedule
which sometimes elicited responses bearing on the question of social and
economic equality.

II. HOW TO ACCOUNT FOR ONE'S OWN STATUS?

It is my thesis that attitudes toward equality rest in the first instance
upon one's attitude towards one's own status. Like a large number of social
beliefs, attitudes towards equality take their direction from beliefs about
the self, the status of the self, one's self-esteem or lack thereof. It is necessary, therefore, first to explore how people see themselves in American hierarchical society.

The American culture and the democratic dogma have given to the
American public the notion that "all men are created equal." Even more
insistently, the American culture tells its members: "achieve," "compete,"
"be better, smarter, quicker, richer than your fellow men"; in short, "be
unequal." The men I interviewed had received these inequalitarian messages,
some eagerly, some with foreboding. Having heard them, they must account
for their status, higher than some, lower than others. They must ask themselves, for example, "Why didn't I rise out of the working class, or out of
the 'housing project class,' or out of the underpaid office help class?" And,
on the other hand, "Why am I better off than my parents? or than the
fellows down the road in the low rental project? or the fellows on relief?"
Men confronted with these questions adopt a variety of interesting answers.

Is it up to me? The problem of accounting for status is personally important for these men only if they think that their decisions, effort, and energy make a difference in their position in life. Most of my subjects accepted
the view that America opens up opportunity to all people; if not in equal

proportions, then at least enough so that a person must assume responsibility for his own status. . . .

III. REDUCING THE IMPORTANCE OF THE STRUGGLE

When something is painful to examine, people look away, or, if they look at it, they see only the parts they want to see. They deny that it is an important something. So is it often with a person's class status when the reference is upward, when people must account not for the strength of their position, but for its weakness. How do they do this?

In the first place they may *insulate themselves,* limit their outlook and range of comparisons. . . . A second device for reducing the importance of class position is to *deny its importance.* This is not to deny the importance of getting ahead, but to limit this to the problem of job classification, or occupational choice—nothing so damaging to the self-esteem as an ordering of persons on a class scale. . . .

A third device for reducing the significance of the struggle for status and "success" is *resignation,* a reluctant acceptance of one's fate. When some men assume this posture of resignation one senses a pose; their secret hopes and ambitions will not down. For others it rings true. . . .

IV. PEOPLE DESERVE THEIR STATUS

If one accepts the view that this is a land of opportunity in which merit will find a way, one is encouraged to accept the status differences of society. But it is more than logic which impels our men to accept these differences. There are satisfactions of identification with the going social order; it is easier to accept differences which one calls "just" than those that appear "unjust"; there are the very substantial self-congratulatory satisfactions of comparison with those lower on the scale. Thus this theme of "just desserts" applies to one's own group, those higher, and those lower.

So Kuchinsky says: "If you're a professor, I think you're entitled to get what you deserve. I'm a painter and I shouldn't be getting what you're getting." Furthermore, confidence in the general equity of the social order suggests that the rewards of one's own life are proportionate to ability, effort, and the wisdom of previous decisions. On ability, Costa, a machine operator, says:

I believe anybody that has the potential to become a scientific man, or a professor, or a lawyer, or a doctor, should have the opportunity to pursue it, but there's a lot of us that are just made to run a machine in a factory. No matter what opportunities some of us might have had, we would never have reached the point where we could become people of that kind. I mean everybody isn't Joe DiMaggio. . . . But the most usual mistake or deficiency accounting for the relatively humble position is failure to continue one's education due to lack of family pressure ("they should have made me"), or youthful indiscretion, or the demands of the family for money, or the depression of the thirties.

THE UPPER CLASSES DESERVE TO BE UPPER.   Just as they regard their own status as deserved, so also do they regard the status of the more eminently successful as appropriate to their talents. Rapuano, an auto parts supply man, reports:

Your income—if you're smart, and your ability calls for a certain income, that's what you should earn. If your ability is so low, why hell, then you should earn the low income. ["Do you think income is proportionate to ability now?"] I would say so. Yes.

But there is a suggestion in many of the interviews that even if the income is divorced from talent and effort, in some sense it is appropriate. Consider Sokolsky again, a machine operator and part-time janitor, discussing the tax situation:

Personally, I think taxes are too hard. I mean a man makes, let's say $150,000. Well, my God, he has to give up half of that to the government—which I don't think is right. For instance if a man is fortunate enough to win the Irish Sweepstakes, he gets 150—I think he has about $45,000 left. I don't think that's right.

Even if life is a lottery, the winner should keep his winnings. . . .
     The concept of "education" is the key to much of the thinking on social class and personal status. In a sense, it is a "natural" because it fits so neatly into the American myth of opportunity and equality, and provides a rationale for success and failure which does minimum damage to the souls of those who did not go to college. Thus in justifying their own positions, sometimes with reference to the interview situation, my clients imply, "If I had gone to college (like you) I would be higher up in this world." Costa, a machine operator, speaks this theme:

Now what would be the advantage of you going 20 years to school so you wind up making $10,000 a year, and me going 8 years to school, making $10,000. You would be teaching the young men of tomorrow, the leaders of tomorrow, and I would be running a machine. You would have a lot more *responsibility to the country as a whole than I would have. Why shouldn't you be rewarded in proportion. . . .*

What is it about education that justifies differences in income? In the above interviews it is clear that education is thought to increase skills which should be suitably rewarded. Furthermore, it appears that the time necessary for educational preparation deserves some reward—a recurrent theme. With education goes responsibility—and responsibility should be rewarded. But there is also some suggestion in the interview material that the pain and hard (unpleasant) work associated with going to school deserves compensation. People who did not like school themselves may be paying homage to those who could stick it out. It is a question whether O'Hara, a maintenance oiler, implies this when he says:

I think a person that is educated deserves more than somebody that isn't. Somebody who really works for his money really deserves it more than somebody that's lazy and just wants to hang around.

In this and other ways, education serves as a peg on which to hang status; and, like "blood," whether a person got the education or not is not his "fault," or at least it is only the fault of an irresponsible youth, not a grown man.

THE LOWER CLASSES DESERVE NO BETTER THAN THEY GET. By and large those in the lower orders are those who are paid daily (not weekly) or are on relief; they live in slums or in public housing projects (but not middle income projects); they do not live respectable lives; they have only grammar school education; they may have no regular jobs. Closer to home, those slightly lower in status are people like "The lady next door who has a little less than I have," the man who can't afford to take care of his kids properly in the project, people who spend their money on liquor, the person with less skill in the same line of work.

The rationale for their lower status turns chiefly on two things: their lack of education and therefore failure to know what they want or failure to understand lifesmanship, and their general indifference. It is particularly this "not caring" which seems so salient in the upper working class mind. This is consonant with the general view that success is a triumph of the will and a reflection of ability. Poverty is for lazy people, just as middle status is for struggling people. . . .

In general, there is little sympathy given to those lower in the scale, little reference to the overpowering forces of circumstance, only rare mention of sickness, death of a breadwinner, senility, factories moving out of town, and so forth. The only major cause of poverty to which no moral blame attaches is depression or "unemployment"—but this is not considered a strikingly important cause in the minds of my clients. They are Christian in the sense that they believe "The poor ye have with you always," but there is no trace of a belief that the poor are in any way "blessed."

V. WHAT IF THERE WERE GREATER EQUALITY OF OPPORTUNITY AND INCOME?

We have examined here the working (and lower middle) class defenses of the present order. They are well organized and solidly built. By and large these people believe that the field is open, merit will tell. They may then deprecate the importance of class, limit their perspectives, accept their situation reluctantly or with satisfaction. They may see the benefits of society flowing to their own class, however they define it. They tend to believe that each person's status is in some way deserved.

How would these lower middle and working class men feel about a change in the social order such that they and their friends might suddenly be equal to others now higher or lower in the social order? Most of them wouldn't like it. They would fear and resent this kind of equality.

ABANDONMENT OF A RATIONALE.   Changing ideas is a strain not to be lightly incurred, particularly when these ideas are intimately related to one's self-esteem. The less education one has, the harder it is to change such ideas. Painfully these men have elaborated an explanation for their situation in life; it helps explain things to their wives who take their status from them; it permits their growing children to account for relative social status in school; it offers to each man the satisfactions of social identity and a measure of social worth. Their rationales are endowed with moral qualities; the distribution of values in the society is seen as just and natural. While it gives satisfactions of an obvious kind to those who contemplate those beneath them, it also gives order and a kind of reassurance, oddly enough, to those who glance upwards towards "society" or "the four hundred." This reassurance is not unlike the reassurance provided by the belief in a Just God while injustices rain upon one's head. The feudal serf, the Polish peasant, the Mexican peon believed that theirs was a moral and a "natural order"— so also the American working man.

THE PROBLEM OF SOCIAL ADJUSTMENT.   Equality would pose problems of social adjustments, of manners, of how to behave. Here is Sokolsky, unprepossessing, uneducated, and nervous, with a more prosperous brother in the same town. "I'm not going to go over there," he says, "because every time I go there I feel uncomfortable." On the question of rising from one social class to another, his views reflect this personal situation:

I think it's hard. Let's say—let's take me, for instance. Supposing I came into a lot of money, and I moved into a nice neighborhood—class—maybe I wouldn't know how to act then. I think it's very hard, because people know that you just—word gets around that you . . . never had it before you got it now. Well, maybe they wouldn't like you . . . maybe you don't know how to act.

The kind of equality with others which would mean a rapid rise in his own status is a matter of concern, mixed, of course, with pleasant anticipation at the thought of "telling off" his brother.

Consider the possibility of social equality including genuine fraternization, without economic equality. Sullivan, a railroad fireman, deals with this in graphic terms:

What is the basis of social class? Well, things that people have in common . . . Money is one, for instance, like I wouldn't feel very comfortable going around with a millionaire, we'll say . . . He could do a lot and say a lot— mention places he'd been and so on—I mean I wouldn't be able to keep up with him . . . and he wouldn't have to watch his money, and I'd have to be pinching mine to see if I had enough for another beer, or something.

And, along the lines of Sokolsky's comments, Sullivan believes that moving upwards in the social scale is easier if one moves to a new place where one has not been known in the old connection. Flynn holds that having the right interests and conversational topics for the new and higher social group will make it possible—but otherwise it could be painful. Kuchinsky, the house painter, says "I suppose it would feel funny to get into a higher class, but I don't believe I would change. I wouldn't just disregard my friends if I came into any money." Clinging to old friends would give some security in that dazzling new world.

De Angelo, a factory operative, also considers the question of whether the higher status people will accept the *arriviste,* but for himself, he dismisses it:

I wouldn't worry much about whether they would accept or they wouldn't accept. I would move into another class. I mean—I mean—I don't worry much about that stuff. If people don't want to bother with me, I don't bother with them, that's all.

These fears, while plausible and all too human on the face of it, emerged unexpectedly from the interview material designed to capture ideas and emotions on other aspects of class status. They highlight a resistance to equalitarian movements that might bring the working class and this reject-ing superior class—whether it is imaginary or not—in close association. If these were revolutionaries, one might phrase their anxieties: "Will my victims accept me?" But they are not revolutionaries.

These are problems of rising in status to meet the upper classes face to face. But there is another risk in opening the gates so that those of moderate circumstances can rise to higher status. Equality of opportunity, it appears, is inherently dangerous in this respect: there is the risk that friends, neigh-bors, or subordinates will surpass one in status. O'Hara has this on his mind. Some of the people who rise in status are nice, but:

You get other ones, the minute they get a little, they get big-headed and they think they're better than the other ones—where they're still—to me they're worse than the middle class. I mean, they should get down, because they're just showing their illiteracy—that's all they're doing.

Sokolsky worries about this possibility, too, having been exposed to the slights of his brother's family. But the worry over being passed by is not important, not salient. It is only rarely mentioned.

DEPRIVATION OF A MERITORIOUS ELITE.   It is comforting to have the "natural leaders" of a society well entrenched in their proper place. If there were equality there would no longer be such an elite to supervise and take care of people—especially "me." Thus Woodside, our policeman, reports:

I think anybody that has money—I think their interest is much wider than the regular working man. . . . And therefore I think that the man with the money is a little bit more educated, for the simple reason he has the money, and he has a much wider view of life—because he's in the knowledge of it all the time.

Here and elsewhere in the interview, one senses that Woodside is glad to have such educated, broad-gauged men in eminent positions. He certainly opposes the notion of equality of income. Something similar creeps into Johnson's discussion of social classes. He feels that the upper classes, who "seem to be very nice people," are "willing to lend a helping hand—to listen to you. I would say they'd help you out more than the middle class [man] would help you out even if he was in a position to help you out." Equality, then, would deprive society, and oneself, of a group of friendly, wise, and helpful people who occupy the social eminences.

THE LOSS OF THE GOALS OF LIFE.   But most important of all, equality, at least equality of income, would deprive people of the goals of life. Every one of the fifteen clients with whom I spent my evenings for seven months believed that equality of income would deprive men of their incentive to work, achieve, and develop their skills. These answers ranged, in their sophistication and approach, across a broad field. The most highly educated man in the sample, Farrel, answers the question "How would you feel if everyone received the same income in our society?" by saying:

I think it would be kind of silly. . . . Society, by using income as a reward technique, can often insure that the individuals will put forth their best efforts.

He does not believe, for himself, that status or income are central to motivation—but for others, they are. Woodside, our policeman, whose main concern is not the vistas of wealth and opportunity of the American dream, but rather whether he can get a good pension if he should have to retire early, comes forward as follows:

I'd say that [equal income]—that is something that's pretty—I think it would be a dull thing, because life would be accepted—or it would—rather we'd go stale. There would be no initiative to be a little different, or go ahead.

Like Woodside, Flynn, a white collar worker, responds with a feeling of personal loss—the idea of such an equality of income would make him feel "very mad." Costa, whose ambitions in life are most modest, holds that equality of income "would eliminate the basic thing about the wonderful opportunity you have in this country." Then, for a moment the notion of his income equalling that of the professional man passes pleasantly through his mind: "don't misunderstand me—I like the idea"; then again, "I think it eliminates the main reason why people become engineers and professors and doctors."

Rapuano, whose worries have given him ulcers, projects himself into a situation where everyone receives the same income, in this case a high one:

If everyone had the same income of a man that's earning $50,000 a year, and he went to, let's say 10 years of college to do that, why hell, I'd just as soon *sit on my ass as go to college and wait till I could earn $50,000 a year, too. Of course, what the hell am I going to do to earn $50,000 a year—now that's another question.*

But however the question is answered, he is clear that guaranteed equal incomes would encourage people to sit around on their anatomy and wait for their pay checks. But he would like to see some levelling, particularly if doctors, whom he hates, were to have their fees and incomes substantially reduced.

THAT THESE SACRIFICES SHALL NOT HAVE BEEN IN VAIN. The men I talked to were not at the bottom of the scale; not at all. They were stable bread-winners, churchgoers, voters, family men. They achieved this position in life through hard work and sometimes bitter sacrifices. They are distinguished from the lower classes through their initiative, zeal and responsibility, their willingness and ability to postpone pleasures or to forego them entirely. In their control of impulse and desire they have absorbed the Protestant ethic. At least six of them have two jobs and almost no leisure. In answering questions on "the last time you remember having a specially good time" some of them must go back ten to fifteen years. Nor are their good times remarkable for their spontaneous fun and enjoyment of life. Many of them do not like their jobs, but stick to them because of their family responsibilities—and they do not know what else they would rather do. In short, they have sacrificed their hedonistic inclinations, given up good times, expended their energy and resources in order to achieve and maintain their present tenuous hold on respectability and middle status.

Now in such a situation to suggest that men be equalized and the lower orders raised and one's own hard-earned status given to them as a right and not a reward for effort, seems to them desperately wrong. In the words of my research assistant, David Sears, "Suppose the Marshall Plan had provided a block and tackle for Sisyphus after all these years. How do you think he would have felt?" Sokolsky, Woodside, and Dempsey have rolled the stone to the top of the hill so long, they despise the suggestion that it might have been in vain. Or even worse, that their neighbors at the foot of the hill might have the use of a block and tackle.

THE WORLD WOULD COLLAPSE. As a corollary to the view that life would lose its vigor and its savor with equality of income, there is the image of an equalitarian society as a world running down, a chaotic and disorganized place to live. The professions would be decimated: "People pursue the higher educational levels for a reason—there's a lot of rewards, either financial or social," says Costa. Sullivan says, "Why should people take the headaches of responsible jobs if the pay didn't meet the responsibilities?" For the general society, Flynn, a white collar man, believes that "if there were no monetary incentive involved, I think there'd be a complete loss. It would stop all development—there's no doubt about it." McNamara, a bookkeeper, sees people then reduced to a dead level of worth: with equal income "the efforts would be equal and pretty soon we would be worth the same thing." In two contrasting views, both suggesting economic disorganization, Woodside believes "I think you'd find too many men digging ditches, and no doctors," while Rapuano believes men would fail to dig ditches or sewers "and where the hell would we be when we wanted to go to the toilet?"

Only a few took up the posssible inference that this was an attractive, but impractical ideal—and almost none followed up the suggestion that some equalization of income, if not complete equality, would be desirable. The fact of the matter is that these men, by and large, prefer an inequalitarian society, and even prefer a society graced by some men of great wealth. As they look out upon the social scene, they feel that an equalitarian society would present them with too many problems of moral adjustment, interpersonal social adjustment, and motivational adjustment which they fear and dislike. But perhaps, most important, their life goals are structured around achievement and success in monetary terms. If these were taken away, life would be a desert. These men view the possibility of an equalitarian world as a paraphrased version of Swinburne's lines on Jesus Christ, "Thou hast conquered, oh pale equalitarian, and the world has grown gray with thy breath."

VI. SOME THEORETICAL IMPLICATIONS

Like any findings on the nature of men's social attitudes and beliefs, even in such a culture-bound inquiry as this one, the new information implies certain theoretical propositions which may be incorporated into the main body of political theory. Let us consider seven such propositions growing more or less directly out of our findings on the fear of equality:

(1) The greater the emphasis in a society upon the availability of "equal opportunity for all," the greater the need for members of that society to develop an acceptable rationalization for their own social status.

(2) The greater the strain on a person's self-esteem implied by a relatively low status in an open society, the greater the necessity to explain this status as "natural" and "proper" in the social order. Lower status people generally find it less punishing to think of themselves as correctly placed by a just society than to think of themselves as exploited, or victimized by an unjust society.

(3) The greater the emphasis in a society upon equality of opportunity, the greater the tendency for those of marginal status to denigrate those lower

than themselves. This view seems to such people to have the factual or even moral justification that if the lower classes "cared" enough they could be better off. It has a psychological "justification" in that it draws attention to one's own relatively better status and one's own relatively greater initiative and virtue.

(4) People tend to care less about *equality* of opportunity than about the availability of *some* opportunity. Men do not need the same life chances as everybody else, indeed they usually care very little about that. They need only chances (preferably with unknown odds) for a slightly better life than they now have. Thus: Popular satisfaction with one's own status is related less to equality of opportunity than to the breadth of distribution of some opportunity for all, however unequal this distribution may be. A man who can improve his position one rung does not resent the man who starts on a different ladder half way up.

These propositions are conservative in their implications. The psychological roots of this conservatism must be explored elsewhere, as must the many exceptions which may be observed when the fabric of a social order is so torn that the leaders, the rich and powerful, are seen as illegitimate— and hence "appropriately" interpreted as exploiters of the poor. I maintain, however, that these propositions hold generally for the American culture over most of its history—and also, that the propositions hold for most of the world most of the time. This is so even though they fly in the face of much social theory—theory often generalized from more specialized studies of radicalism and revolution. Incidentally, one must observe that it is as important to explain why revolutions and radical social movements do *not* happen as it is to explain why they do.

The more I observed the psychological and physical drain placed upon my sample by the pressures to consume—and therefore to scratch in the corners of the economy for extra income—the more it appeared that competitive consumption was not a stimulus to class conflict, as might have been expected, but was a substitute for or a sublimation of it. Thus we would say:

(5) The more emphasis a society places upon consumption—through advertising, development of new products, and easy installment buying—the more will social dissatisfaction be channeled into intra-class consumption rivalry instead of inter-class resentment and conflict. The Great American Medicine Show creates consumer unrest, working wives, and dual-job-holding, not antagonism toward the "owning classes."

As a corollary of this view: (6) The more emphasis a society places upon consumption, the more will labor unions focus upon the "bread and butter" aspects of unionism, as contrasted to its ideological elements.

We come, finally, to a hypothesis which arises from this inquiry into the fear of equality but goes much beyond the focus of the present study. I mention it here in a speculative frame of mind, undogmatically, and even regretfully:

(7) The ideals of the French Revolution, liberty and equality, have been advanced because of the accidental correspondence between these ideals and needs of the bourgeoisie for freedom of economic action and the demands of the working class, very simply, for "more." Ideas have an autonomy of their own, however, in the sense that once moralized they persist even if the social forces which brought them to the fore decline in strength. They become "myths"—but myths erode without support from some major social stratum. Neither the commercial classes nor the working classes, the historical beneficiaries of these two moralized ideas (ideals or myths), have much affection for the ideals in their universal forms. On the other hand, the professional classes, particularly the lawyers, ministers, and teachers of a society, very often do have such an affection. It is they, in the democratic West, who serve as the "hard core" of democratic defenders, in so far as there is one. It is they, more frequently than others, who are supportive of the generalized application of the ideals of freedom and equality to all men. This is not virtue, but rather a different organization of interests and a different training. Whatever the reason, however, it is not to "The People," not to the business class, not to the working class, that we must look for the consistent and relatively unqualified defense of freedom and equality. The professional class, at least in the American culture, serves as the staunchest defender of democracy's two greatest ideals.

Ethnic and Party Affiliations of Candidates as Determinants of Voting

LEON J. KAMIN

The process of electoral choice in a representative democracy ultimately confronts the voter with a ballot form presenting a number of alternative candidates among whom he must choose. The bases upon which such choices are made are an obvious concern of political theory and also a legitimate subject of psychological inquiry. Political theory tends to stress party affiliation as a rational determinant of such choices; political parties are said to represent distinctive programmes of action, and the voter, by choosing the candidate of the appropriate party, expresses his preference among these

Reprinted from *The Canadian Journal of Psychology*, vol. 12 (1958), pp. 205–13 by permission of the author and the University of Toronto Press.

programmes. There are, however, many other factors which undoubtedly influence the voter's choice.

Rationally irrelevant factors such as a candidate's personal appearance, mannerisms, and sex may influence voters in one direction or another. Another factor is perhaps of greater moment; practical politicians assert with confidence the importance of the ethnic affiliations of candidate and of voter. Voters of French descent are said to prefer candidates of French origin, voters of Jewish descent, Jewish candidates, and so on. The basis for such assertions lies largely in the analysis of actual election returns: French-speaking districts tend to return French-speaking candidates, Jewish districts Jewish candidates.

The study of such factors by analysis of actual elections suffers from inherent difficulties. Thus, if an Anglo-Saxon district traditionally returns an Anglo-Saxon Liberal, it is by no means clear whether this is because the candidate is Anglo-Saxon, is Liberal, wears a goatee, or all of these. We cannot, of course, intervene in actual elections to separate such confounded factors, but we can arrange artificial elections in such a way as to separate those factors whose effects we wish to study.

The essential technique of the present study was to approach voters in the context of a public opinion poll before an actual parliamentary election, and ask them to make a choice among fictitious candidates for a fictitious office. The personal characteristics of the "candidates" could obviously be of no influence in such a choice; hence, by varying in permutation their alleged ethnic and party affiliations, clear tests of the relative importance of these factors could be made. Although the conclusions drawn from the study are limited to the specific samples employed, the methodology may be of more general interest.

METHOD

The respondents' voting choices were obtained by door-to-door canvassing during May and June, 1957, before the June parliamentary election. The canvasser, carrying a cardboard "ballot box" and a sheaf of mimeographed ballot forms, asked the householder if he were a registered voter. If so, the canvasser explained that an attempt was being made to predict the outcome of the forthcoming election. The householder was asked to participate in the poll by accepting a ballot form, marking his choices, and depositing the ballot anonymously in the box. The refusal rate was very low and, in any event, has no bearing on the following analyses.

There were two separate polls, one conducted in the city of Kingston and one in the city of Cornwall. The Kingston canvasser was a native English speaker, and was instructed to avoid households with nameplates obviously suggesting French descent. The composition of the Kingston population makes it certain that very few of the respondents were ethnically French, and suggests that the majority were Scottish, English, and Irish. The Cornwall canvasser was a native French speaker, instructed to remain within a French-speaking neighbourhood. The Kingston ballots were in English, the Cornwall ballots in French. We shall refer to the repondents in the two cities as, respectively, "English" and "French."

The general form of the ballots employed is illustrated in Figure 1, which reproduces *one* of the forms used in Kingston. The ballot presents two separate contests. The first is genuine, giving the names and party affiliations of the actual candidates for parliament. The names and parties of the true candidates were never tampered with, though on some ballot forms there was no mention of political parties. The second contest, for "Federal Solicitor," is wholly fictitious. The parties attributed to the three fictitious candidates were permuted on different ballot forms. There were some ballot forms which made no mention of parties; on forms of this type the orders in which the three fictitious names appeared were permuted.

The canvasser was thus equipped with a number of different ballot forms. Within any given neighbourhood, he used the various forms in sequence as he progressed from house to house. The data analyses will be based on comparisons between different ballot forms, and for this purpose the technique assures equivalent samples for different forms. Independently of this, an attempt was made to sample geographic neighbourhoods in such a

FIGURE 1.   ONE FORM OF THE BALLOT EMPLOYED IN KINGSTON. ALTERNATE FORMS OMITTED MENTION OF POLITICAL PARTIES, ROTATED POSITIONS OF FICTITIOUS CANDIDATES ON THE BALLOT, AND PERMUTED COMBINATIONS OF FICTITIOUS CANDIDATES AND PARTIES.

The Public Opinion Centre

We are trying to predict the results of the next election. We are *not* interested in how you, as an individual, vote. But we would appreciate it greatly if you filled out this form and, in private, dropped it into the interviewer's box. Thank you.

If a federal election were to be held today for the following two offices, for which candidate would you vote?

For MEMBER OF PARLIAMENT, FROM KINGSTON:
HENDERSON, William J.   (LIBERAL)   _____
KIDD, Thomas A.   (PROGRESSIVE CONSERVATIVE)   _____
MILLARD, J. Allan   (C.C.F.)   _____

For FEDERAL SOLICITOR, FROM KINGSTON:
CARTER, Stanley F.   (PROGRESSIVE CONSERVATIVE)   _____
LAVOISIER, René   (LIBERAL)   _____
McINTYRE, Robert H.   (C.C.F.)   _____

way as to be roughly representative of the entire city. The distribution of respondents' choices in the genuine contest, it may be noted, corresponded very closely to the votes later cast in the real election in the city.

The Cornwall ballots were of the same general construction as the Kingston ballots, though the names of the true candidates for parliament were, of course, different. The fictitious office was termed "Conseilleur Juridique Fédéral." The three fictitious candidates, whose political parties and positions on the ballot were permuted, were Lucien Beaulieu, Robert H. Harris, and René Lavoisier. The canvasser made no attempt to obtain a representative sample of the city of Cornwall, remaining instead within a single French-speaking neighbourhood. In this neighbourhood different ballot forms were used in sequence to obtain equivalent samples.

When, as sometimes occurred, a respondent remarked that he had never heard of the office of "Federal Solicitor," or did not know the candidates, the canvassers remained non-committal. When pressed on this score—a rare occurrence—they explained that they merely worked for the polling agency, and were not familiar with details of the poll. The canvassers were instructed to give the name, address, and telephone of the experimenter to any respondent who requested a fuller explanation. The one respondent who asked for this information did not in fact contact the experimenter.

Within Kingston, it was assumed, the names Carter and McIntyre would be categorized as English, and the name Lavoisier as French. Within Cornwall, the names Beaulieu and Lavoisier should be categorized as French, and Harris as English. The analyses will focus especially on votes for the odd, "contra-ethnic" candidate.

RESULTS

The Kingston sample included six hundred individuals whose ballot forms made no mention of political parties. Thus, in the fictitious contest, any deviation of the choices of these respondents from a chance distribution must be attributed either to the names of the candidates or to the order in which the names appeared. To separate these possibilities the three names were presented equally often in each of the six possible permutations.

The first point of interest is that 241 (40 per cent) of these respondents, all of whom had indicated a choice in the true parliamentary contest, failed to vote in the fictitious contest. The following analysis is thus based on the 359 respondents who did vote. Table I indicates, in terms of both number and percentage of votes, the division of votes among the three candidates, with position on the ballot counterbalanced. There are, clearly, systematic preferences among the three fictitious names. The deviation of the votes from an even three-way division was assessed by chi-square. The chi-square, with 2 df, is 82.12, p much less than .001. The Lavoisier vote, as expected, is by

TABLE I. DISTRIBUTION OF VOTES IN KINGSTON SAMPLE
WITH NO PARTIES ON BALLOT

	Total Vote	*Percentage*
Candidate		
Carter, Stanley F.	133	37.0
Lavoisier, René	44	12.3
McIntyre, Robert H.	182	50.7
Ballot position		
First	152	42.3
Second	128	35.7
Third	79	22.0

far the smallest; however, when McIntyre and Carter alone are considered, McIntyre is selected significantly more often (p < .01).

Table I also indicates, for the same respondent, the division of votes among the three ballot positions, with names of candidates counterbalanced. There is a marked effect of position on the ballot. The chi-square, assuming the theoretical model of an even three-way split among positions, is 23.33, with 2df, p < .001. The main effect is a severe depression of the third ballot position, the difference between the first two positions alone falling short of significance.

The ballots of this sample had been so marked as to permit identification of the sex of the respondent. Analysis revealed no significant differences whatever between sexes as to preferences for names or for ballot positions.

There was an additional Kingston sample of three hundred whose ballots assigned political parties to each of the fictitious candidates. There were forty-three respondents (14 per cent) who failed to vote. Thus, in Kingston, more respondents vote in a fictitious election if candidates are assigned parties than if not (p < .001). The question of major interest, however, is whether systematic differences among candidates' names still occur when candidates are assigned parties. The critical candidate for analytical purposes is Lavoisier, who appeared on one hundred ballots as a Liberal, on one hundred as a Progressive Conservative, and on one hundred as a C.C.F. candidate, with ballot position held constant.

Table II presents, first, the proportion of votes for and against the Progressive Conservatives, both when Lavoisier is the Conservative candidate and when he is not. These proportions, submitted to a chi-square test, do not differ significantly. The table also indicates the proportion of votes for and against the Liberals, both when Lavoisier is the Liberal candidate and when he is not. These proportions do not differ significantly. These analyses in-

TABLE II. ANALYSIS OF VOTES OF KINGSTON SAMPLE
WITH PARTIES ON BALLOT

	Total Vote		*Percentage*	
P.C. Candidate	*For P.C.*	*Against P.C.*	*For P.C.*	*Against P.C.*
Lavoisier	44	36	55.0	45.0
Carter or McIntyre	87	90	49.1	50.9
Liberal Candidate	*For Libs.*	*Against Libs.*	*For Libs.*	*Against Libs.*
Lavoisier	37	51	42.0	58.0
Carter or McIntyre	82	87	48.5	51.5

dicate that the classifications by party and by candidate's name are independent. That is, the proportion of votes cast for a party is not significantly
affected by the name of the party's candidate. This despite the fact that, in
the absence of a party label, a clear order of preference exists among the
names.

The C.C.F. vote in the sample was so small (2 per cent) as to make an
analysis for this party impossible. Parenthetically it may be noted that, in
terms of votes for the genuine parliamentary contest, there were no significant differences among the various sub-samples to which different ballot
forms were distributed.

In the French sample, in Cornwall, 126 people were given ballots which
made no mention of parties. There were eighteen failures to vote in the
fictitious contest (13 per cent). This percentage is smaller than that in Kingston, but no attempt was made to match the samples for socio-economic
status or other variables. Table III indicates, for this sample, the distribution
of votes among the candidates, with position on the ballot counterbalanced.
There exists, as in Kingston, a systematic preference: the chi-square, with

TABLE III. DISTRIBUTION OF VOTES IN CORNWALL SAMPLE
WITH NO PARTIES ON BALLOT

	Total Vote	*Percentage*
Candidate		
Beaulieu, Lucien	72	66.7
Harris, Robert H.	17	15.7
Lavoisier, René	19	17.6
Ballot position		
First	40	37.0
Second	44	40.9
Third	24	22.2

2 df, is 54.06, p>.001. While Harris, as expected, polls the lowest vote, Lavoisier does not do so significantly better; Beaulieu is by far the preferred candidate. Table III also indicates a significant effect of position on the ballot in Cornwall, similar to that in Kingston. The third position is significantly depressed; the chi-square, with 2 df, is 6.22, p < .05.

There was an additional Cornwall sample of sixty-eight whose ballots assigned parties to the fictitious candidates. There were eleven failures to vote (16 per cent). This percentage does not differ significantly from the equivalent Kingston sample, or from the party-less Cornwall sample. Table IV presents, first, the proportion of votes for and against the Progressive Conservatives, both when Harris (now the critical candidate) is the Conservative candidate and when he is not. These proportions, submitted (because of the small N in some cells) to Fisher's exact test, do not differ significantly. The table also presents the proportion of votes for and against the Liberals when Harris is and is not the Liberal candidate; again, by Fisher's exact test, there is no significant difference between these proportions. There was only one C.C.F. vote in this sample, precluding any analysis. Thus, as with the English Kingston sample, the proportion of votes cast for a party is not affected by the name of the party's candidate, despite a marked preference among the names presented without parties.

TABLE IV. ANALYSIS OF VOTES OF CORNWALL SAMPLE
WITH PARTIES ON BALLOT

	Total Vote		*Percentage*	
P.C. Candidate	*For P.C.*	*Against P.C.*	*For P.C.*	*Against P.C.*
Harris	0	19	0.0	100.0
Beaulieu or Lavoisier	5	33	13.2	86.8
Liberal Candidate	*For Libs.*	*Against Libs.*	*For Libs.*	*Against Libs.*
Harris	14	3	82.4	17.6
Beaulieu or Lavoisier	37	3	92.5	7.5

DISCUSSION

The over-all results of the study are clear. With both English and French samples, when respondents are requested to choose among fictitious candidates for a fictitious office, they are markedly influenced both by the candidates' names and by the order in which the names appear on the ballot. Within each ethnic group, a name with ethnic connotations opposite to the respondents' is under-chosen, as is the last name in a three-person list. When, however, the same names are presented but associated with political parties, both the English and French groups are guided by party identification of the candidate, and name as such cannot be demonstrated to have a significant effect.

The precise significance of the preference orders among names is difficult to specify. Although it does not seem surprising that Lavoisier fares poorly among the English, and Harris among the French, the preferences of the English for McIntyre over Carter and of the French for Beaulieu over Lavoisier were not expected. With hindsight, it seems reasonable to assume that Lavoisier, unlike Beaulieu, is not truly a *canadien* name; indeed, a few French respondents overtly remarked that, knowing none of the candidates, they "might as well vote for a *canadien,* Beaulieu." The English respondents volunteered no bases for their choices.

The candidates' names differ, of course, in terms of sheer familiarity to the respondents, as well as with regard to ethnic connotations. Although it is difficult to separate ethnic value and familiarity, it seems worthwhile to stress that there is no reason to equate preference orders among the names with ethnic *prejudice*. The vote distribution does not indicate an active rejection of opposite ethnic groups any more than it indicates an active "prejudice" against the third ballot position. Psychologically, these data are reminiscent of experimental studies of perception; the importance of minimal, irrelevant cues is exaggerated when the normally determining cues are deliberately excluded.

The results of this study are limited by the nature of the samples and conditions employed. Whether similar results would obtain in cities of different cultural composition, for other ethnic groups, in provincial and municipal elections, and so on, is an open question. The technique employed in this study, however, seems capable of answering many such questions, and may be of value both to social scientists and to practical politicians.

We should note, finally, that the ballot actually employed in Canadian parliamentary elections is of such a form as to maximize "irrational" determinants of voting choice. The ballot does not indicate the party affiliations of candidates, nor is position on the ballot counterbalanced. These, of course, are the conditions which maximize "ethnic voting" and the position effect. The present data, taken in conjunction with the political theory on which democracy rests, could support strong arguments for the inclusion of party affiliation on the ballot, and for counterbalancing of positions.

SUMMARY

Within the context of a public opinion poll before a genuine parliamentary election, English- and French-speaking respondents were asked to choose among three fictitious candidates for a fictitious office. The candidates' names were varied with regard to ethnic connotations and to position on the ballot. Within both English and French groups there were marked tendencies to under-choose candidates whose names had "alien" ethnic connotations, or who appeared last on the ballot. When, however, with new samples, the same names were permuted with political parties, both English and French samples were guided by the candidates' party affiiliations; name had no significant effect.

CHAPTER THREE

SOCIAL BASES
OF
POLITICAL BEHAVIOR

IN Chapter Two it was suggested that personality is the result of interaction between original nature and social environment. The material in that section focused on personality as a determinant of political behavior. It was noted, however, that the extent to which personality is a major variable for behavior depends on the context in which it occurs. Political situations may so structure behavior as to suppress personality differences and produce patterns of response in which large numbers of individuals assume essentially the same roles. This may be due to the fact that the situation leaves little room for personality differences. The act of voting is a case in point, for while there is choice in such matters, alternatives are drastically restricted.

Further examples of this theory are presented by Donald Matthews. While no one would suggest the absence of personality differences in the United States Senate, he shows that certain types of behavior are called for by particular group norms or folkways. As Matthews indicates, success in goal attainment is significantly related to the degree of conformity one exhibits in such situations. All of this is consonant with the teaching of social psychology that the average individual is highly sensitized to his peer groups and to the subgroup in the society of which he is a member. These influences are so strong that they may overcome biological and basic personality differences. Thus, if a Negro is reared in Chinese society, he will develop attitudes and habits which reflect the values of Chinese culture.

As might be expected, situational pressures do not affect all individuals in the same way. The selection by Eleanor Maccoby *et al.* indicates that young people are unusually responsive to the political pressures of the moment. This suggests the possibility that youth may be able to play a greater role in mediating change than their elders. Of course, older people, too, are influenced by contemporary environmental pressures as Edward Shils shows in his piece on the legislator; but the Maccoby finding reflects the fact that personality is developed primarily in early rather than later life. Consequently, it appears that the older one becomes, the greater the influence of past rather than present experience in determining behavioral response.

One who studies the political process cannot afford to ignore the social variables in the background of the decision-maker. The presence of certain social background characteristics not only influence the behavior of the individual possessing them, but may also make the individual more or less attractive to others with whom he interacts. An example of the latter is shown by Schmidhauser in his study of Supreme Court justices. The evidence reveals that a particularized set of social background characteristics have been unusually salient for presidents making appointments to the Court.

Finally, as Fenton and Vines reveal, social variables may serve to differentiate geographical areas in terms of the behavioral responses of the population to particular contemporary problems.

Youth and Political Change

ELEANOR E. MACCOBY, RICHARD E. MATTHEWS, ANTON S. MORTON

In each presidential election occurring in the mid-twentieth century, approximately one-ninth of the people eligible to vote are young people who are eligible to cast a presidential ballot for the first time, having had their twenty-first birthdays since the last presidential election. These young people are of great interest to social scientists and political practitioners alike, not only because they constitute a large enough group to carry considerable weight in any particular election outcome, but because it is possible that the political allegiances which they form early in their voting careers will be perpetuated for many years, and thus have an impact upon a series of elections. We do not know a great deal about changes in the voting pattern of individual citizens, or groups of citizens, as they grow older and accumulate voting experience. Nor do we know how many elements of the political

Reprinted from *The Public Opinion Quarterly,* vol. 18 (1954–55), pp. 23–39 by permission of the publisher. Copyright 1954 by *The Public Opinion Quarterly.*

ideology formed in late adolescence and early adulthood are retained for a life-time. It is a reasonable hypothesis, however, that young people, being less bound than older people by habit and old political ties, will be more responsive to the political pressures of the moment, so that they might play a greater role in mediating political change than their elders.

What do we already know concerning the political behavior of young people? With varying degrees of certainty, the following facts have been fairly well established:

1. *A smaller percentage of young people go to the polls than do people in older age groups.*
2. *In his choice of candidate, a young person tends to be similar to his parents.*
3. *Despite the agreement with their parents, young people as a group have been more Democratic in party choice than older voters, at least since 1936.*

An interesting question is whether the young person's preference for the Democratic party means that he is less conservative in his ideology than older voters. In general, of course, there is a correlation between the liberal-conservative dimension and party choice, but the existing evidence does not point as strongly to a liberal ideology among the young, as might be expected. Centers found a slight tendency for young people among the upper occupational groups to be more liberal, but among the laboring groups, the young were no more liberal than the old. Lazarsfeld found greater conformity to one's group with increasing age, so that older Catholics were more strongly Democratic, old Protestants more strongly Republican, than younger people in these two religious groups. He suggested that increasing age brings about greater social conservation, rather than greater political conservatism.

In any case, an anomaly in the existing findings remains to be explained, and this is the fact that youth is consistently more Democratic than the older generations, while at the same time young people tend to follow in the political footsteps of their parents. Lubell has proposed an interesting hypothesis to explain this situation. He points out that over the last two decades, children of immigrants have come of age; their parents were not eligible voters. Furthermore, the working-class urban masses, with their higher birthrate, have contributed disproportionately to each new crop of first-time voters. Possibly, young people vote proportionally just as their parents do, and it is the differential rates of population growth among the different social classes which explain the fact that young people as a whole have been consistently more Democratic than the older age groups. On the other hand, it is possible that young people tend to start their political careers with a more "left" or liberal ideology, and become more conservative as they grow older and acquire a larger stake in the existing state of affairs. Possibly, both these factors operate jointly to produce a high proportion of Democrats among the young.

Some important questions to be answered by research, then, are: 1) To what extent do young people follow their parents' lead politically? 2) When they do differ from their parents in politics, do they move primarily in the Democratic direction, or are there counter-balancing changes in both directions? and 3) When the young person does take up a political position different from that of his parents, what are some of the psychological and sociological variables associated with the change? The present study has been focused upon these questions, in an effort to advance our understanding of the political behavior of young people.

THE STUDY

The study was conducted in Cambridge, Massachusetts just after the presidential elections of November, 1952. Interviews were conducted with 339 people aged 21-24 inclusive—a group eligible to vote in a presidential election for the first time in 1952. Originally, a probability sample of people within the desired age range was selected from the police lists of Cambridge, which are compiled in January of every year, and are intended to record the name, age and sex of every adult resident of Cambridge at the time of listing. In the course of interviewing, however, the list was found to be badly out of date and consequently the young people finally interviewed cannot be considered to be a representative sample of the young people of Cambridge. However, the main objective of the study was not to produce descriptive statistics about Cambridge but to examine relationships between variables. For such purposes, the range of the sample is more important than its representativeness.

By way of background for the report which follows, it may be useful to present here the voting record for the city of Cambridge in the 1952 elections:

76 per cent of those eligible to vote cast a ballot in the presidential contest.
41.8 per cent voted for Eisenhower (among those voting for one of the two major Presidential candidates).
35.5 per cent voted for Lodge, the Republican senatorial candidate.
37.1 per cent voted for Herter, the Republican candidate for Governor.

It may be seen that even in a year in which the Republicans swept the country, and in which Eisenhower carried the state of Massachusetts (which has been Democratic for many years), Cambridge remained heavily Democratic. The margin for the Democrats was smaller than in previous years, however.

The following report must be interpreted, then, in the light of the fact that the study was conducted in a Democratic stronghold (predominantly working class), in a year which saw a major swing toward the Republican Party.

POLITICAL PREFERENCES: PARENT AND CHILD

National poll data have consistently shown that youth are more Democratic than older age groups. This was true even in 1952 although Eisenhower carried a much larger proportion of the young vote than had earlier Republican candidates. It has not been clear, however, whether individuals change during their lifetime (switching from the Democratic to the Republican Party as they grow older), whether the ranks of the Democrats in the young age bracket are being swelled through the higher birth-rate in the lower Socio-Economic Status (SES) urban groups and by the arrival at voting age of the children of immigrants, or whether both factors are operating.

If it is true that people change party allegiance in the Republican direction as they grow older, then it should follow that young people, as a group, would be more Democratic than their own parents. To check this, young voters were asked for their own party preferences and their choice of presidential candidates; they were also asked these two items of information about each of their parents. Of course, there were some instances in which the young person had lost contact with a parent, or for some other reason did not know his parents' political preferences. Data are presented in Table 1 for the cases in which the young person could report the party choice of his parents.

As may be seen from Table 1, there is high agreement between the party choice of the young voter and that of his parents, but the agreement is higher when the parents are Democrats. This would suggest a slight shift on the part of the younger generation as a whole toward the Democratic Party, if there were as many Republican as Democratic parents.

In a Democratic stronghold like Cambridge, there are so many more sets of Democratic than Republican parents, that the small proportion of young people switching from Democratic to Republican Party allegiance more than offsets (numerically) the larger proportion of young people switching from the Republican allegiance of their parents into the Democratic party, so that over the sample as a whole, there were slightly fewer (not significantly) Democratic young people than Democratic parents. On the whole, however, the agreement of young people with the party choice

TABLE 1. RELATIONSHIP BETWEEN PARTY CHOICE OF YOUNG
VOTER AND THAT OF HIS PARENTS

		FATHERS	
Respondents	*Republican*	*Democrat*	*Independent*
Republican	60%	12%	30%
Democrat	26	81	35
Independent	14	7	35
Total	100%	100%	100%
N	58	192	17
		MOTHERS	
Respondents	*Republican*	*Democrat*	*Independent*
Republican	71%	9%	23%
Democrat	22	83	50
Independent	7	8	27
Total	100%	100%	100%
N	56	201	26

of their parents is high: 74 per cent of those who can report their fathers'
party preference prefer the same party, and 76 per cent choose the same
party as their mothers'. In 86 per cent of the cases where the parents are
both of the same party, son or daughter chooses that party.

Parenthetically, it should be noted that there is no evidence of the traditional "father dominance" in political matters. There are only 21 instances
in the sample in which the father and mother disagree on their choices of
political party, but when they do, the young person is slightly more likely
(not significantly) to follow the mother's preference than the father's. When
agreement with parents is studied according to the sex of the child, it appears that while the daughters are most responsive to the influence of the
mother, sons are as likely to follow the mother as the father when parents
disagree.

While we have seen considerable agreement between political preferences of the first-time voter and those of his parents, there exists a group of
young people who choose a different party or a different presidential candidate than their parents, or both. What are the forces which might influence
a young person to abandon the political orientation of his parents? The first
step in studying this problem was to develop a score which would reflect
the extent to which the young person had changed from the political position of his parents. This score is called the Index of Political Change. Six
items of information were considered for the score: the respondent's party
choice and presidential choice, his mother's party choice and presidential

choice, and his father's party choice and presidential choice. Numerical values were assigned to each difference between the young person and either of his parents and these values were added, so that the highest score on political change would go to the young person who differed with both parents on both candidate and party choice. Differences on party choice were given twice as much weight as differences on candidate choice, on the assumption that party choice is a more pervasive indicator of political position than the preference for any particular candidate. Shifts away from the parents' political preferences were also labeled according to whether they were shifts away from a Democratic position and toward a Republican position, or vice versa.

What factors might produce a change on the part of the young person from the political orientation of his parents? The first hypothesis tested was one related to youthful rebellion. It has been popularly assumed that some young people are radical because they are throwing off the shackles of parental authority in their late adolescence. A reasonable assumption would be that the more rigid the control which the parents attempt to exercise over the teen-aged youth, the more he will feel the impulse to rebel and reject parental values when he is in a position to do so. An attempt was made in the current study to measure the strictness and rigidity of control exercised by the parents over the respondents when they were in their teens, and something about the reaction of the young person to his parents' effort at control.

As may be seen in Table 2, it is the children of the parents who attempt to exercise strictest control who most often change away from the political preference of their parents.

The highest conformity to parental political values is found among the group who were subject to moderate parental control. For the young person who is left rather completely on his own, conformity is less—presumably because his decisions are made more independently of family knowledge or influence. And conformity is also less for the rigidly-controlled group. Thus we see that maximum conformity by the young person to the political values of his family occurs when his parents have been neither laissez faire nor authoritarian in their dealings with him—when they have taken an interest in him and attempted to guide him, but have used moderate pressure via persuasion rather than strong pressure by command or force.

Although there are too few cases to make a definitive test, it is interesting that the effects of parental training methods on political conformity seem greatest when the parents have a high level of interest in politics. Presumably, when parents do not consider politics important, their children will choose some other area of values in which to signify their loyalty or register their protest.

TABLE 2. RELATIONSHIP BETWEEN AMOUNT OF PARENTAL
CONTROL AND THE INDEX OF POLITICAL CHANGE

	"In your case, when you were in your teens, did your family want to have quite a lot to say about your friends and the places you went and so on, or were you pretty much on your own?"		
Index of political change by young voter	*Parents had a lot to say*	*About average amount to say*	*Parents left respondent on his own*
Major change in Republican direction	18%	7%	9%
Minor change in Republican direction	14	10	17
No change, family Republican	12 ⎱ 50*	9 ⎱ 69*	11
No change, family Democratic	38 ⎰	60 ⎰	45
Minor change in Democratic direction	7	7	9
Major change in Democratic direction	11	7	9
	100%	100%	100%
Number of cases	74	69	140

*The 19% difference between the "no change" groups in the first two columns is significant at the .05 level, using a two-tailed test.

Among the strictist families, the change is largely toward being more Republican than the parents. This is unexpected, since "adolescent revolt" has been presumed to lead to leftward, rather than rightward, movement. It must be noted, however, that the strictest parental control was found at the lower SES levels, where the parents are heavily Democratic in political orientation. If the young person is to adopt a different set of political values than that of his parents, he *must* change toward the Republican party, unless he wants to go into the fringe parties, which very few young people do. (Only one member of our sample voted for the Progressive Party candidates.)

The fact that parental control is stricter in the low SES group raises the question whether the relationship found in Table 2 could be an artifact of SES: that is, possibly both political change and strict control are found mostly at the lower SES levels, in which case of course the relationship between control and change would be difficult to interpret. Analysis shows that political change is slightly more common at the *upper* SES levels, so that the relationship in Table 2 is not an artifact of SES.

It is true, however, that the relationship between the degree of parental control and the frequency of the young people's change away from parental politics is found almost exclusively at the lower SES. That is, among the working-class group, young people changed most from their parents' political positions when parental control was strict and when the young people resented this fact. At the higher SES levels, this tends not to be the case.

It appears, then, that when young people at the lower SES level change away from the political preferences of their parents, the change is at least partly motivated by revolt against over-strict control. At the upper SES level, while there is as much or more change on the part of young people, it is *not* a function of the atmosphere in the home where they grew up, and other factors must be sought.

What about the depth, or generality, of the change away from parental politics which is engendered in the "revolt" group? Possibly, these young people simply give themselves a different party label from their parents, or choose a different presidential candidate, without changing any of the ideology which one would ordinarily expect to underlie political preferences. Possibly, on the other hand, the spirit of revolt goes much deeper, and takes the form of a basic shift in ideology (toward the right or left) which is then reflected in vote and party choice. Unfortunately, the study provided no measure of the ideology of the young voter's parents. The young voter himself, however, was asked three questions adapted from Centers' ideology questions, and it is possible to compare the "revolt" group with the "non-revolt" group at a given SES level in their ideology (See Table 3).

There is a shift in the conservative direction among the young people who resent parental control, and who were shown earlier to be changing away from the party preference of their parents (changing largely in the direction of becoming more Republican). Two other ideology questions, one on public versus private ownership of power facilities and one on security versus individual initiative, both showed shifts in the same direction on the part of the "revolt" group, although the shifts were somewhat smaller.

TABLE 3. RELATIONSHIP BETWEEN PARENTAL CONTROL
AND IDEOLOGY, AT THE LOW SES LEVEL

For low SES group only: "In strikes and disputes between working people and employers, do you usually side with the workers or the employers?"	*Believe parents interfere too much*	*Believe parents do not interfere too much*
Workers	47%	67%
Lean toward workers, reservations	21	17
Sometimes one, sometimes other	19	14
Lean toward employers, reservations	9	2
Employers	4	—
	100%	100%
Number of cases	43	64

It appears likely, then, that shifts away from parental political preferences on the part of young people who resent parental control are accompanied by (or perhaps preceded by) some changes in general politico-social attitudes.

PEER GROUP INFLUENCE

We have been examining parental influence on voting. What about the influence of the young person's peers: friends, fellow-workers, and spouse? As Table 4 shows the young voter agrees on choice of party most highly with his spouse, next most highly with his friends, and least often with his fellow workers.

TABLE 4. RELATIONSHIP BETWEEN PARTY CHOICE OF YOUNG VOTER AND THAT OF HIS FRIENDS, FELLOW WORKERS, AND SPOUSE*

| | *Young Voter's Party Choice* | | |
	Republican	*Democrat*	*Independent*
Friends Mostly:			
Republican	52%	12%	24%
Democrat	28	74	52
Independent or 50-50	20	14	24
	100%	100%	100%
Number of cases**	71	203	29
Fellow Workers Mostly:			
Republican	35%	27%	42%
Democrat	42	52	25
Independent or 50-50	23	21	33
	100%	100%	100%
Number of cases**	48	132	24
Spouse:			
Republican	49%	4%	28%
Democrat	33	95	44
Independent	18	1	28
	100%	100%	100%
Number of cases**	33	103	18

*The young voter was asked the party preference of his spouse, and whether he thought his friends and fellow workers were mostly Republicans or mostly Dmeocrats.

**The numbers of cases vary because only part of the sample were married, and a sizeable group of the sample (mostly women) were not working and therefore had no fellow workers. Almost all the sample had a group of friends whose political orientation they could discuss.

Seventy-seven per cent of the married young voters had the same party preference as their spouses; 64 per cent had the same party preference as the majority of their friends, and 46 per cent of those who worked agreed in party choice with the majority of their fellow-workers. In a heavily Democratic area like Cambridge, Republican young people cannot or do not surround themselves as easily with like-minded friends and fellow workers as do the Democrats, or else, possibly the young Republicans tend to assume that the people around them are Democrats unless they have positive knowledge to the contrary.

Of course, the amount of agreement on party choice does not tell anything about the extent and direction of influence. Possibly, the higher agreement with friends than fellow workers means that people have more freedom of choice as to friends than fellow workers, and that they tend to choose like-minded friends. Another possibility is that friends exert more influence upon each other—change one another's minds about politics more—than do members of work groups.

In an effort to trace lines of influence, the young voter was asked how much he talked about politics with his friends, fellow workers, and spouse. The amount of political discussion was fairly high with friends and spouse, lower with fellow workers, where we have seen that there is less agreement on party preference. When we relate the amount of discussion to the amount of agreement on politics, we find that people who prefer the same party as their fellow workers tend to talk politics with them quite a bit, while those who have a different political position than their fellow workers less often engage in political discussion at work. (This difference is significant at the .05 level. The opposite situation tends to hold true within the home of young married couples: when they disagree on politics, they discuss them extensively, while with agreement, politics become a less central subject of discussion. Among friends discussion is as common when they are of a different party as when they are of the same party.

The findings on political discussion are interesting when viewed from the standpoint of group dynamics. A hypothesis among students of group dynamics is that when a group is highly cohesive and a topic is central to the attainment of group goals, disagreement will produce discussion and mutual influence. If a group is not cohesive, and/or the topic is not central to its goals, disagreement will cut off discussion of the topic, or lead people to leave the group. Among the peer groups studied here it is reasonable to assume that the husband-wife team is the most cohesive, the group of friends the next most cohesive, and the work group the least cohesive in terms of the strength of the individual's desire for the approval of the group. The centrality of politics as a topic relevant to the functioning of the group is difficult to assess for these three groups, but we might expect that politics is least relevant to the work group, which has presumably been brought together for other reasons than agreement on politics, while friendships and marriage ties are presumably formed at least partly because of like-mindedness on a number of issues. Of course, if one views political alignment as an expression of membership in an economic interest group, one's political position *could* be viewed as central to the functions of his work group. In any case, our data suggest that the husband-wife team is a cohesive group and that political agreement is important to the smooth functioning of the group, so that disagreement produces discussion and mutual influence. On the other hand, the work group is either not cohesive or political views are irrelevant to the functions of the group, for disagreement on political matters cuts down discussion and thus prevents the work group from being a potent source of political influence. The friendship group occupies a position mid-way between the spouse and the work group in the extent of its probable influence in political matters.

We have seen that the young voter less often agrees with his friends on politics than he does with his parents. It is interesting, however, that the friends appear to exert more influence if the young person is resentful of parental control.

While the number of cases is small, there is evidence of inter-action between home atmosphere and the influence of friends: once the psychological ground work for change is laid in over-strict home control, the young person becomes more responsive to the political orientation of his friends in his choice of party and candidate.

The Legislator and his Environment

EDWARD A. SHILS

Congressional investigating committees have brought about valuable reforms in American life. They have performed services which no other branch of the government and no private body could have accomplished. They have also—like any useful institution—been guilty of abuses. Like many institutional abuses, these have been products of the accentuation of certain features which have frequently contributed to the effectiveness of the investigative committee. In the following essay, we shall not concern ourselves with the description of these abuses, nor with the ways in which cer-

Reprinted from *The University of Chicago Law Review*, vol. 18 (1951-52), pp. 571-84 by permission of The University of Chicago Press. Copyright 1951 by The University of Chicago.

tain valuable practices, when pushed to an extreme, have become abuses. These abuses have included intrusions in spheres beyond the committees' terms of reference, excessive clamor for publicity, intemperate disrespect for the rights of witnesses, indiscriminate pursuit of evidence, sponsorship of injudicious and light-hearted accusations, disregard for the requirements of decorum in governmental institutions, and the use of incompetent and unscrupulous field investigators. Here we shall take as our task the exploration of factors which may assist in understanding some of these peculiarities and excesses of congressional investigations.

In the view here taken these excesses arise out of the conditions of life of the American legislator: the American constitutional system itself, the vicissitudes of the political career in America, the status of the politician, the American social structure and a variety of other factors. This analysis does not claim to be a complete picture of the social pattern of the American legislator; it is not intended to be an exhaustive analysis. It seeks only to point out those factors which have produced certain features of the investigative process—especially the tone of acrimony, of hostility toward witnesses and of disregard for the standards of propriety and respect which are even more necessary in political democracies than in other systems of government.

We shall accordingly begin with an exposition of some of the sources of strain on the legislator. Then we shall go further into the manner in which these strains become intensified in the relations between politicians on the one hand and administrators, intellectuals, and, occasionally, business men on the other.

I

In the United States as in any other large democratic government, the burden on the legislator is great. The volume of legislation is vast and its complexity beyond the judgment of laymen. Even an expert could not hope to understand and master fully all the bills which are produced. This is particularly true in the United States where many bills are produced on the same subject and where individual legislators often have their own legislative ambitions, in addition to the program of their party leaders. The legislator is overwhelmed by his legislative work alone, the amount aggravating the difficulty. He frequently votes on measures on which he has not formed his own judgment and on which he has not had his judgment authoritatively and reassuringly formed for him by his party organization. The fact that he leaves so much uncovered has a disquieting effect on him; it causes him to feel that matters are slipping beyond his control.

The structure of the American party system and its manifestation in Congress accentuate the strains on the American legislator. He is very much on his own. The national party does not arrange his candidacy; it has little control over the machine on which the congressman depends for his re-election; and its financial aid for the conduct of his campaign is much less than adequate. He must keep his machine going. Like an ambassador who is uneasy that his enemies at home are undoing his work and undermining his position while he is away, the legislator must always keep his eye on the machine at home—fearing that it might break out of his control during his absence in Washington.

American constituents, at least a sector of them, are often very out-spoken in their demands. The American legislator is moreover hypersensitive to the faintest whisper of a constituent's voice. Unable to depend on the national party for re-election, he must cultivate and nurture his constituency more than legislators in other democratic countries where constituents are less clamorous and parties are stronger at the center. . . .

In addition to trying to please those whom he sees, he is constantly harried in his mind's eye by those whom he does not see or from whom he does not hear. His remoteness from them does not make him less sensitive to their sentiments or fearful of their displeasure. The distance from the voter and his anonymity make the sensitivity even greater and more delicate. The nature of the recruitment process favors the man with a delicate ear for the voters' sentiments, and an eagerness to gain their approbation. American politics favors the person who can present himself as a man of the people, who is proud that he deviates from them in no significant way and who fears that any known deviations would be interpreted as snobbery or stand-offishness.

This eagerness to gratify an unseen constituency and to rank high in their favor helps us to understand why it is that legislators who have no strong convictions on a given topic might sometimes be among its most fervent investigators. They do so simply because they believe it will appeal to their constituents and because they cannot allow any rival for the affection and votes of their constituents to pre-empt this theme.

Far from his home base and insecure about his tenure and support, he is hard put to find a procedure for keeping in touch with his constituents and fixing himself in their minds. The congressional investigation is often just the instrument which the legislator needs in order to remind his constituents of his existence. That is the reason why investigations often involve such unseemly uses of the organs of publicity. Publicity is the next best thing to the personal contact which the legislator must forego. It is his substitute offering by which he tries to counteract the personal contact which his rivals at home have with the constituents. . . .

To these particular strains in the vocational life of an American legislator should be added the more general strains. For one thing the career of the professional politician is full of hazards. In all democracies the legislator is recurrently in danger of not being re-elected. In the event of being unsuccessful he must go back to a career which he has neglected. In the United States very few of our professional politicians are recruited from the classes which live from inherited wealth. If he is in the professions or in business he will have to make up the distance which his contemporaries have gained on him. Although he might have improved certain "connections," some of his skill other than political skill might well have deteriorated. Whatever the effect on his skill he faces the humiliation of return as a political failure, and the need to begin at a lower level than those who were his equals a few years before. Moreover, since our politicians do not come from classes which have as part of their tradition a normal expectation of entering a political career, they tend to a greater extent to be selected from among persons who enjoy the game of politics, to whom it has a special psychological appeal. For such persons, the threat of exclusion from politics through failure is especially menacing. Thus the situation of the political career in the United States makes legislators faced with the possibility of failure take eager refuge in devices which will recommend them to their constituents. Well publicized activity as a member of an investigative committee is one of these devices.

Even when successful, however, the professional politician in the United States cannot always have the pleasure and comfort of feeling that he is participating in a highly honored profession. The fact that he is so often made into an errand boy or a handmaiden to his constituents is indicative of their attitude towards him and of his attitude towards himself. Government in the United States, where established institutions are not usually objects of deep reverence, is far from the most esteemed of institutions. Living off the public treasury, from the taxpayers' money, whether as legislator or administrator, has until recently been rather looked down upon by the hard-working taxpayer and his newspaper spokesmen. This view is still at work in American public opinion. The image of the politician in the organs of mass communication is not a laudatory one. Pomposity, vanity, an unbalanced sense of importance and occasionally sheer dishonesty are part of the traditional American conception of the professional politician—although the reality has been far different. Even though this popular image has been changing in the past decades, the term "politician" still has a derogatory overtone. The occasional outbursts of an excessive desire to please on the one hand and of vindictive aggressiveness on the other are both products of this perception by the professional politician of his ambiguous status. The legislator's suspicion of the administrator as one who lives wastefully on the taxpayers' money is also an expression of his discomfiture concerning his own ambiguous status.

Congressional investigations often provide favorable occasions for the manifestation of this deep-lying distrust. It is not only the social status of politics that influences the legislator's mood. The geographical location of the center of national political life also has its effect. The almost exclusive position of politics as the chief employment of Washington has an influence on the life of the legislator. It means that he is forced to live almost entirely in an atmosphere of politics. It is true of course that many enjoy this type of life with its incessant stress on influence, rivalry, ambition and frustration—it sharpens political wits and has a brilliance of its own. It does however strengthen and even overdevelop the political orientation of men who have already entered voluntarily upon such a career. By political orientation is meant that exclusive preoccupation with political events to the point where every human activity becomes evaluated not in terms of its intrinsic value but in terms of its political significance. In Washington legislators must associate in their leisure hours almost entirely with other legislators or with journalists, administrators, and business men whose presence in Washington is almost always evidence of their own predominantly political interests. In such a society where the talk is invariably centered about who is getting what from whom, both the sensitivity and the insecurity of the legislator are increased. It strengthens his tendency to interpret everything in political terms and to look on the world as engaged at every moment in arranging political combinations, intended to advance some individual or group and to ruin another. This type of social life offers no respite from the tensions and anxieties of the individual legislator's own political career—it provides a stimulant rather than a soothing calm. The gossip and rumors agitate him and cause him to worry more about his own political fortunes. Hearing so much of what others are doing or are having done for them to secure their political fortunes, he feels he must exert himself more to establish and advance his own prestige. Whoever blocks him is his enemy. Whoever has a deficiency, real or imputable, which can be attacked in the name of a major political value, becomes a fair target in the competition to keep oneself politically afloat.

As a result of these factors—not all of which operate equally for all our legislators—the life of the American politician holding a seat in the Senate or in the House of Representatives is far from an easy one. He is always confronted with more demands on him than he can satisfy; he is always in danger of displeasing someone and he is never sure of just what it will take to please them or how he can do it when he knows what it is; he is always dependent on someone else's judgment for his equanimity and for his security. The result is a state of stress and disquiet, often flaring up into rage and sometimes into vindictiveness.

The emotional moods and the deeper attitudes to which they become fixed enter very intimately into the conduct of congressional investigations. The chief victims of congressional investigation are administrative officials and political dissenters, with big business men occasionally emerging as targets. We shall now deal with them in that order.

II

The traditions of the American Congress and the outlook of our congressmen are the products of a free society in which it was neither necessary nor desirable that large powers be assigned to the executive branch of the government. The inevitability of the delegation of power is often intellectually acknowledged by our legislators but there is also resentment against this necessity and a deep unwillingness to accept it. As we have already indicated, the bureaucrat or the administrator is regarded as the usurping rival of the legislator. General laws, when implemented in detail by administrators, often work hardships on particular constituents. The legislator is often unable to persuade the administrator to remove that hardship. In many cases the derogation of his power and status which this implies is bitterly felt by the legislator and animosity against particular administrators and against the executive branch and bureaucracy in general is fostered.

This attitude is also affected by the gradual diminution of the patronage system in the recruitment of the federal civil service. A civil servant appointed by patronage is the creature of the legislator. The prevailing atmosphere of the American political system, despite the establishment of the merit system in the federal civil service, is still that of patronage. The important role in the national parties of local and state "machines," subsisting on patronage, is responsible for this. A legislator who has passed through the lower levels of the party on his way upward still tends to expect civil servants to respond to him as though they are personally beholden to him. The fact that this is not so is well appreciated by the ordinary administrator and manifested in his behavior.

The contact between legislators and administrators who appear before the various standing committees and subcommittees is often frustrating to the legislator. There is seldom the element of direct challenge to the personal status of the legislator but the authoritative and self-assured way in which the administrator disposes of his own knowledge and the legislator's questions can also become a source of uneasiness. The administrator deals self-confidently with a matter which the legislator does not always grasp with the same measure of self-confidence. When the subject matter of the hearings is one about which the legislator already has some grievances, the result is apt to be a further rankling of his sentiments. The resulting "soreness" occasionally reveals itself in the support and conduct of investigations directed against the particular administrator and against bureaucrats in general.

This particular friction is, in part, one of the by-products of the merit system. The civil servant, particularly the civil servant of the level called before congressional committees, tends to be considerably more educated and probably of a higher social and economic status as regards his origin, than the legislator who is requesting a service of him or interrogating him. He is as we have indicated not only more expert in the matter at hand but he usually, either wittingly or unwittingly, is also more the master of the situation than the legislator. Resentment against those whose fortunate accidents of birth gave them educational opportunities which were not available to the legislator is heightened—it certainly was heightened during the Roosevelt administration—by an attitude of personal, social and intellectual superiority on the part of the administrator. This sense of superiority very often does not exist at all but is nonetheless often assumed to exist and is as bitterly resented.

The concurrent elevation of the educational level of the civil service and the delegation of vast legislative powers to a resourceful and ingenious executive only reinforced a difficulty which is endemic in the American constitutional system—namely, the sharp, personal separation of the legislative and executive branches. The fact that the leaders of the executive branch—the President to some extent, and even more, his cabinet members (except generally the relatively insignificant Postmaster General)—cannot usually be regarded as "one of the boys" deepens the breach between the legislators and the executive branch. It increases the likelihood of misunderstandings which accumulate and which cannot easily be cleared up by informal personal interchange, or prevented by the existence of close personal relations or friendship.

Some of these frictions are in the nature of our constitutional situation. If legislators are intended to watch over the execution of the laws they pass and to scrutinize the laws recommended to them by the executive branch, some friction will necessarily exist. It is however exaggerated by the adventitious element of the legislator's representation of the private interests of particular constituents. It is also driven further by the fact that except for the personal intercessions and questioning in committees, the American legislator has no control over what he regards as injustices or inefficiencies in the working of the administrative system. He must intervene personally, often at the cost of much time and energy, or he must attempt to hold up the appropriation of an entire section of the administration. If he fails in the first and the second alternative is not available to him, he has only the investigative committee left to him. It is certainly not always easy to start such a committee and a long accumulation of hurts and grievances will usually have been felt before the committee can be created and got under way. He must wait until enough other legislators think the issue is a good one or until, for some other reason, enough other legislators are willing to allow him to go ahead. The long period of waiting and the gradual fusion of resentments from a great variety of sources make it more likely that the investigation will be rough. Even if he is not on the committee himself, he will often support it because it is a vicarious way of soothing the many hurts he has experienced. There is little opportunity for the release of pressure by moderate means, such as the question period in the House of Commons, which provides a regular opportunity for the airing of small injustices and prevents an accumulation first of personal animosity and then of animosity in general. The possibility of having a particular wrong corrected imposes a sense of responsibility on the person who is trying to bring about the correction. If the situation has been allowed to go so far that accusations are generalized and no immediate corrections expected—when the legislator feels that he is shouting into the wind—then his accusations will become louder and angrier and his wrath will be less easily and efficiently appeased. Yet this is the atmosphere in which investigations are too often launched.

The strains which arise from our constitutional system and our cultural background are aggravated during periods of strong executive leadership and expansion of the executive. Strong executive leadership appears, while it is in operation, to cure the ailments, but under our present conditions it nonetheless leads inevitably to aggravation. The dry fruit of this aggravation is harvested in the period of weakest leadership. And jealous though they are of their powers and prerogatives, legislators normally renounce some of them during periods of national crisis. This was what happened under the administration of Franklin Roosevelt. His brilliant personality and self-confidence in confronting the domestic crisis of the thirties and the succeeding international crisis encouraged as great a delegation of power as any American Congress has ever participated in. Legislative regret and resentment over this delegation was already gathering force in the late 1930's. Pressure accumulated because of the insolence and brilliance of the exceptional group of energetic administrators and advisors whom the President gathered round him. The demand for a redress of the balance—for revenge against the disrespectful usurpers—grew through the thirties and was scarcely held in check by the continuation of the crisis and the exceptional personal and political capacities of the late President. His replacement by Mr. Truman and the renaissance of demands for normality after the war released the flood of resentment which had been storing up against the chief executive and against the bureaucrats. . . .

III

It must not be thought that the strong emotions of uneasy legislators are reserved only for bureaucrats. Congressmen conducting investigations are not always the friends of the existing economic system or of the "vested interests" of big business. In the main, congressional investigations, even when they are hostile to great economic organizations, usually treat individual business men politely. It is also probably true that in this most recent period where the various categories of the legislator's internal and foreign enemies have preoccupied them, "big business" has been treated rather respectfully. It is not always so however. Congress in its sentiments is disposed to sympathize with the small business man and to look with suspicion on the great organizations. Legislators in the United States are disproportionately of small town origin and their values too are those of the small town society. Big business represents a negation of these values. Moreover in addition to these fundamental sentiments and principles which favor small business, many of the legislator's errands on behalf of constituents are conducted for small business men. Not all the grievance which flows from injustice or rebuff is directed toward the bureaucrat. Some of it goes towards big business.

On the other hand big business represents the successful culmination of the aspirations of the small business man; he who sympathizes with the latter cannot withhold some admiration from the former. Many of the great American industrial achievements which make legislators proud of their American nationality are the achievements of "big business men." Their attitude towards big business is therefore ambivalent. Big business is vast, impersonal and often creates hardships for their small business constituents. Moreover it very often works through sophisticated lobbyists whose personal charm and favor do not always eradicate the guilty feeling of having allowed oneself to be seduced by the "vested interests," and do in fact generate guilt for having yielded to their blandishments. As a result of this ambivalence in loyalties to the different strata of the business community, legislative attitudes towards big business are more fluctuating than they are towards bureaucrats, intellectuals and subversives. When the tide turns against the big business man, as it did for instance in the 1930's, and they become the objects of investigation, the violence of tone and the acrimonious method of conducting an inquiry can reach the extremes which the investigations of other targets have reached since the Second World War.

IV

In the tense atmosphere of the legislative investigation, where accumulated passions are released against potential or imagined enemies, each ac-

cusingly worded question or hostilely intended general statement sets the
stage for more bitter accusations and more violent denunciation. The pattern of discourse already too prevalent in American political life—that a
point cannot be made unless it is overstressed and reiterated in the strongest
posible terms—has been further developed by congressional investigations
and made into the standard currency of American legislative and political
argument. Legislators who feel relatively little animosity against their opponents use this language because it has become a convention of their profession or because to be heard in the clamor of sensational words, they too
must speak sensationally. . . .

The Folkways of the United States Senate: Conformity to Group Norms and Legislative Effectiveness

DONALD R. MATTHEWS

The Senate of the United States, we are told, is a "club." The image, while
hopelessly imprecise and occasionally quite misleading, does have at least
one advantage: it underscores the fact that there are unwritten but generally accepted and informally enforced norms of conduct in the chamber.
These folkways influence the behavior of senators to a degree and in directions not yet fully understood. "There is great pressure for conformity in
the Senate," one member (mercifully varying the simile) has recently said.
"It's just like living in a small town." And, as in small-town life, so too in
the Senate there are occasional careers to be made out of deliberate nonconformity, sometimes only skin-deep, but sometimes quite thorough-going.

Political scientists know this in a general way. But, judging from the
dearth of literature on the subject, they have deemed legislative folkways
either unworthy of their attention or beyond their analytic powers. Journalists and legislators—close observers and participants—are acutely aware
of their importance, and have written about the Senate's folkways. While
some of their efforts have shown real insight, most such writings merely
reaffirm the existence of the norms without telling us what they are about.
Thus, most of the basic questions about the folkways of the Senate, and
other legislative bodies, remain unanswered. What, specifically, do the unwritten rules say? Why do they exist? In what ways do they influence the

Reprinted from *The American Political Science Review,* vol. 53 (December
1959), pp. 1064-89 by permission of the publisher. Copyright 1959 by The American
Political Science Association.

behavior of senators? How, concretely, are they enforced? What kinds of senators obey the folkways? Which ones do not, and why? What are the political consequences of the folkways?

These are difficult questions for an outsider to analyze. Only those who have served in the Senate—and perhaps not even all of them—are likely to grasp the folkways in all their complexity. Yet, if we are ever to understand the behavior of legislators, a beginning must be made in the systematic analysis of the subject. . . .

(1) The first rule of Senate behavior—and the one most widely recognized off the Hill—is that new members are expected to serve an unobtrusive apprenticeship.

The freshman senator's subordinate status is impressed upon him in many ways. He receives the committee assignments the other senators do not want. The same is true of his office suite and his seat in the chamber. In committee rooms he is assigned to the end of the table. He is expected to do more than his share of the thankless and boring tasks of the Senate, such as presiding over the floor debate or serving on his party's Calendar Committee. According to the folkways of the Senate, the freshman is to accept such treatment as a matter of course. . . .

(2) There are two kinds of Congressmen—show horses and work horses. If you want to get your name in the paper, be a show horse. If you want to gain the respect of your colleagues, keep quiet and be a work horse.

Senator Carl Hayden of Arizona remembers being told this when he first came to the Congress many years ago. It is still true.

The great bulk of the Senate's work is highly detailed, dull and politically unrewarding. According to the folkways of the Senate, it is to these tasks that a senator *ought* to devote a major share of his time, energy and thought. Those who follow this rule are the senators most respected by their colleagues. Those who do not carry their share of the legislative burden or who appear to subordinate this responsibility to a quest for publicity and personal advancement are held in disdain. . . .

(3) According to the folkways of the Senate, a senator should not try to know something about every bill that comes before the chamber or try to be active on a wide variety of measures. Rather, he ought to specialize, to focus his energies and attention on the relatively few matters that come before his committees or that directly and immediately affect this state. "When you come to the Senate," one administrative assistant said, "you have to decide which street corner you are going to fight on."

In part, at least, senators *ought* to specialize because they *must*: "Thousands of bills come before the Senate each Congress. If some senator knows

the fine details of more than half a dozen of them, I've never heard of him."
Even Robert A. Taft, who won much of his legislative reputation by his
phenomenal mastery of the details of bills on the floor could not escape the
rule, and generally let foreign affairs alone. And even when a senator re-
stricts his attention to his committee work, the job is more than one man
can do. . . .

Moreover, modern legislation is complex and technical. It comes before
the Senate in crushing quantity. The committee system and specialization—
in a word, a division of labor within the chamber—increase expertise and
decrease the average senator's work load to something approaching manageable proportions. When a senator refuses to "go along" with specialization,
he not only challenges the existing power structure, but also decreases the
expert attention which legislative measures receive.

(4) The Senate exists to solve problems, to grapple with conflicts.
Sooner or later, the hot, emotion-laden issues of our time come before it.
Moreover, senators as a group are ambitious and egocentric men, chosen
through an electoral battle in which a talent for invective, righteous indignation, "mud-slinging" and "engaging in personalities" are often assets.
Under these circumstances, one might reasonably expect a great deal of
manifest personal conflict and competition in the Senate. Such conflict does
exist, but its sharp edges are blunted by the felt need—expressed in the
Senate folkways—for courtesy.

A cardinal rule of Senate behavior is that political disagreements should
not influence personal feelings. This is not an easy task; for as one senator
said, "It's hard not to call a man a liar when you know that he is one."

Fortunately, a number of the chamber's formal rules and conventions
make it possible for the senator to approximate this ideal—at least so far as
overt behavior is concerned. The selection of committee members and chairmen on the basis of their seniority neatly by-passes a potential cause of grave
dissension in the Senate. The rules prohibit the questioning of a colleague's
motives or the criticism of another state. All remarks made on the floor are,
technically, addressed to the presiding officer: "Mr. President, . . ." serves
as a psychological barrier between antagonists. Senators are expected to
address each other not by name but by title—Earle C. Clements does not
disagree with Irving M. Ives but rather the Senior Senator from Kentucky
disagrees with the Senior Senator from New York. . . . Courtesy, far from
being a meaningless custom as some senators seem to think it is, permits
competitors to cooperate. The chaos which ensues when the folkway is
ignored testifies to its vital function.

(5) Every senator, at one time or another, is in a position to help out
a colleague. The folkways of the Senate hold that a senator ought to provide
this assistance—and that he be repaid in kind.

A man gets elected to the Senate on some kind of platform. He has made some promises or pledges that he will get this or that thing done. Then he gets down here and finds that nobody else gives a damn about his projects. What can he do? He either must back down on his promises or begin log-rolling. At first, I was pretty cynical when I found this was necessary. But then I realized that this was the kind of compromise necessary to govern a nation like this.

The most important aspect of this pattern of reciprocity is, no doubt, the trading of votes. Occasionally, this is exhibited for all to see. . . .

(6) Most institutions demand an emotional investment from their members. The Senate is no exception. Senators are expected to *believe* that they belong to the greatest legislative and deliberative body in the world. They are expected to be a bit suspicious of the President and the bureaucrats and just a little disdainful of the House. They are expected to revere the Senate's personnel, organization and folkways and to champion them to the outside world.

And most of them do, whether out of conviction or for the good of the order. "The most remarkable group that I have ever met anywhere," "the most able and intelligent body of men that it . . . [has] . . . been my fortune to meet," "the best men in political life today,": thus do senators typically describe their colleagues. The Senate as an institution is usually described in similar superlatives.

A senator whose emotional commitment to Senate ways appears to be less than total is suspect. One who brings the Senate as an institution or senators as a class into public disrepute invites his own destruction as an effective legislator. One who seems to be using the Senate for the purposes of self-advertisement and advancement obviously does not belong. Senators are, as a group, fiercely protective of and highly patriotic about the Senate.

This, after all, is not a great deal different from the school spirit of P.S. 34, or the morale of a military outfit, or the "fight" of a football team. But, as we shall see, its political consequences are substantial. For some senators are in a better position than others to develop this emotional attachment.

(7) We have seen that normative rules of conduct—called here folk-ways—exist in the Senate. Moreover, we have seen that they perform important functions. They provide motivation for the performance of legislative duties that, perhaps, would not otherwise be performed. They discourage long-windedness in a chamber of one hundred highly verbal men, dependent upon publicity, and unrestrained by any formal limitations on debate. They encourage the development of expertise and division of labor and discourage those who would challenge it. They soften the inevitable personal conflict of

a legislative body so that adversaries and competitors can meet (at the very least) in an atmosphere of antagonistic cooperation or (at best) in an atmosphere of friendship and mutual respect. They encourage senators to become "compromisers" and "bargainers" and to use their substantial powers with caution and restraint. Without these folkways the Senate could hardly operate in anything like its present form.

Yet they are not universally accepted or adhered to: indeed, there is some covert hostility toward them. If most senators do observe them, why don't all? This we shall try to explain in the following pages.

PREVIOUS TRAINING AND EXPERIENCE.   Senators often express pride in the fact that their chamber is "democratic.". . .

A former governor who becomes a senator is often accustomed to a higher salary, more power and perquisites, a grander office, a larger staff, and more publicity than the freshman senator enjoys. He is likely to find the pace of legislative life slow and be frustrated by the necessity of cooperating with 99 equals (most of them at first far more equal than he). To move from the governorship of one of the larger states to the role of apprentice senator is, in the short run, a demotion. The result for the one-time governors is a frequent feeling of disillusionment, depression and discouragement.

I moved from one world to another [a former governor now in the Senate says]. Back home everything revolved, or seemed to revolve, around the Governor. I had a part in practically everything that happened. There was administration. There was policy making. But down here there was just a seat at the end of the table.

At the same time, the other senators complain that the former governors ". . . are the hardest group to handle; they come down here expecting to be big shots," and that they often are unwilling to realize that "they are just one of the boys." Some governors, they feel, never make the adjustment; a larger number make it slowly and painfully.

It is possible to subject this hypothesis to a rough empirical test. Crude indices of conformity can be obtained by counting the number of speeches senators make and by determining the extent to which the bills they introduce are on similar or disparate subjects. . . .

In giving floor speeches during the 83d and 84th Congresses, the ex-governors were more vocal than the former congressmen, state legislators, ex-judges and men with no office-holding experience. The former local government officials and federal executives, on the other hand, gave even more floor speeches than the erstwhile governors. In legislative specialization, only the ex-judges appear to have had a narrower range of legislative interests

than the governors. Indeed, of the other senators, only the former congressmen and state legislators came even close to matching them in this respect.
Thus, if our indices of conformity are reliable, the governors *as a group* seem
to "go along" with the Senate folkways fairly well.

But it is the governors from the larger states, coming to the Senate with
national reputations, who seem to find their initial experiences in the chamber
especially trying. Moreover, their record for conformity to the folkways is
bad. While they do tend to specialize quite highly, they are extremely active
on the floor—even when compared to other senators from similar states. . . .

There is another peculiar feature about the former governors in the
Senate: those with low seniority conform to the folkways more closely than
those with high seniority. The higher the seniority of the ex-governors the
more active they were in floor debate while just the opposite is true among
the former representatives. Both the ex-governors and ex-representatives become more specialized as seniority increases, yet the former congressmen with
high seniority specialize considerably more than the high seniority governors.
While the numbers involved are too small to warrant generalization the same
pattern is suggested for the former local officials and federal executives: those
with high seniority conform less than the junior men. The one-time judges
and state legislators, on the other hand, seem to follow the pattern of congressmen: the senior men conform more than the youngsters.

Among the present crop of senators at any rate, prolonged exposure to
the folkways seems to have resulted in a high degree of conformity among
the former congressmen, state legislators and judges but *not* among former
governors, federal executives, and local government officials. . . .

The amateur politicians—distinguished business and professional men
who entered politics relatively late in life and became senators with little
political experience—face many of the same problems as the former governors, compounded by their relative ignorance of political ways. One must
learn to be a senator and the amateurs have a great deal to learn. They are
more likely to ignore the folkways regarding floor activity and legislative
specialization than are the professionals. Moreover, the amateurs usually
must learn how to be legislators in less time than those who follow other
career lines to the Senate: they are the oldest group of freshmen in age. A
relatively young man can afford to be patient, to devote two or four or six
years to learning the ropes and climbing the seniority ladder. A sixty-year-old
man, with sufficient vigor to win election to the Senate and a distinguished
career back of him, is not so likely to take the long view. At any rate, a
larger proportion of the men elected to the Senate relatively late in life tend
to "talk too much" than is the case for the others. Thus we find a curious
situation in the Senate. The greater a man's pre-Senate accomplishments
(either in or out of politics) and the greater his age at election, the less

likely he is to conform. For these reasons, a sort of reverse snobbism is quite widespread in the Senate. As one old-timer said, "We are skeptical of men who come to the Senate with big reputations." From the standpoint of protecting the Senate folkways, this skepticism is justified.

POLITICAL AMBITIONS. Higher political ambitions—and for senators this means a desire to become either President or Vice-president—can also lead to nonconformity.

First of all, strong and exhalted ambitions are likely to lead to restiveness during the period of apprenticeship. A national following is seldom made by "being seen and not heard" or through faithful service on the District of Columbia Committee. In order to overcome this initial handicap, the highly ambitious freshman may resort to extreme and unsettling tactics as, for example, Senator Kefauver is thought by his colleagues to have done in his crime investigations, and Senator McCarthy certainly did in his "crusade" against Communism. His legislative duties are likely to be neglected in the ceaseless quest for publicity and personal advancement. His ears are likely to be ". . . attuned to noises outside the workaday drone of the Senate chamber." And since the senator with higher ambitions is almost invariably shooting for the Presidency, he is likely to be attuned to the voices of somewhat different groups than are most senators. Close presidential elections are won and lost in the doubtful states containing large metropolitan populations. Popularity in these areas is generally a prerequisite for nomination and election to the Presidency. Yet these very groups are the ones underrepresented in the Senate, the ones most often at odds with its present power structure. Thus, to the extent that ambitious senators *anticipate* the wants of possible future constituents, they find themselves challenging the Senate *status quo.*

Of the most obvious presidential aspirants during the 83d and 84th Congresses all save Symington gave more floor speeches than the average Senator and all pursued a wider range of legislative interests.

It should be immediately admitted, however, that the list of presidential aspirants used here is based entirely upon common report—latent presidential ambitions smolder in the breasts of senators not included. Moreover, the list includes both floor leaders, and the folkways regarding floor speaking and specialization are necessarily and greatly relaxed for the incumbents of these specialized positions. Finally, an occasional senator is able to be both a serious presidential candidate and a highly regarded and effective senator—Senators Taft, Johnson and Knowland are the most conspicious examples within recent years. Yet Taft was never nominated, at least in part because he was a "Senate man." Knowland seems to have found the conflict between the expectations of his Senate colleagues and his presidential ambitions too much to bear. Senator Johnson's presidential chances appear to be low for somewhat the same reasons as Taft's. As a general rule, it seems that a man who entirely adheres to the Senate folkways has little chance of becoming President of the United States. . . .

POLITICAL IDEOLOGY. Senators are, of necessity, tolerant of differences of opinion. A senator's political views make less difference to his acceptance or lack of it by his colleagues than is generally realized. Yet a senator's stance on political issues *does* make it easier (or harder) for him to conform to the folkways and thus, indirectly, influences his prestige and effectiveness in the chamber.

The folkways of the Senate, as we have already seen, buttress the *status quo* in the chamber. And the distribution of power within the chamber results in generally conservative policies. Thus the liberals are more likely to challenge Senate norms than the conservatives. "A reformer's life is perhaps not easy anywhere," one close observer of the Senate has remarked. "In the Senate it can be both bitter and fruitless. . . ."

A man elected to the Senate as a "liberal" or "progressive" or "reformer" is under considerable pressure to produce legislative results in a hurry. The people who voted for him are not likely to be happy with small favors—dams built, rivers dredged, roads financed—but want major national legislative policy changed. Yet as a freshman or a junior senator, and many never become anything else, the liberal is in no position to do this alone. If he gives in to the pressure for conformity coming from the folkways, he must postpone the achievement of his liberal objectives. If he presses for these objectives regardless of his junior position, he will become tabbed as a nonconformist, lose popularity with his colleagues and, in most cases, his legislative effectiveness as well.

The conservative does not face this problem. He has committed himself to fewer changes in basic policies: he finds the strategic positions in the Senate occupied by like-minded senators regardless of which party organizes it. He is able to identify more strongly with the folkways of the chamber and side more easily with the Congress in its running feud with a generally more liberal President. Nor is he, as is the liberal, so dependent on the support of broad, often unorganized groups which can be reached only through the mass media. At any rate, the liberals seem to talk considerably more and to specialize less than senators of different political persuasion. Conservatives can afford to be quiet and patient. Reformers—by definition—find it difficult to be either.

(8) All this would be very "interesting" but not particularly important to serious students of politics if the Senate folkways did not influence the distribution of power within the chamber.

But the senators believe, rightly or wrongly, that without the respect and confidence of their colleagues they can have little influence *in the Senate.* "You can't be effective," they said over and over again, "unless you are respected—on both sides of the aisle." And the safest way to obtain this respect is to conform to the folkways, to become a "real Senate man." Those who do not, run a serious risk. "In the Senate, if you don't conform, you don't get many favors for your state. You are never told that, but you soon learn."

In order to test this hypothesis, a crude index of "Legislative Effectiveness" was constructed for the 83d and 84th Congresses by calculating the proportion of all public bills and resolutions introduced by each senator that were passed by the Senate. While such an index does not pretend to measure the overall power or influence of a senator, it does seem to reflect his efficiency as a legislator, narrowly defined. And, to the extent that the concept as used on Capitol Hill has any distinct meaning, "effectiveness" seems to mean the ability to get one's bills passed.

The less a senator talks on the Senate floor, and the narrower a senator's area of legislative interest and activity, the greater is his "effectiveness." Moreover, the types of senators who, as we have already seen, tend not to conform have considerably less impact on the chamber's legislative output than the conformists. Conformity to the Senate folkways does, therefore, seem to "pay off" in concrete legislative results. . . .

SUMMARY AND CONCLUSION

There are unwritten rules of behavior, which we have called folkways, in the Senate. These rules are *normative,* that is, they define how a senator ought to behave. Nonconformity is met with moral condemnation, while senators who conform to the folkways are rewarded with high esteem by their colleagues. And partly because of this fact, the conformists tend to be the most influential and effective members of the Senate.

These folkways, we have suggested, are highly functional to the Senate social system since they provide motivation for the performance of vital duties and essential modes of behavior which, otherwise, would go unrewarded. They discourage frequent and lengthy speechmaking in a chamber without any other effective limitation on debate, encourage the development of expertise and a division of labor in a group of overworked laymen facing unbelievably complex problems, soften the inevitable personal conflicts of a problem-solving body, encourage bargaining and the cautious use of awesome formal powers. Without these folkways, the Senate could hardly operate with its present organization and rules.

Nonetheless, the folkways are no more perfectly obeyed than the traffic laws. Abstractly stated, the reasons for non-conformity seem to be three:

1. Men become senators at different stages in life after varying kinds of careers. The ease and frequency with which they conform is affected by these differences in their recruitment. Senators elected relatively early in life with considerable political experience seem to conform most readily and often. Not all professional politicians find the adjustment equally easy, however. Former legislators and judges seem to adjust most easily while governors from the larger states and federal executives often find the Senate a psychological demotion, their administrative skills irrelevant, their perceptions of the political process at odds with Senate realities. Amateur politicians, men who have entered politics relatively late in life after distinguished business and profesional careers, have the hardest time of all.

2. The senators differ, too, in the level of their political aspirations. Most of them think of Senate service as the climax to their political lives. A minority, however, have their eyes firmly focused on an even bigger prize, the Presidency. Not only does this weaken their identification with the chamber and its ways: it also causes them to identify with a national constituency demanding modes of behavior which are sometimes subversive to the folkways.

3. All senators belong to, or identify with, many other groups in addition to the Senate and the expectations and demands of these other groups sometimes conflict with the folkways. The most powerful of these groups is undoubtedly the senator's constituents—both present and potential. But the ability of a senator's constituents to employ their ultimate sanction varies considerably. For example, incumbent senators are rarely defeated in one-party states. Men from this kind of state need be less responsive to their constituents and thus are able to conform to the folkways more often and thoroughly than men from competitive two-party areas. Moreover, some senators are far less likely than others to be caught in the middle of cross-presures from constituency and legislative peers. The Senate is organized in a way that greatly exaggerates the power of rural, conservative interests. The folkways justify and buttress the *status quo* in the chamber. Thus rural conservatives are less often caught in the squeeze of conflicting constituency-folkway demands than are the liberal senators from urban states. When confronted with such a conflict situation, a senator must choose between conforming to the folkways and thus appearing to "sell out," or gaining popularity back home at the expense of goodwill, esteem and effectiveness in the Senate—a course which diminishes his long run ability to achieve what his constituents demand. For this reason, conflicts between the immediate demands of constituents and peers are by no means automatically resolved in favor of constituents.

It would be a mistake to assume that the folkways of the Senate are unchangeable. Their origins are obscure, but sparse evidence scattered throughout senatorial memoirs suggests that they have changed little since the late

18th or early 19th century. Certainly the chamber's small membership and gradual turnover is conducive to the transmission of such rules virtually unchanged from one generation to the next. Yet the trend in American politics seems to be toward more competitive two-party politics; a greater political role for the mass media of communications and those skilled in their use; larger, more urban constituencies. All these are factors which presently encourage departure from the norms of Senate behavior. Thus nonconformity to the folkways may increase in the future, if the folkways remain unchanged. Moreover, the major forces which presently push senators toward nonconformity tend to converge upon a relatively small group of senators. This is a far more unstable situation than the random distribution of such influences —and hence of nonconforming behavior—among the entire membership of the Senate.

The Justices of the Supreme Court:
A Collective Portrait

JOHN R. SCHMIDHAUSER

For many years, students of the Supreme Court of the United States have stressed the importance of the social and economic background of appointees to the nation's highest tribunal. More recently, controversy over the Supreme Court's decision in *Brown* v. *Board of Education* served to raise the issue (among others) of the prior judicial experience (or lack of it) of such appointees. This emphasis upon personal qualifications and characteristics is a manifestation of the twentieth century shift in American jurisprudence from the unrealistic acceptance of the mechanistic theory of judical interpretation to frank acknowledgment of the subjective element in the decision-making process.

The recognition of the subjective and its possible implications was perhaps best stated by Robert K. Carr when he wrote nearly two decades ago that "it is entirely possible that a careful examination of the personalities and the economic and social backgrounds of the eighty men who have served on the Supreme Court would prove to be as valuable and realistic an approach to the American Constitution as the more usual law school approach which lays so much emphasis upon the study of cases, the rule of *stare decisis,* and

Reprinted from *The Midwest Journal of Political Science,* vol. 3 (February 1959), pp. 1–57 by permission of the Wayne State University Press. Copyright 1959 by Wayne State University Press.

of fixed legal principles." The growing recognition of the importance of subjective factors in judicial interpretation is generally regarded as intellectually desirable. However, the uses made of background data have varied in accordance with the intellectual sensitivity of the user. Some, such as Carr and Frankfurter, while eschewing the mechanistic, have been cautious in their assessments of the influence of social background factors. In quite a different vein, others have assumed a rather close relationship between background factors and judicial interpretation. Fred Rodell's striking reference to Roger Brooke Taney is illustrative—"There is not one of his decisions as Chief Justice . . . but can be traced, directly or indirectly, to his big-plantation birth and background."

One thing is clear. Investigation of the relative influence of social background factors upon judicial interpretation has scarcely progressed beyond the speculative stage. In the 1930's, for example, Cortez A. M. Ewing gathered a great deal of biographical data relating to some elements in the social background of Supreme Court members, but made no serious effort to determine meaningful relationships between the justices' backgrounds and their judicial behavior. By far the greatest amount of attention has been focused upon the writing of biographies of Supreme Court members. These studies, while contributing necessary and exceedingly valuable information and analyses of individual court members, have not ordinarily concerned themselves with the question of the significance of background factors.

The sustained intellectual interest in judicial biography demonstrated in the past three decades has, however, opened up hitherto limited opportunities for the investigation of this subject. . . . The Court's membership may be treated collectively to determine basic recruitment factors and the place of the Court in American politics and society. . . .

THE PRIOR JUDICIAL EXPERIENCE OF MEMBERS OF THE SUPREME COURT

In recent years a great deal of attention has been focused upon the question whether individuals should have judicial experience before they are considered eligible for appointment to the Supreme Court of the United States. President Eisenhower, after his appointment of Earl Warren, imposed such a standard, choosing Harlan, Brennan and Whittaker from the federal or state benches. On April 30, 1956, Senator Smathers proposed that Congress formalize this policy by adopting a statutory requirement that all future appointees to the Supreme Court have at least five years judicial experience either in an inferior federal court or in the highest court of a state. It may be assumed that the similarity of objectives does not reflect a similarity of motives. The ostensible justifications for these proposals were identical, however. Both the President and the Congressional supporters of prior judicial experience argued that individuals possessing such experience are more likely to develop attitudes of restraint which, at least by implication, are alleged to be lacking in "political" appointees. For Southern Congressmen the matter is put somewhat differently. With the shadow of *Brown* v. *Board of Education* looking over them, they bitterly urge the selection of men who will base decisions, according to this argument, upon "law," not "sociology." It may be properly suspected that those who urge this method of selection consciously or subconsciously assume that "good" judges are those who are apt to render decisions in accordance with the ideological predilections of the sponsors of this change in method of judicial selection.

The contemporary advocacy of prior judicial experience as a prerequisite for Supreme Court appointment is only the most recent of the manifestations of the fact that advocacy of particular methods of judicial selection is inexorably related to desires for ideological control of the Court. This may be made more apparent by an analysis of the type of men on the Supreme Court who have had prior judicial experience. Well over fifty per cent of the justices had served in a judicial capacity at some time before appointment to the Supreme Court, but only slightly more than twenty-five per cent had had really extensive judicial careers. It is upon this latter group of justices whose life careers prior to appointment to the Supreme Court had been primarily judicial that attention will be centered.

The considerations which governed the choice of these judicially-trained men varied according to changing circumstances. During the period of Jeffersonian and Jacksonian dominance of the national administration, Supreme Court appointments were often viewed with an eye to the local responsibilities of the justices while on circuit duty. Thus acquaintance with the peculiarities of the land laws of the states within a circuit was occasionally considered a prerequisite, as, for example, in the choices of Thomas Todd and Robert Trimble. Particularly before 1891, experience in the "federal specialities," such as admiralty law, was also of importance. However, it is not at all clear that experience on an inferior federal court or a state court is necessary to or intimately related to the sort of service performed on the nation's highest court. As Justice Frankfurter has ably put it,

The Supreme Court is a very special kind of court. 'Judicial service' as such has no significant relation to the kinds of litigation that come before the Supreme Court, to the types of issues they raise, to qualities that these actualities require for wise decision.

Frankfurter clearly recognized that it might be argued that even "if experience on a state [or inferior federal] court does not adequately prepare even the greatest judges for the problems . . . of the Supreme Court, judicial experience intrinsically fosters certain habits of mind and attitudes . . . which are indeed preconditions for the wise exercise of the judicial function of the Supreme Court." Justice Frankfurter himself dealt with this by stating that fewer justices without prior judicial experience "dallied with political ambition" than those who possessed such experience. However, the problem of political ambition whether directed toward the Presidency or, as is frequently overlooked, toward promotion to the Chief Justiceship, represents only one facet of a broader ideological problem. To put it bluntly, there is little evidence to support the view that individuals with primarily judicial careers before selection to the Supreme Court were more objective than those without such experience. And this was generally true whether they cherished political ambitions or not.

There are several historical factors which support this conclusion. First, appointment to an inferior federal judgeship has generally been in the nature of a political reward for recognized partisans. The process of selection of inferior federal judges, which has always been essentially based on patronage, is hardly conducive to the choice of judges who are apt to be aloof to party or ideological issues. Secondly, the choice of prominent state judges similarly draws upon men who usually have had to make strong party and ideological commitments in order to achieve high judicial office in their states. This has been less true in some states than others, but, generally speaking, high state judicial office has required party and ideological commitments whether the posts be appointive or elective. Furthermore, the biographies of many of the prominent state judges who achieved a position on the nation's highest court bear this out. Men like Justices Catron or Davis, despite the fact that they served in state judicial posts for much of their adult careers, were primarily political managers.

Finally, the men chosen for the Supreme Court from the inferior federal bench or higher state courts have almost uniformly been strong ideological partisans. Justice David Brewer's often-quoted declaration that the paternalistic system of government is odious, is illustrative of the kind of partisanship which was part of the make-up of most of the justices who had extensive judicial experience before their Supreme Court appointment. The penchant for presidents to appoint such men, especially during the periods 1862-1888 and 1889-1919 (when such appointees comprised 45% of the Supreme Court), reflected not a desire to choose men who were aloof, but rather a purposeful determination to select known ideological partisans. As inferior federal judges or state judges, men like Field, Brewer, Strong, Brown, Howell Jackson, Pitney, or Lurton, made their reputations as individuals who were apt to take a conservative view on government regulation of private enterprise and in some cases, as stern judicial administrators in their treatment of labor unions. For presidents looking for Supreme Court appointees with these qualities, service on the inferior federal bench or higher state courts provided a readily available index to the assessment of the personal and intellectual qualities of potential candidates. Similarly, such prior judicial experience provided the sort of knowledge of individual career patterns desired by interest groups which have, particularly since the Civil War, sought to influence appointments to the Supreme Court.

There is little in the history of the Supreme Court to suggest that justices with prior judicial experience were more objective or better qualified than those who lacked such experience. As a matter of fact, despite the examples of Holmes and Cardozo, some of the Supreme Court's most distinguished members, notably Marshall, Story, Taney, Curtis, Campbell, Miller, Bradley, Hughes, Brandeis and Stone, were totally lacking in this experience before their appointments to the Supreme Court.

THE SIGNIFICANCE OF SOCIAL AND POLITICAL BACKGROUND FACTORS

The presidential choice of a member of the Supreme Court has always been an object of great public attention contemporaneously and a subject of keen interest to public law commentators and historians after the event. Most treatments have centered attention upon the reasons, ostensible or real, for the individual selections made by a particular president. It is important, however, to consider the collective aspects of the judicial selection process in order, first, to establish the pattern of recruitment, and secondly to examine in tentative fashion some of the possible relationships between social and political background factors and decision-making tendencies.

Throughout American history there has been an overwhelming tendency for presidents to choose nominees for the Supreme Court from among the socially advantaged families. The typical Supreme Court justice has invariably been white, generally Protestant with a penchant for a high social status denomination, usually of ethnic stock originating in the British Isles, and born in comfortable circumstances in an urban or small town environment. In the earlier history of the Court, he very likely was born in the aristocratic gentry class, while later he tended to come from the professionalized upper middle-class. While nearly two-thirds of his fellows were selected from politically-active families, a third of his fellows were chosen from families having a tradition of judicial service. In college and legal education, the average justice was afforded opportunities for training and associations which were very advantageous. It seems reasonable to assume that very few sons of families outside the upper or upper-middle social and economic classes have been able to acquire the particular type of education and the subsequent professional, and especially, political associations which appear to be unwritten prerequisites for appointment to the nation's highest tribunal.

Educational opportunity emerges as a crucial ingredient in judicial recruitment. Every member of the Supreme Court was the recipient of law training and a great number were afforded college or university educations prior to their law training. Law training not only fulfilled an unwritten educational requirement for judicial appointment, but frequently represented an important stage in the development of individual political careers. Especially in the periods before the widespread acceptance of law schools as the primary centers for legal education, the internship of subsequent members of the Supreme Court in the law offices of prominent practitioners afforded the student not only a unique educational opportunity and valuable professional associations, but frequently the political sponsorship of men who held high office or were influential in the councils of their political organizations.

The influence of family background, while less tangible in certain respects, may be considered of great importance. In an economic sense, birth in a family in comfortable circumstances was generally a precondition for the advanced educational opportunities afforded most Supreme Court members. However, it is important to note that the families of the justices generally were not of the type one identifies with the modern middle class, a type which has become increasingly apolitical, interested more in comfort and economic security than in the assumption of social responsibility. On the contrary, a high percentage of the families of the justices demonstrated a very deep sense of social responsibility and political involvement. It would be a gross over-simplification to assume a direct transferal of the particular political attachments of these families to their sons. Yet, the biographical data on the justices evidences a considerable conditioning of broad attitudes toward social and political participation. One finds in Chief Justice Harlan Fiske Stone's statement of his personal attitude toward social responsibility an excellent summary of a view common to virtually all of the justices and to most of their families. As Stone put it:

. . . *it is . . . important . . . that we do not seek escape from our problems by leaving them to be solved by chance, or by those who have no more responsibility for their solution than ourselves. We should hold firmly to the belief that man by his very nature is bound to find the answers to his difficulties by intelligent, courageous, diligent intellectual effort. For that there is no substitute in the world in which we live.*

Although selection to the Supreme Court has not usually involved the patronage considerations ordinarily associated with judicial appointment to the inferior federal courts, it has generally involved basically political considerations. Just as training in law has been a necessary educational step in the achievement of a Supreme Court appointment, so has political activism been a virtual precondition for such an appointment. The degree of political involvement of aspirants to the Supreme Court has, of course, varied considerably. In a large number of instances the justices, prior to their appointments, not only held high political office, but were deeply involved in party and campaign management and had close political associations and personal ties with the men who later nominated and appointed them. Thus political activism of a rather intense kind emerges as a necessary stage in career ascent to the Supreme Court.

Political involvement before Supreme Court appointment ordinarily serves as an effective medium for the identification of the political, social and economic values of prospective Court members by interest groups seeking to assure the ideological soundness of new appointees. For example, the strong intervention by the President of the Chicago and Northwestern Railroad and the Union Pacific Railroad, William B. Ogden, with the Lincoln Administration in behalf of Noah Swayne coincided with the rapid growth of corporate influence at all levels of government in the Civil War and post-Civil War eras. The endorsement of Swayne by Ogden marked the beginning of a period of substantial railroad influence in the appointment of Supreme Court justices.

The appointment of men with prior judicial experience, especially those with extensive careers in the inferior federal courts or the state courts, was of great importance in particular historical periods. These appointments frequently served the practical function of identifying ideological partisans as did selection from the ranks of the openly avowed political activists.

The picture that emerges in the pattern of recruitment of Supreme Court justices is one which emphasizes the intimacy of judicial and political affairs. Since the most important function of the Supreme Court is the settlement of fundamentally political issues, the political background of the justices undoubtedly represents a very necessary and valuable source of experience and training.

It is not at all clear that the social and political background factors in themselves may serve as reliable indicators of precise patterns of judicial behavior. Explanations based entirely upon the causal influence of such factors as family, economic and social status, ethnic background or religious affiliation could scarcely take into account such important considerations as the impact upon individual justices of the traditions of the Supreme Court itself, or that interaction of intelligent and frequently forceful personalities which has been an integral part of the internal procedure of the Court. Complete dependence upon background factors would also ignore the complexity and subtlety of intellect and motivation which is part of the collective picture of the ninety-one individuals who sat on the high bench.

The difficulty is illustrated by looking at the overall judicial reputations of the nine justices of humble origin. It might be argued, for example, that the choice of men of humble origin for the Supreme Court could scarcely be considered dangerous to the rights of private property because the group included James Wilson, John McLean, John Catron, Pierce Butler, and James Byrnes. Perhaps one would be tempted to accept the acid comment made by a contemporary concerning Catron's personal characteristics as a sociological explanation of the decision-making predilections of these justices. Catron was described as "profoundly aristocratic in all his habits and bearing *as all men raised to wealth and station by concurrence of accidents.*" Yet as appealing as such a pat explanation seems, there are certain difficulties inherent in the unqualified use of such biographical data. For one thing, the overall judicial reputations of the other four justices of humble origin—Henry Baldwin, Samuel F. Miller, Sherman Minton and Earl Warren—can hardly be accounted for by this explanation. Furthermore, a variety of other explanations involving such things as political associations, educational conditioning or ideological commitments to nationalism or states' rights, might appear just as plausible as the emphasis upon family background.

It would be a serious mistake, however, to conclude that the background factors have had no influence upon judicial behavior whatsoever. The social attitudes of families in the gentry class or professionalized upper middle-class, and particularly the traditions of the families with judicial associations, may be accounted subtle factors influencing the tone and temper of judicial decision-making. While such influence can not ordinarily be traced in cause and effect formulas in specific decisions, it frequently emerges in the careers of individual justices as setting implicit limits on the scope of theoretical decision-making possibilities. Justice Frankfurter once wrote that "by the very nature of the functions of the Supreme Court, each member of it is subject only to his own sense of trusteeship of what are perhaps the most revered traditions in our national system." If it is in this sense that the Supreme Court is the keeper of the American conscience, it is essentially the conscience of the American upper middle-class sharpened by the imperative of individual social responsibility and political activism, and conditioned by the conservative impact of legal training and professional legal attitudes and associations.

Negro Registration in Louisiana

JOHN H. FENTON and KENNETH N. VINES

The 1944 action of the Supreme Court voiding the white primary ended the last effective legal block to Negro voter registration in the South. After that, resort to legal steps to block Negro registration was either outlawed by the courts or else could only be a delaying device. In the state of Louisiana, however, the decision in *Smith* v. *Allwright* did not result in Negro registration comparable to white registration. In 1956, twelve years later, 30 percent of the potential Negro voting population was registered, compared to 73 percent of the whites. This study is an investigation of some factors in that discrepancy, and in particular, of the differences in registration between Catholic and Protestant areas.

An important characteristic of Negro registration in Louisiana is the extreme range of variation to be found among the several parishes. Table I shows 17 parishes with fewer than 20 percent of the eligible Negroes registered, and 11 parishes with 70 percent or more of the potential Negro vote registered. Therefore, the statewide "average" percentage of Negro registration has little meaning without more detailed interpretation.

Among the factors responsible for these differences is the religio-cultural variable. Louisiana offers a unique opportunity to study the influence

TABLE I.   LOUISIANA PARISHES BY PERCENTAGE OF NEGROES
21 AND OVER REGISTERED, 1956

Registration Percentage	Number of Parishes
0– 9	7
10– 19	10
20– 29	9
30– 39	6
40– 49	5
50– 59	13
60– 69	3
70– 79	6
80– 89	3
90–100	2

Reprinted from *The American Political Science Review*, vol. 51 (1957), pp. 704–13 by permission of the publisher. Copyright 1957 by The American Political Science Association.

of this variable on the registration aspect of race relations. Catholicism is dominant in southern Louisiana and Protestantism in northern Louisiana. The two regions are very nearly separate worlds. Other variables enter, but this one is the focus of this paper.

The material for this study was gathered from Census Reports and from specialized and local sources on the cultural characteristics of Louisiana. Sixteen parishes were visited throughout the state, chosen to represent different degrees of Negro registration, different socio-economic areas, and different religio-cultural areas. Interviews were conducted with state and parish officials and local political leaders, both white and Negro.

I. THE RELIGIO-CULTURAL VARIABLE

Every Louisianian is aware of the religious complications of his state's politics. It has usually been thought, though experience provides exceptions, that only Protestants can be elected to state-wide offices or as congressmen from the north Louisiana districts; and only Catholics can be elected to major offices in south Louisiana. The Catholicism of Louisiana is predominantly French, and it is said that a French name is worth 50,000 votes in south Louisiana in a state-wide election.

Roughly the southern 25 parishes form French Catholic Louisiana while the remaining parishes in the north are predominantly Protestant and Anglo-Saxon. The French parishes remain French-Catholic because of their assimilation of extraneous cultural elements entering the area.

As Table II indicates, Negro registration in percentages of potential eligibles, is more than twice as great in Louisiana's French-Catholic parishes as in its non-French parishes. In only two of the 25 French-Catholic parishes are less than 20 percent of the eligible Negroes registered, whereas in 13 of the 39 non-French parishes less than 20 percent of the potential Negro vote is registered. In seven of the French-Catholic parishes Negro registration is 70 percent or more, while only four of the non-French-Catholic parishes equal or exceed the 70 percent mark. Yet no significant differences exist between the two groups of parishes with respect to Negro-White population balance or to urbanism.

The reasons for the different reaction of French and non-French population groups to Negro registration seem, in large part, to be due to fundamentally different attitudes of each culture toward the Negro. Both Negro and white leaders agree that social attitudes toward the Negro differ in the two cultures.

Some objective evidence of this difference is to be found in these facts: (1) at political meetings in southern Louisiana crowds are often racially mixed, even at indoor meetings, whereas in northern Louisiana such crowds

TABLE II.   NEGRO REGISTRATION BY RELIGIO-CULTURAL
SECTIONS OF LOUISIANA, 1956

	French-Catholic Parishes[1]	Non-French Parishes[2]
Number of Negroes registered	70,488	90,922
Potential Negro vote	138,000	390,000
Percentage of Negroes registered	51	23
Mean of parishes—percentage of Negroes in total population	32	38
Mean of parishes—percentage of urbanism	30	26
Mean of parishes—percentage of Catholics among all religions[3]	83	12

[1] French parishes: Acadia, Ascension, Assumption, Avoyelles, Calcasieu, Cameron, Evangeline, Iberis, Iberville, Jefferson, Jefferson Davis, Lafayette, LaFourches, Plaquemines, Pointe Coupee, St. Bernard, St. Charles, St. James, St. John the Baptist, St. Landry, St. Martin, St. Mary, Terrebonne, Vermilion, West Baton Rouge. Definition of French parishes taken from T. Lynn Smith and Homer L. Hitt, *The People of Louisiana* (Baton Rouge, 1952), p. 143.
[2] Predominantly Anglo-Saxon Protestant.
[3] From 1926 *Census of Religious Bodies,* the most reliable source available. It is recognized that the figures contain a bias because of the difference between Catholic and Protestant practice in counting children as members of the church. However, the purpose of the figures is to show differences in degree of Catholicism.

are always segregated; (2) the Citizens' Council organizations have comparatively little support in French-Catholic Louisiana, while in northern Louisiana, as a Madison Council official put it, "Here the Citizens' Councils are the prominent people"; (3) racially hybrid communities occur more frequently in south Louisiana than in north Louisiana.

It should be emphasized that the people of French-Catholic Louisiana are not in favor of integration. Yet they do evidence, people and leaders alike, a permissive attitude toward Negro participation in political affairs that is generally lacking in the northern parishes. These permissive attitudes seem to stem in large part from the social and religious practices of the Catholic Church. The Church looks upon segregation as a sin, and Archbishop Rummel of New Orleans has led the clergy in an all-out doctrinal attack on the practice. Catholic clergy cite the "catholic" character of the Church as the reason for its advanced stand on racial issues and emphasize the fact that the Protestant churches are national in origin and tend to be exclusive in character, whereas the Catholic Church is more universal in both its background and orientation. Many Catholics also point to the effect of the Church on the Negro as a reason for the high percent of Negro registration in Catholic parishes. According to this argument, the Catholic Negro enjoys religious and ethical training which is identical with that re-

ceived by the white community, and from a well-educated priest. Therefore, the Catholic Negro's value system more nearly approaches that of the
white community than does that of the Protestant-Negro, and, accordingly,
he is more readily accepted by the greater community.

Since the Catholic Church attempts to build a Catholic culture wherever it exists by providing educational, recreational, and fraternal organizations for its members, the influence of the Church as a social institution is
great. It appears to be the principal, in many areas the only, unsegregated
social institution in Louisiana. In the French parishes where Catholicism has
been the major formative factor in the culture for many years, it has been,
Catholics say, important in producing the permissive attitudes of the people toward the political and social activities of the Negro.

In north Louisiana, on the other hand, one finds little or no objective
evidence that the dominant Protestant religion has aided in the creation of
tolerant attitudes toward Negro political activity. Negro leaders in these areas
rarely cited white Protestant ministers as friends of the Negro, and seldom
referred to a Potestant church as an ameliorative factor in the easing of
racial tensions. Although most Protestant national organizations are opposed
to racial prejudice and segregation, their position has not effected many
changes in the attitudes of local congregations. Protestant churches, in contrast to the authoritative control by the Catholic heirarchy, are dominated
by local congregations, and Protestant ministers, though often mindful of
national pronouncements on segregation, must remain passive on such
matters so as not to offend their flocks.

Although the mean percent of Negro registration is low in north
Louisiana, there are parishes with large Negro registration. As Table III
shows, this usually occurs where Negroes are not an important part of the

TABLE III. RELATION BETWEEN PERCENTAGE OF TENANCE, PERCENTAGE OF
NEGRO POPULATION, AND PERCENTAGE OF NEGROES REGISTERED IN FRENCH
AND NON-FRENCH PARISHES OF LOUISIANA, 1956

Percentage of Tenancy	Number of Parishes		*Mean Percentage of Negro Population*		*Mean Percentage of Negroes Registered*	
	French	*Non-French*	*French*	*Non-French*	*French*	*Non-French*
50 and over	6	11	34	52	65	11
40–49	0	4	—	43	—	23
30–39	7	6	33	39	48	25
20–29	5	6	23	36	67	36
10–19	7	9	34	25	43	53
0– 9	0	3	—	19	—	59

population, that is, where there are few Negroes, little economic tenancy, and no heritage of a plantation society.

When the parishes of northern Louisiana are grouped into areas, this correspondence of a high rate of tenancy and concentration of Negro population to a low Negro registration becomes clearly evident and significant. In the North-Central cut-over pine section where the percentage of Negroes in the total population (mean of parishes, 24 percent) and prevalence of tenancy (17 percent) is relatively low, there is a great deal of Negro registration (55 percent). In this area, there has been little fear of the Negro as a political force, and the society tends to be pluralistic.

The Mississippi Delta area, in northeast Louisiana, is the section with the highest rate of tenancy (60 percent), the greatest proportion of Negroes (51 percent), and the lowest Negro registration (11 percent) in the state. It remains a plantation society. There are plantation owners in Tensas and Madison parishes who take pride in the resemblance between the plantations of 1856 and 1956, in terms of the physical appearance of the Negro and his cabin, and of the social and economic relationships between Negro and white.

The survival of this kind of society depends upon excluding the Negro from all political and economic power. Outsiders are assured that the Negro happily accepts the existing power structure, and strenuous efforts are made to demonstrate the mutual advantages which accrue from it.

Thus in non-French Louisiana, Negro registration varies with the number of Negroes present and the nature of the economy. In a plantation economy, a tight power structure exists which makes it possible to exclude Negroes from the polls. In addition the numerical strength of Negroes in such communities arouses real or imagined fears of possible Negro rule if he should obtain the ballot.

As Table III indicates, the economic structure of many of the French-Catholic parishes differs from that of the northern portion of the state. In French-Catholic Louisiana the Negro is not typically in a tenant-master relationship to the white community. Rather, his position is that of a free wage-earner. The reason is that much of southern Louisiana is engaged in the production of cane sugar, which does not lend itself to the tenant system of farming.

The free wage-earner is more remote from his master than is the tenant farmer, and thus (at least in prosperous times) enjoys greater social and economic freedom. Therefore, the difference in the economies of the two regions undoubtedly exercises an important conditioning effect on Negro registration.

However, even in those French-Catholic parishes where a plantation economy does exist the percent of Negro registration tends to be considerably above that of the northern plantation parishes. In three French-Catholic parishes (St. Landry, Pointe Coupee, and West Baton Rouge) both the percentage of Negro population and the percentage of tenancy is 45 or more. The percentage of Negro registration exceeds 20 in all three parishes and reaches a level of 87 in St. Landry. This highlights the importance of the French-Catholic religio-culture in producing a permissive attitude toward Negro registration.

II. THE EFFECT OF NEGRO-WHITE POPULATION BALANCE

Perhaps the most widely accepted belief concerning Negro registration in the South is that the amount will vary inversely to the proportion of Negroes in the local population. According to this theory, areas with large Negro populations, (1) were most passionately attached to the cause of the Confederacy, and (2) because of the greater number of Negroes have more reason to fear Negro voting. The theory concludes that the centers of Negro population will be the last to extend the suffrage to the Negro.

Table IV shows that there is certainly no uniform correlation between the proportion of parish population Negro and the proportion of Negroes registered. However, at the extreme ends of the scale, the relationship is significant. The four Louisiana parishes with no Negro registration—Tensas, Madison, West Feliciana, and East Carroll, neighboring parishes in the Mississippi Delta area—are the only parishes with over 60 percent Negro population. In the parishes with less than 29 percent Negro population there is a significant increase in the percentage of Negro registration. However, in ten parishes with a majority of Negro population (50 to 59 percent) the mean percentage of Negroes registered (37 percent) slightly

TABLE IV.   RELATION BETWEEN NEGROES IN TOTAL POPULATION AND
NEGRO REGISTRATION IN PARISHES OF LOUISIANA, 1956

Percentage of Negroes in Total Population	Number of Parishes			Mean Percentage of Negroes Registered		
	Total	French	Non-French	Total	French	Non-French
60 and over	4	—	4	0	—	0
50–59	10	4	6	37	44	33
40–49	8	3	5	33	57	19
30–39	19	6	13	32	47	25
20–29	12	6	6	52	51	53
10–19	10	5	5	62	65	59
0– 9	1	1	—	94	94	—

exceeds that for the two intervals with fewer Negroes (40 to 49 percent and 30 to 39 percent).

Table IV also shows that the presence or absence of large numbers of Negroes has a similar effect on Negro registration in French and non-French parishes. However, as the table indicates, the range of variation tends to be much narrower in the French than in the non-French parishes. Of course, the degree of economic tenancy is another variable present in this figure, a factor which has already been discussed.

In conclusion, it can be definitely stated that, in Louisiana, the simple fact of the presence of a high proportion of Negroes and a tradition of a plantation economy (such as in St. Landry parish) does not necessarily militate against the registration of Negroes in sizeable numbers, especially where a French-Catholic culture predominates.

III. THE EFFECT OF URBANISM

Contrary to the widely held belief that Negro registration in the South is concentrated in urban areas, Table V indicates that no clear relationship exists in Louisiana between the degree of urbanism and the extent of Negro registration.

TABLE V.   RELATION BETWEEN URBANISM AND WHITE AND NEGRO REGISTRATION, FOR STATE AND BY RELIGIO-CULTURAL SECTIONS, LOUISIANA, 1956

| Percentage of Urbanism | Number of Parishes | | | Mean Percentage Registered of Potential Vote | | | | | |
| | | | | Negro | | | White | | |
	Total	Fr.	Non-Fr.	Total	Fr.	Non-Fr.	Total	Fr.	Non-Fr.
70 and over	5	2	3	29	43	20	64	70	60
50–69	4	3	1	45	48	35	75	78	69
40–49	8	2	6	27	67	13	78	79	77
30–39	10	3	7	46	54	42	84	84	84
20–29	14	8	6	49	61	33	90	91	88
10–19	6	3	3	28	43	13	88	89	87
0– 9	17	4	13	43	53	40	92	93	90

The reason, in all probability, for the stereotype about urbanism and Negro registration is that those few Negroes who were registered to vote prior to 1944 resided in the large urban centers. In addition, the first increases in Negro registration after 1944 largely occurred in urban areas. The urban areas of the state contain the largest concentration of professional and business Negroes, equipped to provide leadership toward registration; and the cities provide, one might imagine, an environment of political competition better suited to encourage Negro political participation.

As Table V indicates, however, Negro registration in Louisiana is, if anything, lower in the large urban centers than in the more rural portions of the state. The table also shows that an identical though more pronounced pattern obtains for white registration too. Taking the religio-cultural areas of the state separately, the same relationship between urbanism and registration exists in both regions as in the state as a whole, but with both Negro and white registration in the French parishes tending to be either equal to or higher than registration in the non-French parishes.

Negro registration tends to be lower in the urban than the rural areas for a variety of reasons. Many an urban Negro is rootless, and tends to feel little identification with his community or his fellow Negroes; his leadership often works at cross purposes, and is particular rather than general. In addition, local interest in registration and voting tends to be more intense in Louisiana's rural areas, where the election of a sheriff is an important event, than in the urban areas. All of these factors tend, also, to operate on the level of white registration.

Even though the urban centers do not provide favorable environments for securing a high proportion of Negro registration, the "pilot" role of activities in urban centers toward launching Negro registration is important. In all parishes studied the registration of Negroes was initiated by business and professional Negroes residing in the major urban center of the parish. In the event resistance to Negro registration made it necessary to resort to legal and political action, the city provided the resources and locus for suits against the registrar, for requests to the F.B.I. to investigate reluctant registrars, and for bargains which might be negotiated with court-house politicians.

IV. THE POLITICAL FACTOR

The first concern of every politician is to be elected and reelected to office. Therefore, the existence in any community of a reservoir of untapped voters tends to act as a magnet on politicians in search of votes. The Negro vote in Louisiana, however, was not exploitable until the Supreme Court declared the white primary laws unconstitutional. After 1944, Louisiana politicians could legally pursue the Negro vote.

In all the Louisiana parishes except those with the very largest cities, political power and interest center in the courthouse of the parish seat. The dominant political figure in the courthouse is the sheriff, whose election occasions the most interest and largest voter turnout in the parish. Where Negro registration has occurred in large numbers, the sheriff has almost invariably been friendly to the idea.

The process by which this political variable helps bring Negroes to the polls works generally as follows. Community attitudes must, first of all, be permissive with respect to Negro registration. If the white community is strongly and unalterably opposed to Negro voting, the sheriff or other politician will rarely venture to seek the Negro vote. Instead, as in the Mississippi parishes with no registration, the sheriff will help keep the Negroes away from the polls. This is true because the politician fears the reaction of his townspeople to Negro registration and because he, too, generally shares the dominant attitude.

Secondly, the sheriff, by the very nature of his office, is subject to manifold temptations relating to law enforcement, particularly, in Louisiana, to the classic "payoff" to permit gambling. When a sheriff permits gambling, he is charged with corruption of his office by the good government, middle-class voters of his community. In this event the sheriff is compelled to turn to lower socio-economic groups or to marginal groups in the community for support.

After Negro leaders have initiated the movement for registration and thus demonstrated their group's potential voter strength, the sheriff or other official can then use to his own profit the power of his office to prevent interference with registration, or else later encourage registration drives and voter turnout campaigns. In many parishes the Negro vote has become a "balance of power" factor.

Finally, the reward of the Negro for his vote is respect from the politicians and attendance at Negro political meetings, cessation of police brutality, and promises made and often kept regarding such matters as street improvements and better school facilities. It is ironical that this advance may thus result from an alliance of shady white and underdog Negro elements against the more "respectable" white segment of the community.

The political factor is also important as an inhibiting influence. For example, in the two French parishes (Terrebonne and Plaquemines) with a rate of Negro registration below 20 percent, the local sheriff has been instrumental in keeping the Negroes from the polls. In these cases, the sheriff is unalterably opposed to Negro voting, primarily out of fear that it will cost him the election, and, consequently, he uses the power of his office to prevent registration. In all probability, a different sheriff could permit Negro registration without suffering a serious reaction from the white community.

V. CONCLUSIONS

This paper is concerned with the problem of differences in the political behavior of the South toward the Negro. These differences have been studied, here, through an analysis of Negro registration for voting in Louisiana. Negro registration is basically related to Southern politics not only because it is the fundamental step for the Negro toward the power of the ballot box but also because it appears to be vitally related to the willingness or unwillingness of specific societies to allow the Negro an equal place in the community. The evidence indicates that Southern attitudes and practices toward the Negro are in large part a function of the culture in which the relationships occur. Our inquiry here is whether religio-cultural variables in the South, long celebrated as the "Bible-belt" of the nation, are related to Negro-white political relationships insofar as these can be defined by practices and attitudes toward Negro registration.

The findings of this study emphasize the importance of religio-cultural factors in defining white attitudes and practices toward Negro registration. In the southern French-Catholic parishes the percentage of Negroes registered is more than twice as great as in the northern Anglo-Saxon Protestant parishes. Socio-economic factors, urbanism and Negro-white population balance, account for some of the difference. Yet where non-religious cultural factors are held constant, as in cotton plantation areas with large Negro populations, the religio-cultural variable emerges as a clearly influential factor in Negro registration.

First-hand observations in the parishes of Louisiana support the statistical evidence that Negro registration is related to the type of religio-cultural area involved. Permissive attitudes toward Negro registration in French-Catholic parishes seem expressive of the basic value that the Negro is spiritually equal in a Catholic society. Such a view of man's relation to man, a scheme of elementary justice implicit in a Catholic society, some Catholics maintain, is sustained by traditional Catholic theology and actively promoted by the Church in Louisiana. There is little evidence in the Protestant parishes of cultural values assigning the Negro a spiritually equal place in the community or of activity by the church itself toward these values.

Dr. Frank Tannenbaum has written a brilliant exposition of the comparative treatment of the Negro in North and South America, maintaining that differences are in large part a function of the respective Protestant and Catholic cultures. Curiously, the religio-cultural analysis has been largely neglected in race-relations analysis of the United States, even though the role of the Protestant ethic, for instance in economic behavior and intellectual development, has been well stated.

It is not the intention of the authors to urge religious determinism in this paper but to maintain that, on the evidence, the politics of Negro registration in Louisiana can be understood only by consideration of religio-cultural variables with other relevant factors. In consequence we suggest that religio-cultural analysis may be useful in understanding the whole of

Southern politics. Excepting Maryland, possibly, the type of analysis employed here would not be possible in other Southern states due to the lack of distinctive religio-cultural areas. Some attention could be given, however, to the general problem of the Protestant ethic in the South and its involvement with political behavior.

PART II

Conceptual Approaches to Political Behavior

Chapter Four

SYSTEMS ANALYSIS

IN Part One of this volume, a focus on political behavior as an approach to the study of politics was considered. To do this, it was necessary to become concerned with such questions as: What is the behavioral approach? What is political behavior? What are the bases of political behavior? To what extent can differences in the psychological and social bases of behavior be used to explain its many variations? In Part Two attention will be devoted to some of the major concepts used in the analysis of political behavior. It is fitting to begin with the concept of *system,* since it is sufficiently broad to subsume (if one wishes) most other formulations. *Systems analysis* is sometimes referred to as functionalism or structural functionalism. Two major contributors to systems theory are Talcott Parsons and Marion J. Levy, Jr.

Parsons' emphasis is on action as a frame of reference and starting point for his system. Action for Parsons is simply behavior (political or otherwise) oriented toward specific goals. Collective action organized around relations of a plurality of actors leads to a social system when value orientation standards become shared. The basic unit in the system is *role,* and the social system is merely a network of roles. Every social system assumes interaction among system elements (roles) which Parsons calls the first law of social process. Moreover, such interactions tend toward stability or equilibrium over time. The papers in this section exemplify the use of systems theory in political science.

The Parsons selection suggests the possible uses of an economic model for political analysis. David Easton, on the other hand, adapts the social system model to a political system. A political system of action, like any other system, is characterized by input-conversion-output processes which operate in terms of a particular goal orientation. Easton concerns himself with the political relationships necessary for the continuation of the input-conversion-output process. Gabriel Almond's work is even more closely related to the action theories of Parsons and Edward Shils. His primary concern is the comparison of political systems using the Parsons-Shils conceptualizations. The Almond piece is quite suggestive, particularly in the rather striking comparison of role structures in various political systems.

The paper on homeostatic tendencies in the United States Supreme Court was written especially for this volume. It attempts to utilize systems theory in a concrete, empirical research project. The focus here is also on action. The work adopts (within the limitations of the data) Almond's suggestion that political institutions or persons performing political roles may be fruitfully viewed "in terms of what it is that they do, why they do it, and how what they do is related to and affects what others do." It is also an attempt to produce evidence for the equilibrium tendencies which systems theory predicts.

The paper by Robert K. Merton reflects the viewpoint of the structural-functionalists such as Marion Levy, whose work, in turn, is an amplification of the Parsonian theory. Levy contends that a structural requisite of a system is a pattern of action necessary for the system's continued existence. A functional requisite, on the other hand, is a generalized condition necessary for the maintenance of the system. Structural requisites would include such things as goal orientation and stratification. The functional requisites of any society are said to include the meeting of biological needs, role differentiation and assignment, and the control of disruptive behavior.

From this frame of reference, one expects every system to perform a function and indeed to exist for that very purpose. The failure of the system to adequately perform its specific function leads to its disruption and breakdown. The failure of any existing system to meet a felt social need will call into play a new system whose function may or may not be obvious to all observers. The Merton paper illustrates this point of view by delineating the social role of the political machine. This piece is a simple, yet excellent, example of functional theory in use. Although political machines may now be essentially relics of the recent past, Merton's use of them may add to our understanding of systems analysis.

Power, Party and System

TALCOTT PARSONS

The political aspect of a social system may be thought of as centered on the generation and distribution of power. Power may, for the present purposes, be conceived as the capacity of the society to mobilize its resources in the interest of goals, defined as positively rather than permissively sanctioned by the system as a whole—goals that are "affected with a public interest." The amount of its power is an attribute of the total system and is a function of several variables. These, as I conceive them, are the *support* that can be mobilized by those exercising power, the *facilities* they have access to (notably the control of the productivity of the economy), the *legitimation* that can be accorded to the positions of the holders of power, and the relatively *unconditional loyalties* of the population to the society in its politically organized aspects. It is above all the factor of support which will be the center of concern here. In a modern, differentiated society the most important "producers" of power on the collectivity level, though by no means the sole ones, are those who hold responsible positions in what we call the structure of government—here, of course, the federal government. . . .

I have defined power as the capacity of a social system to mobilize resources to attain collective goals. A total society's paramount "goal" must be conceived on a very high level of abstraction. It is a function primarily of two sets of factors, the institutionalized value system of the society and the exigencies of the situation. Together they define states of affairs that need to be changed in the interest of a higher level of value-implementation. The specificity of a societal goal will vary greatly for different societies, but in any case there will be many subgoals that vary as functions of a societal development and the manifold relations of the society to the situation.

The value system of the contemporary United States centers on what may be called "instrumental activism." It is oriented to control the action situation in the interest of range and quality of adaptation, but with more economic than political emphasis. In goal definition it is highly indefinite and pluralistic, being committed to a rather general direction of progress or improvement, without any clearly defined terminal goal. Economic production is highly valued as the most immediate focus of adaptive capacity. Beyond that, however, we value particularly technology and science as means to productivity, and the maximization of opportunity for individuals and

Reprinted from *American Voting Behavior,* edited by Eugene Burdick and Arthur J. Brodbeck (1959), pp. 81–93 by permission of the publisher. Copyright 1959 by The Free Press of Glencoe, Illinois.

subcollectives (manifested above all in concern with health and education).
Moreover, we have a special set of attitudes toward organization and authority which might be summed up as involving, on the one hand, a pragmatic
acceptance of authority in the interest of limited specifically approved goals,
but, on the other hand, an objection to any pretensions of generalized superiority of status.

The over-all goal of American society (in a special technical sense)
may then be tentatively defined as the *facilitation* of effective adaptive development of the society and of the societal conditions associated with it.
It centers on economic development, but definitely includes the integrative
conditions which are relevant. At the next lower level of specifications,
American society stresses the more immediate facilitation of production and
the development of productivity, the effective ordering of political organization itself, the furthering of effective integration of the social system, and
the promoting of conditions on the level of opportunity for operation of the
system and adjustment of personalities.

The generation and allocation of power in a society occurs through a
set of structures and processes, a subsystem parallel to the economy which
we may call the "polity." It is essentially a functional-relational system, controlled by institutional patterns and controlling collectivities and roles. The
relevant institutional patterns are those governing the hierarchical ordering
of social statuses, authority, and the compulsory regulation of "private" activities. The focus of the collectivity structure is clearly government, though
there is a political as well as economic component in all collectivities in the
society. Government is that complex of collectivities which have political
primacy. This means that governmental organizations primarily, in their
relations to the rest of the society, generate power and make it available to
the rest of the society.

Like the economy, the polity is an analytically distinct subsystem of
the society. It too is conceived to stand in relations to other parts of the society which involve the interchange of inputs and outputs over its boundaries. Of these interchanges, one is of primary importance for present
purposes. It may be characterized through a comparison between the functions of government and those of the polity. On the federal level, which
alone will concern us here, the main functions of government are relatively
clearly set forth in the Constitution itself. The most important concern the
conduct of foreign relations, the regulation of commerce between the states,
the enforcement of rights (personal freedom, opportunity, property), the
ensuring of justice and internal order, and the promotion of the "general
welfare." Broadly, this constitutional mandate is to implement within a
certain framework the goals of the society as sketched above.

The functions of the polity, as contrasted with those of government I conceive to center in creating the conditions necessary if those assuming responsibility in government are to be able to assume and discharge this responsibility. Given the American value system these may be said to be: (1) the legitimation of the powers of government and the statuses of its various subcollectivities and offices; (2) the requisite share in the control of the basic facilities available in the society, especially control of the productivity of the economy through the establishment of "rights to intervene"; and (3) the mobilization of "support" for the assumption, by office holders in government, of leadership roles and the corresponding responsibilities for formulation of more specific goals and their implementation.

The theoretical analysis of this chapter concerns the third of these conditions of responsible leadership. I shall call this the "goal-attainment" process of the polity as a system. *Its* goal, which must be distinguished from that of the society as a whole as sketched above, is to generate power in the political sense, i.e., to mobilize "resources" that can be used to implement societal goals. There are two main levels on which this goal is (more or less effectively) achieved. The more general is the provision of effective *leadership* in the goal-specification and goal-implementation processes on the requisite collective level. The more specific is arriving at *decisions* which are binding on the society as a politically organized collectivity. For present purposes the subsystem that functions as recipient of these outputs of the polity may be referred to as the "public."

We are, however, speaking of a boundary-interchange process and must be concerned not only with outputs from the polity but also with the inputs to the polity from the public—which on the one hand are essential factors in its functioning, on the other are in certain ways contingent on its performance. I should like to suggest that support (point 3 above) is the appropriate input category (from public to polity) which matches the outputs of provision of leadership and making of decisions. At the more general level, the support that is exchanged with and contingent upon leadership is *generalized*. It takes the form of broadly based confidence in those assuming responsibility for leadership in governmental affairs which is necessary to enable them to act with real power, i.e., to make necessary and far-reaching decisions responsibly in the sense that elements of the population affected will accept the consequences. Such consequences inevitably include burdens and obligations that affect some elements adversely and bear unevenly on different groups. On the lower level of generality, the relevant type of support which corresponds to decision-making may be said to be the *advocacy of policies*. By this I mean an accepting attitude on a level more general than that of specific decisions but less general than that of an "administration" in the American or a "Government" in the British sense (which is a term of generalized support).

In the above formulation I am thinking self-consciously in terms of a parallel with the corresponding boundary-interchange of the economy: the one involved vis-à-vis the household with labor as a factor of production and the production of consumers' goods. On the higher level of generalization the primary output of the economy to the household is the production of *income* in the monetary sense—in the labor case, wage income. On the lower level it is the production of specific commodities made available to consumers. The corresponding inputs to the economy from the household are, on the high level, labor in the factor sense and, on the lower level, consumers' spending.

These relations of interchange of inputs and outputs—on the one hand, between the economy and the household—may be represented diagrammatically in a simply way as follows:

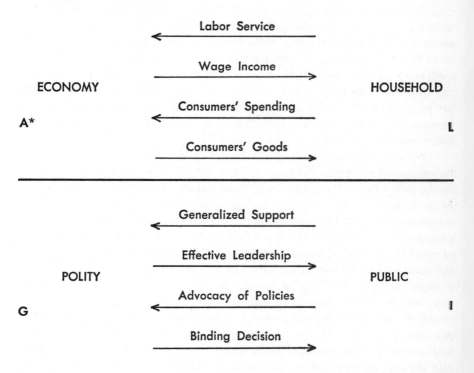

*For an explanation of the notation, A, G, I, L, see final section of this chapter entitled: Technical Note.

. . . . Let us now attempt to apply this abstract analytical scheme to some familiar facts of American political structure. I have stated that the focus of political organization on the collectivity level is government, in our case the federal government. The boundary-interchange just outlined is that set of processes by which control of the federal government is decided, its major policies are worked out, and public attitudes toward them are influenced and brought to bear. The focus of the mechanisms by which the processes work out is what we call the party system. At the support level the most important single process on the side of the public is voting because, under our constitutional system, this decides who is to assume the primary roles of responsible leadership.

There are of course many other influences on leadership: media of opinion, behind-the-scenes persuasion and threats, financial interests, etc. But voting is the central focus of the process of selection of leadership and hence in one sense all other influences must channel their effects *through* the voting process.

The most important fact about the American situation is the existence on the national level of the *two*-party system which, with some interruptions, has proved stable over a long period. This means that the presidency must at any given time be occupied by the candidate of one of the two parties, and that the majority party in each house of Congress has the opportunity to "organize" its house through the speakership (in the case of the House of Representatives) and chairmanships and majorities of committees. In spite of the looseness of party discipline there can be no doubt of the overwhelming importance of this two-party structure.

Within the complex of operation of the two-party system this analysis, in line with the empirical studies with which it is concerned, will be confined to the voting processes which determine the incumbency of the presidency. It is of course vital to realize that the process of electing the President, considered as a system, is only part of a larger one. It has been noted that a variety of influences operate to determine the decisions of voters. But even where the voting mechanism itself is concerned, voting for presidential candidates is only part of the voter's function and opportunity. The separation of powers means that he also votes for congressional candidates and for state and local offices.

A salient fact of American politics is that there is only a rough correlation between party votes for President and for these other offices. The looseness of party discipline and the plural voting opportunities provided in the American system mean that in no sense can the determination of the presidency be considered a *closed* system. For example, tensions generated by being forced to choose between only two candidates for President may be expressed in supporting for other offices candidates not in sympathy with the presidential candidate, or candidates of the opposing party. Empirical statements made in the following analysis should always be qualified with these considerations in mind.

Nevertheless I think it is legitimate to consider the voting process by which Presidents are elected as authentically a *social system*. It is a set of processes of action and interaction which may be treated in terms of specific modes of interdependence which can be analytically separated from other influences. Futhermore, in our system, the Presidency is the focus of integration of the political system as a whole. Of course the concrete data that will be reviewed are affected by factors emanating from outside this particular system—including the other voting processes in other subsystems of the political structure. But in principle this is true of any social system that is a subsystem of a larger one, i.e., less than the total society.

To return to the substantive discussion, the main function of political organization is the facilitation of effective action on collective levels. The two-party system may be regarded as a mechanism that makes possible a certain balance between effectiveness through relative centralization of power, and mobilization of support from different sources in such a way that there is genuine contingency—the supporter is offered a real alternative. Dictatorships naturally are different; their concern is to avoid losing support lest the opposition become dangerous, and there is a strong tendency to use coercive measures in coping with actual or feared opposition. But the two-party system, as has often been pointed out, makes it possible for the holders of power to be changed without upsetting the system. Naturally this depends on definite institutional conditions, notably the acceptance of electoral results by the losing side without impairment of basic loyalties, and the restraint of winners from using their power to suppress opposition. It depends overwhelmingly on the firm institutionalization of such "rules of the game."

All this I take for granted. The point of present interest is that the two-party system, as distinguished from a many-party system or one of an indefinite number of shifting factions, has certain implications for the structure of support in its relation to leadership. This way of structuring the situation forces a high level of *generalization* of support on the one side, of responsibility on the other. This is particularly true in a society with a social structure as diverse as the American, in economic, class, occupational, regional, ethnic, religious, and other terms. Support, focusing on the presidency, must be given to one of two party candidates: the alternative is a "protest" vote for a minority-party candidate, or nonparticipation altogether. Many votes are motivated by more particularized considerations having to do with specific interest groups, etc. But *whatever* their motivation on lower levels of generality, all the votes have to be *counted* as support for the party candidate and his administration, and on some level for the power of the party in Congress. This point brings out in one context very sharply the difference in significance between the problem of the *motivation* of the individual voter, and of the *consequences* of his vote for the political system. . . .

What I have called the generalization of support is parallel to the "mobility of labor," the readiness to co-operate in the production of goods and services that do not themselves satisfy one's own personal needs or those of one's family. The individual worker must in an important sense relinquish control of the product of his labor. Similarly the political supporter, in our case the voter, must not claim direct control of the consequences of his vote; if he did, political support would be reduced to a "barter" basis and the political integration of a complex social system would become impossible. What then does the voter receive which is analogous to the money income of the worker? He receives the expectation that many *kinds* of measures that he approves will be implemented if his candidate wins, but without exact specification of particular policies. The directional orientation of a party candidate is a kind of political "currency" which, if he wins, will improve the probabilities that a *kind* of direct political action, over which the voter does not have direct control but which *in general* he favors, will be taken. In taking money wages for his work and relinquishing control of the product, the worker evidences "faith" that by spending the money he will be able to get something he values as much or more than the product of his work. Similarly the voter evidences faith that, if his candidate wins, the "way things will go" will be relatively in accord with his wishes, but he cannot directly control the specific decisions that will be taken.

This generalized support is, I have noted, a fundamental ingredient of power. It, along with the other ingredients, is used to help produce concrete decisions, binding on the collectivity, which are analogous to specific goods. The support is necessary because without it the decisions could not be responsible, i.e., could not be made to "stick." But if the support is to be of any "use," its consequences must eventuate in concrete decisions that deal effectively with the real problems of the collectivity. The quality and quantity of these decisions and of their consequences in turn justify the acts of faith involved in giving political support. But it is the *aggregate value* of such decisions, not their particularities, which is the basis of the community's political "income" from its commitments of support.

Perhaps it is worth while to carry the parallel between the economic and the political one step further. The keynote of economic organization has rightly been said to be the division of labor. Through it the individual "producer" makes a sacrifice and receives a gain. The sacrifice is essentially one of self-contained independence; he can no longer meet his own needs from his own efforts and resources. The gain is one of "efficiency." He gets more by pooling competence and resources with others than if each operated alone on a self-sufficient basis. In the political case the axis is the differentiation of responsibility. The giver of support makes a sacrifice—loss of immediate control of collective decisions that affect his own interest; he "delegates" this control to the holders of power. But he also receives a gain, which is his share in the benefits of the *effectiveness* with which collective action can be taken. If the responsibility of every voter, including the President, for collective action were exactly equal, in effect *no* collective action would be taken at all. But in exchange for this gain the voter has to take his chances that the *particular* decisions in which he is most directly interested will be forthcoming.

A built-in element of the conflict of interest is always present in any system of the economic division of labor—for example, the terms of the contract of employment. But this is greatly accentuated in the political case because of the commitment of the collectivity as a whole which is involved. At the leadership-support level this is, in our system, dramatized by the duality of the parties and the fact that in an immediate presidential election, what is gained by one—namely electoral victory—is by definition lost by the other. Hence there are inherently divisive potentialities in political "competition" which are not present to the same degree in economic competition. The control of such divisive potentialities is, in our society, attained through the institutionalization of the two-party system referred to above.

So far we have attempted to do two things. The first was to outline a general model of the relation between the organization of leadership and the mobilization of support in a political system. The second was to apply this to the main facts of the American two-party system so far as it involved the processes of election to the presidency. It is clear that the operation of such a system is dependent on the firm institutionalization of the "rules of the game" by which certain standards of fairness are insured, by which the losing party accepts the legitimacy of electoral victory of the winner, and by which in turn the winners do not use the power of the state to make it imposible for the losers to have a real chance of winning in future elections.

In addition to this condition of general institutionalization, it follows, I think, from the above analysis that there are certain further conditions necessary to the successful operation of a democratic two-party system. These conditions may be stated in the following four propositions:

1) There must be mechanisms by which the average voter can come to a "responsible decision that is meaningful to him. He must not, in too many cases, withdraw to nonvoting, nor be too susceptible to appeals that would be grossly disruptive of the stability of the system. Since the intellectual problems involved in a rational solution are not practicably soluble, my thesis is that the mechanisms are typically nonrational. They involve stabilization of political attitudes *in terms of association with other members of the*

principal solidary groups in which the voter is involved. In terms of party affiliation this may be called "traditionalism." The traditionalistic operation of nonrational mechanisms is a condition of the stability of the system. That they root in the solidary groupings of the society follows from the fact that support is mobilized from the integration subsystem of the society.

2) Pure traditionalism, however, would result in a rigidity of the system which would be incompatible both with the shift of conditions under which problems of public goal-specification and attainment must be posed and with the necessity, for a two-party system, that there be realistic opportunities for each party to win in its bid for leadership through the election of a President. A certain proportion of voters must shift from time to time in party allegiance, if a flexible balance is to be maintained. The data show that this takes place mainly through what has been called above the "indifference" reaction—the voting change of people under cross-pressures who show relatively low levels of interest in the campaign and have difficulty in making their decisions. This finding will be interpreted as in line with the importance of solidary groupings as foci of poltical loyalties. It is a mechanism which on the whole minimizes the dangers of instability, inherent in political shifting. But it is primarily a condition of effective attainment of *new* goals as they become salient.

3) Under two-party conditions a limited polarization of the electorate is essential—a choice between only two realistic alternatives is offered. This means that the inherently divisive potentialities of political power-struggle are increased. There must clearly be mechanisms which prevent this polarization from producing a progressively deepening rift in the electorate. In the subsequent discussion, it will be shown that there are two main foci of such mechanisms. First, there is the supraparty consensus referred to above, which institutionalizes the duality of party organization, prescribing rules of political fair play. Second, there is the involvement of voting with the solidary groups in the society in such a way that, though there is a correlation, there is no *exact* correspondence between political polarization and other bases of differentiation. Hence, pushing the implications of political difference too far activates the solidarities between adherents of the two parties which exist on other, nonpolitical, bases so that members of the political majority come to defend those who share other of their interests but differ from them politically. These mechanisms serve the effective integration of the system.

4) American society is not static, but dynamically evolving. The political system must be adapted to this fact and must include mechanisms of adjustment to social change. Under American conditions the main autonomous processes of social change do not operate through government, but largely through the development of the economy. The business element, which is the core of this process of change, tends to be politically conserva-

tive because positive use of the powers of government has been felt, since the early thirties, to imply interference with the process. The left, on the other hand, is relatively residual, tending to gather together those elements in the society on whom the problems and difficulties arising from the dynamic process impinge, and who see in governmental action an opportunity to remedy their situations. There must be mechanisms in the political system which mediate the balance between right and left without running the risk that either set of elements will be oppressively overwhelmed by the other. They are mechanisms that are essential to adapt the system to *changes in the structure of the society.*

An Approach to the Analysis of
Political Systems

DAVID EASTON

The study of politics is concerned with understanding how authoritative decisions are made and executed for a society. We can try to understand political life by viewing each of its aspects piecemeal. We can examine the operation of such institutions as political parties, interest groups, government, and voting; we can study the nature and consequences of such political practices as manipulation, propaganda, and violence; we can seek to reveal the structure within which these practices occur. By combining the results we can obtain a rough picture of what happens in any self-contained political unit.

In combining these results, however, there is already implicit the notion that each part of the larger political canvas does not stand alone but is related to each other part; or, to put it positively, that the operation of no one part can be fully understood without reference to the way in which the whole itself operates. I have suggested in my book, *The Political System,* that it is valuable to adopt this implicit assumption as an articulate premise for research and to view political life as a system of interrelated activities. These activities derive their relatedness or systemic ties from the fact that they all more or less influence the way in which authoritative decisions are formulated and executed for a society.

Once we begin to speak of political life as a system of activity, certain consequences follow for the way in which we can undertake to analyze the

Reprinted from *World Politics,* vol. 9 (1956–57), pp. 383–400 by permission of the author and the publisher.

working of a system. The very idea of a system suggests that we can separate political life from the rest of social activity, at least for analytical purposes, and examine it as though for the moment it were a self-contained entity surrounded by, but clearly distinguishable from, the environment or setting in which it operates. In much the same way, astronomers consider the solar system a complex of events isolated for certain purposes from the rest of the universe.

Furthermore, if we hold the system of political actions as a unit before our mind's eye, as it were, we can see that what keeps the system going are inputs of various kinds. These inputs are converted by the processes of the system into outputs and these, in turn, have consequences both for the system and for the environment in which the system exists. The formula here is very simple but, as I hope to show, also very illuminating: inputs—political system or processes—outputs. These relationships are shown diagrammatically in Figure I. This diagram represents a very primitive "model" —to dignify it with a fashionable name—for approaching the study of political life.

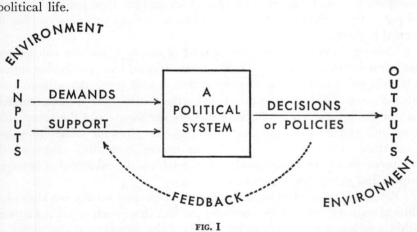

FIG. I

Political systems have certain properties because they are systems. To present an over-all view of the whole approach, let me identify the major attributes, say a little about each, and then treat one of these properties at somewhat greater length, even though still inadequately.

(1) PROPERTIES OF IDENTIFICATION. To distinguish a political system from other social systems, we must be able to identify it by describing its fundamental units and establishing the boundaries that demarcate it from units outside the system.

(a) Units of a political system. The units are the elements of which we say a system is composed. In the case of a political system, they are

political actions. Normally it is useful to look at these as they structure themselves in political roles and political groups.

(b) Boundaries. Some of the most significant questions with regard to the operation of political systems can be answered only if we bear in mind the obvious fact that a system does not exist in a vacuum. It is always immersed in a specific setting or environment. The way in which a system works will be in part a function of its response to the total social, biological and physical environment. . . . The boundary of a political system is defined by all those actions more or less directly related to the making of binding decisions for a society; every social action that does not partake of this characteristic will be excluded from the system and thereby will automatically be viewed as an external variable in the environment.

(2) INPUTS AND OUTPUTS. Presumably, if we select political systems for special study, we do so because we believe that they have characteristically important consequences for society, namely, authoritative decisions. These consequences I shall call the outputs. If we judged that political systems did not have important outputs for society, we would probably not be interested in them.

Unless a system is approaching a state of entropy—and we can assume that this is not true of most political systems—it must have continuing inputs to keep it going. Without inputs the system can do no work; without outputs we cannot identify the work done by the system. The specific research tasks in this connection would be to identify the inputs and the forces that shape and change them, to trace the processes through which they are transformed into outputs, to describe the general conditions under which such processes can be maintained, and to establish the relationship between outputs and succeeding inputs of the system.

From this point of view, much light can be shed on the working of a political system if we take into account the fact that much of what happens within a system has its birth in the efforts of the members of the system to cope with the changing environment. We can appreciate this point if we consider a familiar biological system such as the human organism. It is subject to constant stress from its surroundings to which it must adapt in one way or another if it is not to be completely destroyed. In part, of course, the way in which the body works represents responses to needs that are generated by the very organization of its anatomy and functions; but in large part, in order to understand both the structure and the working of the body, we must also be very sensitive to the inputs from the environment.

In the same way, the behavior of every political system is to some degree imposed upon it by the kind of system it is, that is, by its own structure and internal needs. But its behavior also reflects the strains occasioned by the specific setting within which the system operates. . . .

(3) DIFFERENTIATION WITHIN A SYSTEM. As we shall see in a moment, from the environment come both energy to activate a system and information with regard to which the system uses this energy. In this way a system is able to do work. It has some sort of output that is different from the input that enters from the environment. We can take it as a useful hypothesis that if a political system is to perform some work for anything but a limited interval of time, a minimal amount of differentiation in its structure must occur. In fact, empirically it is impossible to find a significant political system in which the same units all perform the same activities at the same time. The members of a system engage in at least some minimal division of labor that provides a structure within which action takes place.

(4) INTEGRATION OF A SYSTEM. This fact of differentiation opens up a major area of inquiry with regard to political systems. Structural differentiation sets in motion forces that are potentially disintegrative in their results for the system. If two or more units are performing different kinds of activity at the same time, how are these activities to be brought into the minimal degree of articulation necessary if the members of the system are not to end up in utter disorganization with regard to the production of the outputs of interest to us? We can hypothesize that if a structured system is to maintain itself, it must provide mechanisms whereby its members are integrated or induced to cooperate in some minimal degree so that they can make authoritative decisions. . . .

Among inputs of a political system there are two basic kinds: demands and support. These inputs give a political system its dynamic character. They furnish it both with the raw material or information that the system is called upon to process and with the energy to keep it going.

The reason why a political system emerges in a society at all—that is, why men engage in political activity—is that demands are being made by persons or groups in the society that cannot all be fully satisfied. In all societies one fact dominates political life: scarcity prevails with regard to most of the valued things. Some of the claims for these relatively scarce things never find their way into the political system but are satisfied through the private negotiations of or settlements by the persons involved. Demands for prestige may find satisfaction through the status relations of society; claims for wealth are met in part through the economic system; aspirations for power find expression in educational, fraternal, labor, and similar private organizations. Only where wants require some special organized effort on the part of society to settle them authoritatively may we say that they have become inputs of the political system.

Systematic research would require us to address ourselves to several key questions with regard to these demands.

(1) How do demands arise and assume their particular character in

a society? In answer to this question, we can point out that demands have their birth in two sectors of experience: either in the environment of a system or within the system itself. We shall call these the external and internal demands, respectively.

Let us look at the external demands first. I find it useful to see the environment not as an undifferentiated mass of events but rather as systems clearly distinguishable from one another and from the political system. In the environment we have such systems as the ecology, economy, culture, personality, social structure, and demography. Each of these constitutes a major set of variables in the setting that helps to shape the kind of demands entering a political system. For purposes of illustrating what I mean, I shall say a few words about culture.

The members of every society act within the framework of an ongoing culture that shapes their general goals, specific objectives, and the procedures that the members feel ought to be used. Every culture derives part of its unique quality from the fact that it emphasizes one or more special aspects of behavior and this strategic emphasis serves to differentiate it from other cultures with respect to the demands that it generates. As far as the mass of the people is concerned, some cultures, such as our own, are weighted heavily on the side of economic wants, success, privacy, leisure activity, and rational efficiency. Others, such as that of the Fox Indians, strive toward the maintenance of harmony, even if in the process the goals of efficiency and rationality may be sacrificed. Still others, such as the Kachins of highland Burma, stress the pursuit of power and prestige. The culture embodies the standards of value in a society and thereby marks out areas of potential conflict, if the valued things are in short supply relative to demand. The typical demands that will find their way into the political process will concern the matters in conflict that are labeled important by the culture. For this reason we cannot hope to understand the nature of the demands presenting themselves for political settlement unless we are ready to explore systematically and intensively their connection with the culture. And what I have said about culture applies, with suitable modifications, to other parts of the setting of a political system.

But not all demands originate or have their major locus in the environment. Important types stem from situations occurring within a political system itself. Typically, in every on-going system, demands may emerge for alterations in the political relationships of the members themselves, as the result of dissatisfaction stemming from these relationships. For example, in a political system based upon representation, in which equal representation is an important political norm, demands may arise for equalizing representation between urban and rural voting districts. Similarly, demands for changes in the process of recruitment of formal political leaders, for modifications of the way in which constitutions are amended, and the like may all be internally inspired demands. . . .

(2) How are demands transformed into issues? What determines whether a demand becomes a matter for serious political discussion or remains something to be resolved privately among the members of society? The occurrence of a demand, whether internal or external, does not thereby automatically convert it into a political *issue*. Many demands die at birth or linger on with the support of an insignificant fraction of the society and are never raised to the level of possible political decision. Others become issues, an issue being a demand that the members of a political system are prepared to deal with as a significant item for discussion through the recognized channels in the system.

The distinction between demands and issues raises a number of questions about which we need data if we are to understand the processes through which claims typically become transformed into issues. For example, we would need to know something about the relationship between a demand and the location of its initiators or supporters in the power structures of the society, the importance of secrecy as compared with publicity in presenting demands, the matter of timing of demands, the possession of political skills or know-how, access to channels of communication, the attitudes and states of mind of possible publics, and the images held by the initiators of demands with regard to the way in which things get done in the particular political system. Answers to matters such as these would possibly yield a conversion index reflecting the probability of a set of demands being converted into live political issues.

If we assume that political science is primarily concerned with the way in which authoritative decisions are made for a socetiy, demands require special attention as a major type of input of political systems. I have suggested that demands influence the behavior of a system in a number of ways. They constitute a significant part of the material upon which the system operates. They are also one of the sources of change in political systems, since as the environment fluctuates it generates new types of demand-inputs for the system. . . .

Inputs of demands alone are not enough to keep a political system operating. They are only the raw material out of which finished products called decisions are manufactured. Energy in the form of actions or orientations promoting and resisting a political system, the demands arising in it, and the decisions issuing from it must also be put into the system to keep it running. This input I shall call support. Without support, demands could not be satisfied or conflicts in goals composed. If demands are to be acted upon, the members of a system undertaking to pilot the demands through to their transformation into binding decisions and those who seek to influence the relevant processes in any way must be able to count on support from others in the system. . . .

What do we mean by support? We can say that A supports B either when A acts on behalf of or when he orients himself favorably toward B's goals, interests, and actions. Supportive behavior may thus be of two kinds. It may consist of actions promoting the goals, interests, and actions of another person. We may vote for a political candidate, or defend a decision by the highest court of the land. In these cases, support manifests itself through overt action.

On the other hand, supportive behavior may involve not external observable acts, but those internal forms of behavior we call orientations or states of mind. As I use the phrase, a supportive state of mind is a deepseated set of attitudes or predispositions, or a readiness to act on behalf of some other person. It exists when we say that a man is loyal to his party, attached to democracy, or infused with patriotism. What such phrases as these have in common is the fact that they refer to a state of feelings on the part of a person. No overt action is involved at this level of description, although the implication is that the individual will pursue a course of action consistent with his attitudes. Where the anticipated action does not flow from our perception of the state of mind, we assume that we have not penetrated deeply enough into the true feelings of the person but have merely skimmed off his surface attitudes. . . .

(1) THE DOMAIN OF SUPPORT

Support is fed into the political system in relation to three objects: the community, the regime, and the government. There must be convergence of attitude and opinion as well as some willingness to act with regard to each of these objects. Let us examine each in turn.

(a) THE POLITICAL COMMUNITY. No political system can continue to operate unless its members are willing to support the existence of a group that seeks to settle differences or promote decisions through peaceful action in common. The point is so obvious—being dealt with usually under the heading of the growth of national unity—that it may well be overlooked; and yet it is a premise upon which the continuation of any political system depends. To refer to this phenomenon we can speak of the political community. At this level of support we are not concerned with whether a government exists or whether there is loyalty to a constitutional order. For the moment we only ask whether the members of the group that we are examining are sufficiently oriented toward each other to want to contribute their collective energies toward pacific settlement of their varying demands. . . .

(b) THE REGIME. Support for a second major part of a political system helps to supply the energy to keep the system running. This aspect of the system I shall call the regime. It consists of all those arrangements that regulate the way in which the demands put into the system are settled and the way in which decisions are put into effect. They are the so-called rules of the game, in the light of which actions by members of the system are legitimated and accepted by the bulk of the members as authoritative. Unless there is a minimum convergence of attitudes in support of these fundamental rules—the constitutional principles, as we call them in Western society—there would be insufficient harmony in the actions of the members of a system to meet the problems generated by their support of a political community. The fact of trying to settle demands in common means that there must be known principles governing the way in which resolutions of differences of claims are to take place.

(c) THE GOVERNMENT. If a political system is going to be able to handle the conflicting demands put into it, not only must the members of the system be prepared to support the settlement of these conflicts in common and possess some consensus with regard to the rules governing the mode of settlement; they must also be ready to support a government as it undertakes the concrete tasks involved in negotiating such settlements. . . .

The fact that support directed to a political system can be broken down conceptually into three elements—support for the community, regime and government—does not mean, of course, that in the concrete case support for each of these three objects is independent. In fact we might and normally do find all three kinds of support very closely intertwined, so that the presence of one is a function of the presence of one or both of the other types. . . .

If a system is to absorb a variety of demands and negotiate some sort of settlement among them, it is not enough for the members of the system to support only their own demands and the particular government that will undertake to promote these demands. For the demands to be processed into outputs it is equally essential that the members of the system stand ready to support the existence of a political community and some stable rules of common action that we call the regime.

(2) QUANTITY AND SCOPE OF SUPPORT

How much support needs to be put into a system and how many of its members need to contribute such support if the system is to be able to do the job of converting demands to decisions? No ready answer can be offered. The actual situation in each case would determine the amount and scope required. We can, however, visualize a number of situations that will be helpful in directing our attention to possible generalizations.

Under certain circumstances very few members need to support a system at any level. The members might be dull and apathetic, indifferent to the general operations of the system, its progress or decisions. In a loosely connected system such as India has had, this might well be the state of mind of by far the largest segment of the membership. Either in fact they have not been affected by national decisions or they have not perceived that they were so affected. They may have little sense of identification with the present regime and government and yet, with regard to the input of demands, the system may be able to act on the basis of the support offered by the known 3 per cent of the Western-oriented politicians and intellectuals who are politically active. In other words, we can have a small minority putting in quantitatively sufficient supportive energy to keep the system going. However, we can venture the hypothesis that where members of a system are putting in numerous demands, there is a strong probability that they will actively offer support or hostility at one of the three levels of the system, depending upon the degree to which these demands are being met through appropriate decisions.

Alternatively, we may find that all the members of a system are putting in support, but the amount may be so low as to place one or all aspects of the system in jeopardy. Modern France is perhaps a classic illustration. The input of support at the level of the political community is probably adequate for the maintenance of France as a national political unit. But for a variety of historical and contemporary reasons, there is considerable doubt as to whether the members of the French political system are putting in anything but a low order of support to the regime or any particular government. This low amount of support, even though spread over a relatively large segment of the population, leaves the French political system on somewhat less secure foundations than is the case with India. There support is less widespread but more active—that is, quantitatively greater—on the part of a minority. As this illustration indicates, the amount of support is not necessarily proportional to its scope.

It may seem from the above discussion as though the members of a political system either put in support or withhold it—that is, demonstrate hostility or apathy. In fact, members may and normally do simultaneously engage in supportive and hostile behavior. What we must be interested in is the net balance of support.

To this point I have suggested that no political system can yield the important outputs we call authoritative decisions unless, in addition to demands, support finds its way into the system. I have discussed the possible object to which support may be directed, and some problems with regard to the domain, quantity, and scope of support. We are now ready to turn to the main question raised by our attention to support as a crucial input:

how do systems typically manage to maintain a steady flow of support? Without it a system will not absorb sufficient energy from its members to be able to convert demands to decisions.

In theory, there might be an infinite variety of means through which members could be induced to support a system; in practice, certain well-established classes of mechanisms are used. Research in this area needs to be directed to exploring the precise way in which a particular system utilizes these mechanisms and to refining our understanding of the way in which they contribute to the making of authoritative policy.

A society generates support for a political system in two ways: through outputs that meet the demands of the members of society; and through the processes of politicization. Let us look at outputs first.

(1) OUTPUTS AS A MECHANISM OF SUPPORT

An output of a political system, it will be recalled, is a political decision or policy. One of the major ways of strengthening the ties of the members to their system is through providing decisions that tend to satisfy the day-to-day demands of these members. Fundamentally this is the truth that lies in the aphorism that one can fool some of the people some of the time but not all of them all of the time. Without some minimal satisfaction of demands, the ardor of all but the most fanatical patriot is sure to cool. The outputs, consisting of political decisions, constitute a body of specific inducements for the members of a system to support that system.

Inducements of this kind may be positive or negative. Where negative, they threaten the members of the system with various kinds of sanctions ranging from a small monetary fine to physical detention, ostracism, or loss of life, as in our own system with regard to the case of legally defined treason. In every system support stems in part from fear of sanctions or compulsion; in autocratic systems the proportion of coerced support is at a maximum. For want of space I shall confine myself to those cases where positive incentives loom largest.

Since the specific outputs of a system are policy decisions, it is upon the government that the final responsibility falls for matching or balancing outputs of decisions against input of demand. But it is clear that to obtain the support of the members of a system through positive incentives, a government need not meet all the demands of even its most influential and ardent supporters. Most governments, or groups such as political parties that seek to control governments, succeed in building up a reserve of support. This reserve will carry the government along even though it offends its followers, so long as over the extended short run these followers perceive the particular government as one that is in general favorable to their interests. One form that this reserve support takes in Western society is that of party loyalty, since the party is the typical instrument in a mass industrialized society for mobilizing and maintaining support for a government. However, continuous lack of specific rewards through policy decisions ultimately leads to the danger that even the deepest party loyalty may be shaken. . . .

Thus a system need not meet *all the demands* of its members so long as it has stored up a reserve of support over the years. Nor need it satisfy even *some of the demands* of all its members. Just whose demands a system must seek to meet, how much of their demands, at what time, and under what conditions are questions for special research. We can say in advance that at least the demands of the most influential members require satisfaction. But this tells us little unless we know how to discover the influentials in a political system and how new sets of members rise to positions of influence. . . .

(2) POLITICIZATION AS A MECHANISM OF SUPPORT

It would be wrong to consider that the level of support available to a system is a function exclusively of the outputs in the form of either sanctions or rewards. If we did so conclude, we could scarcely account for the maintenance of numerous political systems in which satisfaction of demands has been manifestly low, in which public coercion is limited, and yet which have endured for epochs. Alternately, it might be difficult to explain how political systems could endure and yet manage to flout or thwart urgent demands, failing thereby to render sufficient *quid pro quo* for the input of support. The fact is that whatever reserve of support has been accumulated through past decisions is increased and reinforced by a complicated method for steadily manufacturing support through what I shall call the process of politicization. It is an awkward term, but nevertheless an appropriately descriptive one.

As each person grows up in a society, through a network of rewards and punishments the other members of society communicate to and instill in him the various institutionalized goals and norms of that society. This is well known in social research as the process of socialization. Through its operation a person learns to play his various social roles. Part of these goals and norms relate to what the society considers desirable in political life. The ways in which these political patterns are learned by the members of society constitute what I call the process of politicization. Through it a person learns to play his political roles, which include the absorption of the proper political attitudes. . . . In stable systems the support that accrues through these means adds to the reservoir of support being accumulated on a day-to-day basis through the outputs of decisions. The support obtained through politicization tends to be relatively . . . independent of the vagaries of day-to-day outputs.

When the basic political attachments become deeply rooted or institutionalized, we say that the system has become accepted as legitimate. Politicization therefore effectively sums up the way in which legitimacy is created and transmitted in a political system. And it is an empirical observation that in those instances where political systems have survived the longest, support has been nourished by an ingrained belief in the legitimacy of the relevant governments and regimes.

What I am suggesting here is that support resting on a sense of the legitimacy of a government and regime provides a necessary reserve if the system is to weather those frequent storms when the more obvious outputs of the system seem to impose greater hardships than rewards. Answers to questions concerning the formation, maintenance, transmission, and change of standards of legitimacy will contribute generously to an understanding of the way in which support is sufficiently institutionalized so that a system may regularly and without excessive expenditure of effort transform inputs of demand into outputs of decisions.

Comparative Political Systems

GABRIEL A. ALMOND

What I propose to do in this brief paper is to suggest how the application of certain sociological and anthropological concepts may facilitate systematic comparison among the major types of political systems operative in the world today. . . .

The problem to which this paper is a tentative and provisional answer is the following. With the proliferation of courses and special studies of specific "governments" and groupings of governments on an area or other bases, is it possible to set up and justify a preliminary classification into which most of the political systems which we study today can be assigned? The classifications which we now employ are particularistic (e.g., American Government, British Government, the Soviet Union, and the like); regional (e.g., Government and Politics of the Far East, Latin America, and the like); or political (e.g., the British Commonwealth, Colonial Government,

Reprinted from *The Journal of Politics,* vol. 18 (1956), pp. 391–409 by permission of the author and the publisher. Copyright 1956 by The Southern Political Science Association.

and the like) ; or functional (e.g., the comprehensive comparative efforts limited to the European-American area, such as Finer and Friedrich, and the specific institutional comparisons such as comparative parties, and comparative administration).

Anyone concerned with this general problem of classification of political systems will find that all of the existing bases of classification leave something to be desired. Dealing with governments particularistically is no classification at all. A regional classification is based not on the properties of the political systems, but on their contiguity in space. The existing structural classifications, such as democracy-dictatorship, parliamentary-presidential systems, two-party and multi-party systems, often turn out to miss the point, particularly when they are used in the strikingly different political systems of the pre-industrial areas. There may be a certain use therefore in exploring the possibilities of other ways of classifying political systems. What is proposed here is just one of these ways, and because of the uneven state of our knowledge is necessarily crude and provisional.

In my own efforts to stand far off, so to speak, and make the grossest discriminations between types of empirical political systems operative in the world today, I have found a fourfold classification to be most useful: the Anglo-American (including some members of the Commonwealth), the Continental European (exclusive of the Scandinavian and Low Countries, which combine some of the features of the Continental European and the Anglo-American), the pre-industrial, or partially industrial, political systems outside the European-American area, and the totalitarian political systems. This classification will not include all the political systems in existence today, but it comes close to doing so. It will serve the purpose of today's discussion, which is not that of testing the inclusiveness of this classification but rather the usefulness of sociological concepts in bringing out the essential differences between these political systems.

The terms which I shall use in discriminating the essential properties of these classes have emerged out of the Weber-Parsons tradition in social theory. I shall try to suggest why I find some of these concepts useful. First, a political system is a system of *action*. What this means is that the student of political systems is concerned with empirically observable behavior. He is concerned with norms or institutions in so far as they affect behavior. Emphasizing "action" merely means that the description of a political system can never be satisfied by a simple description of its legal or ethical norms. In other words, political institutions or persons performing political rôles are viewed in terms of what it is that they do, why they do it, and how what they do is related to and affects what others do. The term *system* satisfies the need for an inclusive concept which covers all of the patterned actions relevant to the making of political decisions. Most political scientists use the term *political process* for these purposes. The difficulty with the term *process* is that it means any patterning of action through time. In contrast to *process,* the concept of *system* implies a *totality* of relevant units, an interdependence between the interactions of units, and a certain stability in the interaction of these units (perhaps best described as a changing equilibrium).

The unit of the political system is the rôle. The rôle, according to Parsons and Shils, ". . . is that organized sector of an actor's orientation which constitutes and defines his participation in an interactive process." It involves a set of complementary expectations concerning his own actions and those of others with whom he interacts. Thus a political system may be defined as a set of interacting rôles, or as a structure of rôles, if we understand by *structure* a patterning of interactions. The advantage of the concept of *rôle* as compared with such terms as *institutions, organizations,* or *groups,* is that it is a more inclusive and more open concept. It can include formal offices, informal offices, families, electorates, mobs, casual as well as persistent groupings, and the like, in so far as they enter into and affect the political system. The use of other concepts such as those indicated above involves ambiguity, forced definitions, (such as groups) or residual categories. Like the concept of system it does not prejudice our choice of units but rather enables us to nominate them on the basis of empirical investigation.

While there appear to be certain advantages in these concepts of political system and rôle for our purposes, they confront the political scientist with a serious problem. While he intends the concept to have a general application, Parsons appears to have had before him in elaborating the concept the model of the primary group—family, friendship, and the like —and not complex social systems, the units of which are collectivities and not individual actors. . . .

My own conception of the distinguishing properties of the political system proceeds from Weber's definition—the legitimate monopoly of physical coercion over a given territory and population. The political systems with which most political scientists concern themselves all are characterized by a specialized apparatus which possesses this legitimate monopoly, and the political system consists of those interacting rôles which affect its employment. There are, of course, simpler societies in which this function of maintenance of order through coercion is diffuse and unspecialized; it is combined with other functions in the family and other groupings. While these systems are also properly the subject matter of political science, there are few political scientists indeed with the specialized equipment necessary to study them. . . .

The task of describing a political system consists in characterizing all the patterned interactions which take place within it. It takes us beyond the legal system into all the rôles which occur and involves our defining these rôles in action or behavioral terms. The concept of system implies that these rôles are interdependent and that a significant change in any one rôle affects changes in the others, and thereby changes the system as a whole. Thus the emergence of pressure groups in the present century produced certain changes in the party system and in the administrative and legislative processes. The rapid expansion of executive bureaucracy was one of the factors that triggered off the development of legislative bureaucracy and pressure group bureaucracy. Changes in the rôle of political communication have transformed the electoral process, the behavior of parties, the legislature, the executive. The concepts of system and of interdependence lead us to look for these changes when any specific rôle changes significantly. It suggests the usefulness of thinking at the level of the system and its interdependence rather than in terms of discrete phenomena or only limited bilateral relationships, or relationships occurring only within the formal-legal rôle structure.

. . . . Every political system is embedded in a set of meanings and purposes. We speak of "attitudes toward politics," "political values," "ideologies," "national character," "cultural ethos." The difficulty with all these terms is that their meanings are diffuse and ambiguous. The concepts of orientation to action and of the pattern variables are useful since they at least attempt logical distinctness and comprehensiveness. It is not essential for my purposes to go into the modes of orientation of action, or into the "pattern variables" in detail. Parsons and Shils tell us that any orientation to politics involves three components: the first is perception, or *cognition;* the second is preference, involvement, or affect (*cathexis*) ; the third is evaluation or choice through the application of standards or values to the cognitive and affective components. By *cognition* is meant the knowledge and discrimination of the objects, events, actions, issues, and the like. By *cathexis* is meant the investment of objects, issues, etc., with emotional significance, or affect. By *evaluation* is meant the manner in which individuals organize and select their perceptions, preferences, and values in the process of establishing a position *vis-à-vis political action.*

Every political system is embedded in a particular pattern of orientations to political action. I have found it useful to refer to this as the *political culture.* There are two points to be made regarding the concept of political culture. First, it does not coincide with a given political system or society. Patterns of orientation to politics may, and usually do, extend beyond the boundaries of political systems. The second point is that the political culture is not the same thing as the general culture, although it is related to it. Because political orientation involves cognition, intellection, and adaptation to external situations, as well as the standards and values of the general culture, it is a differentiated part of the culture and has a certain autonomy. Indeed, it is the failure to give proper weight to the cognitive and evaluative factors, and to the consequent autonomy of political culture, that has been responsible for the exaggerations and over-simplifications of the "national character" literature of recent years.

THE ANGLO-AMERICAN POLITICAL SYSTEMS

The Anglo-American political systems are characterized by a *homogeneous, secular* political culture. By a secular political culture I mean a multi-valued political culture, a rational-calculating, bargaining, and experimental political culture. It is a homogeneous culture in the sense that there is a sharing of political ends and means. The great majority of the actors in the political system accept as the ultimate goals of the political system some combination of the values of freedom, mass welfare, and security. . . .

A secularized political system involves an individuation of and a measure of autonomy among the various rôles. Each one of the rôles sets itself up autonomously in political business, so to speak. There tends to be an arms-length bargaining relationship among the rôles. The political system is saturated with the atmosphere of the market. Groups of electors come to the political market with votes to sell in exchange for policies. Holders of offices in the formal-legal rôle structure tend to be viewed as agents and instrumentalities, or as brokers occupying points in the bargaining process. The secularized political process has some of the characteristics of a laboratory; that is, policies offered by candidates are viewed as hypotheses, and the consequences of legislation are rapidly communicated within the system and constitute a crude form of testing hypotheses. Finally, because the political culture tends to be homogeneous and pragmatic, it takes on some of the atmosphere of a game. A game is a good game when the outcome is in doubt and when the stakes are not too high. When the stakes are too high, the tone changes from excitement to anxiety. While "fun" is frequently an aspect of Anglo-American politics, it is rarely a manifestation of Continental European politics; and, unless one stretches the definition, it never occurs at all in totalitarian politics.

RÔLE STRUCTURE IN THE ANGLO-AMERICAN POLITICAL SYSTEMS

The rôle structure in this group of political systems is (1) highly differentiated, (2) manifest, organized, and bureaucratized, (3) characterized by a high degree of stability in the functions of the rôles, and (4) likely to have a diffusion of power and influence within the political system as a whole.

With regard to the first point, each one of the units—formal governmental agencies, political parties, pressure groups and other kinds of voluntary associations, the media of communication, and "publics" of various kinds—pursues specialized purposes and performs specialized functions in the system. As was already pointed out, each one of these entities is more or less autonomous—interdependent, but autonomous. . . .

Secondly, this rôle structure is manifest and on the surface. Most of the potential "interests" have been organized and possess bureaucracies. Thirdly, there is in contrast to some of the other systems a relatively high degree of stability of function in the various parts of the structure. Bureaucracies function as bureaucracies, armies as armies, parliaments as parliaments. The functions are not ordinarily substitutable as among these various institutions and organizations, in contrast to some of the other systems. This is another way of saying that the political division of labor is more complex, more explicit, and more stable. There are, of course, striking differences between the British and American versions in these respects. For the American system is at the same time more complex and less stable than the British. There are, for example, many more pressure groups and types of pressure groups in the United States for reasons of size, economic complexity, and ethnic and religious heterogeneity. Furthermore there is more substitutability of function in the American system, more policy-making by pressure groups and the media of communication, more intervention in policy-making through the transient impact of "public moods." But again if we are comparing the Anglo-American system with, for example, the pre-industrial or partially industrial systems, the British and American systems will stand out by virtue of their similarities on the score of complexity, manifestness, and stability of rôle structure.

Finally the Anglo-American type of political system is one in which there is a diffusion of power and influence. This is only partially expressed in the formal legal phraseology of a democratic suffrage and representative government. There is an effective as well as a legal diffusion of power, resulting from a system of mass communications, mass education, and representation by interest groups. Here again the British and American versions differ sharply in terms of formal governmental structure, the relations between parties and pressure groups, and the system of communication and education. The net result is a more centralized, predictable rôle structure in Britain than in the United States. . . .

RÔLE STRUCTURE IN THE PRE-INDUSTRIAL
POLITICAL SYSTEMS

The characteristics of the pre-industrial political systems may be brought out more clearly and systematically in an analysis of the political rôle structure which is more or less characteristic.

There is first a relatively low degree of structural differentiation. Political interest often tends to be latent and when it emerges into politics often takes the form of spontaneous, violent action. Political parties are unstable; they fragment and consolidate, appear and disappear. There is ordinarily only a rudimentary specialized system of communication. Unless there is a bureaucracy left by a Western colonial power, the bureaucratic structure may be only partially developed.

Secondly, because of the absence of a stable and explicit rôle structure, there is likely to be a high degree of *substitutability* of rôles. Thus bureaucracies may take over the legislative function, and armies may and often do the same. A political party may pre-empt the policy-making function, or a mob may emerge and take the center of the policy-making stage for a brief interval. In other words, in contrast to the Anglo-American political systems, there is no stable division of political labor.

A third and most important aspect of these political systems is the mixing of political rôle structures. Thus there may be a parliament formally based on a set of legal norms and regulations; but operating within it may be a powerful family, a religious sect, a group of tribal chieftains, or some combination of these. These are elements of the traditional rôle structure operating according to their own traditional norms. The student of these political systems would be greatly misled if he followed Western norms and expectations in describing such a decision-making system. What would be corruption in a Western parliament would be normatively oriented conduct in a "mixed parliament" of the kind often found in the regions outside of the Western-European American area. . . .

TOTALITARIAN POLITICAL SYSTEMS

The totalitarian political culture gives the appearance of being homogeneous, but the homogeneity is synthetic. Since there are no voluntary associations, and political communication is controlled from the center, it is impossible to judge in any accurate way the extent to which there is a positive acceptance of the totalitarian order. One can only say that in view of the thorough-going penetration of the society by a centrally controlled system of organizations and communications, and the special way in which coercion or its threat is applied, the totalitarian system, in contrast to the others, tends to be non-consensual. This is not to say that it is completely non-consensual. A completely coercive political system is unthinkable. But if one were to place the totalitarian system on a continuum of consensual-non-consensual it would be located rather more at the non-consensual end of the continuum than the others described here. Unlike the other systems where some form of legitimacy—whether traditional, rational-legal, or charismatic—underlies the acquiescence of the individual in the political system, in the totalitarian order the characteristic orientation to authority tends to be some combination of conformity and apathy. This type of political system has become possible only in modern times, since it depends on the modern technology of communication, on modern types of organization, and on the modern technology of violence. Historic tyrannies have no doubt sought this kind of dominion but were limited in the effectiveness of their means. Totalitarianism is tyranny with a rational bureaucracy, a monopoly of the modern technology of communication, and a monopoly of the modern technology of violence.

RÔLE STRUCTURE IN TOTALITARIAN POLITICAL SYSTEMS

I believe Franz Neumann in his *Behemoth* was one of the first students of totalitarianism who rejected the *monocratic* model as being useful in understanding these systems. He spoke of the peculiar shapelessness of the Nazi régime, of the fact that there was no stable delegation of power among the bureaucracy, party, the army, the organizations of big business, and the like. He concluded, as you recall, that there was no state under the Nazis. I believe what he meant to say was that there was no *legitimate* state. Later students of totalitarianism such as Hannah Arendt, Merle Fainsod, Carl Friedrich, Alex Inkeles, and Barrington Moore, Jr., have been led to similar conclusions about totalitarianism in general, or about Soviet totalitarianism. Hannah Arendt has painted the most extreme picture, which, while an exaggeration, is useful analytically. She argues that the "isolation of atomized individuals provides not only the mass basis for totalitarian rule, but is carried through at the very top of the whole structure." The aim of this process of atomization is to destroy solidarity at any point in the system and to avoid all stable delegations of power which might reduce the freedom of manoeuver of those at the very center of the system. "As techniques of government, the totalitarian devices appear simple and ingeniously effective. They assure not only an absolute power monopoly, but unparalleled certainty that all commands will always be carried out; the multiplicity of the transmission belts, the confusion of the hierarchy, secure the dictator's complete independence of all his inferiors and make possible the swift and surprising changes in policy for which totalitarianism has become famous."

There are thus at least two distinctive characteristics of the totalitarian rôle structure: (1) the predominance of the coercive rôles, and (2) the functional instability of the power rôles—bureaucracy, party, army, and secret police. The predominance of the coercive rôle structure is reflected in its penetration of all of the other rôle structures. Thus all forms of organization and communication become saturated with a coercive flavor. This predominance of coercion is reflected in the celebrated definition of the state as "bodies of armed men" in Lenin's *State and Revolution*. It is also reflected in the doctrine of the "potential enemy of the state," a conception under which almost any behavior may be arbitrarily defined as disloyal behavior. This eliminates the predictability of the impact of coercion and renders it an omnipresent force, however limited its application may be in a quantitative sense.

The functional instability among the power rôles has as its main purpose the prevention of any stable delegation of power, and the consequent diffusion of power and creation of other power centers. This pattern was apparently quite marked in the development of the Nazi régime and has been observable in the uneasy balance established in the Soviet Union between party, bureaucracy, army, and secret police. In the nature of the case there must be a stabler delegation of power among the economic allocative rôles, but even these rôles are penetrated by the coercive rôle structure and manipulated within limits. A third class of rôles is illustrated by the electoral process and the representative system, as well as the practice of "self-criticism" in the party. While there is a set of norms under which these activities are supposed to influence power and policy-making, they are rather to be understood as mobilizing devices, as devices intended to create a façade of consent.

THE CONTINENTAL EUROPEAN POLITICAL SYSTEMS

We refer here primarily to France, Germany, and Italy. The Scandinavian and Low Countries stand somewhere in between the Continental pattern and the Anglo-American. What is most marked about the Continental European systems is the fragmentation of political culture; but this fragmentation is rather different from that of the non-Western systems. For in the non-Western systems we are dealing with mixed political cultures involving the most striking contrasts. The Western political culture arising out of a very different development pattern is introduced bodily, so to speak, from the outside. In the Continental European systems we are dealing with a pattern of political culture characterized by an uneven pattern of development. There are significant survivals, "outcroppings," of older cultures and their political manifestations. But all of the cultural variations have common roots and share a common heritage.

In view of this developmental pattern it may be appropriate to speak of the Continental European systems as having political sub-cultures. There is indeed in all the examples of this type of system a surviving pre-industrial sub-culture (e.g., the Catholic *Ancien Régime* areas in France, Southern

Italy, and the Islands, and parts of Bavaria). The historical background of all three of these systems is characterized by a failure on the part of the middle-classes in the nineteenth century to carry through a thorough-going secularization of the political culture. Thus another political sub-culture in these political systems constitutes remnants of the older middle classes who are still primarily concerned with the secularization of the political system itself. A third group of political sub-cultures is associated with the modernized and industrialized parts of these societies. But because they emerged in an only partially secularized political culture, their potentialities for "political market" behavior were thwarted. As major political sub-cultures there are thus these three: (1) the pre-industrial, primarily Catholic components, (2) the older middle-class components, and (3) the industrial components proper. But the political culture is more complex than this. Since in the last century the political issues have involved the very survival of these sub-cultures, and the basic form of the political system itself, the political actors have not come to politics with specific bargainable differences but rather with conflicting and mutually exclusive designs for the political culture and political system. This has involved a further fragmentation at the level of ideology and political organizations. Thus the pre-industrial, primarily Catholic element has both an adaptive, semi-secular wing and an anti-secular wing. The middle classes are divided into conservative wings in uneasy alliance with clerical pre-republican elements, and left-wings in uneasy friendship with socialists. Finally, the industrial workers are divided according to the degree of their alienation from the political system as a whole. The organized political manifestations of this fragmented political culture take the form of "movements" or sects, rather than of political parties. This means that political affiliation is more of an act of faith than of agency.

Perhaps the most pronounced characteristic of the political rôle structure in these areas is what one might call a general alienation from the political market. The political culture pattern is not adapted to the political system. For while these countries have adopted parliaments and popular elections, they are not appropriately oriented to these institutions. The political actors come to the market not to exchange, compromise, and adapt, but to preach, exhort, convert, and transform the political system into something other than a bargaining agency. What bargaining and exchanging does occur tends to take the form of under-the-counter transactions. Thus demoralization (*"transformism"*) is an almost inescapable consequence of this combination of political culture and system. In contrast, the normatively consistent, morally confident actor in this type of political system is the *militant* who remains within the confines of his political sub-culture, continually reaffirms his special norms, and scolds his parliamentarians.

This suggests another essential characteristic of this type of rôle structure, which places it in contrast to the Anglo-American. There is not an individuation of the political rôles, but rather the rôles are embedded in the sub-cultures and tend to constitute separate sub-systems of rôles. Thus the Catholic sub-culture has the Church itself, the Catholic schools, propaganda organizations such as Catholic Action, Catholic trade unions, or worker organizations, a Catholic party or parties, and a Catholic press. The Communist sub-culture—the sub-culture of the political "alienates"—similarly has a complete and separate system of rôles. The socialist and "liberal" sub-cultures tend in the same direction but are less fully organized and less exclusive. Thus one would have to say that the center of gravity in these political systems is not in the formal legal rôle structure but in the political sub-cultures. Thus "immobilism" would appear to be a normal property of this kind of political system, and it is not so much an "immobilism" of formal-legal institutions as a consequence of the condition of the political culture. Needless to say, this portrayal of the Continental European political system has been exaggerated for purposes of contrast and comparison.

Two other general aspects of the rôle structure of these countries call for comment. First, there is a higher degree of substitutability of rôles than in the Anglo-American political systems and a lesser degree than in the non-Western systems. Thus parties may manipulate pressure groups in the sense of making their decisions for them (the Communist case); interest groups such as the Church and Catholic Action may manipulate parties and trade unions; and interest groups may operate directly in the legislative process, although this last pattern occurs in the Anglo-American system as well. The "immobilism" of the formally political organs often leads to a predominance of the bureaucracy in policy-making.

A second general characteristic, which is a consequence of the immobilism of the political system as a whole, is the ever-present threat of what is often called the "Caesaristic" breakthrough. As in the non-Western area, although the situations and causes are different, these systems tend always to be threatened by, and sometimes to be swept away by, movements of charismatic nationalism which break through the boundaries of the political sub-cultures and overcome immobilism through coercive action and organization. In other words, these systems have a totalitarian potentiality in them. The fragmented political culture may be transformed into a synthetically homogeneous one and the stalemated rôle structure mobilized by the introduction of the coercive pattern already described. . . .

The Functions of the Political Machine

ROBERT K. MERTON

In view of the manifold respects in which political machines, in varying degrees, run counter to the mores and at times to the law, it becomes pertinent to inquire how they manage to continue in operation. The familiar "explanations" for the continuance of the political machine are not here in point. To be sure, it may well be that if "respectable citizenry" would live up to their political obligations, if the electorate were to be alert and enlightened; if the number of elective officers were substantially reduced from the dozens, even hundreds, which the average voter is now expected to appraise in the course of town, county, state and national elections; if the electorate were activated by the "wealthy and educated classes without whose participation," as the not-always democratically oriented Bryce put it, "the best-framed government must speedily degenerate";—if these and a plethora of similar changes in political structure were introduced, perhaps the "evils" of the political machine would indeed be exorcized. But it should be noted that these changes are often not introduced, that political machines have had the phoenix-like quality of arising strong and unspoiled from their ashes, that, in short, this structure has exhibited a notable vitality in many areas of American political life.

Proceeding from the functional view, therefore, that we should *ordinarily* (not invariably) expect persistent social patterns and social structures to perform positive functions *which are at the time not adequately fulfilled by other existing patterns and structures,* the thought occurs that perhaps this publicly maligned organization is, *under present conditions,* satisfying basic latent functions. A brief examination of current analyses of this type of structure may also serve to illustrate additional problems of functional analysis.

SOME FUNCTIONS OF THE POLITICAL MACHINE

Without presuming to enter into the variations of detail marking different political machines—a Tweed, Vare, Crump, Flynn, Hague are by no means identical types of bosses—we can briefly examine the functions more or less common to the political machine, as a generic type of social organization. We neither attempt to itemize all the diverse functions of the political machine nor imply that all these functions are similarly fulfilled by each and every machine.

The key structural function of the Boss is to organize, centralize and maintain in good working condition "the scattered fragments of power" which are at present dispersed through our political organization. By this centralized organization of political power, the boss and his apparatus can satisfy the needs of diverse subgroups in the larger community which are not adequately satisfied by legally devised and culturally approved social structures.

To understand the role of bossism and the machine, therefore, we must look at two types of sociological variables: (1) the *structural context* which makes it difficult, if not impossible, for morally approved structures to fulfill essential social functions, thus leaving the door open for political machines (or their structural equivalents) to fulfill these functions and (2) the subgroups whose distinctive needs are left unsatisfied, except for the latent functions which the machine in fact fulfills.

STRUCTURAL CONTEXT: The constitutional framework of American political organization specifically precludes the legal possibility of highly centralized power and, it has been noted, thus "discourages the growth of effective and responsible leadership. The framers of the Constitution, as Woodrow Wilson observed, set up the check and balance system 'to keep government at a sort of mechanical equipoise by means of a standing amicable contest among its several organic parts.' They distrusted power as dangerous to liberty: and therefore they spread it thin and erected barriers against its concentration." This dispersion of power is found not only at the national level but in local areas as well. "As a consequence," Sait goes on to observe, "when *the people or particular groups* among them demanded positive action, no one had adequate authority to act. The machine provided an antidote."

The constitutional dispersion of power not only makes for difficulty of effective decision and action but when action does occur it is defined and hemmed in by legalistic considerations. In consequence, there developed "a much *more human system* of partisan government, whose chief object soon became the circumvention of government by law. . . . The lawlessness of the extra-official democracy was merely the counterpoise of the legalism of the official democracy. The lawyer having been permitted to subordinate democracy to the Law, the Boss had to be called in to extricate the victim, which he did after a fashion and for a consideration."

Officially, political power is dispersed. Various well-known expedients were devised for this manifest objective. Not only was there the familiar separation of powers among the several branches of the government but, in some measure, tenure in each office was limited, rotation in office approved. And the scope of power inherent in each office was severely circumscribed. Yet, observes Sait in rigorously functional terms, "Leadership is necessary; and *since* it does not develop readily within the constitutional framework, the Boss provides it in a crude and irresponsible form from the outside."

Put in more generalized terms, *the functional deficiencies of the official structure generate an alternative (unofficial) structure to fulfill existing needs somewhat more effectively.* Whatever its specific historical origins, the political machine persists as an apparatus for satisfying otherwise unfulfilled needs of diverse groups in the population. By turning to a few of these subgroups and their characteristic needs, we shall be led at once to a range of latent functions of the political machine.

FUNCTIONS OF THE POLITICAL MACHINE FOR DIVERSE SUBGROUPS.   It is well known that one source of strength of the political machine derives from its roots in the local community and the neighborhood. The political machine does not regard the electorate as an amorphous, undifferentiated mass of voters. With a keen sociological intuition, the machine recognizes that the voter is a person living in a specific neighborhood, with specific personal problems and personal wants. Public issues are abstract and remote; private problems are extremely concrete and immediate. It is not through the generalized appeal to large public concerns that the machine operates, but through the direct, quasi-feudal relationships between local representatives of the machine and voters in their neighborhood. Elections are won in the precinct.

The machine welds its link with ordinary men and women by elaborate networks of personal relations. Politics is transformed into personal ties. The precinct captain "must be a friend to every man, assuming if he does not feel sympathy with the unfortunate, and utilizing in his good works the resources which the boss puts at his disposal." The precinct captain is forever a friend in need. In our prevailing impersonal society, the machine, through its local agents, fulfills the important social *function of humanizing and personalizing all manner of assistance* to those in need. Foodbaskets and jobs, legal and extra-legal advice, setting to rights minor scrapes with the law, helping the bright poor boy to a political scholarship in a local college, looking after the bereaved—the whole range of crises when a feller needs a friend, and, above all, a friend who knows the score and who can do something about it,—all these find the ever-helpful precinct captain available in the pinch.

To assess this function of the political machine adequately, it is important to note not only that aid *is* provided but *the manner in which it is provided*. After all, other agencies do exist for dispensing such assistance. Welfare agencies, settlement houses, legal aid clinics, medical aid in free hospitals, public relief departments, immigration authorities—these and a multitude of other organizations are available to provide the most varied types of assistance. But in contrast to the professional techniques of the welfare worker which may typically represent in the mind of the recipient the cold, bureaucratic dispensation of limited aid following upon detailed investigation of *legal* claims to aid of the "client" are the unprofessional techniques of the precinct captain who asks no questions, exacts no compliance with legal rules of eligibility and does not "snoop" into private affairs.

For many, the loss of "self-respect" is too high a price for legalized assistance. In contrast to the gulf between the settlement house workers who so often come from a different social class, educational background and ethnic group, the precinct worker is "just one of us," who understands what it's all about. The condescending lady bountiful can hardly compete with the understanding friend in need. In *this struggle between alternative structures for fulfilling the nominally same function* of providing aid and support to those who need it, it is clearly the machine politician who is better integrated with the groups which he serves than the impersonal, professionalized, socially distant and legally constrained welfare worker. And since the politician can at times influence and manipulate the official organizations for the dispensation of assistance, whereas the welfare worker has practically no influence on the political machine, this only adds to his greater effectiveness. More colloquially and also, perhaps, more incisively, it was the Boston ward-leader, Martin Lomasny, who described this essential function to the curious Lincoln Steffens: "I think," said Lomasny, "that there's got to be in every ward somebody that any bloke can come to—no matter what he's done—and get help. *Help, you understand; none of your law and justice, but help.*"

The "deprived classes," then, constitute one subgroup for whom the political machine satisfies wants not adequately satisfied in the same fashion by the legitimate social structure.

For a second subgroup, that of business (primarily "big" business but also "small"), the political boss serves the function of providing those political privileges which entail immediate economic gains. Business corporations, among which the public utilities (railroads, local transportation and electric light companies, communications corporations) are simply the most conspicuous in this regard, seek special political dispensations which will enable them to stabilize their situation and to near their objective of maximizing profits. Interestingly enough, corporations often want to avoid a chaos of uncontrolled competition. They want the greater security of an economic czar who controls, regulates and organizes competition, providing that this czar is not a public official with his decisions subject to public scrutiny and public control. (The latter would be "government control," and hence taboo.) The political boss fulfills these requirements admirably.

Examined for a moment apart from any moral considerations, the political apparatus operated by the Boss is effectively designed to perform these functions with a minimum of inefficiency. Holding the strings of diverse governmental divisions, bureaus and agencies in his competent hands, the Boss rationalizes the relations between public and private business. He serves as the business community's ambassador in the otherwise alien (and sometimes unfriendly) realm of government. And, in strict business-like terms, he is well-paid for his economic services to his respectable business clients. In an article entitled, "An Apology to Graft," Lincoln Steffens suggested that "Our economic system, which held up riches, power and acclaim as prizes to men bold enough and able enough to buy corruptly timber, mines, oil fields and franchises and 'get away with it,' was at fault." And, in a conference with a hundred or so of Los Angeles business leaders, he described a fact well known to all of them: the Boss and his machine were an *integral part* of the organization of the economy. "You cannot build or operate a railroad, or a street railway, gas, water, or power company, develop and operate a mine, or get forests and cut timber on a large scale, or run any privileged business, without corrupting or joining in the corruption of the government. You tell me privately that you must, and here I am telling you semi-publicly that you must. And that is so all over the country. And that means that we have an organization of society in which, *for some reason,* you and your kind, the ablest, most intelligent, most imaginative, daring, and resourceful leaders of society, are and must be against society and its laws and its all-around growth."

Since the demand for the services of special privileges are built into the structure of the society, the Boss fulfills diverse functions for this second subgroup of business-seeking-privilege. These "needs" of business, as presently constituted, are not adequately provided for by conventional and culturally approved social structures; consequently, the extra-legal but more-or-less efficient organization of the political machine comes to provide these services. To adopt an *exclusively* moral attitude toward the "corrupt political machine" is to lose sight of the very structural conditions which generate the "evil" that is so bitterly attacked. To adopt a functional outlook is to provide not an apologia for the political machine but a more solid basis for modifying or eliminating the machine, *providing* specific structural arrangements are introduced either for eliminating these effective demands of the business community or, if that is the objective, of satisfying these demands through alternative means.

A third set of distinctive functions fulfilled by the political machine for a special subgroup is that of providing alternative channels of social mobility for those otherwise excluded from the more conventional avenues for personal "advancement." Both the sources of this special "need" (for social mobility) and the respect in which the political machine comes to help satisfy this need can be understood by examining the structure of the larger culture and society. As is well known, the American culture lays enormous emphasis on money and power as a "success" goal legitimate for all members of the society. By no means alone in our inventory of cultural goals, it still remains among the most heavily endowed with positive affect and value. However, certain subgroups and certain ecological areas are notable for the relative absence of opportunity for achieving these (monetary and power) types of success. They constitute, in short, sub-populations where "the cultural emphasis upon pecuniary success has been absorbed, but where there is *little access to conventional and legitimate* means for attaining such success. The conventional occupational opportunities of persons in (such areas) are almost completely limited to manual labor. Given our cultural stigmatization of manual labor, and its correlate, the prestige of white-collar work, it is clear that the result is a tendency to achieve these culturally approved objectives *through whatever means are possible.* These people are on the one hand, "asked to orient their conduct toward the prospect of accumulating wealth [and power] and, on the other, they are largely denied effective opportunities to do so institutionally."

It is within this context of social structure that the political machine fulfills the basic function of providing avenues of social mobility for the otherwise disadvantaged. Within this context, even the corrupt political machine and the racket "represent the triumph of amoral intelligence over morally prescribed 'failure' when the channels of vertical mobility are closed or narrowed *in a society which places a high premium on economic affluence, [power] and social ascent for all its members.*" As one sociologist has noted on the basis of several years of close observation in a slum area:

The sociologist who dismisses racket and political organizations as deviations from desirable standards thereby neglects some of the major elements of slum life. . . . He does not discover the functions they perform for the members [*of the groupings in the slum*]. *The Irish and later immigrant peoples have had the greatest difficulty in finding places for themselves in our urban social and economic structure. Does anyone believe that the immigrants and their children could have achieved their present degree of social mobility without gaining control of the political organization of some of our largest cities? The same is true of the racket organization.* Politics and the rackets have furnished an important means of social mobility for individuals, who, because of ethnic background and low class position, *are blocked from advancement in the "respectable" channels.*

This, then, represents a third type of function performed for a distinctive subgroup. This function, it may be noted in passing, is fulfilled by the *sheer* existence and operation of the political machine, for it is in the machine itself that these individuals and subgroups find their culturally induced needs more or less satisfied. It refers to the services which the political apparatus provides for its own personnel. But seen in the wider social context we have set forth, it no longer appears as *merely* a means of self-aggrandizement for profit-hungry and power-hungry *individuals,* but as an organized provision for *subgroups* otherwise excluded from or handicapped in the race for "getting ahead."

Just as the political machine performs services for "legitimate" business, so it operates to perform not dissimilar services for "illegitimate" business: vice, crime and rackets. Once again, the basic sociological role of the machine in this respect can be more fully appreciated only if one temporarily abandons attitudes of moral indignation, to examine in all moral innocence the actual workings of the organization. In this light, it at once appears that the subgroup of the professional criminal, racketeer or gambler has basic similarities of organization, demands and operation to the subgroup of the industrialist, man of business or speculator. If there is a Lumber King or an Oil King, there is also a Vice King or a Racket King. If expansive legitimate business organizes administrative and financial syndicates to "rationalize" and to "integrate" diverse areas of production and business enterprise, so expansive rackets and crime organize syndicates to bring order to the otherwise chaotic areas of production of illicit goods and services. If legitimate business regards the proliferation of small business enterprises as wasteful and inefficient, substituting, for example, the giant chain stores for hundreds of corner groceries, so illegitimate business adopts the same businesslike attitude and syndicates crime and vice.

Finally, and in many respects, most important, is the basic similarity, if not near-identity, of the economic role of "legitimate" business and of "illegitimate" business. *Both are in some degree concerned with the provision of goods and services for which there is an economic demand.* Morals aside, they are both business, industrial and professional enterprises, dispensing goods and services which some people want, for which there is a market in which goods and services are transformed into commodities. And, in a prevalently market society, we should expect appropriate enterprises to arise whenever there is a market demand for certain goods or services.

As is well known, vice, crime and the rackets *are* "big business." Consider only that there have been estimated to be about 500,000 professional prostitutes in the United States of 1950, and compare this with the approximately 200,000 physicians and 350,000 professional registered nurses. It is difficult to estimate which have the larger clientele: the professional men and women of medicine or the professional men and women of vice. It is, of course, difficult to estimate the economic assets, income, profits and divi-

dends of illicit gambling in this country and to compare it with the economic
assets, income, profits and dividends of, say, the shoe industry, but it is altogether possible that the two industries are about on a par. No precise figures
exist on the annual expenditures on illicit narcotics, and it is probable that
these are less than the expenditures on candy, but it is also probable that
they are larger than the expenditure on books.

It takes but a moment's thought to recognize that, *in strictly economic
terms,* there is no relevant difference between the provision of licit and of
illicit goods and services. The liquor traffic illustrates this perfectly. It would
be peculiar to argue that prior to 1920 (when the 18th amendment became
effective), the provision of liquor constituted an economic service, that from
1920 to 1933, its production and sale no longer constituted an economic
service dispensed in a market, and that from 1934 to the present, it once
again took on a serviceable aspect. Or, it would be *economically* (not morally) absurd to suggest that the sale of bootlegged liquor in the dry state of
Kansas is less a response to a market demand than the sale of publicly
manufactured liquor in the neighboring wet state of Missouri. Examples of
this sort can of course be multiplied many times over. Can it be held that
in European countries, with registered and legalized prostitution, the prostitute contributes an economic service, whereas in this country, lacking legal
sanction, the prostitute provides no such service? Or that the professional
abortionist is in the economic market where he has approved legal status and
that he is out of the economic market where he is legally taboo? Or that
gambling satisfies a specific demand for entertainment in Nevada, where it
constitutes the largest business enterprise of the larger cities in the state, but
that it differs essentially in this respect from motion pictures in the neighboring state of California?

The failure to recognize that these businesses are only *morally* and not
economically distinguishable from "legitimate" businesses has led to badly
scrambled analysis. Once the economic identity of the two is recognized,
we may anticipate that if the political machine performs functions for
"legitimate big business" it will be all the more likely to perform not dissimilar functions for "illegitimate big business." And, of course, such is
often the case.

The distinctive function of the political machine for their criminal,
vice and racket clientele is to enable them to operate in satisfying the economic demands of a large market without due interference from the government. Just as big business may contribute funds to the political party
war-chest to ensure a minimum of governmental interference, so with big
rackets and big crime. In both instances, the political machine can, in
varying degrees, provide "protection." In both instances, many features of
the structural context are identical: (1) market demands for goods and

services; (2) the operators' concern with maximizing gains from their enterprises; (3) the need for partial control of government which might otherwise interfere with these activities of businessmen; (4) the need for an efficient, powerful and centralized agency to provide an effective liaison of "business" with government.

Without assuming that the foregoing pages exhaust either the range of functions or the range of subgroups served by the political machine, we can at least see that *it presently fulfills some functions for these diverse subgroups which are not adequately fulfilled by culturally approved or more conventional structures.*

Several additional implications of the functional analysis of the political machine can be mentioned here only in passing, although they obviously require to be developed at length. First, the foregoing analysis has direct implications for *social engineering*. It helps explain why the periodic efforts at "political reform," "turning the rascals out" and "cleaning political house" are typically (though not necessarily) short-lived and ineffectual. It exemplifies a basic theorem: *any attempt to eliminate an existing social structure without providing adequate alternative structures for fulfilling the functions previously fulfilled by the abolished organization is doomed to failure.* (Needless to say, this theorem has much wider bearing than the one instance of the political machine.) When "political reform" confines itself to the manifest task of "turning the rascals out," it is engaging in little more than sociological magic. The reform may for a time bring new figures into the political limelight; it may serve the casual social function of reassuring the electorate that the moral virtues remain intact and will ultimately triumph; it may actually effect a turnover in the personnel of the political machine; it may even, for a time, so curb the activities of the machine as to leave unsatisfied the many needs it has previously fulfilled. But, inevitably, unless the reform also involves a "re-forming" of the social and political structure such that the existing needs are satisfied by alternative structures or unless it involves a change which eliminates these needs altogether, the political machine will return to its integral place in the social scheme of things. *To seek social change, without due recognition of the manifest and latent functions performed by the social organization undergoing change, is to indulge in social ritual rather than social engineering.* The concepts of manifest and latent functions (or their equivalents) are indispensable elements in the theoretic repertoire of the social engineer. In this crucial sense, these concepts are not "merely" theoretical (in the abusive sense of the term), but are eminently practical. In the deliberate enactment of social change, they can be ignored only at the price of considerably heightening the risk of failure.

A second implication of this analysis of the political machine also has a bearing upon areas wider than the one we have considered. The paradox has often been noted that the supporters of the political machine include both the "respectable" business class elements who are, of course, opposed to the criminal or racketeer and the distinctly "unrespectable" elements of the underworld. And, at first appearance, this is cited as an instance of very strange bedfellows. The learned judge is not infrequently called upon to sentence the very racketeer beside whom he sat the night before at an informal dinner of the political bigwigs. The district attorney jostles the exonerated convict on his way to the back room where the Boss has called a meeting. The big business man may complain almost as bitterly as the big racketeer about the "extortionate" contributions to the party fund demanded by the Boss. Social opposites meet—in the smoke-filled room of the successful politician.

In the light of a functional analysis all this of course no longer seems paradoxical. Since the machine serves both the businessman and the criminal man, the two seemingly antipodal groups intersect. This points to a more general theorem: *the social functions of an organization help determine the structure (including the recruitment of personnel involved in the structure), just as the structure helps determine the effectiveness with which the functions are fulfilled.* In terms of social status, the business group and the criminal group are indeed poles apart. But status does not fully determine behavior and the inter-relations between groups. Functions modify these relations. Given their distinctive needs, the several subgroups in the large society are "integrated," whatever their personal desires or intentions, by the centralizing structure which serves these several needs. In a phrase with many implications which require further study, *structure affects function and function affects structure.*

Homeostatic Tendencies in the
United States Supreme Court

S. SIDNEY ULMER

This paper presupposes the desirability of integrating theory and research in political science. The research reported herein, which is basically an attempt to illustrate the usefulness of systems theory in analyzing certain empirical data associated with the behavior of Supreme Court justices, is consonant with that aim.

This selection was written especially for this volume.

I

The Supreme Court of the United States is ideal for the kind of analysis undertaken here for the following reasons: (1) It is a small group of manageable proportions. (2) The variables which interact in this group are subject to quantification. (3) The activity of the group collectively and individually is recorded in considerable detail. (4) The records of activity are highly accessible.

As a small group, the Supreme Court may be classified as a combination work group and colleague group, but the emphasis undoubtedly is properly placed on the former. The Supreme Court as a system consists of a set of interdependent processes of action and interaction. As such these processes are internal, but as a subsystem they are conditioned by the external systems (the environment). The internal and external systems combined constitute the total social system of the group.

The Court is an open rather than a closed system. An open system features a continual materials exchange with the environment. Such interchange is necessary to maintain the energy level necessary for system survival. Thus the Court as an open system is a boundary-interchange system characterized by input-conversion-output. Systems theory postulates that the action of a system is functionally oriented in terms of societal goals Talcott Parsons has defined the over-all goal of American society as the *facilitation* of effective adaptive development of the society and of the societal conditions associated with it.

This interpretation of the aim of American society focuses primarily on the range and quality of adaptation. It defines not so much a committed society as a society interested in facilitating adjustments and accommodations of the diverse elements of which it is composed. As a subsystem, the function of the Supreme Court is to contribute to the attainment of these goals. The output of the Court is designed to do this by (1) allocating societal values and (2) legitimizing such allocations whether made by itself or other governmental institutions. The appropriate input category for this particular output would include all those communications processes which inform the court as to the institutionalized value system of the society and changes in that system. This follows from the fact that effective allocation and legitimization can occur only within the framework of generalized support furnished by the institutionalized value system.

The survival of a system depends upon its effectiveness in performing its social function. Patterns of interaction among system components represent a response to this challenge and attempts of the system to make the proper adjustments for the effective production of the necessary output.

Relative to environment, these patterns tend toward a steady state which if achieved absolutely would represent the maximal response of the system to the demands upon it. Homeostatic tendencies are to be expected among interaction patterns in the United States Supreme Court if the Court is subject, as has been suggested, to conceptualization as a system.

At least three types of social equilibria may be identified. Equilibrium is *stationary* if the parameters of the system are held constant in a given interval of time and no variable changes its position. *Dynamic* equilibrium encompasses change in environment as well as change in the relationships among system components. If, however, the *rate* of change is constant or if the change has a pattern that continually repeats or maintains itself, equilibrium is attained. Equilibrium is *stable* and *dynamic* if subsequent to any disturbance the system components tend to resume their original relationships. Equilibrium in the Supreme Court must be dynamic since the Court is an open boundary-interchange system. If the Court were a closed system and no new elements were introduced, the interaction processes would continue unchanged until expenditure of energy led to complete stagnation.

With the Supreme Court this is not the case. New elements are continually being introduced. Basically, this consists of the introduction of new information and new members. The continual input of new elements makes stationary equilibrium impossible. Activity within the system cannot be expected to cease. The introduction of a new element disturbs the expectations of one or more group members which leads to attempts at adjustment toward a steady state. Parsons has described this phenomenon in the following words: "The action of one of the members, or a situational event perceived by one or more of the members, introduces a new element, which is a disturbance; this evokes reaction which may be opposite in direction in the sense that it tends to restore equilibrium or may be similar in direction in that it tends further to disturb equilibrium. The complexity of interdependence of the elements in the system is such that very seldom will one reaction completely restore equilibrium. Even in relatively stable systems there may be a long series of such action-reaction processes which, however, will tend to narrow in range, leading toward a stable state. This tendency . . . will, however, be continually interrupted by the introduction of a whole series of new elements into the system, not only the initial ones" (Parsons, Bales, and Shils, pp. 71-72). Thus while we expect to find evidence of equilibrium in certain behavior patterns in the Court, intermittent disturbances in the patterns are to be anticipated. The intention here is not, however, to engage in a complete systems analysis of the Supreme Court. In order to simplify the empirical problem, the analysis will be limited to the processes of interaction which structure the power relations among the justices of the Court. Also a very limited attempt will be made to show how the findings may be related to goal attainment in a functional model.

As Easton has pointed out, the prime requisite for such an analysis is the quantification of the relevant variables. The Shapley-Shubik power index* is suited for this purpose. Shapley and Shubik define the power of a member of a group making decisions by majority rule as the probability that the member is critical to the successful coalition. For a series of decisions, the mean is used as a numerical criterion in terms of which members of a decision-making group may be ranked. If one applies this measuring device to the decisions of the Supreme Court made during each term, he is able to rank the justices on the Shapley-Shubik index. The Shapley-Shubik procedure is an operational definition which gives a numerical measure of certain relationships among the members of a group.

In this analysis the primary concern is whether or not these relationships tend to stablize over time. Evidence bearing on this point may be derived in several ways. One such way is to rank each of nine Supreme Court positions on the Shapley-Shubik power index. Rank orders have been computed for each term from 1888 through 1958. This seventy-year span was then divided into seven periods by tenure of Chief Justice which gave seven courts in the time span, headed respectively by Fuller, White, Taft, Hughes, Stone, Vinson, and Warren. It is interesting to know whether these courts taken individually evinced tendencies toward a steady state in the power relations among their respective members. But relations among positions must be dealt with, since during each court period changes in personnel occurred. The use of positions does not materially affect the analysis, since the interest here lies in tendencies toward the equilibrium of behavior patterns rather than in individual justices. The procedure, therefore, is to compute the rank order of each justice for each term of the court. When a change in personnel occurs, the incoming justice assumes the position occupied by his outgoing predecessor. A different approach would be to define a court as extending over any period of time during which the composition of the group remains unchanged. The procedure used at this point, however, enables one to investigate the role of the Chief Justice in a way that cannot be reached using the alternative conceptualization.

Table I is inserted at this point to illustrate the form of the data to be analyzed for each court. This particular data is for the Stone Court which sat from 1941 through 1945 inclusively. The insertions RU and BU in the Table show two personnel changes during the period: Rutledge replaced Byrnes in 1942 and Burton replaced Roberts in 1945. As soon as

*A detailed explanation of the index may be found on pp. 384–86 in this volume.

TABLE I. RANK ORDER OF SUPREME COURT POSITIONS
ON SHAPLEY-SHUBIK POWER INDEX:
STONE COURT—1941–1945

Term	BY	FR	MU	RE	ST	JA	RO	BL	DO
1941	1	2	3	4	5	6	7	8	9
	RU								
1942	9	3	8	2	1	5	4	7	6
1943	4	5	8	3	1	2	9	6	7
1944	2	4	7	1	6	3	9	8	5
							BU		
1945	7	8	1	6	9	4	3	2	5
Rj	22	22	27	16	22	20	32	31	32

Code: BY — Byrnes
FR — Frankfurter
MU — Murphy
RE — Reed
ST — Stone
JA — Jackson
RO — Roberts
BL — Black
DO — Douglas
RU — Rutledge
BU — Burton

Rj — Sum of Ranks

the data for all seven courts is compiled in this form interesting relationships appear. First, we observe that some justices tend consistently to maintain a high power position and others a low power position even though the time span of their service extends over several different courts. Over the period covered by the 1888-1958 terms, eight justices served through two or more courts. For all practical purposes a ninth (Burton) may be included since he left the Warren Court in October, 1958. Van Devanter and Reed served respectively through the White and Taft Courts and the Stone and Vinson Courts. The former ranked third in power on the White Court and second on the Taft Court. Reed, on the other hand, ranked first on the Stone Court and tied for second on the Vinson Court. At the other end of the spectrum are Black and Douglas, who served through the Stone and Vinson Courts and, of course, are still sitting on the Warren Court. Douglas turns up with the lowest rank on all three courts, while Black ranks seventh on all three. This is, indeed, remarkable when it is remembered that the tenure of these three courts extended from 1941 to the present.

As for the other five justices, a greater variation is observed among the power ratings on different courts. But in four of the five cases, the movement is toward a lower ranking in the second court than on the first. Thus Holmes moved from position four on the White Court to position six on the Taft Court; McReynolds shifted from the fifth to the eighth position on the Taft and Hughes Courts; Jackson, who ranked second on the Stone Court could do no better than sixth on the Vinson Court; and Burton showed a shift from second to fifth position respectively on the Vinson and the Warren Courts. The exception to the two tendencies indicated by the cross-court justices is Frankfurter whose record shows that a lost position may be regained. From a third position on the Stone Court, Frankfurter moved down to seventh on the Vinson Court, but came back to fourth place on the Warren Court. Thus from this analysis one notes two tendencies: (1) A tendency for some justices to stabilize at a certain positional level. (2) A tendency for some justices to move downward on the power indices through time.

The foregoing applies between courts. If the entire career of each justice is observed for the purpose of ascertaining rank-order stability and movement both within and across court lines, some striking results emerge. We begin by eliminating all justices who served less than six years. The number of terms served by each of the remaining thirty-nine justices is halved and the mean power rank for the first career-half is compared with that for the second. As soon as the data is so arranged a natural break line seems to fall between those justices appointed prior to the New Deal and those appointed subsequently. Of twenty-seven pre-New Deal justices, seventeen had a higher mean power rank in the second period than in the first. But of twelve post-New Deal justices, only one had a higher mean rank in the second period. Although the first distribution is not statistically significant, it suggests a tendency for upward movement through time. The second distribution suggests a tendency for downward movement through time and is statistically significant at .05 ($X^2 = 4.1$). This leads one to suspect a disparity in the balance of the variables operating in the pre-New Deal situation and those operating in the post-New Deal era.

A possible interpretation is that in the earlier period the accumulated experience of the individual judge was of importance in the interaction patterns which determined rank on the power index. In the subsequent period, on the other hand, the circumvention of accumulated experience was precisely what the New Deal was designed to accomplish. It is consistent with the data to think that the judge of the Supreme Court in the second era evaluated the efforts of his colleagues in much more realistic terms—that he was more concerned with whether proffered solutions to social problems were practical than with their legal and logical implications. Other possible interpretations of the data for the post-1932 period are: (1) The power of the judge tapers off in the twilight of his career as a result of age, infirmity, and declining interest in social problems. (2) The timidity of new judges inclines them to gravitate toward the majority position in the beginning of tenure. This would illustrate Dahl's concept of "chameleon" behavior. (3) New justices reflect the climate of the times with which the Court is generally in step, but, while public opinion changes and the direction of Court policy-making changes, the attitudes of sitting judges change more slowly which inevitably pushes them toward dissenting roles. (4) Judges grow more conservative and exhibit greater attitudinal rigidity as time passes.

When the data on all seven courts is compiled in the form illustrated in Table I, we may proceed to the next step in the analysis which consists of determining the degree of movement among ranks in each of the courts, proceeding then to a cross-court comparison. It is obvious that some degree of concordance could occur as a matter of pure chance, and an adequate measure must take such a fact into consideration. A statistical measure of agreement among a set of data of this type is Kendall's coefficient of concordance expressed by the formula $W = \dfrac{S}{1/12k^2 \ (N^3 - N)}$ where S is equal to the sum of squares of the observed deviations from the mean of Rj; k is equal to the number of sets of rankings; N is equal to the number of entities ranked; and $1/12k^2 \ (N^3 - N)$ is equal to the maximum possible sum of the squared deviations. Analysis of the seven courts reveals that the degree of concordance among the power positions in each court could have occurred by chance less than 1 in 100 times in two courts; less than 1 in 1,000 times in four courts; and approximately 70 in 100 times in the remaining court. Thus, it is concluded that the degree of stability exhibited by six of the seven courts is statistically significant and very unlikely to have occurred by chance. The one exception is the Stone Court in which the power shifts were so numerous and of such magnitude that the residual interagreement was most likely a chance occurrence. One infers at this point that six of the seven courts show pronounced equilibrium tendencies insofar as the range of movement among power positions is concerned. Since this is precisely what systems theory would lead one to suspect, it is not necessary to belabor the point. One notes in passing, however, that the evidence here is consonant with the suggestion that the Supreme Court may be viewed as a system with certain intracourt patterns of behavior tending toward a steady state.

The relative stability of the seven courts is summarized in Table II. One concludes from the Table that the normal tendency of power relations within a court is to stabilize. If so, it is necessary to explain, if possible, the only exception to the generalization—the Stone Court—which sat from 1941 through 1945. Evidence bearing on the problem may be derived by

TABLE II. STABILITY OF POWER POSITIONS ON SEVEN SUPREME COURTS 1888–1958:*
BY TENURE OF CHIEF JUSTICES

Court	Tenure	W	X^2	Sig. Level	(X^2A-X^2N)**
Fuller	1888–1909	.27	43.20	.001	17.08
Taft	1921–1929	.55	39.40	.001	13.28
Vinson	1946–1952	.58	32.48	.001	6.36
White	1910–1920	.32	28.42	.001	2.30
Hughes	1930–1940	.27	23.76	.010	3.67
Warren	1953–1958	.47	22.56	.010	2.47
Stone	1941–1945	.18	7.20	.700	

   *—in terms.
   **—Chi square value actually observed less the value necessary for the level of significance indicated.

ascertaining the factors which account for the varying degree of stability running through the rank orders. The attempt is not made at this point to identify "cause," but only to reveal relationships which, in the nature of things, are subject to varying interpretations. Bivariate analysis was conducted with fifteen variables which were hypothesized as being dependent on stability (the independent variable). Results were negative on ten of these, but significant relationships were found between stability and five of the hypothesized variables. Since the stability of a court depends on the stability of its members, it is plausible to look for factors which might be thought to promote stable behavior of the individual.

   One of the five variables was suggested by the numerous bills introduced in Congress in the past few years designed to restrict or limit the United States Supreme Court. Among these has been a series of bills which would require service as a judge on a state or Federal court for those nominated to the Supreme Court. These bills, in effect, predict that such prior judicial experience affects subsequent judicial behavior. Specifically, their authors seem to think that such experience promotes proper attitudes toward precedent and the rate at which the Constitution should be allowed to grow and develop. Such claims are not evaluated here, but it is asked whether this type of experience is significantly related to the stability of the individual justices and, thus, of the court on which they sat. By ranking each court in terms of the number of justices with prior judicial service who served during the court span, a rank-order coefficient of .680 is established. This degree of relationship could occur by chance about seven times in a hundred, but when the courts are ranked in terms of the total years of prior judicial service, represented by members of the Court during its entire span, the co-efficient increases to .800, which has a chance probability of less than two times in a hundred.

The second and third variables positively associated with the stability of the courts were suggested by the role of the Chief Justice in the Court's decision-making processes. Enough has been written about this role to warrant a query as to whether the behavior of the Chief Justice is of consequence for the behavior of members of his court. A positive association was found to exist between stability of the Court and the stability of the Chief Justice. The correlation coefficient of .750 justifies the inference that the more stable the Chief Justice, the more stable his court in the period 1888-1958.

The number of years covered by the court under study and the relative age at which the Chief Justice assumed office were also found to be positively associated with court stability ($r = .721$ and .715 respectively). Since each court was defined in terms of the tenure of the Chief Justice it is inferred that the longer the Chief Justice served the more stable his court became. It must be remembered, however, that the Kendall W expresses the average stability of each court over its entire period. While the inference is to be interpreted in that light, it encompasses the view that such average stability tends to increase with length of service.

The finding, that the more youthful the Chief Justice at assumption of office the more stable his court, suggests that physical and mental vigor are characteristics of the Chief Justice which play some role in promoting stability in power relations. It is not implausible to expect a youthful Chief Justice to expend a greater degree of energy toward minimizing invariant group relations than a Chief Justice who is bordering on senility or who has reached the plateau of placid disinterest.

Finally, it was noted that if the geographical origins of the members of each court were classified as East or West, the number of Western justices serving on each court was inversely related to the degree of stability exhibited by the Court. This relationship seems trivial at first glance, but something could possibly be made of the differences between the informal culture of the West and the relatively formal culture of the East. The products of these two regions could be expected to carry into the Court the attitudes toward personal relationships that prevail in each region. The disparity between these attitudes might very well lead to the production of interpersonal tensions which the Kendall W would reflect. But it is not desirable to push this interpretation too far. Clearly the finding in respect to prior judicial experience is much less trivial and if corroborated by other data and other studies it could have significant policy implications.

On balance the most important interpretation that may be made from the bivariate analyses is that the role of the Chief Justice is perhaps more significant than is generally conceded. John P. Frank has said that "The Chief Justice of the United States is not a number one man among a group of subordinates. He is *primus inter pares,* first among equals. He casts only one vote, and that vote carries no more authority, no more weight, than that of the most junior Justice, except as his own personality and abilities influence other members of the Court" (Frank, p. 70). If this is true, the data presented here suggest that the Chief Justices serving in the period 1888-1958 were (with the exception of Stone) men of strong personality and first-rate abilities who exerted steady and effective influence on those who served with them.

The seemingly anomalous position of the Stone Court can be explained in two ways. First, the Stone Court ranks seventh on all five of the variables that have been identified. This alone is persuasive, but it may be buttressed by qualitative data bearing on Stone's ability as an effective leader of his Court. That such data is relevant here is suggested by the high degree of movement by Stone on the power index, movement which has been shown to be significantly related to the stability of the Court as a whole. In fact, the stability of the Chief Justice is an aspect of power not measured by the Shapley-Shubik index. Thibaut and Kelley say that ". . . when a person has high power. . . . He is subject neither to much external behavior control nor to large swayings in his expressive behavior. Therefore, such a person is likely to appear to others as 'inscrutable'. The converse seems also tenable: an inscrutable person, one who shows little variation in mood or enigmatical changes in behavior, will be viewed as powerful. Much expressive behavior, on the other hand, is said to be a 'sign of weakness' " (Thibaut and Kelley, p. 123).

In this sense, then, behavioral stability in itself is an aspect of power —an aspect which seems related to leadership skills. An examination of Stone in this light is revealing. For a start, we may note that the bench Stone headed was the most frequently divided, the most openly quarrelsome in history. Why was this? Certainly the facts suggest that Taft's assertion in 1929 that Stone was not a leader and that he would have a good deal of difficulty in massing the court was remarkably prophetic. Taft, of course, was competent to speak about leadership; his own ability as a leader is reflected in the large number of instances in which other justices went along, although disagreeing with his decisions. Stone's paucity of the qualities which make a leader is most clearly seen when he is compared to other Chief Justices.

The most important functions of Chief Justices are presiding over conferences, making opinion assignments, and keeping acrimony in the group to a minimum. Measured in these terms, the failure of Stone is outstanding. Chief Justice Hughes was a master of the conference and possessed the ability to master at one time the details of hundreds of cases which enabled the Court to dispense with the business at hand in short order. Under Hughes the Saturday conferences lasted four hours, but under Stone they sometimes extended for four days. It is said that Stone's clerks prepared his statements to the conference, and that the other justices could tell which of the clerks prepared the notes from the length of time Stone took to state the cases. Fuller, White, and Taft were quite adept at controlling flare-ups in conference and in minimizing their effects by skillfully turning the discussion at the proper moment. Fuller, particularly, was outstanding in this respect: "He ran his conferences extremely well, and in his close attention to the management of the administrative side of the Court Fuller may have been one of its outstanding presiding officers. The stories of how Fuller stopped a quarrel that was developing between Harlan and Holmes; how he handled the unpleasant duty of persuading the senile Field to retire; how he dissuaded Holmes from using a certain word that might have annoyed the other Justices;—all these incidents led Fuller's biographer to conclude that, though Fuller was not the greatest intellect ever to guide the Court, 'he was an extraordinary Chief Justice in his relations with his colleagues' " (Frank, p. 85).

Chief Justice Vinson was weak in technical ability, but he was a likeable and diplomatic person, qualities which he used to advantage to ameliorate the excessive tensions he inherited from the Stone period. These tensions testify further to Stone's weakness as a Chief Justice. He came to a Court characterized by efficiency and a high level of unanimity developed under Hughes' dominant leadership. But, almost immediately the Court began to deteriorate and was much more frequently divided than before. The stridency of tone which crept into the opinions of some of the justices on the Stone Court was almost completely unknown during Hughes' tenure. Personal relations among the justices seemed to reach a new low. The conference under Stone became a wrangling affair and not without reason. John P. Frank has pinpointed the personal characteristics which made Stone so difficult to work with: "A partisan battler himself, he could not rise above the fray to bring calm leadership into the controversies of others . . . he was given to tactless comments about his colleagues. Stone condemned almost every colleague he had, whether Republican or Democrat, both in the Old Court and in the New Deal days" (Frank, pp. 80-81).

Under Warren, the Court seems to be operating at an efficient level, both in quantity and quality of opinions. However, Warren has not been completely successful in bringing harmony to the competing blocks of justices which inhabit his Court. This probably accounts to some extent for the fact that the Warren Court ranks sixth in stability among the seven courts, although it should be noted that this does not put the Warren Court in the same class as that of Stone.

II

It has now been shown that among seven courts of the Supreme Court stability of power relationships was the general rule. For the analysis courts were defined in terms of the tenure of the Chief Justice, and work was done with positions rather than with individual justices. A slightly different conceptualization will furnish additional evidence for the thesis. A court may be defined for this phase of the investigation as a group of justices serving together for a certain period of time. Of course, many courts may be described in this way and they may differ considerably both as to the number of members and the length of time spanned by their collective service. The purpose here is to show that though one shifts to a slightly different focus, evidence of stability is not lost by the shift. To make the point three courts are defined as follows: (1) Court I covered the period 1926-1930 and consisted of Justices Van Devanter, Sutherland, McReynolds, Butler, Stone, Holmes, and Brandeis. (2) Court II sat from 1946 through 1952 and was composed of Justices Jackson, Vinson, Reed, Burton, Black, Frankfurter, and Douglas. (3) Court III is the smallest of the courts defined; it consisted of the last three justices listed for Court II, plus Warren and Clark. Court III spanned the five terms from 1954 to 1958. Instead of dealing with the absolute ranks of nine Supreme Court positions on the power index, we focus on the relative ranks of the justices involved in each court as it progressed through time.

One asks whether, relative to each other, the justices tended toward a rank order stabilization. The degree of stability (or lack of movement) in a series of terms is measured by the difference between unity and the coefficient which expresses the rank order correlation between the first term in the series and each other term, i.e., $S = 1$ minus r. This constitutes a *stability index*. The index values for each of the three courts are plotted in Charts 1 through 3, corresponding to Courts I, II, and III. From Chart 1 it is evident that the power relations on Court I were highly stabilized. The level of stability is high despite the fact that the Court was composed of four conservatives and three liberals. While these two groups had pronounced differences in attitude and outlook when making decisions, the power roles of the members were seemingly well defined. Courts II and III

CHART I

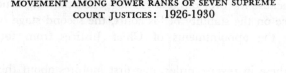

MOVEMENT AMONG POWER RANKS OF SEVEN SUPREME
COURT JUSTICES: 1926-1930

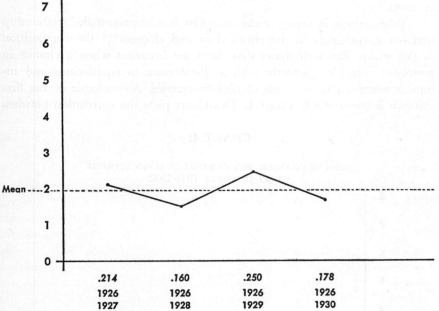

also exhibited a high degree of stability, as is seen in the accompanying charts. In fact, the highest point on the stability index is reached by Court II in the 1948 and 1949 terms. But Courts II and III show a greater range of movement about the mean value and thus were less stable than Court I. It will be noted that the mean stability of each of the three courts falls at about the same point, varying from 1.96 to 2 on the stability index. Thus a second type of evidence is found for the thesis that power relations on the Supreme Court tend toward homeostasis.

Systems theory states that stable systems are subject to disruption, and Parsons has argued that such disruption is so continuous in a boundary-interchange system that equilibrium is never attained, but only approached. In view of the many disruptive influences that may be thought to play upon the Supreme Court, it is surprising that the power relations examined evidenced the stability noted. The explanation may be that in their impressionistic manner observers tend to overemphasize the effect of, or improperly identify, these disturbing elements. In order to show how one may be more precise about such matters, the impact of the most obvious new element being continually introduced into the system, new personnel, will be investigated. Because the previous analysis suggested that the Chief Justice has great influence on the stability of his court, the second stage of the inquiry will separate the appointments of Chief Justices from total personnel changes.

Taking these in reverse order, one first inquires about the relationship between disturbances in the equilibrium and changes in the composition of the group. Research shows that there are instances when a change in personnel coincides perfectly with a disturbance in equilibrium and instances when a change seems of no consequence. An example of the first instance is contained in Chart 4. This Chart plots the correlation between

CHART II

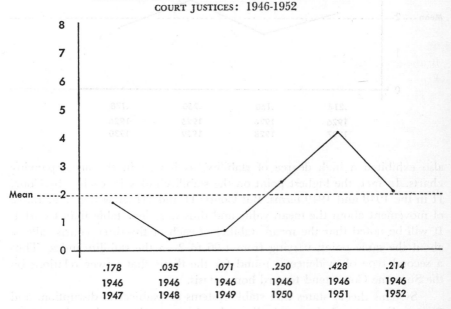

MOVEMENT AMONG POWER RANKS OF SEVEN SUPREME
COURT JUSTICES: 1946-1952

each pair of terms moving from 1904 to 1914. The encircled figures show that eight appointments were made in this period and that seven of the eight were associated with marked disturbances. Only one of the appointments, that of White in 1910, involved a change in Chief Justices. This data suggests that in the period 1904-1914 a change in Court personnel was likely to cause a disturbance in the power relations of the nine Supreme Court positions. Since all the values below the center line represent negative correlations, the movement in the ranks associated with personnel changes was obviously of considerable magnitude. Yet, the 1911 personnel change shows that some appointments are not disturbing elements. This is to be expected, since the "fit" of the new appointee is likely to be the key factor, rather than a mere change in group composition. The data in Chart 4 suggests that the "fit" of most of the justices appointed in the period 1904-1914 was not conducive to continued maintenance of the prevailing steady state tendencies.

The second part of this inquiry is concerned with the possible impact of a change in Chief Justices on the relative power relations among individual justices. For this purpose two additional courts are defined which meet the following conditions: (1) The members of a court serve continually through the period. (2) The period covered by a court is the final years of tenure for one chief justice and the beginning years of tenure for another. (3) The period of "final years" is a period characterized by a high degree of stability among the justices. In this way, we start with stable relations, we change Chief Justices and observe the effect, if any, on stability. The two courts cover the periods 1926-1932 and 1950-1955. The first of these courts was staffed by Van Devanter, McReynolds, Sutherland, Brandeis, and Stone. The latter court consisted of Clark, Black, Reed, Frankfurter, and Douglas. Thus what happened to relative power relations as Hughes replaced Taft and Warren replaced Vinson is observed.

The movement in the rank orders may be measured as before by the stability index using the first term in each series as a point of reference. In Chart 5, 1926 is used as a base and each year is correlated with that term. The shaded columns in the Chart show a high degree of stability from 1926 through 1928. In 1929 Hughes replaced Taft and the rank order of the power relations is shaken, but very slightly. The degree of variation from 1926 as a reference point is slightly less in 1930 and 1931 and returns to a rate of change in 1932 that is identical to that for the 1926-1928 period. When the movement for each pair of terms is plotted as represented in the lined columns, a slightly different curve results. This curve shows, as expected, that the rank order in 1929 was more consonant with that of 1928 than was the 1928 term with that of 1927. The measure here magnifies the amount of movement, since it measures upward and downward movement through a series of terms, rather than the extent to which the variables tend to cluster around a reference point. In short, it measures changes in a moving or dynamic equilibrium with no fixed point of reference, while the alternate measure is tied to a persistent base.

The value of the year-to-year measure lies in the fact that it alerts one to the formation of a new equilibrium. For as soon as a low rate of change from year-to-year is seen, one inquires as to whether the low rate

CHART III

MOVEMENT AMONG POWER RANKS OF FIVE SUPREME
COURT JUSTICES: 1954-1958

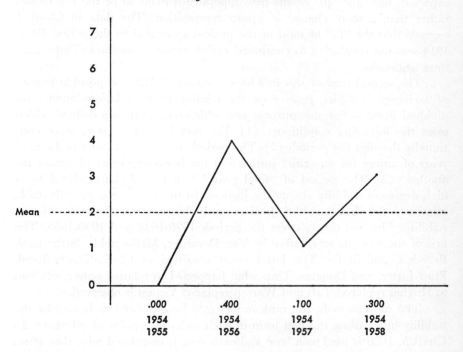

results from absolute rank similarity between one of the rank orders and those following. When one term is frozen as the basic point of reference and the equilibrium is disturbed, the establishment of a new equilibrium cannot be ascertained by continuing to plot S with the initial base. One infers from the charts on the Taft-Hughes shift that the change caused very little disturbance in court power relations and that what little disturbance was evident was dissipated by 1930. At that point, the rank order again correlates highly with that of the equilibrium evident in the 1926-1928 period.

An examination of the Vinson-Warren shift reveals a different pattern. An equilibrium seems to have been established in the three-year period 1950-1952. Warren's addition to the group in the 1953 term seems to have had a more serious impact than the Taft-Hughes shift in the 1929 session. What is more revealing, the disturbance initiated in the 1953 term became more pronounced in the following year. In the 1955 term the disturbance begins to abate, but is still at a relatively high level. If one turns to the year-to-year rate of change, as plotted in the lined columns on Chart 6, he sees that the absolute rank difference between the 1953 and 1952 terms

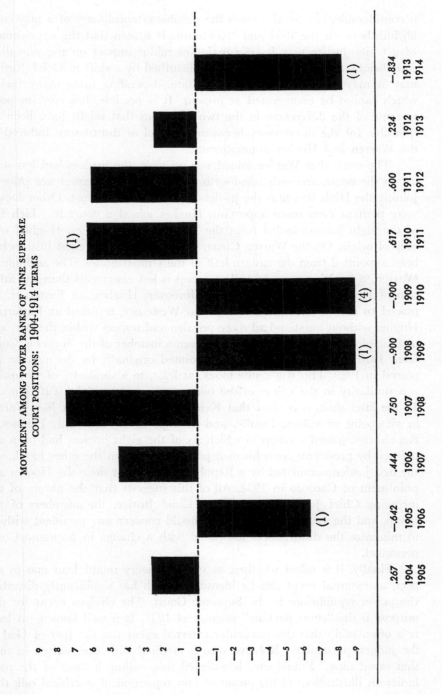

CHART IV

MOVEMENT AMONG POWER RANKS OF NINE SUPREME
COURT POSITIONS: 1904-1914 TERMS

is considerable, but he also notes the possible establishment of a new equilibrium between the 1954 and 1955 terms. It is seen that the appointment of a Chief Justice may have a major or minor impact on the prevailing equilibrium, and that the equilibrium disturbed by a shift in Chief Justices may or may not return to its initial state, depending upon many factors which cannot be enumerated at present. It is possible, however, to point to some of the differences in the two situations that might have been responsible for the discrepancy between the level of disturbance induced by the Warren and Hughes appointments.

The court that Warren joined was younger, the justices had less service on the court, and only one-fourth as much judicial experience prior to joining the High Bench as the justices on the Hughes Court. Other factors were perhaps even more important. Hughes joined a court in which five of the eight justices hailed from the Eastern United States, Hughes' own area of origin. On the Warren Court, however, six of the eight justices had been appointed from the eastern half of the United States. The addition of Warren, a far Westerner, to such a group is less congruous than the addition of Hughes to the earlier court. Moreover, Hughes, an Easterner, replaced an Easterner, while Warren, a far Westerner, replaced an Easterner. Hughes without question had more prestige and respect within the Bar, and in general, than Warren. Hughes had been a member of the Supreme Court from 1910 to 1916. He had been appointed originally by the man he replaced in 1929. This is a crude index, at least, to a similarity of viewpoint —a similarity in the values of the two men as construed by Taft himself. In the later shift, it is clear that Kentucky's Vinson was not like Warren in viewpoint or values. Finally, and perhaps most important, Hughes, a Republican, joined a group in which six of the eight justices had been appointed by presidents from his own party. Warren, on the other hand, was the first justice nominated by a Republican president since the Hoover appointment of Cardozo in 1932. All of this suggests that the nature of the incoming Chief Justice, the outgoing Chief Justice, the members of the group, and the external environment should concern any president wishing to minimize the disturbances associated with a change in Supreme Court personnel.

Finally, it is asked whether, as systems theory might lead one to expect, an external event can be identified which has significantly disturbed the power equilibrium in the Supreme Court. The obvious event for this purpose is the "court packing" attempt of 1937. It is well known (at least it is often said) that this particular external event put the fear of God in the judges, particularly Roberts, who is credited with the "switch in time that saved nine." Frankfurter has denied this, calling it "one of the most ludicrous illustrations of the power of lazy repetition of uncritical talk that

CHART V

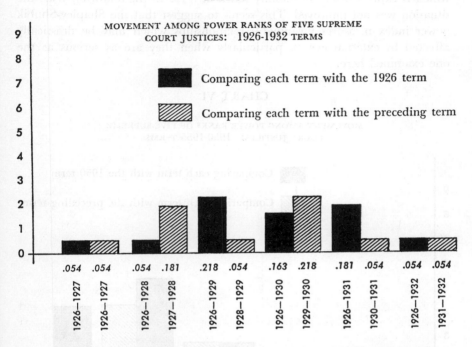

MOVEMENT AMONG POWER RANKS OF FIVE SUPREME
COURT JUSTICES: 1926-1932 TERMS

■ Comparing each term with the 1926 term

▨ Comparing each term with the preceding term

a judge with the character of Roberts should have attributed to him a change of judicial views out of deference to political considerations" (Frankfurter, 104 U.P.L.R. 311). But almost every indicator yet devised supports the contention that Roberts was a vacillating justice who was in effect a "satellite" of Hughes and, thus, the most likely judge to switch positions as a result of external and internal pressure. At any rate, it is well known that Hughes and Roberts were the "swing" justices in the 1936 term. Certainly, if the investigatory techniques used here have any validity at all, they should reflect the 1937 disturbance within the Court, regardless of whether or not the individuals most seriously affected are identified.

At this point still another court is defined which is composed of Hughes, Roberts, McReynolds, Butler, Brandeis, Cardozo, and Stone. These are the seven justices who served throughout the 1931-1937 terms. It happens that the period covered by the four terms (1931-1935) was one of remarkably high stability. The degree of movement in the power ranks in respect to the order established in 1931 was limited to less than .215 on the stability index. The mean variation was only .096 for the four years. On February 5, 1937 (the latter part of the 1936 term), Franklin D. Roosevelt brought forth his plan to reorganize the Supreme Court. The event coincides with a remarkable disturbance in the Court's power equilibrium, a disturbance which is expressed on the stability index at .719. In the following year, the situation was not improved. This seems to suggest that the Shapley-Shubik power index measures meaningful relationships which may be drastically affected by external events, particularly when they are as serious as the one examined here.

CHART VI

MOVEMENT AMONG POWER RANKS OF FIVE SUPREME COURT JUSTICES: 1950-1955 TERMS

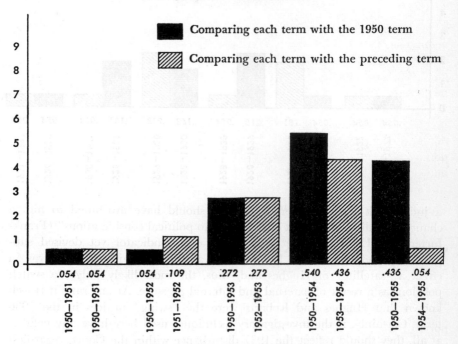

Finally, it is not impossible to "fit" the evidence of the stability of Supreme Court power roles to a functional model. It has been previously suggested that the Court is a subsystem of the total social system and that power relations constitute a subsystem of the Court. If one accepts, for purposes of illustration, the definition of societal goals offered by Parsons, one may ask whether and in what way the Supreme Court contributes to these goals. It has been suggested that one of the Court's primary functions is to allocate values and to legitimize such allocations by itself and other governmental institutions. However, this function must be pursued within the framework of general support furnished by the institutionalized value system of the community.

The Supreme Court performs this function through its influence on the development of the law. Influence, however, is not exerted equally by all justices. The Shapley-Shubik power index is a reflection of the varying degrees of participation by the justices in molding the law. The position of a justice on the index is not unilaterally determined. This is not to suggest that the individual justice has no control over his power status, but basically the position of a particular justice on the index is determined by the interactions between the justice and his colleagues. A justice can assume a high power position only if his associates interact with him in a particular manner.

If the Court as a system is pursuing the function suggested and is doing so within the limitations set by the systems external to it, the interaction which occurs will promote on the index those justices whose attitudes and values seem most consonant with those of the institutionalized value system. Observation of the rank orders of individuals lends some credence to this view. The most obvious example would seem to be the case of Douglas who has occupied the eighth or ninth position on the index in every term since 1947 with one exception. If the reasoning presented in this article is valid, the interpretation would be that the Court as a system has operated to minimize the influence of Douglas in shaping the law during this ten-year period. Moreover, it has done so because of the disparity between his values and attitudes and those called for by the institutionalized value system of the total community. Stability in a role, once established, suggests lack of change in the relative value disparity from year to year.

In conclusion, it has been suggested that certain theoretical concepts may be used to advantage in the analysis of certain patterns of behavior in the United States Supreme Court. It has been shown that when the Court is conceptualized as a small-group system, evidence may be found for some of the relational characteristics predicted for such groups by general systems theory. The possibility of a functional explanation of these relationships has also been raised. This paper represents, therefore, an exploratory and some-what crude effort to narrow the chasm which tends to exist between theory and empirical research.

It is recognized, of course, that this work is far from the kind of formal systems analysis which considers the multiples of variables interacting in a total social system. But one must begin with the simple and progress to the complex. If the simplest social system consists of interaction between "alter" and "ego," an analysis of the stability of power relations among Supreme Court justices does not seem out of order; is is thought that such relational patterns furnish a useful point of departure for more complex analyses.

The purpose has not been to establish or to identify a state of general equilibrium for the Supreme Court as a total system. Merely, an attempt has been made to show that *evidence* for homeostatic tendencies in certain

CHART VII

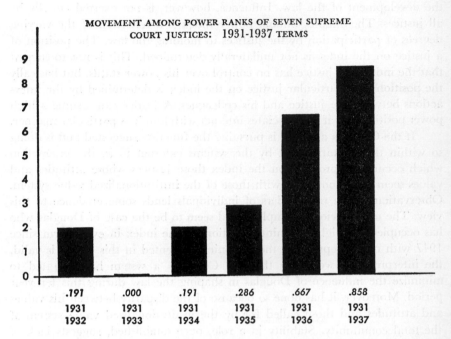

MOVEMENT AMONG POWER RANKS OF SEVEN SUPREME
COURT JUSTICES: 1931-1937 TERMS

relational patterns may be adduced. From this evidence it may be inferred
that in some respects particular patterns of interaction on the Court tend
toward *stable* as well as *dynamic* equilibrium.

CHAPTER FIVE

GROUPS

FOR some time now, group concepts have been an important focus of political analysis. In an earlier period political research centered on the role of pressure groups in democratic society. More recent times have witnessed a growing emphasis on the interdependence of social behavior patterns. One effect of this has been the increasing frequency with which group oriented studies have appeared. Using the work of Arthur E. Bentley as a base, David Truman and others have developed the external approach which views the group from outside as a cell in the social organism and societies as essentially collectivities of groups. The political interest groups discussed by Alfred de Grazia and Clement Vose are of this type, as are the voluntary and involuntary groups studied so assiduously by sociologists. The societies-as-groups school is little concerned with internal organization, although some awareness of internal relationships is reflected in the dichotomy between primary and secondary groups. These terms distinguish groups primarily on the basis of warm-personal and cool-impersonal characteristics. As McClosky and Dahlgren point out in their treatment of party loyalty, *primary group* is a useful concept for political analysis.

An alternative approach is that of the group dynamicists who focus on groups as societies. For this school the internal approach is endemic and little attention is given to the social roles of groups in the social system.

Groups are studied as relevant environments for individual behavior. The interaction of group members is observed in order to identify behavior patterns and the factors which influence them. This approach is exemplified by Eloise Snyder and others in analyzing Supreme Court behavior. Considering the Supreme Court as a *small group,* these researchers have discovered behavior patterns of sufficient stability and persistence as to suggest possible predictive value. This work clearly shows the relevance of the small group concept for those in political science whose research interests are oriented toward behavior.

The primary problems which small group theorists presently face lie in the great disagreements that now exist concerning the basic variables, concepts, or facts with which laws will deal. Some of the variables that have served as foci of research are: group roles, group size, group norms, power, prestige, and status. An important approach has been that of Robert F. Bales which stresses action, interaction, and situation. Homans, Chapple, Whyte, and others who share this view hold that over a period of time the interactions among individual members of a group form a system or pattern of relationships. Such systems are said to be characterized by differentiation of access to resources and control of system parts, as well as by stratification of status positions. The focus of research then becomes the internal relationships and the factors in the internal and external situation which modify them. Thus the group may be seen as a small system or as a subsystem of the total society. As such, the propositions of general systems theory are clearly applicable.

Central to this type of inquiry is the notion of equilibrium, a concept of considerable importance in the mechanical sciences. This concept and approach gained prominence in sociological research through Herbert Spencer's theory of the rhythm of motion and the work of Pareto and others who made the idea of equilibrium central to their research. The assigning of such a critical role to equilibrium analysis is said to be justified by the desirability of unifying the sciences. It is said that all scientific research deals with determinant systems which strive for homeostasis or some kind of balance among the variables interacting in the system. General systems theory, it is urged, is adequate for research in all systems, and equilibrium is the central concept for systems analysis.

The equilibrium model in the social sciences has had greatest use in the fields of sociology, anthropology, and economics. Yet, while disguised in such terms as adjustment, accommodation, or balance of power, the concept has underlain much of the work in political science. It has been shown in a previous selection (Ulmer, "Homeostatic Tendencies in the United States Supreme Court") that a small group such as a collegial court may exhibit behavior patterns which tend toward a stable state. In his article

on the group concept, David Truman argues persuasively that the equilibrium tendencies predicted by general systems theory may be observed in
a wide variety of political and apolitical groups. Thus we see some continuity
between the work of the systems theorists and those whose research is focused
on a particular type of system, such as the large or small group.

The Group Concept

DAVID B. TRUMAN

If the uniformities consequent upon the behavior of men in groups are the
key to an understanding of human, including political, behavior, it will be
well to specify somewhat more sharply what is involved when the term
"group" is used. An excessive preoccupation with matters of definition will
only prove a handicap. "Who likes may snip verbal definitions in his old
age, when his world has gone crackly and dry." Nevertheless, a few distinctions may be useful.

We find the term "group" applied in two broad senses. Both popularly
and in much technical literature it is used to describe any collection of individuals who have some characteristic in common. These are sometimes
known as categoric groups. In this sense the word is applied to persons of a
given age level, to those of similar income or social status, to people living
in a particular area, as Westerners, and to assortments of individuals according to an almost endless variety of similarities—farmers, alcoholics,
insurance men, blondes, illiterates, mothers, neurotics, and so on. Although
this sense of the word may be useful, it omits one aspect of peculiar importance. The justification for emphasizing groups as basic social units, it
will be recalled, is the uniformities of behavior produced through them.
Such uniformities do not depend immediately upon such similarities as those
mentioned above, but upon the relationships among the persons involved.
The significance of a family group in producing similar attitudes and behaviors among its members lies, not in their physical resemblance or in their
proximity, as such, to one another, but in the characteristic relationships
among them. These interactions, or relationships, because they have a certain character and frequency, give the group its molding and guiding powers. In fact, they are the group, and it is in this sense that the term will be
used.

A minimum frequency of interaction is, of course, necessary before a group in this sense can be said to exist. If a motorist stops along a highway to ask directions of a farmer, the two are interacting, but they can hardly be said to constitute a group except in the most casual sense. If, however, the motorist belongs to an automobile club to the staff of which he and the other members more or less regularly resort for route information, then staff and members can be designated as a group. Similarly, groups in the first sense—collections of people with some common characteristic—may be groups in the proper sense if they interact with some frequency on the basis of their shared characteristics. If a number of mothers interact with one another as they tackle problems of child training, whether through a club or through subscription to a mothers' periodical, they have become a group, though the two forms differ in structure and frequency of interaction. If the members of any aggregation of blondes begin to interact as blondes, alcoholics as alcoholics (or former addicts), people over sixty as aged—they constitute groups. That is, under certain recurring conditions they behave differently with each other than with brunettes, teetotalers, or the young. In fact, the reason why the two senses of the term "group" are so close is that on the basis of experience it is expected that people who have certain attributes in common—neighborhood, consanguinity, occupation—will interact with some frequency. It is the interaction that is crucial, however, not the shared characteristic.

These groups, or patterns of interaction, vary through time in a given society, and they obviously differ sharply in different societies. Why this variation occurs has been only incompletely ascertained, since comparative studies of simple cultures are relatively few and competent comparative analyses of complex cultures are virtually nonexistent. The most satisfactory hypothesis, however, indicates that the relative complexity of such interactions depends upon the degree of diversity in the everyday business of living. The latter in turn reflects refinement in the techniques by which the society adapts to its environment and the degree of specialization and division of labor that these techniques involve. In a simple society in which all activities—economic, religious, political—are carried on within the family, the division of labor is rudimentary, the techniques are simple, and the patterns of interaction are few and standardized. The latter become more complex as the routine activities of existence alter in conformity with altered techniques for dealing with the environment.

Variations in the division of labor are nowhere more striking than in the activity of house building. An Eskimo igloo is usually constructed by a single family, each man erecting the structure of snow blocks with the aid of his wife and sons. Division of labor is slight, and the interactions among the participants—the patterns of superordination and subordination—are simple. Frequently among a sedentary farming people, however, such as the Riffians of North Africa, relatively elaborate and permanent dwellings are constructed by work parties in which a fairly complex division of labor occurs, based upon more developed techniques and differences in the skill with which particular individuals can perform the various operations:

Among Riffians, some of the men will bring stones, others will nick them into shape and set them in the walls, while still others puddle clay for the mortar. When the walls are up, two men . . . climb up and set the ridgepole and rafters in place. Meanwhile other men have been cutting young alders and other small saplings near the stream; they peel these and hand them up in bundles. Most of the men have now climbed to the roof, and they tie these sticks to the rafters to form a foundation for the clay.

It is a considerable step from this moderately complex division of labor to the elaborate activities necessary in the construction of an ordinary American house. The collection, preparation, and transportation of materials, the elaborate behavior involved in procuring and readying the site, and the welter of specialties that contribute to its erection bespeak a series of complicated interaction patterns.

The complexity and variation of group life among human cultures apparently grow out of the daily activities of their participants and reflect the kinds of techniques that the cultures have developed for dealing with the environment. These techniques, however, are not confined to those directly utilized in providing food, clothing, and shelter. The invention of a written language and its diffusion through a population include techniques of at least equal importance. Similarly, group patterns in a culture in which the priest, or *shaman,* deals with the crises and problems arising from birth, sickness, death, flood, drought, earthquakes, thunderstorms, and eclipses of the sun and moon will be far simpler than the group patterns of a culture where these crises are separately dealt with by various specialists. The activities of the shaman, and those of his functional descendant, the specialized scientist, consist of techniques for adjustment to the environment fully as much as do those of the farmer, the weaver, and the bricklayer. The skills of shaman and scientist are parts of different group patterns and their resulting attitudes and behavioral norms.

In any society certain of these group patterns will be characterized by "a relatively high degree of stability, uniformity, formality, and generality. . . ." These are customarily designated by the term *institution.* The word does not have a meaning sufficiently precise to enable one to state with confidence that one group is an institution whereas another is not. Accepted examples, however, include the courts, legislatures, executives, and other political institutions, families, organized churches, manufacturing establishments, transportation systems, and organized markets. All of these, it will be noted, are rather highly organized (formality) ; examples of the same type of institution show the same patterns (uniformity) ; and these patterns are characteristic of, though not necessarily peculiar to, a particular society, such as the American (generality).

The institutionalized groups that exemplify these behavior patterns, and the patterns themselves, represent almost by definition an equilibrium among the interactions of the participants. In a typical American family, for example, it will be accepted almost unconsciously and without discussion that the male parent will almost always make certain kinds of decisions for the family group, such as what kind of automobile tires to purchase, whether they can afford a new washing machine, and how much money can be spent on the family vacation. He will be expected to take the lead in such actions, and the rest of the family will accept his decisions. The mother will make many more decisions affecting the children than will the father. The husband, moreover, will follow her lead in such things as home decoration, the color of a new car, and the guests to be included at a dinner party. These and the other expected patterns of interaction that make up the institutional group are normally in balance, or in a state of equilibrium. The same situation applies to any institutionalized group, although perhaps in a somewhat more complicated fashion, whether political, economic, or religious.

An equilibrium of this sort must be worked out within an institutionalized group or an institution if it is to survive. That is, the equilibrium must be achieved along standardized lines if the pattern is not to be radically altered or if the particular group is not to be irrevocably disrupted, as, for example, in the case of a family by the separation or divorce of man and wife. It is characteristic of such balanced groups that if the equilibrium is disturbed by some event outside the group, the equilibrium will be restored when the disturbance is over. This tendency to maintain or revert to equilibrium is what is meant by the stability of an institution. The existence of the equilibrium and its stability presumably can be measured by observing the consistency of interaction patterns. Although such observations have been made for simple groups and in a general way for more complicated ones, the possibilities in this area are largely still to be explored. The basic propositions, however, have been sufficiently tested to give them strong presumptive validity.

Although institutionalized groups are characterized by stability, that is, by the tendency to revert to an equilibrium among the interactions of the participants following a disturbance from outside the group, not all disturbances are followed by a return to such a balance. If the disturbance is of great intensity or if it persists over a long period of time, a quite different pattern of interactions is likely to be established in place of the previous one. How serious the interruption must be and how long it must last in order to produce an alteration of the pattern are matters for careful observation, precise or approximate depending upon the use to which the observations are to be put.

An obvious example can be seen in the case of a family that loses one of its members through death. Since the remainder of the group can no longer interact with the deceased, any subsequent stable interaction pattern in the group will differ sharply from the preceding one. The possibilities of establishing a new and stable pattern will depend in part upon the role of the deceased in the previous balance. That is, it will be far more difficult if a parent or an only child has been withdrawn from the group, since relationships with a parent or only child will have constituted a very large segment of the total behavior pattern of the remaining members of the family. The death of one of eight or ten children, however, may be far less disruptive, since almost inevitably a major portion of the total interactions in the group will not have depended upon one of eight or ten children.

If the removal of one member of a family group is not permanent, but temporary, a quite different situation will result. If the male parent is obliged to be away from the rest of the family for a short period of time or if his breadwinning activities temporarily require him to spend less time in the family than has been customary, the equilibrium of the group will be disturbed. The pattern and frequency of interactions will be altered. When the husband-father has returned from his travels, however, or when his duties permit him again to participate in the group with normal frequency, the previous balance probably will be restored.

In the strictly political sphere there are obvious parallel instances of the effects of disturbances in established patterns of interaction. Thus the death or unexpected resignation of the "boss" of a highly organized political "machine" constitutes a serious disturbance to the group. It will be followed by a more or less prolonged tussle among aspiring successors. Unless some stable new pattern is established under the leadership of one of the previous "boss's" henchmen, the group will disintegrate into competing factions. Similarly, take the case of a trade association whose principal function is the fixing of prices. If it finds its methods outlawed as a result of government action, this disturbance will result in the disappearance of the group unless equilibrium is re-established in one of three ways. First, the group may secure the repeal of the disturbing decision. Second, new methods of performing the function may be developed. Third, an entirely different set of functions may be developed. The first of these results in a restoration of the disturbed pattern, whereas the second and third produce new patterns of interaction.

An important point must be kept in mind in talking of patterns, equilibriums, and the like. These terms do not refer to a mystical entity like a "group mind" that suffers, changes, and dies. A group is "real" in the sense that the interactions that are the group can be observed, and these terms are convenient ways of describing interactions. But one is dealing with the activities of individuals too. To draw any other inference is to become involved in the literally false and disastrously misleading distinction between "the individual" and "society." When men act and interact in consistent patterns, it is reasonable to study these patterns and to designate them by collective terms: *group, institution, nation, legislature, political party, corporation, labor union, family,* and so on. Similarly, it is reasonable for some purposes to study particular individuals, as do the clinical and individual psychologists. But these are merely two approaches to the same thing, not separate entities. Men exist only in society; society is the interactions of men.

It follows, therefore, that when one speaks of a disturbance in an institutional pattern, one refers as well to a disturbance in the individual organisms whose activities have made up the pattern. One of the features of an institutionalized group, as has been noted, is its persistence. It may be thought of as a habit and as being made up of certain habitual activities of a number of individuals. When the pattern is interrupted, there is disturbance or frustration in varying degrees of the habits of the participants, a circumstance that is always unpleasant and may be extremely painful. One may study the consequences for the affected individuals or the changes in the interaction patterns or both, but "the equilibrium of the internal environment [the organism], the equilibrium of the individual in relation to others, and the equilibrium of the group are similar and related phenomena."

When the equilibrium of a group (and the equilibriums of its participant individuals) is seriously disturbed, various kinds of behavior may ensue. If the disturbance is not too great, the group's leaders will make an effort to restore the previous balance. As we shall see in more detail later, this effort may immediately necessitate recourse to the government. Other behaviors may occur if the disturbance is serious to the point of disruption. These may be classified in various ways for different purposes. In the present context three broad types of behavior may be distinguished on the basis of their effect upon the existing or potential groups involved. In the first place, the participants may individually engage in various kinds of inappropriate or aberrant or compensatory substitute activities: complaining, rumor-mongering, phantasies, alcoholism, drug addiction, indiscriminate aggression, and the like. Thus, in a revolutionary situation where the equilibriums of a wide range of institutions have been disturbed or disrupted, there is a constant possibility that large segments of the populace will engage in undisciplined loafing, irresponsible violence, or other activities useless to a successful revolutionary movement. It is the task of revolutionary leadership to limit such behavior by providing new and "constructive" forms of interaction in the place of those that have been disrupted. Similarly, a sudden change in the relations (interactions) between management and workers in a factory, initiated by the former, may at first result in gossiping, griping, and picking on scapegoats. The adolescent, whose roles are in a highly fluid state alternating between those of an adult and those of a dependent child and necessarily involving disequilibrium, will frequently indulge in daydreams and phantasies. These substitutive activities may be harmless or may have neurotic consequences, depending on the situation.

Secondly, the disturbed individuals may increase their activities in other groups in order to restore some sort of personal balance. Thus a state of disequilibrium in the family group may be compensated for by increased interaction in the work group (longer hours at the office) or in a recreational group (increased attendance at meetings of a bowling league, woman's club, and the like).

The third type of behavior that may result from a serious disequilibrium is the formation of new groups that may function to restore the balance. For present purposes this type is the most important of the three, especially if a considerable number of individuals is affected, since these new groups are likely to utilize political means of achieving their objectives. They are likely to become political groups, although they need not do so. Adolescents who cannot establish a stable set of relationships in family groups may join others of the same age level in informal or formal clubs or gangs. This behavior is particularly likely where the adolescent adjustment is made more difficult by special problems such as arise for American-born children of immigrant parents, or for young men and women who are unable to establish stable and satisfactory relationships in an economic group. Among adults new groups are likely to develop or old ones to grow and increase their activity where a serious disequilibrium is produced in family and work groups by a depression or similar economic crisis. Farm movements throughout American history have developed and reached their peaks of strength in times of great economic distress, such as the 1870's and the early 1920's.

When Japanese Americans and Japanese aliens resident on the West Coast were ruthlessly uprooted from their homes in early 1942 and sent to relocation centers, the disruption of established equilibriums was profound.

In his distinguished study of the relocation camp at Poston, Arizona, Leighton found ample evidence to this effect: "Although social patterns did exist, some new and some old, more prominent was disarticulation and the *absence of the accustomed habits of human relationship.* People were strangers to each other in a strange situation and *did not know what to expect.*" (Italics added.) This imbalance involved not only the family groups, work groups, and neighborhood groups but more inclusive institutions such as the nation itself. That is, the attitudes and behavior of wide segments of the American people, especially in the West, with whom Niseis in particular had been accustomed to interact peacefully and on a basis of considerable equality, sharply contradicted what most of the victims had been accustomed to expect. The imbalance was not temporary or minor, but persistent and inclusive: "Most aspects of life were lived with acquaintances made since coming to Poston and every individual and every family was trying to adjust to a society that had no framework and no stability. Hardly anyone had a confident expectation as to how anybody with whom he worked or had contact would behave from week to week." Out of this situation a series of new groups emerged, some spontaneously and some under the guidance of the camp's administrators. Among the former were gangs that administered beatings to alleged informers.

Examples of the emergence of new groups in compensation for disturbances in the equilibrium of existing institutionalized groups can be drawn from simpler societies as well as the more complex. When government officials and missionaries arrived in the Papua Territory, New Guinea, in the 1920's, they attempted to alter the ways of the natives and particularly to keep them from holding some of their customary religious ceremonies. The resulting disturbance in the established patterns of interaction was followed by the development of a series of religious movements that spread over New Guinea.

When one views any society as a sort of mosaic of groups, one is confronted with a bewildering array of groups that may be classified in different ways. Thus various characteristic activities seem to be carried on in one group that make it different from another in that particular respect. The examples used in the preceding paragraphs are sufficient illustration. Similarly, although it is an observable fact that all groups involve the same fundamental process, the interaction of individuals, they seem to differ from one another in the form that this process takes—for example, in the degree of formality. In the pursuit of meaning and understanding, students of society, particularly sociologists, have classified groups on these and other bases, distinguishing and defining classes of groups. These efforts have varied with the purposes, skills, and insights of the classifiers. In addition to the category "institution," which has been examined briefly above, various sub-categories have been designated on the basis of fairly obvious differences of function—the family, economic groups, political groups, and religious groups. On somewhat different bases distinctions are drawn among crowds, publics, assemblies, organizations, mobs, primary groups, secondary groups, in-groups, out-groups, and a host of others.

Nature and Prospects of
Political Interest Groups

ALFRED de GRAZIA

An interest group may be defined as a privately organized aggregation which attempts to influence public policy. "Interest" implies the existence of "disinterest." The "politics of interest groups" therefore would suggest a "politics of disinterest groups." But there is no politics of disinterest groups. "Disinterested" groups and politics are impossible. Therefore, insofar as politics is the politics of groups, all politics is the politics of interest groups. However, the word "interest" may be placed on an adjectival continuum of "how intensely," or "how interested," or "how involved," are the members of the group. If we could begin the history of the concept over again, we might discover that the term "political group" would be more useful than the term "interest group." Conversely, the term "pressure group" seems to exaggerate the degree of political activity of many interest groups, and the word "lobby" is far too limited for the concept. Yet it is better not to argue over terms at all provided only that we have understood from our verbal exercise that the term "interest" has a shady past. It contains the notion of a limited and prejudiced cause and came into use originally as a supposed contrast to rational, free, and formally constitutional institutions of political force and effect.

Many thousands of interest groups can be found. The United States has probably more per thousand population than any other country of the world. Even so, recent studies are revising upwards the ratio of interest groups to population in parliamentary regimes such as England and France, as well as in less industrialized areas such as Spain, Egypt, and India.

The number of interest groups in a society seems to depend upon the diversity of sentiment in the population with respect to those things that

Reprinted from *The Annals of the American Academy of Political and Social Science,* vol. 319 (September 1958), pp. 113–22 by permission of the author and the publisher.

might fall within the scope of governmental action. If there are numerous religions, there tend to be numerous religious interest groups. The United States and Lebanon well exemplify this situation. The number also depends upon and is positively related to the habit of informal association, the degree of freedom of association, and the unavailability of formal governmental machinery to incorporate interests.

Interest groups have all degrees of organizational stability and formality. Groups may be informally united on a single, transient issue or may be exceedingly complicated and long-lived, as for instance the Roman Catholic Church, which is older than any of the states within which it dwells. Interest groups may exist within the government as well as outside of it; civil service unions, scientific associations of executives, an informal committee to secure a new administrative procedure or a new enactment—these are instances.

Interest groups are privately organized. Hence, they stand in contrast to constitutional and legislatively enacted institutions. They originate as, and tend to be, nongovernmental, nonlegitimate, and nonauthoritative organizations. Thus the activity of a South Side Neighborhood Development League is not viewed by people as prescribed by law or as permitting and conveying much psychological compulsion.

However, legitimacy and authority are not the monopoly of the state. They are subjective relations that prevail between individuals of differing statuses. Hence interest groups may possess both legitimacy and authority to varying degrees, competing, in unusual cases such as a gang or a religious body, with the state. The state in contemporary times derives much of its legitimate authority from its claim—rightly or wrongly—to represent the interest of all and to its compulsory jurisdiction over all.

Everyday writing about interest groups classifies them by function or subject matter, such as professional, agricultural, labor, and business and also subclassifies them further. It is now apparent that interest groups are formed with respect to all functions of society and that such a classification roughly parallels the occupational, attitudinal, and demographic stratification of society. An interest group tends to originate wherever political relevance affects an aggregate. There can be little theoretical value therefore in the endless enumeration and description of interest groups divided by subject matter. Probably the key idea implicit in the common functional classification is that certain functional categories of society hold great power. Political science is perforce fascinated by the largest and strongest interest groups, and these correspond to the greatest functional institutions.

Whether a particular interest group has much or little power depends essentially upon its place in the total way of life of the population—churches in a society of the devout, automobile manufacturers in a "society on wheels," and so forth—but also upon the other general features of a society: the degree of separation of formal powers of government, the strength or weakness of formal authority, the degree of legitimacy accorded formal authority, and the lack of representation of the interests in the representative structure of government.

Knowledge of these elements allows one to guess whether an interest group possesses great power. Other factors are less important, unless one needs detailed and short-run comparisons. Thus many conditions will dictate the precise form, degree of organization, kind of policy orientation, and the quality of leadership of each interest group and larger classes of groups.

ORIGIN OF INTERESTS

But it is time to go back to the beginning and ask from where an interest comes. Relying upon some recent convincing studies of perception by Jean Piaget, Jerome Brunner and others, one may believe that involvement with an object at the least accompanies, if it does not precede, the perception of the object. An infant will see his nursing bottle in a place where it rests unnoticed by adults. One is interested in God before one strives to perceive the Hand of God. The Gospel preaches that first was the Word, "and the Word was made flesh, and dwelt among us." Far from this, but strangely not so far, Sigmund Freud speaks of the feeling of a vast oneness in the universe that leads a person to God. From infancy to old age, the law that interest precedes perception seems to rule man's actions. Concern with politics or with some reward associated with being concerned with politics goes before learning who the party leaders are and what a party is up to.

It is because perception is so conditioned by involvement that we can dispense with a politics of disinterest as opposed to a politics of interest and can assume that every action a man takes in politics must be an interested action. All groups in which he participates are interest groups in the true sense that he is interested in them. (He may not find the interest agreeable, of course.) Some hold his interest more than others, and there must indeed be some minimum flicker of attention and reference to indicate he is a member of the group.

An example would be "age groups," so called, which might better be called age groupings. Assuredly the whole population belongs to statistical age groups, classified to one's desire by years, decades, or otherwise. There are also behavioral features of an age grouping; even unawares, the old may be conservative or some other thing by contrast with the young. This is still not a group. But if there is an awareness, then there is a group; if a young person says: "We young people are tired of the Democrats," he speaks as a member of a group, without proper name or organization but still a group, because he refers to it and acts in its role. Beyond this type of group come the more organized groups, the Youth for Christ, the Young Democrats, the Junior Chamber of Commerce, and many others. There are in some societies, especially "primitive" ones, formal orders or parliaments of the young that recognize and accord political responsibilities to them. So a trait such as age can lend itself to every shade of group-ism from least to most, and so can every other trait that distinguishes one person from another.

It is important to note that a very general bifurcation of theory in political science, sociology, and social psychology is being attacked here. For it is asserted or assumed by many that there is a politics of individuals that opposes a politics of groups. For instance, if a man votes for a general as President because he respects the special talents a military man may possess, he is said to act as an individual. This action is supposed to be theoretically different from the action of a Negro who votes for a friend of Negroes. Is it then true that political theory must be based upon the individual or upon both the group and the individual, but not upon the group alone? Perhaps contemporary theory does so, and therefore bumps along like a cart mounted on a wheel and a skid.

It is correct to say that a person almost never gives himself fully to any group to which he belongs, whether it be one of the formal governmental groups or one of the barely conscious groupings such as age. Nor does he ever have an attitude that is completely determined by any group. A person is far too complicated for that to happen. It cannot be denied therefore that the sum of all groups and groupings is not "all." Indeed, excluded from the simplistic group theory of political behavior are most people as they behave most of the time.

Yet let us dissect our individual's non-group sentiments. Are they not in the last analysis a personal, private and, in an absolute sense, unique combination of his group roles? For instance, may not one man be, say, an "old-socialist-atheist-majoritarian" and another man a "young-Christian-socialist-pluralist," whereupon both share roles as socialists but never think and act socialist in the same way? Suppose that the two become involved in politics as members of two opposing factions of the socialist patry that are based upon the issue of anticlericalism. Then we say, of course, that the groups accurately reflect the men; but they in turn are much more than these two traits. Each may hate everything else about his faction except the mode of representation accorded his opinion on religion. Hence we still have in the elaborate internal differentiation of our two men a great reservoir of potential reorganization, regrouping, and weakening or strengthening of the intensity of a view or an action on an issue. This fact is at once a political and a methodological warning: it tells the politically unwary that a group's bonds are rarely unbreakable and the student of politics that the actuality of individuals is not to be pictured by a simple group theory.

The proponents of group theory can correctly assert their perspective only by admitting two sets of facts. First, the group dissolves at its participant edges and also at its core in the individual person. Its existence is measured in the person by the intensity of his association with it and hence among an aggregate of persons by a frequency distribution of such measures. Secondly, group forces can combine within individuals to create an interest that is not within the scope and domain of any particular group that makes up the coalition. The behavior and opinions of a man who is both a localistic Chicagoan and an American are conditioned by both such identities even though he may be representing Chicago in negotiations with the United States government; that is, he might be internally compelled to ask for less for Chicago. The character of group alliances changes the meaning of the struggle although the particular groups rest unchanged. Athens alone against Persia may represent individualism against despotism; Athens and Sparta against Persia may represent Western Civilization against the East. Tariff-protected businesses working against low tariffs suggest selfishness, but high-tariff businessmen, labor leaders, and politicians all working against low tariffs would represent a conception of the national interest.

The "interest of all" is the conscious involvement of the members of the largest aggregate in society. (Analogous logic may be used for the "national interest," the "general interest," the "interest of the greatest number.") Insofar as all may feel American, they are to that degree Americans and dependent upon their role as Americans. Insofar as all may think of themselves favorably as Americans, "pro-American" is the interest of all. Insofar as all are divided into two groups who dispute whether Hawaiians are Americans, the interest of all remains divorced from a position on this issue. The national government is supposed to represent the interest of all. But this interest conveys only a vague and limited agreement among nearly all Americans. It becomes an extremely strong interest when it does unite a program to its sentiment, as when everyone wants peace when war is threatened. But such is rare.

So "the interest of all" generally consists of the acceptance of the symbols and behaviors of the government. It comes from the involvement that most or all feel in the group that is the nation. The "interest of all" is as conceivably measurable as any other group affiliation and should not, therefore, be regarded as a different species. If it does not suffice to represent all people all of the time, it merely exhibits the problem of all groups: their limited hold over their members and their restricted concord on particular issues introduced to group concern.

ORGANIZATION OF INTEREST AND POWER

The organization of political interest and political power, when viewed historically, takes a form that adheres to the theory of interest groups hitherto recited in its logical, psychological, and social aspects.

Every societal and political order is interest based. Important economic interests, for instance, are always to be found. Charles Beard, in his historical essay, *The Economic Basis of Politics,* thought he had discovered that the wealthy ran everything. But he merely affirmed and confused a monumental truism. The classical writers were careful to delineate the sources of power of the ruling classes in Greek states and later in Rome. The medieval estates allocated political rights and privileges, or denied them, to their members. Often the free-trade element, the Jewish element, and the foreign element might not aspire to legitimate power as groups, though they might act as pressure groups; and as individuals they might take on roles in the larger political spheres. The power of guilds in the medieval cities is well known. One medieval scholar has discovered an intriguing list of interest groups behind the legislation of a medieval English parliament. Local governments lobbied actively.

Throughout history, interest groups have been more or less visible and forceful from time to time. The principal factor in their visibility is ideology. It is ideology that legitimates power and political activity. Power without the legitimacy that is conferred by the ideology of the period is naked. When power is naked, it is ashamed and others are ashamed of it. Groups that lack legitimacy but possess political force represent naked power and are ashamed of themselves. Standing by our definition of interest groups as nongovernmental aggregates, we can observe one very large and long cycle of visibility, attributable in part to the relative legitimacy or disrepute of private associations. The cycle begins in the late medieval period when groups were strong, organized, and respected; descends into a period following the Enlightenment when groups were maligned and suppressed; and ends in an upswing of groupism in which we are presently found.

THE IDEOLOGICAL FIGHT AGAINST GROUPS. The victory of the proponents of free enterprise in the eighteenth century in England, France, and America, to be followed by the great parliamentary revolution of the nineteenth century in Europe, and to be hopelessly emulated in the constitutions of practically all other countries who lacked the essential ingredient of a vigorous free enterprise as the interest basis for the constitutional formal revolution, can be construed as the legitimizing of the pre-existing interest groups founded upon the commercial and industrial revolution. The shift of power from the House of Lords to the House of Commons in England, from the executives to the legislatures there and elsewhere, occurred as the new interests sought housing in the state. At this age of history, the assembly or parliament offered itself as the housing; but, like the hermit crab, an interest can move into various types of shells.

Yet the legislative revolutions were only a part of the Enlightenment, which was a vast ideological revolution based upon the beliefs in equality and individualism, and the legislatures only temporarily controlled the great historical transformation. Incarnate in Enlightenment ideology was a reaction against interest groups that went far beyond the mere nonlegitimacy of the interests who sponsored and led the legislative revolutions in England, France, and America. Added to the typical distaste for other interest groups that the new ruling interests who were ensconced in the parliaments displayed, was the hostility against groups implied in the Enlightenment's beliefs in liberty, equality, and individualism. The age of rationalistic mass democracy was on hand, to be portrayed on the historical stage by the Jeffersonians and Jacksonians in America; by the suffragists, laborites, and intellectuals in England; and by the socialist-communist parties in Europe. Beginning in the nineteenth century there might be no interests apart from the interests of the mass of people, however cloudy such a concept might be. An equally accepted but opposite belief was that the individual, a solitary wayfarer in life and politics, could govern himself without belonging to any cohesive groups. The two beliefs might be simultaneously held, for they are psychologically, if not politically, consistent. In the individualism and utilitarianism of Benthamism all interests break down. Little thought goes to the mass authoritarianism or majoritarianism that was the inevitable denouement. Whereas the mass public had never before been seriously regarded as the active agent in legislative processes, the People was now sculpted into a massive monolithic interest group. The older interests which could not be destroyed—aristocracy and Church—were stripped of formal and secular authority. The French, with rationalistic thoroughness, passed laws prohibiting the formation of religious and functional associations. Laws against labor unions were partly a logical development of the new ideology. Prohibitions against lobbying were also congruent. In early United States history the formal conditions of entering the legal and medical professions were scanty, and medical societies were forbidden to exercise professional power.

The envisioned society was a practical absurdity, but men have never successfully distinguished between a practical absurdity and a glorious and instructive ideal. No people tried as assiduously as the Americans to make the anti-interest ideology part of their political lives, and the great heat with which discussions of interest groups are conducted in the United States evidences our great internal fire on this question.

Yet, in a contradictory way, America is world-renowned for its hospitality to voluntary associations. It has been called a nation of joiners and, although this picture may be exaggerated—since about half the people belong to no formal voluntary group—we certainly do exceed all other nations in our penchant and ability to form new groups, many of which have political effect. Thus we are creating on the one hand what we consistently have opposed on the other.

THE IRREPRESSIBLE GROUPISM.   Consequently we have been accomplishing a fantastic feat of producing a new order of modern society while stoutly espousing the old society. More than this, we have been creating the only society that can compete successfully with world communism, while espousing an ideology that has been shown to contribute, consciously or unwittingly, to dictatorship in the name of the masses.

Although most writings by American scholars are hostile to interest groups or accept them as an inevitable manifestation of *Realpolitik,* evidence of the transforming of American politics by such groups is abundant. Many legal specialists now practice administrative law on behalf of interests affected by the enlarging administrative establishment. Every industry of any consequence has its trade associations who are continuously engaged in setting forth the lowest common denominator of industrial policy and tactics. The Catholic Church, which has undergone a considerable revival of vigor and influence while separate from the government, now widely circulates and urges the principles of pluralism. If we were to have measures of extent and trend in the vocabulary and argumentation of everyday politics, civic work and welfare work in the thousands of local communities in America as well as at the seats of government, we should discover that an increasing and very heavy proportion of all references to support that is sought or held is described in the language of groups rather than of individuals. Whether in the economic sphere, the religious sphere, the recreational sphere, the political sphere, or the military sphere, the individual policy is rare and the collective policy is everywhere.

The technique of organizing new formal associations, usually by incorporating for profit or not-for-profit, is increasingly well known, and numbers of such groups are annually organized. Legislatures have a most perplexing task in prescribing rules for the political conduct of such organizations. It will not be long before the laws in relation to their political conduct will break down insofar as they seek to prohibit that conduct. However, they will constantly increase in number and in detail as they seek to regulate behavior. Because the interest groups of today have risen as disreputable challenges to rationalistic, majoritarian, democratic structures, they have imitated the constitutionalism of those structures. The almost invariable oligarchy of the interest group is almost never manifest in the formal credentials that the group presents to the society. Or, if it is, it appears only in fine print that may provide for an officer to succeed himself, or for a system of weighted votes in accord with the actual power of the leadership, or for some other oligarchic device.

The popular nineteenth-century theory of democracy has never made room for a nondemocratic constituent element. It is as if the body had decided that it was working poorly as a mass of disconnected and specialized organs and cells and decreed that every cell would be like every other cell and every organ like every other one. So in its first surrender to the principle of the interest groups in modern life, rationalistic mass democracy decreed merely that interest groups might exist only if they were organized as replicas of the largest political configuration.

The results have been pathetic. Myriad small tyrannies and oligarchies have formed in groups organized so as to mirror the larger constitution. These may be contributing to deterioration in the constitution of the larger democracy. It might benefit the morale of the governmental element of the modern state as well as that of the constituent elements if the state were to recognize a diversity of organizational forms. It would not necessarily credit one as better than the other, but would recognize that an oligarchy in a corporation, in a military unit, or in a church may be continuously better than a democracy without prejudicing the value of democracy in another place and at another level. Although the intellectual terror of the human being at having to embrace several conflicting directives in different environments should be always feared, a type of man may be visualized, and indeed may be quite common, who can simultaneously play the rules of several different games which correspond to his different roles in life. He may so conduct himself without personal disorganization. Sebastian de Grazia, in his book, *The Political Community,* ascribes much civic disharmony to the conflict of religious and economic directives. Such conflict, however, is less deleterious to social harmony than is the more general condition of interpersonal hostility and lack of love for oneself and others, which, it must be said, he also asserts strongly.

A NEW KIND OF DEMOCRACY

I believe that in pluralism and a rational organization of interests can be discovered a new kind of democracy upon which a superior society may be founded. Such a society would derive its most desirable democratic elements from an initial equality of opportunity. It would teach groups to view themselves not as outlaws nor as the clubs of little boys imitating their big brother, the state, but as integral parts of a whole in which they pursue their useful and dignified way. So long as we suppress rather than educate the group formations of American life, we lower the quality of their membership and activities. We distort their operational code by forcing them to mold it absurdly to the main theory of the democratic state produced by the Enlightenment.

But then to preserve the maximum of individuality and to ward off the stultifying rigidities of estate and corporative systems, we must prepare a vastly enlarged and much more sophisticated theory of organizations that views generously the free formation and dissolution of groups and permits movement of individuals from one group to another. Diverse evils must be combatted: the compulsive power of a church to hold its members, the keeping of classes or races "in their place" as subordinate estates, the compulsive domination of a cartel over the formation of new businesses, and the compulsive grip of a limited pension plan on a worker's free movement from job to job.

Despite the misadventures of syndicalism, fascism—whether political or clerical—and the pork-barrel of geographical or functional interests, an associational democracy is possible. In the new age, to respond keenly and poignantly to the dreams of Jefferson, Mazzini, and Trotsky is as natural as identifying with the troubadors and knights of old; yet those dreams, when they lead to action, move fatally toward bureaucratic, socialist, and communist statism. It appears to me that the future of the followers of Christ and of the heirs of the Renaissance moves along with the perfecting of ways of organizing and operating myriad interest and pressure groups and assembling them into a productive, free, and creative community. The philosophers of some form of pluralism have been so many and varied— federalists, Catholics, pragmatists, guild socialists, and fascists—that the mechanical liberalism or socialism of contemporary social scientists seems to be needlessly unimaginative and inadequate.

The fatal political deficiency of associational democracy to the present time has been the general conviction that it would be incapable of suppressing special pressures in accord with some general vision of the state or world community. I feel that political scientists who have presented the simplistic theory of associations have done a disservice, even when they have contributed much to our objective knowledge of politics and even when they described the positive benefits of group politics. They have made of politics a mere grab bag of organized groups. They have failed to see that our troubles are in ourselves and not in our groups. We should be able, by a social and civic education appropriate to the theory of the associational democracy, to raise a generation able to perceive and involve itself in a series of roles ranging from occupational and neighborhood associations to the functions of a national and world citizen. If we did so, we would naturally introduce sympathies that would constantly arbitrate the disputes between the special interests that arise and are resolved in the personality. We would induce a higher and more general level of integration in each individual's contribution to the policies of collective action. Groups would not then domineer their parochial membership; they would be understood and controlled within their members' bosoms. And group leaders, too, moderated by their followers and disciplined to the larger meanings of their roles, would turn less to piracy on the social main.

The transition from individualized to modern group political processes was not accompanied by a deterioration in political morality nor by a shift from a broad vision of political policy to a narrow one. The Association of American Railroads can compare itself favorably in these respects with the promoters of the great early railroads such as Leland Stanford. All the more remarkable, then, are the fervid efforts of the leaders of associations and groups to represent themselves as individuals of the old stripe. I suppose that the association leadership would say that they are compelled to fight the government and its pernicious influences upon their members' rights and efficiency of operation, and that they must use the only rhetoric that conveys meaning to the public: the rhetoric of the state against the individual. That is only one of a thousand illustrations, regrettably, that a major task lies before political science, the task of creating an ideological climate able to assimilate the diverse justifications and descriptions of interest-group life into a new theory of associational democracy. Such theory, preceding an ideology and developing into a new ideology, may establish the only political order that in this century and that to come can compete successfully with socialism and communism, in America and in the world.

Litigation as a Form of
Pressure Group Activity

CLEMENT E. VOSE

The conventional judicial process is distinguished from legislative and administrative processes by features which forbid, conceal, or control the participation of organized pressure groups. Justice Robert H. Jackson warned that "perhaps the most significant and least comprehended limitation upon

Reprinted from *The Annals of the American Academy of Political and Social Science,* vol. 319 (September 1958), pp. 20–31 by permission of the Author and the publisher.

the judicial power is that this power extends only to cases and controversies." This limitation has meant that the Supreme Court of the United States refuses to provide advisory opinions and avoids what judges are fond of calling "political questions." It cannot be overstressed that the Supreme Court's only power is to decide lawsuits between adversaries with real interests at stake. Under the case system that marks American jurisprudence, a court is a "substantially passive instrument, to be moved only by the initiative of litigants." This contrasts with the power of the President and the Congress to deal with any subject as desired.

Despite this limiting prerequisite, the Supreme Court does possess considerable control over the particular cases to be decided. The Judiciary Act of 1925 gave the Court almost complete discretionary control of its appellate business through grant or denial of the writ of certiorari. This statute settled the modern principle that the Supreme Court's function was

not to see justice done in every case, but to decide the more important policy issues presented within the frame of a "case" or "controversy," concerning the federal balance, the relations of the branches of the federal government, or the fundamental rights of the individual in relations to government.

Elaborating upon the function of deciding important policy issues, Chief Justice Fred M. Vinson, in 1949, told the bar that the Supreme Court is interested only in "those cases which present questions whose resolution will have immediate importance beyond the particular facts and parties involved." Vinson added that "what the Court is interested only in is the actual practical effect of the disputed decision—its consequences for other litigants and in other situations." This meant that lawyers whose petitions for certiorari were granted by the Supreme Court were representing not only their clients, "but tremendously important principles, upon which are based the plans, hopes and aspirations of a great many people throughout the country."

It is the thesis of this article that organizations—identifiable by letterhead—often link broad interests in society to individual parties of interest in Supreme Court cases. Since the American judicial system is built upon specific cases with specific facts, it is assumed that study of the role of specific organizations is relevant to understanding.

REASONS ORGANIZATIONS GO TO COURT

Organizations support legal action because individuals lack the necessary time, money, and skill. With no delays a case takes an average of four years to pass through two lower courts to the Supreme Court of the United States. A series of cases on related questions affecting the permanent interest of a group may extend over two decades or more. The constant attention that litigation demands, especially when new arguments are being advanced, makes the employment of regular counsel economical. This may be supplemented by a legal staff of some size and by volunteer lawyers of distinction. Parties also pay court costs and meet the expense of printing the record and briefs. Organizations are better able to provide the continuity demanded in litigation than individuals. Some individuals do maintain responsibility for their own cases even at the Supreme Court level, but this is difficult under modern conditions.

The form of group participation in court cases is set by such factors as the type of proceeding, standing of the parties, legal or constitutional issues in dispute, the characteristics of the organization, and its interest in the outcome. Perhaps the most direct and open participation has been by organizations which have been obliged to protect their own rights and privileges. Robert A. Horn has shown that a modern constitutional law of association has developed out of Supreme Court cases concerning churches, trade unions, political parties, and other organizations. The cases have sometimes placed organizations as parties, but more often the organization supports a member or an officer in litigation. One example must suffice.

The constitutional concept of religious freedom has been broadened in recent years by the Supreme Court decisions in cases involving members of the sect known as Jehovah's Witnesses. Most of the cases began when a Jehovah's Witness violated a local ordinance or state statute. Since 1938, the Witnesses, incorporated as the Watch Tower Bible and Tract Society and represented by its counsel, Hayden Cooper Covington, have won forty-four of fifty-five cases in the United States Supreme Court. As a result Jehovah's Witnesses now enjoy

the rights to solicit from house to house, to preach in the streets without a license, to canvass apartment buildings regardless of the tenants' or owners' wishes, to be recognized as ministers of an accredited religion and thus be exempt from the draft, to decline to serve on juries, and to refuse to salute or pledge allegiance to the flag.

THE NAACP

Since 1909 the National Association for the Advancement of Colored People has improved the legal status of Negroes immeasurably by the victories it has won in more than fifty Supreme Court cases. During its early years, the NAACP relied upon prominent volunteer lawyers like Moorfield Storey, Louis Marshall, and Clarence Darrow to represent Negroes in the courts. Limited success coupled with its failure to win gains from Congress led the NAACP in the 1930's to make court litigation fundamental to its program. A separate organization, the NAACP Legal Defense and Educational Fund, was incorporated for this purpose. The goal of the NAACP was to make Negroes "an integral part of the nation, with the same rights and guarantees that are accorded to other citizens, and on the same terms." This ambition meant that beginning in 1938 Thurgood Marshall as special counsel for the NAACP Legal Defense and Educational Fund held what was "probably the most demanding legal post in the country."

In aiming to establish racial equality before the law on a broad basis, the Legal Defense Fund has not functioned as a legal aid society. Limited resources have prevented the Fund from participating in all cases involving the rights of Negroes. As early as 1935 Charles Houston, an imaginative Negro lawyer who preceded Marshall as special counsel, set the tone of NAACP efforts when he declared that the legal campaign against inequality should be carefully planned "to secure decisions, rulings and public opinion on the broad principle instead of being devoted to merely miscellaneous cases."

By presenting test cases to the Supreme Court, the NAACP has won successive gains protecting the right of Negroes in voting, housing, transportation, education, and service on juries. Each effort has followed the development of new theories of legal interpretation and required the preparation of specific actions in the courts to challenge existing precedent. The NAACP Legal Defense Fund has accomplished these two tasks through the co-operation of associated and allied groups. First, as many as fifty Negro lawyers practicing in all parts of the country have been counsel in significant civil rights cases in the lower courts. Many of these men received their legal education at the Howard University Law School in Washington, D.C., and have shared membership in the National Bar Association since its founding in 1925. These common associations have contributed to the consensus among Negro lawyers on timing their quest for equality through litigation. Second, the NAACP has long benefited from its official advisory group, the National Legal Committee composed of leading Negro and white lawyers. Today Lloyd Garrison is Chairman of the National Legal Committee of forty-five attorneys located in twenty three cities. This is the nucleus of the many volunteers in many fields who have contributed ideas, often at national conferences, to the planning of litigation. Third, other organizations with no direct connection with the Legal Defense Fund have sponsored a few cases. State and local chapters of the NAACP have often aided Negroes who were parties in cases, especially in the lower courts. The

St. Louis Association of Real Estate Brokers was the chief sponsor of the important restrictive covenant case of *Shelley v. Kraemer*. A Negro national college fraternity, Alpha Phi Alpha, sponsored quite completely the successful attack on discrimination in interstate railway dining cars.

INDIVIDUAL TEST CASES. Winning new constitutional protections for Negroes has depended on the development of individual test cases with a Negro as party in each. There is no chronicle of the human interest stories contained in the roles of Negroes in historic Supreme Court cases. But what is known reveals many difficulties to be inherent in improving the legal status of a group of fifteen million persons through individual court cases. In a suit by a single plaintiff, the case may become moot as the passage of time makes the remedy sought inapplicable. This danger, though avoided by the co-operation of state officials, was created in the Missouri Law School case of 1938 when the plaintiff Lloyd Gaines, disappeared just as the case was completed. Also the concerted efforts of authorities to deny Negroes participation in the Texas white Democratic primary kept Dr. L. A. Nixon from voting even though he was the plaintiff in two Supreme Court victories. Furthermore there is always the temptation for compromise by the original plaintiff which would accomplish his narrow purpose but stop the litigation before the broad constitutional issue was before the appellate court.

These dangers were largely overcome in the School Segregation Cases when federal court actions were instituted by individual plaintiffs both on their own behalf and on behalf of persons similarly situated. Since 1955, in the expanding litigation over race relations, the class action has become a procedural device of growing importance. Rule 23 (a) of the Federal Rules of Civil Procedure provides under certain circumstances that

If persons constituting a class are so numerous as to make it impracticable to bring them all before the court, such of them, one or more, as will fairly insure the adequate representation of all may, on behalf of all, sue or be sued.

One authority has said that "school segregation is a group phenomenon which is peculiarly suited to resolution as a class action." As Negroes enter a new generation of litigation, their cases are apt increasingly to take the form of the class action.

THE AMERICAN LIBERTY LEAGUE

The experience of the American Liberty League, organized in 1934 by conservative businessmen to oppose the New Deal, provides another variation on the theme of organizations in litigation. When the League proved unable to prevent enactment of economic regulation by Congress, a National Lawyers' Committee was formed to question the constitutionality of the legislation. In August 1935, the National Lawyers' Committee of fifty-eight members announced plans to prepare a series of reports to the public on whether particular federal laws were "consonant with the American constitutional system and American traditions." These reports "would be of a strictly professional nature and would in no case go into the question of social and economic advisability or the need for constitutional change to meet new conditions." This intention led the Committee during the next two years to conclude that a dozen New Deal statutes were unconstitutional.

The most celebrated Liberty League "brief" prepared by the National Lawyers' Committee questioned the constitutionality of the National Labor Relations Act. That analysis was prepared by a subcommittee of eight attorneys under the chairmanship of Earl F. Reed. It was then submitted to the other members and made public by Raoul E. Desverine, Chairman of the entire group, on Constitution Day, 1935. The reports of the Committee were given wide publicity through press releases, the distribution of pamphlets, and radio talks by leading conservative lawyers like James M. Beck. Critics of these reports feared that they had two purposes: "to influence the federal courts when such legislation shall be presented for consideration" and "to arouse public sentiment so that confidence in the courts will be impaired should the legislation be held constitutional."

Members of the National Lawyers' Committee of the American Liberty League, but not the organization itself, participated in litigation. The Committee's first public announcement had stated that "it will also contribute its services in test cases involving fundamental constitutional questions." Although the intention was to offer free legal services to citizens without funds to defend their constitutional rights, members of the National Lawyers' Committee actually represented major corporations which challenged the constitutionality of New Deal legislation in the Supreme Court. Earl F. Reed simply adapted the Liberty League report to apply to the specific facts of the case when he represented the Jones and Laughlin Steel Corporation against the National Labor Relations Board. Another member of the National Lawyers' Committee, John W. Davis, represented the Associated Press in a companion case.

AIDING THE GOVERNMENT DEFENSE

Judicial review in the United States constitutes an invitation for groups whose lobbying fails to defeat legislation to continue opposition by litigation. The NAACP has taken advantage of this in questioning state segregation laws, and, especially before 1937, business groups of various sizes—the American Liberty League, trade associations, and corporations—contested the constitutionality of state and federal regulatory legislation. This exploitation of judicial review has been balanced by the practice of victorious groups in legislation continuing to support administrative agencies in charge of enforcement. When statutes are challenged, organizations often support the Justice Department in Washington or a state Attorney General in defending them. This is to say that when losers in legislation have brought test cases in the courts, the legislative winners have aided the official legal defense.

THE NATIONAL CONSUMERS' LEAGUE

The efforts of the National Consumers' League to defend the validity of protective labor legislation affords an example of this private organizational aid to the public defense of legislation. Organized by society women in 1899 to improve the lot of women and children in industry, the National Consumers' League sought first to boycott goods produced under substandard conditions and then to persuade state legislatures to control factory practices through legislation. When employers in the hotel and laundry business organized to defeat legislation in the courts, the National Consumers' League, in 1908, organized a Committee on Legislation and Legal Defense of Labor Laws to "assist in the defense of the laws by supplying additional legal counsel and other assistance."

The leaders of the National Consumers' League, especially Mrs. Florence Kelley and Miss Josephine Goldmark, learned to prod state Attorneys General in order to gain adequate defense for statutes under fire in the courts. They also made two positive contributions. First, arrangements were made to provide distinguished outside counsel—most importantly, Louis D. Brandeis; but also Felix Frankfurter, Newton D. Baker, and Dean Acheson—to supervise the preparation of briefs and to make oral arguments for a state. Second, the sociological material which was the mark of the Brandeis brief was prepared by Miss Josephine Goldmark and the staff of the National Consumers' League. The first four briefs that were successful were then collected with additional material and published by Miss Goldmark as *Fatigue and Efficiency*. Attorneys General in states whose labor laws were under attack could then invite Consumers' League attorneys to manage the defense or else use the sociological materials prepared by the League in the preparation of their own brief. As a result, the League contributed to the successful defense of state statutes in more than fifteen important cases.

Like most organizations with a long-range interest in litigation, the National Consumers' League believed that publicity was vital. Criticizing the Illinois Supreme Court for invalidating an eight-hour law for women, Florence Kelley wrote in 1905 that when time

*shall have convinced the medical profession, the philanthropists, and edu-
cators, as experience has already convinced the factory employees themselves, that it is a matter of life and death to young people who form so
large a proportion of their numbers, to have a working day of reasonable
length guaranteed by law, it will be found possible to rescue the fourteenth
amendment to the Constitution of the United States from the perverted
interpretation upon which this decision rests.*

Mrs. Kelley's view was adopted in Illinois in 1910, but the full Consumers' League program of child labor, maximum hour, and minimum wage regulation was not accommodated by the United States Supreme Court for three more decades. In that period the League stressed education on the subject and for this purpose distributed extra copies of its briefs to law schools, colleges, and public libraries.

No catalogue exists of government relations with private interests concerned with the conduct of litigation. The National Consumers' League experience suggests similar practices on other subjects at all government levels. At the municipal level, an attorney for a local milk producers association acted "of counsel" on the city's brief defending a favorable ordinance. At the state level, the segregation interest has been closely associated with various Attorneys General in the South. And a prominent attorney with national standing, John W. Davis, rendered free services to South Carolina in the School Segregation Cases. At the federal level, the Justice Department has often been urged by organizations to initiate action to enforce federal statutes.

ORGANIZATIONS AS "FRIENDS OF THE COURT"

The appearance of organizations as *amici curiae* has been the most noticed form of group representation in Supreme Court cases. This does not concern the technical office of *amicus curiae* for which an attorney is appointed to assist the court in deciding complex and technical problems. Today, the Supreme Court does sometimes, as in formulating its decree in the School Segregation Cases, issue a special invitation to the Solicitor General or to state Attorneys General to act as *amici curiae*. Of interest here is the rule under which individuals, organizations, and government attorneys have been permitted to file briefs and/or make oral argument in the Supreme Court. During the last decade *amici curiae* have submitted an average of sixty-six briefs and seven oral arguments in an average total of forty cases a term.

The frequent entrance of organizations into Supreme Court cases by means of the *amicus curiae* device has often given litigation the distinct flavor of group combat. This may be illustrated by the group representation in quite different cases. In 1943, when a member of the Jehovah's Witnesses challenged the constitutionality of a compulsory flag salute in the schools, his defense by counsel for the Watchtower Bible and Tract Society was supported by separate *amici curiae,* the American Civil Liberties Union and the Committee on the Bill of Rights of the American Bar Association. The appellant state board of education was supported by an *amicus curiae* brief filed by the American Legion. In 1951, in a case testing state resale price maintenance, the United States was an *amicus* against a Louisiana statute while the Commonwealth of Pennsylvania, the Louisiana State Pharmaceutical Association, American Booksellers, Inc., and the National Association of Retail Druggists entered *amici curiae* briefs in support of the statute.

Many *amici curiae* briefs are workmanlike and provide the Court with helpful legal argument and material. Yet writers who favor their use by organizations and recognize that "the *amicus curiae* has had a long and respected role in our own legal system and before that, in the Roman law" believe that many briefs in recent years display a "timewasting character." Another authority has said that after 1947 there were multiplying signs "that the brief *amicus curiae* had become essentially an instrumentality designed to exert extra-judicial pressure on judicial decisions." Concern over this by the members of the Supreme Court was shown in 1946 when Justice Robert H. Jackson, in a dissenting opinion, criticized an *amicus curiae* brief by the American Newspaper Publishers Association:

Of course, it does not cite a single authority not available to counsel for the publisher involved, and does not tell us a single new fact except this one: "This membership embraces more than 700 newspaper publishers whose publications represent in excess of eighty per cent of the total daily and Sunday circulation of newspapers published in this country. The Association is vitally interested in the issue presented in this case, namely, the right of newspapers to publish news stories and editorials pending in the courts."

Justice Jackson told his colleagues, "this might be a good occasion to demonstrate the fortitude of the judiciary."

REGULATION OF ORGANIZATIONS IN THE COURTS

Judges, lawyers, legislators, and citizens have reacted to appearances that organizational activity in court cases touches the integrity of the judicial process. A number of limitations have resulted. But in protecting the legal system against these dangers, regulations may be too harsh on organizations and interfere unduly with the freedom of association their functioning represents. Especially is this true when the barriers against group participation in litigation are erected by legislative bodies, but it is not entirely absent when the rules are established by bar associations or by courts themselves. Some practices by organizations require control, but most of the practices of organizations in conducting litigation are perfectly compatible with an independent judiciary. Life tenure and other traditions of Anglo-American jurisprudence will attend to that. This should be borne in mind in evaluating controls placed on the practices discussed below.

PICKETING OF FEDERAL COURTHOUSES. During the trial of the leaders of the Communist party under the Smith Act in the Federal District Court for the Eastern District of New York located at Foley Square in New York City, picketing and parading outside the court was a daily occurrence. When the Senate Judiciary Committee was considering bills to limit this practice, it received many statements like the following: "Assuming under our form of representative government pressure groups must be tolerated in our legislative and executive branches, I feel there is no good reason why our courts should be subjected to such pressures." In accord with this view, Congress, in 1950, enacted legislation prohibiting any person from parading, picketing, or demonstrating in or near a federal courthouse with the intent of "interfering with, obstructing, or impeding" the administration of justice or of "influencing any judge, juror, witness, or court officer" in the discharge of his duty.

MASS PETITIONS TO THE SUPREME COURT. In 1953, the National Committee to Secure Justice in the Rosenberg Case addressed a petition claimed to have the support of 50,000 persons to the Supreme Court. Among many condemnations of this was one urging that "the Court must consult its own collective conscience on such matters without reference to the number of persons who are willing to sign a petition." No rule prevents groups from such indecorous action but Justice Hugo Black has expressed the intense disapproval of the Supreme Court. In 1951, when granting a stay of execution to Willie McGhee, a Negro under the death penalty in Mississippi, Justice Black lamented the "growing practice of sending telegrams to judges in order to have cases decided by pressure." Declaring that he would not read them, he said that "the courts of the United States are not the kind of instruments of justice that can be influenced by such pressures." Justice Black gave an implied warning to the bar by noting that "counsel in this case have assured me they were not responsible for these telegrams.

ORGANIZATION ABUSE OF THE AMICUS CURIAE FUNCTION. Supreme Court rules long provided that a "brief of an *amicus curiae* may be filed when accompanied by written consent of all parties to a case." Until 1949 permission was freely granted. In that year, the filing of briefs by forty organizations in the case of the "Hollywood Ten" who had declined to testify before the House Un-American Activities Committee was widely regarded as an excessive use of the *amici curiae* procedure. The Supreme Court thereupon called attention to the "rule of consent" by elaborating the procedures and permitting persons denied consent by a party to seek leave from the Court itself to act as *amicus curiae*. The Solicitor General, as the legal representative of the United States in the Supreme Court, took the 1949 rule change to mean that he should exercise the "rule of consent" against persons or groups wishing to be *amici curiae* in all cases. Since the United States government is a party in approximately 50 per cent of all cases before the Supreme Court the universal refusal of consent cut the number of organizations filing *amici curiae* briefs rather drastically. This rigid policy was adhered to by a succession of Solicitors General until August 1952. Complaints by Justices Black and Frankfurter then led the Solicitor General to modify the practice and exercise administrative discretion in passing upon requests of organizations to file briefs *amici curiae*. This practice satisfied a majority of the Supreme Court for its 1949 rule change was incorporated into the full revision of the Court's rules which went into effect on July 1, 1954. However, Justice Black was still dissatisfied and, on adoption of the 1954 rules, declared:

. . . *I have never favored the almost insuperable obstacle our rules put in the way of briefs sought to be filed by persons other than the actual litigants. Most of the cases before this Court involve matters that affect far more than the immediate record parties. I think the public interest and judicial administration would be better served by relaxing rather than tightening the rule against* amicus curiae *briefs.*

The standard governing grant or denial of consent to file *amicus curiae* briefs has been elaborated upon in a statement of policy issued by the Office of the Solicitor General. While espousing a liberal attitude, the Solicitor General frowns on applicants with "a general, abstract or academic interest" in a case and on "a brief which is 'a vehicle for propaganda efforts.' " Nor is a brief that merely repeats the argument of the parties well regarded. On the other hand, consent is given "where the applicant has a concrete, substantial interest in the decision of the case, and the proposed brief would assist the Court by presenting relevant arguments or materials which would not otherwise be submitted." Furthermore, in recent years when the Solicitor

General has refused consent, the Supreme Court in some cases has granted permission to an organization to file a brief *amicus curiae.*

Efforts to regulate the indiscriminate filing of *amici curiae* briefs prevent organizations on about ten occasions each term from participating in cases. For example, an American Legion post was refused consent to file an *amicus curiae* brief in the Steel Seizure Case while the Congress of Industrial Organizations was permitted to do so. The most active organizations in filing *amici curiae* briefs in recent years have been the American Civil Liberties Union, the American Federation of Labor-Congress of Industrial Organizations, the American Jewish Congress, and the National Lawyers Guild. Yet under the "rule of consent" by parties to the case each of these organizations has sometimes been denied leave to file briefs.

OFFER OF LEGAL AID BY THE LIBERTY LEAGUE.   The offer of the National Lawyers Committee of the American Liberty League to donate its services in test cases led a critic to make a formal complaint to the American Bar Association. The League was charged with unethical conduct for having "organized a vast free lawyers service for firms and individuals 'bucking' New Deal laws on constitutional grounds." The ABA Committee on Professional Ethics and Grievances ruled, in a formal opinion, that the activities of the Liberty League were perfectly proper, even laudable. The Committee found that neither the substance of the offer, to provide legal defense for "indigent citizens without compensation," nor the "proffer of service," even when broadcast over the radio, was offensive to the ethical code of the American bar.

BARRATRY AND THE NAACP.   Since 1954, eleven Southern states have acted separately through legislation or litigation to restrict the efforts of the National Association for the Advancement of Colored People to proceed with court cases aimed at ending segregation. The NAACP frankly admits the deliberate and conscious use of litigation to secure economic, social, and political gains for Negroes. In some states, registration laws—similar to federal and state lobby registration provisions—require the filing of information by organizations which might participate in desegregation litigation. The common law crime of barratry, usually defined as the fomenting, soliciting, or inciting of unjustified litigation, has been outlawed by new statutes in other states. Legislative investigating committees have sought to expose NAACP practices in litigation as unethical and illegal. State Attorneys General have brought actions against the NAACP in state courts while the NAACP has brought suits in federal courts to secure declaratory judgments and injunctions against the enforcement of state statutes which would restrict their activities.

In June, the Supreme Court overruled as an unconstitutional violation of freedom of association a contempt fine of $100,000 imposed by Alabama on the NAACP for refusing to disclose its membership lists. Two similar Virginia cases have been docketed with petitions for certiorari awaiting action when the Supreme Court convenes for its October 1958 term. In one, the NAACP has asked for review of a Supreme Court of Appeals of Virginia decision enabling a legislative committee to use subpoenas to secure the names of NAACP members and affiliates. In the other case, Virginia has asked the Supreme Court to review the decision of a three-judge federal district court in which the majority concluded the acts punishing barratry and requiring registration could not constitutionally be applied to the normal activities of the NAACP.

CONCLUSION

There is a logical relationship of organizational interest in litigation and the importance of courts in forming public policy. Although courts act only in cases between parties with concrete interests at stake, organizations concerned with the impact of the outcome may become quite active participants. Organizations may do this by sponsoring a "test case" brought in the name of a private party, they may aid the government attorney in a case, or they may file a brief as an *amicus curiae*. Considering the importance of the issues resolved by American courts, the entrance of organizations into cases in these ways seems in order. Indeed the essential right of organizations to pursue litigation would appear to follow from the generous attitude of American society toward the freedom of individuals to form associations for the purpose of achieving common goals. Of course, traditional judicial procedures should be followed and the attorneys for organizations, as well as for individuals, must address their arguments to reason. If these standards of conduct are followed there is no incompatibility between the activity of organizations in litigation and the integrity or independence of the judiciary.

Primary Group Influence on Party Loyalty

HERBERT McCLOSKY and HAROLD E. DAHLGREN

Political science, like other fields of social inquiry, has had an enduring interest in questions of stability and change. This interest—until now prin-

Reprinted from *The American Political Science Review,* vol. 53 (September 1959), pp. 757–76 by permission of the publisher. Copyright 1959 by The American Political Science Association.

cipally expressed in studies of the rise and fall of institutions—has lately been focused increasingly upon individual and group behavior, in a search for the influences that hold men to their political beliefs and affiliations or cause them to shift about. Such influences are important not only for the study of voting and party membership, but for *haute politique* as well—for the great and dramatic questions surrounding political loyalty, conformity, deviation, apostasy, and other states of membership or disaffiliation. Although the research reported below concentrates on the former, it is our hope that it may also cast light upon the latter. It is concerned specifically with primary groups—those small, face-to-face, solidary, informal and enduring coteries that we commonly experience as family, friendship and occupational peer groups.

I. THE POLITICAL ROLE OF PRIMARY GROUPS

The belief that people who associate together come to think alike is now so thoroughly buttressed by research and daily observation that it has become a commonplace. Studies have also shown that the more intimately we relate to our associates, the greater the correspondence between their views and ours. Since we interact most frequently and familiarly with the members of our own primary groups, it is mainly in these groups that our social and political attitudes are anchored. An impressive body of data supports the claim, earlier advanced by social theorists like C. H. Cooley, that the primary group is an essential bridge between the individual and the "great society," serving to transmit, to mediate, to interpret, and, in the end, to sustain society's norms. Primary groups, it now seems plain, are among the principal "carriers" and repositories of cultural beliefs and values. They are instrumental in launching and supporting class, religious, and ethnic identifications, and are even thought to function as intermediaries between consumers and the mass media.

Almost every major voting study furnishes additional proof that primary groups are essential links in the complex process by which political norms are indoctrinated and party preferences implanted. They find, for example, that members of the same primary groups characteristically vote alike, think alike on issues, and affiliate with the same party; that voters in doubt about whom to vote for usually resolve their indecision by embracing the political preferences of their friends; that approximately three out of four young people vote as their parents do; and that the more uniform a group's political outlook the firmer the voting intentions of its members. Homogeneity of opinion among primary group members also affects voting turnout and the level of political curiosity. People who disagree with their families or friends about politics are less apt to vote and less likely to develop or to retain an interest in politics. But primary groups may help to reinforce habits of participation and interest as well as to inhibit them. Patterns of participation, as one study concluded, are "contagious"—likely to be active when voters belong to politically aware groups and apathetic when they belong to politically indifferent ones.

II. THEORY OF PRIMARY GROUP INFLUENCE

The singular influence exerted by primary groups on the behavior of their members arises from a number of attributes that distinguish them from other types of groups. Compared with larger and more impersonal associations whose direct impact is only occasionally or sporadically felt, the members of a primary group enjoy unparalleled opportunities to make their attitudes known, to check, modify, or correct each other's views, and to bring dissenters into line. Their power is further augmented by their extraordinary capacity for rewarding conformity and punishing deviation, and, what is equally important, for doing so immediately, directly, and tangibly. Other associations, in contrast, must rely upon "reinforcements" that are often more distant in time, more dimly perceived, more ambiguous, and likely, therefore (as numerous experiments in the psychology of learning make plain), to be far less effective. Then, too, primary groups enlarge their influence through being able to dispense (or withhold) rewards that are specially valued by their members: more than any other social institution, they have the faculty to satisfy fundamental needs for affection, acceptance, approval, and self-definition, for the grounding of values, and for the resolution of conflicting standards of conduct. Should the use of rewards fail, a primary group may, and often does, win obedience by rejecting or threatening to ostracize the deviants—measures with a potency that increases in proportion as the latter esteem the group or find no alternative groups to turn to.

Primary groups have also been found to play an important part in defining the "social reality" we experience, which means that they not only "structure" certain of the ways in which we perceive the world—itself a powerful source of influence upon us—but that they also furnish us with many of our standards and with an image of ourselves in relation to these standards. Since their portrait of us is obviously important for our happiness, it is not surprising that we usually try to behave as they would like us to. Yielding to a primary group and to its power to define social reality may also help us gain confidence in many of our beliefs. In fact, one reason we fraternize with like-minded people is to reassure ourselves of the wisdom and probity of our opinions. Through the "feed-back" mechanisms of congenial primary alliances we frequently manage to soften the conflict between our opinion preferences on the one side and the empirical realities that crowd in upon us on the other. These alliances also furnish the social support we need to face and to discount the possibility that other people may consider our opinions false, foolish, or even base. The effect of these ministrations is, of course, to increase our dependency upon them and to permit them to impinge even more strongly upon our attitudes.

Some of the pressure for uniformity exerted by primary groups is unintentional, a mere incident of the tendency for people who associate together to arrive at common opinions, especially about subjects that are inherently ambiguous. But much of their influence is deliberate, the result of the group's efforts to realize its goals and to survive. Since the governing of primary groups depends so heavily upon voluntary and informal incentives, they may require a greater measure of agreement than other associations. In a small, face-to-face group, differences of outlook stand out sharply, looming especially large in proportion to the size and intimacy of the group. Disagreements are, furthermore, difficult to confine: the ready accessibility of members to each other heightens the danger that any difference among them may spread to the entire group and divide it severely.

Partly to avoid such catastrophes, the members of small groups quickly set about to resolve disagreements that arise among them. Research has shown, for example, that when disagreements are first discovered, a disproportionate number of comments are addressed to the dissenters in the hope of persuading them to modify their opinions and to restore the group's equilibrium. In general, the intensity of the effort to impose uniformity will depend on the felt relevance of the disputed opinions to the group's activities or goals. The presence of dissension not only interferes with the fulfillment of the group's purposes but also weakens its confidence in its own opinions and hence in its own viability. Finally, primary groups set about to achieve unanimity not merely for the instrumental reasons cited, but for the simple reason that their members have learned to understand things in a certain way and find it puzzling and discomfiting to confront alternative ways of seeing them.

III. HYPOTHESES AND PROCEDURES

We were concerned in the present study not merely to verify anew the connection between group membership and political orientation but to explore the role which primary groups play in strengthening or weakening party loyalty—in the contribution they make to life-long patterns of political support at the one extreme or to political apathy, vacillation, or defection at the other. We began our inquiry with a number of assumptions, *e.g.*, that political preference is rooted in primary group memberships, changing as they change; that the parental family ("family of orientation") functions to sustain as well as to initiate the political affiliations of its offspring; and that other primary groups, such as peers and the "family of procreation" (spouse and children), serve mainly as secondary or reinforcing agents to bolster or undermine the political predisposition implanted by the family of orientation.

The ability of the parental family to stabilize the party affiliations of any of its members would depend most critically, we thought, on the following considerations: (1) the strength of the family's initial political indoctrination; (2) the degree of unity with which its remaining members support its original preferences; (3) the extent to which the family continues to offer opportunities for affection and solidarity ("cohesiveness"); (4) the physical availability of the members to each other ("physical distance") . . . and (5) the degree of correspondence between the political views of one's parental family and one's newer primary group alliances (*e.g.,* friendship and occupational groups and family of procreation).

We anticipated that instability or shifts in party preference would most frequently occur (1) when the parental family has little interest in politics; (2) when one belongs to or enters primary groups with conflicting political norms; (3) when the groups that gave life to the original norms themselves change, experience conflict, or cease for whatever reason to reinforce their earlier views; and, (4) closely related to this, when a voter has become estranged or physically cut off from the groups in which his political outlooks have been anchored.

Systematic inquiry into these and related matters was undertaken in 1953–54 through a field project based on directed, two-hour interviews (conducted by professional interviewers) with a sample of 215 adults in the Twin City area of Minnesota. Since only a minority of voters reject their parents party preferences, special procedures were employed to muster a sample of political "changers" large enough to be statistically useful. Essentially, we proceeded by first drawing a random, cross-section sample of the general population, and by then selecting our final sample from this pool, stratifying it purposely in such a way as to overrepresent the number of voters who favor a different party from their parents.

All respondents were presented with the same interview schedule and, wherever possible, were asked identical questions. The interview inquired in detail into the past and present life of the individual members of the respondent's family, friendship, and occupational groups, their social and intellectual background, their political habits and preferences, etc. A special effort was made to collect all vital information on the respondent's voting history and political attachments. From the copious data yielded by these questions we then constructed indexes for each of the variables that interested us, assigning index scores to each respondent according to the information elicited. Since we were compelled to rely heavily upon recall data—a risky procedure at best—we perferred to ask as many detailed, factual questions as possible, approaching the same core of information from several directions and combining each individual's answers into appropriate index scores. In this way we hoped to catch inconsistencies and to offset somewhat the failures and distortions of memory that time and prejudice are bound to introduce.

More than a dozen indexes were worked out to assess such key variables as: respondent's party stability, modal political orientation of his parental family . . . degree of family cohesion or solidarity, reinforcement by friendship groups and spouse, and so on. The elements from which these measures were fashioned will be set forth as we present the findings concerning them.

IV. RESULTS: THE INFLUENCE OF FAMILY INDOCTRINATION

The observation that three out of four voters adopt the party attitudes of their parents merely begins the analysis of family influence on political preference. Not all voters, for example, maintain their affiliations with equal firmness. Some cling tenaciously to the same party, supporting its candidates regularly and without regard for their individual merit. A smaller number at the other extreme identify with a party but vote only intermittently for its candidates. Here we have called the former "stable" voters and the latter "unstable" voters. A third class of voters, who are less consistent than the "Stables" but more consistent than the "Unstables," have been labelled "moderately stable" voters (or "Moderates").

Whether a voter shifts or remains firm in his party support may depend on a number of political factors, including changes in social conditions and the impact of individual candidates and issues. The influence of these factors is, however, severely circumscribed by a voter's readiness to receive them. Many voters are so unfaltering in their conviction and so deaf to the opposition's appeals that no practical way can be found to disengage them from their habitual attachments; others are held so loosely to a party that any of a number of influences (a dramatic issue, an unfamiliar candidate, a compelling slogan, an alarming rumor, an unfavorable ethnic background, etc.) may be sufficient at the moment to dislodge them. A voter's susceptibility to defection would, we thought, greatly depend on how firmly his party affiliations have been anchored in his primary groups, especially his family. As Table I shows, voters who share their parents' political orientation are far more likely to be consistent in their party support than voters who have rejected parental preferences. Although the latter have re-

TABLE I. STABILITY OF PREFERENCE, WHEN VOTERS AGREE OR
DISAGREE WITH THE PARTY LOYALTIES OF THEIR PARENTS

Respondents are →	Republicans		Democrats		Total	
	Parents Were		Parents Were		Voter Supports Same Party as Parents	Voter Supports Different Party from Parents
	Repub- lican	Demo- cratic	Demo- cratic	Repub- lican		
	(%'s Down)		(%'s Down)		(%'s Down)	
Stable Voters	52.8	17.4	54.0	38.5	53.4	28.6
Moderate Voters	30.2	30.4	32.0	26.9	31.1	28.6
Unstable Voters	17.0	52.2	14.0	34.6	15.5	42.8
Sample Size*	53	23	50	26	103	49

*The sample sizes in this and the following tables vary somewhat. Some of the total sample of 215 voters have been excluded from one or another of our indexes or classifications owing to inappropriateness or lack of reliable information required by the particular index (*e.g.*, voting record, family political background, marriage status, etc.).

nounced the family's political outlook, they are unable to rid themselves of its influence entirely, and have difficulty embracing a new political loyalty without wavering. Only 29 per cent of them become stable voters, compared with 53 per cent stable among voters who continue to support their parents' party. Similarly, 43 per cent of the voters who disown the family's political loyalties are unstable in their adopted preferences, whereas among those who cling to the family party, few (only 16 per cent) turn out to be unstable. Table I also suggests, for reasons we will later consider, that the Republican children of Democratic parents are, on the whole, slightly less stable than the Democratic children of Republican parents.

The present study proceeded on the hypothesis that the primary family not only launches but also helps to sustain the political loyalties of its offspring. Since many voters remain in communication with their families throughout their lifetimes, and since they are likely to have parallel life styles, the family's influence can be expected to endure far beyond the time of the original indoctrination. This expectation is in some measure borne out by the data presented in Table II. There we have grouped our respondents according to the initial and current affiliations of their families, taking into account the modal preferences of the entire family, siblings as well as parents. Those whose family members were predominantly Democratic when the respondent was "in his teens" and who remain primarily Democratic today were placed in the D-D category. Republicans in the

TABLE II. STABILITY OF VOTERS, ACCORDING TO THE CONSISTENCY
OF PARTY LOYALTIES EXHIBITED BY THEIR PARENTAL FAMILIES,
FROM THE TIME VOTERS WERE IN THEIR "TEENS" TO THE
"PRESENT"

Respondent's Preference and Stability	N	*Family Political Preference**		
		R-R	D-D	Conflicted
		(%'s across)		
Stable Republicans	(32)	84.4	6.2	9.4
Moderate Republicans	(23)	60.9	13.0	26.1
Unstable Republicans	(21)	42.9	38.1	19.0
Unstable Democrats	(17)	23.5	35.3	41.2
Moderate Democrats	(26)	11.5	53.8	34.6
Stable Democrats	(37)	10.8	56.8	32.4

*R-R–Family preference has remained consistently Republican over the years.
D-D–Family preference has remained consistently Democratic over the years.
Conflicted–Family preference has varied or shifted over the years.

parallel condition were classified under R-R; while voters whose political backgrounds varied over time in any way were placed in the "Conflicted" column.

These percentage distributions show that a voter's party regularity is strongly affected by the consistency of his family's political preferences. Moving from the Stable Republicans at the one extreme to the Stable Democrats at the other, the frequency of respondents with an R-R pattern of family preference sharply declines, falling from 84 per cent to 11 per cent, while that of respondents with a D-D family background gradually increases, rising from 6 to 57 per cent. The more unstable the voter, in short, the greater the probability that his family has either shifted its past support from one party to the other or has consistently favored the opposition party. The data in the "Conflicted" column also suggest once again that stability among Democrats may be less dependent than Republican stability upon appropriate family influences.

Comparable inferences can be drawn from the data on family "reinforcement"—a term which has reference to the *strength* with which the family has, over the years, reinforced its initial political indoctrination. As can be seen from Table III, party regularity is significantly affected by the strength of reinforcement a voter receives from his family. If his family has been united and steadfast in its support, exhibiting the characteristics of a dependable, homogeneous, and politically aware reference group, he is far more likely to turn out a stable voter than if any or all of these conditions are absent. On a six-point stability measure in which a high score of 6.0 signifies stable support for the parents' party and a low score of 1.0 represents stable support for the opposition party, the strongly reinforced voters have a mean stability score of 4.77 while the weakly reinforced have a score of 3.89. Examination of the distributions and percentages in Table III will show these relationships in greater detail.

TABLE III. VOTER STABILITY AND STRENGTH OF FAMILY REINFORCEMENT
(DEMOCRATS AND REPUBLICANS COMBINED)

| | Family Reinforcement | | |
Respondents' Stability	Strong	Moderate (%'s Down)	Weak
6 Stable Voters—Support Family Party	40.7	45.1	20.0
5 Moderate Voters— " " "	27.1	21.6	25.7
4 Unstable Voters— " " "	13.6	13.7	8.6
3 Unstable Voters—Reject Family Party	8.4	9.8	22.9
2 Moderate Voters— " " "	6.8	2.0	14.3
1 Stable Voter— " " "	3.4	7.8	8.6
Sample Size	59	51	35
Mean Stability Score	4.77	4.75	3.89

Findings from small group research also lead one to expect that reinforcement (and hence family influence) will be greater when its members like one another and are able to see each other often. A voter who is psychologically or physically cut off from his family should be less influenced than one who is frequently exposed to his family and hopes to win or keep its affection. To test this hypothesis a measure was developed for the purpose of classifying respondents into those who satisfy the conditions of high "solidarity" and low "physical distance" (the "favorable" condition) versus those who fail to meet either or both these requirements (the "unfavorable" condition). Comparison of the two groups is presented in Table IV and shows that the hypothesis is strongly supported. Frequent exposure to one's primary family and affection for its members thus have a substantial impact on the nature and stability of party loyalties. Voters who become alienated or separated from their families tend either to renounce its initial political affiliations entirely or to retain them more tenuously. Among voters who share the family's political attachments, 58 per cent of those in the favorable condition, but only 32 per cent in the unfavorable condition, are stable party supporters.

Comparison of voters in the favorable and unfavorable conditions who have *discarded* their family preferences yields similar results, but, as our hypothesis would anticipate, in inverted form, *i.e.,* for such voters family

TABLE IV.   VOTER STABILITY AND FAMILY REINFORCEMENT, UNDER CONDITIONS
"FAVORABLE" AND "UNFAVORABLE" TO REINFORCEMENT
(DEMOCRATS AND REPUBLICANS COMBINED)

Respondents are	Respondents in the "Favorable" Condition Who Support:		Respondents in the "Unfavorable" Condition Who Support:	
	Same Party as Family	Different Party from Family	Same Party as Family	Different Party from Family
	(%'s Down)		(%'s Down)	
Stable Voters	58.1	23.8	32.3	25.0
Moderate Voters	28.4	19.1	44.1	37.5
Unstable Voters	13.5	57.1	23.6	37.5
Sample Size	74	21	34	16

propinquity and solidarity serve to weaken rather than to strengthen party regularity. Among voters who have renounced the family preferences, 57 per cent in the favorable condition, but 37.5 per cent in the unfavorable condition, are unstable. Family solidarity and interaction can thus either strengthen or weaken stability, depending on whether one shares or rejects the family preferences. The stronger the attachment to the family, the greater its influence and the more difficult it becomes to hold firmly to views of which it does not approve. . . .

V. SPOUSE AND FRIENDSHIP GROUP INFLUENCE

Further warranty for some of the foregoing inferences about primary groups can be gained from the data on the spouse and peer groups of our respondents. We find, for example, that a large number (84 per cent) of our married respondents have the same party loyalties as their mates, and that voters who agree with their partners' preferences are considerably more stable (51 per cent of these are stable and 21 per cent unstable; among voters who disagree with their mates, only 14 per cent are stable and 57 per cent are unstable). The spouse also plays an important part in reinforcing the political orientation earlier instilled by a voter's parents. When both the spouse and parents favor the same party, the chances are overwhelming (93 per cent) that a voter will also favor that party; when, however, their political outlooks are diverse, the probability that a voter will remain loyal to his parents' party falls to only 28 per cent.

Conflict between one's parental and acquired families also has a marked effect on the stability of voting, reducing it severely (Table V). The stronger the political interest and preference of the spouse, moreover, the

TABLE V. INFLUENCE OF SPOUSE'S PARTY PREFERENCE ON VOTER STABILITY*

	Family Background is Republican			Family Background is Democratic			Family Background— Combined Samples		
	Spouse's Preference Is:			Spouse's Preference Is:			Spouse's Preference Is:		
	Strongly or Moderately Repub.	Neutral or Weak	Strongly or Moderately Dem.	Strongly or Moderately Dem.	Neutral or Weak	Strongly or Moderately Repub.	Same as Family's —Strong or Moderate	Neutral or Weak	Different from Family's —Strong or Moderate
Respondent's Mean Stability Scores:	5.35	4.00	2.60	5.38	4.50	2.50	5.36	4.20	2.60
Sample Size:	28	15	19	21	12	13	49	27	32

* The measure of spouse's strength of party preference is an index comprised of data on the spouse's level of political interest; frequency of voting; frequency of political discussion; intensity of party feeling; and direction of party preference. The Mean Stability Scores are computed, as before, on the 6 point scale previously described.

greater his or her influence on the respondent's party loyalties. But this influence can work both ways—to increase stability when husband and wife agree in their party attitudes, or to decrease it severely when they disagree. The magnitude of this influence is doubtless a function of the frequency of interactions between husband and wife, and of the solidarity ordinarily achieved by primary groups of this type. As anticipated, there was a tendency for women to switch to their husbands' preferences more often than the reverse. However, our sample of "switchers" was too small to place much confidence in this conclusion.

It should also be noted from Table V that, when family background is taken into account, no difference is found between the stability of voters who marry Democrats and those who marry Republicans. A respondent from a Democratic family who marries a Republican is badly shaken in his voting habits, but no more so, apparently, than a voter from a Republican family who marries a Democrat.

Data on the friends named by our respondents, including friends at work, at church, in neighborhoods, clubs, and other social activities, furnish additional proof of the crucial role which primary groups play in stabilizing political loyalties. As Table VI demonstrates unmistakably, the higher the proportion of friends who support a voter's party, the more stable his preferences: as one reads downward in the left-hand columns, from the Stable Republicans through the moderate and unstable voters to the Stable Democrats, the frequency of Republican peers steadily declines (from 60.8

TABLE VI. RELATION BETWEEN STABILITY OF VOTING PREFERENCE AND
PROPORTION OF DEMOCRATIC AND REPUBLICAN PEERS*

Respondents are: ↓	Total Sample		Voters from Republican Family Backgrounds		Voters from Democratic Family Backgrounds	
	Proportion of Peers who are:		Proportion of Peers who are:		Proportion of Peers who are:	
	Reps	Dems	Reps	Dems	Reps	Dems
	%	%	%	%	%	%
Stable Republicans	60.8	21.2	59.2	20.8	75.0	15.0
Moderate Republicans	43.8	21.6	47.6	21.8	50.0	26.6
Unstable Republicans	36.6	26.0	34.0	24.0	44.6	28.2
Unstable Democrats	27.4	29.2	30.0	36.6	21.4	24.2
Moderate Democrats	23.4	50.6	30.0	52.8	24.6	48.6
Stable Democrats	18.8	53.8	22.0	54.0	18.2	51.4
Sample Size	193		81		70	

* The proportions of peers named whose party preferences were unknown to the respondents have been omitted from this table. In every case, however, it would be the percentage remaining after substracting the proportion of Republican and Democratic peers from 100 per cent: *e.g.*, for the Stable Republicans in the total sample, the party preference of 18.0 per cent of the peers is unknown; for the Unstable Republicans, the proportion is 37.4 per cent.

per cent to 18.8 per cent) while the proportion of Democratic peers uniformly rises (from 21.2 per cent to 53.8 per cent). Whereas stable voters have the highest proportion of peers who share their preferences, the unstable voters draw their friends almost equally from both parties and are subject, therefore, to greater cross-pressure. But they are also politically less aware, they select their friends with less regard for political belief, and they know least about the actual affiliations of their friends; they were unable, for example, to identify the party preferences of 38.6 per cent of their friends, while the comparable figure for the Moderates was 30.2 per cent and for the Stables 23.4 per cent. Whether out of anxiety or apathy, the Unstables seem somewhat more inclined to avoid friendships with people who reveal strong political convictions—a practice which tends to prolong their own instability.

Controlling for family background does not alter the nature or direction of these findings in any important way. Stability, as anticipated, is greatest when the loyalties of one's peers predominantly correspond with (and thus reinforce) the political outlook of one's family. However, when the majority of a voter's peers do *not* support the party favored by his family, the conditional probability is high (over 80 per cent) that he will abandon the family's voting tradition and shift his support to the opposition. Approximately one-third of these "shifters" become stable opposition supporters

The rather impressive power exerted by friends on voting behavior does not mean that they have entirely displaced the family, as a source of influence. In Table VII, we hold friendship preferences constant and vary family background, and find the family continues under all conditions to register an impact upon the preference and stability of the offspring. As the figures show, Republican voters from Republican families are proportionately more stable than voters from Democratic families, even when the latter have as many Republican friends as the former. The same relationships hold for the Democrats when we control for the number of Democratic friends.

TABLE VII. FAMILY INFLUENCE UPON VOTER STABILITY WHEN FREQUENCY OF REPUBLICAN AND DEMOCRATIC FRIENDS IS CONTROLLED

	Percentage of Stable Republican Voters:			*Percentage of Stable Democratic Voters:*	
Proportion of Republican Friends ↓	*From Republican Families*	*From Democratic Families*	*Proportion of Democratic Friends* ↓	*From Democratic Families*	*From Republican Families*
	%	%		%	%
Under 20%	25.0	0.00	Under 20%	25.0	0.00
21%–60%	41.6	0.00	21%–60%	57.7	46.1
61%–100%	69.6	50.0	61%–100%	66.6	44.1
Total Repub. sample	76		Total Dem. sample	75	

In considering the relative influence of family and friends, furthermore, we should keep in mind that the connection between stability and the party preferences of one's peers is not the simple, unilateral relation it may appear at first to be. Cause and effect in this matter are not always easy to distinguish. Our choice of friends is, in some measure at least, governed by our political views, and these in turn have largely been predetermined by our families. Since our families also help to fix our levels of party loyalty, they are indirectly responsible, in part, for the high correlation between voting stability and the party affiliation of friends. Unfortunately, the magnitude of such indirect family influence cannot be assessed and demonstrated in studies of the type we are now considering. Its importance, nevertheless, can safely be assumed.

The data on friendship groups, it should be observed, show no significant or systematic differences in the strength of the influence exerted by Democratic or Republican peers. The correlation between voters stability and the proportion of peers with congruent preferences is .40 (sig. > .001)

for the Republican respondents and .37 (sig.>.01) for the Democratic respondents.

VI. PRIMARY GROUP INFLUENCES COMBINED

So far we have seen that each type of primary group registers its own separate impact on our political loyalties. What happens, however, when they are combined? Our theory suggests that their influence ought to be cumulative, becoming stronger (or weaker) as favorable (or antagonistic) units of reinforcement are added. Warranty for these expectations may be found in Table VIII where combined data are presented for four of the more important variables employed in the study: family reinforcement, social distance, spouse's preference, and peer group influence. Each time one of these factors supported a respondent's party preference, he was assigned a plus (+) score for that variable; each time a variable was in conflict with his preference, he was given a minus (−) score.

It should first of all be noted that group affiliations tend to be mutually reinforcing. When the total number of "reinforcements" were tallied for all respondents, 64 per cent were found to be favorable (+), 24 per cent

TABLE VIII. THE COMBINED EFFECT OF FOUR PRIMARY GROUP INFLUENCES (FAMILY REINFORCEMENT, SOCIAL DISTANCE, SPOUSE, AND PEER GROUPS) ON VOTER STABILITY

Respondents are:	Number of Favorable (+) Reinforcements*			(%'s Down)
	1+	2+'s	3+'s	4+'s
Stable Voters	17.6	35.7	58.1	70.5
Moderate Voters	17.6	32.1	27.9	23.5
Unstable Voters	64.7	32.1	13.9	5.9
Sample Size	17	28	43	17

	Number of Favorable(+) Reinforcements			Voters Who Support Initial Family Preference			Voters Who have Switched from Initial Family Preference		
				Number of Favorable(+) Reinforcements					
	1 or 2 +'s	3 or 4 +'s	(N)	1 or 2 +'s	3 or 4 +'s	(N)	1 or 2 +'s	3 or 4 +'s	(N)
Respondents are: ↓	(%'s Across)			(%'s Across)			(%'s Across)		
Stable Voters	26.0	74.0	(50)	18.9	81.0	(37)	46.1	53.8	(13)
Moderate Voters	42.9	57.1	(28)	36.9	63.1	(19)	66.7	33.3	(6)
Unstable Voters	74.1	25.9	(27)	66.7	33.3	(12)	78.6	21.4	(14)

* Favorable or (+) association with a primary group whose party loyalties are congruent with those of the respondent.

were negative (−), and 12 per cent were neutral. Regular party supporters, however, have experienced a significantly greater proportion of positive reinforcements than unstable supporters, the figures being 82 per cent for the former and 54 per cent for the latter.

Examination of Table IX shows that 74 per cent of the Stables have been exposed to three or more positive reinforcements (out of a possible four), while only 25.9 per cent of the Unstables have been so consistently reinforced. When we compute the percentages vertically, the degree to which stability depends upon the frequency and homogeneity of primary group support becomes, if anything, even more obvious. The probability that a voter will be stable if all his reinforcements are favorable is 70.5 per cent; it declines sharply, however, as the number of his positive scores diminishes—dropping from 70 to 58 to 35 and finally to 17 per cent. Similarly, if all four group reinforcements are favorable, the probability is small (only 5.9 per cent) that a voter will become unstable, whereas it is quite high (64.7 per cent) if only one of the four reinforcements is favorable. Clearly, party loyalty strongly depends upon the ratio of favorable to unfavorable primary group supports.

Controlling for initial family background modifies these results only in detail, for stability rises as reinforcements increase, no matter what political outlook voters have received from their families. Nevertheless, a voter who does not follow his family's preference is less likely to be stable than a voter who does, even when both have been subjected to the same number of subsequent group pressures. The impact of the family's initial indoctrination persists, in short, even if it does not always result in retention of the parents' party.

Correlations were computed which summarize and elaborate these findings somewhat. The simple correlation between family reinforcement and the level of respondent's stability is, to begin with, .27 (sig. .01). If we add social distance and compute a multiple correlation, the figure rises to .41, with similar correlations for Republican and Democratic respondents. When spouse and peer group variables are added, the multiple correlation rises again, this time to .49. Had we also been able to take account of family solidarity and propinquity (which unfortunately we could not, owing to complications involving the small size of the N), these correlations would doubtless be even higher, since family influence is increased, as we have seen, when physical and psychological "distance" are favorable to reinforcement.

VII. SUMMARY AND CONCLUSIONS

The data presented in this paper largely confirm the hypotheses with which the project began and furnish additional support for some of the inferences about primary groups suggested by the Elmira study, the Maccoby study, and others. The findings make it plain that the indoctrination, retention, or shift of party loyalties is significantly related to, and often determined by, family and other primary bonds. Of course, our results do not explain stable or shifting patterns of support in *particular* elections, for these, as Key and Munger correctly point out, require explanations that are more immediately *political, i.e.,* that chiefly take account of issues, candidates, or changing political conditions. What the findings do show, however, is that voters differ widely in their susceptibility to political influence, and that their tendencies to shift or remain stable in response to such influence will vitally depend upon the strength and homogeneity of their primary group affiliations.

Specifically, the following inferences seem warranted from our data:

1. The family is a key reference group which transmits, indoctrinates, and sustains the political loyalties of its members. Voters who support the party favored by their families develop firmer and more consistent habits of party allegiance than voters who renounce the family preference.

2. Family influence on the stability of a voter's preference increases when (a) the party outlooks of its members are homogeneous; (b) political interest and loyalty among the other members are high (this affects direction of preference more than stability, however); and (c) the same family preference has been retained over time. Family influence on party allegiance becomes stronger, in addition, when its members like and often see each other; however, these factors undermine the party loyalty of voters who have rejected the family preference. The family thus serves as a continuing agency for defining the party affiliations of its members. . . .

3. Unless they embody a party viewpoint or life-style that conflicts with the family's outlook, primary groups other than the parental family, such as spouse and peer group associates, operate to reinforce the party loyalties a voter acquires from his family. The more widespread the agreement among them, and the more intense their outlook, the more stable his own party allegiance. Compared with party regulars, unstable voters are less often able to identify the political affiliations of their friends.

4. Disagreements among the several primary groups to which a voter belongs are among the most important sources of party irregularity and defection. Most voters, however, are anchored in a matrix of politically harmonious primary associations—a result, to some extent, of conscious selection and of the tendency for the social environment to bring together people of like views.

5. Democrats and Republicans were observed to differ somewhat in their response to family and other primary group influences, but the differences were neither large nor systematic enough to warrant firm generaliza-

tion. If family political background is allowed to vary freely, Republican voters appear to conform more strongly than Democrats to family influence. They also appear to be less affected by changes in life-style or social mobility—a result consistent with the findings reported by the Elmira study, by Maccoby, and others. These inferences, which imply the greater tenacity of Republican loyalties, are misleading, however, for they overlook the consideration that some of our Republicans and Democrats were initially indoctrinated by families of a contrary political persuasion. When we took this into account and controlled for family party preference, the differences between Democratic and Republican voters either disappeared or reversed themselves: Democrats from Democratic families and Republicans from Republican families proved to be equally stable; while Democrats from Republican family backgrounds turned out, on the average, to be somewhat more stable than Republicans from Democratic backgrounds. Voters whose origins were Democratic, in short, appear more resistant to conversion than voters from Republican backgrounds. These findings could mean either that Democratic families leave a more enduring imprint on the politics of their members or—a more plausible explanation—that the balance of non-family forces in the Twin City community favored the Democrats. On this explanation, the apparently greater tenacity of Democratic family influence would be largely an artifact of our measurement procedures, and would arise from our inability to assess independently other important influences in the community. In any event, the belief that Republicanism is the more magnetic and enduring preference, owing to the higher status of its more visible supporters and its symbolic identification with the middle and upper classes, is not substantiated in our data. The Republican party does tend, on the whole, to be the party of status, but it is not always the preferred or prestige party. Especially since the New Deal, with its strong impact on political affiliation and perceptions, the advantage of being the prestige party belongs, in many communities, to the Democrats.

6. Reference to the role of the community environment underscores the need to observe that primary group memberships cannot, by themselves, account for all the variance in political belief and affiliation, and that other influences, such as economic interest, status needs, the mass media, the behavior of the parties themselves, etc., will often have to be considered. We should also enter the qualification that, having dealt in this research largely with party affiliations, we cannot be certain that the results can be generalized to all forms of political attachment. We have, nevertheless, proceeded on the assumption that the several forms of political support are sufficiently alike so that knowledge gained from the study of party affiliation will prove useful in the investigation of other forms of political loyalty.

The Supreme Court as a Small Group

ELOISE SNYDER

INTRODUCTION

The Supreme Court as a political and social force and as a collection of great individual justices has long been a topic of scholarly research. More recently analyses of the Supreme Court have been made by Jessie Bernard and C. Herman Pritchett. The present study is analytical but differs from preceding studies in that it deals with the Supreme Court as a small group and attempts to discover what group processes are present as the justices solve the important problems brought before them. Specifically, this study attempts to determine whether or not the Supreme Court, a small group charged with the important duty of national decision-making, becomes divided into subgroups or cliques of justices. If cliques of justices are found to be in existence, the present study is concerned with how changes in group alignments occur, how the court "ingests" or assimilates new members, and how new members find their position in the group.

Since the Supreme Court is virtually a battleground for every important social conflict, acting as judge not only of the citizens but of the government itself, the analysis of the Court as a small group would appear to be significant.

METHODOLOGY

In this study the nine justices, who composed the Supreme Court for whatever period of time they existed as a stable, unchanging body, were conceived of as constituting a small group. Each time one of the justices was replaced, due to either death or retirement, a new group was conceived of as being initiated. Therefore, rather than analyzing the data in terms of a specific year such as the 1949 or the 1950 Court, in this study they were analyzed in terms of groups of justices. Thus the court from 1949 to 1953 was viewed as a single small group since the same justices composed the Supreme Court for this period of time.

The method used to determine whether or not the Supreme Court contains cliques of justices was based upon the responses of the justices to the cases heard by them during their stays with the Supreme Court. A clique was considered to be in existence when a group of two or more jus-

Reprinted from *Social Forces,* vol. 36 (March 1958), pp. 232–38 by permission of the author and publisher.

tices consistently tended to respond together in opposition to the other members of the court.

Data for the present study were gathered from volumes 257 to 346 inclusive, of the United States Reports, published by the United States Government Printing Office, in Washington, D.C. The data included the responses of the justices to all cases heard by the Supreme Court from 1921 to 1953 involving one or more of the Amendments to the Constitution of the United States. Over this period approximately 1,148 amendment cases were decided by the Court, presenting approximately 10,332 individual opinions to be analyzed.

These 10,332 individual opinions were the resultants of the extensive considerations given by the justices to the cases argued before the court. For each justice this involved both listening to a detailed case presentation and then attending a session which was held exclusively for the justices. The purpose of this "closed" session is to permit a "thrashing-out" of the various facets of the case in an attempt to reconcile any conflicting points of view held by the justices. At the conclusion of this session each justice presented his final opinion regarding the case under consideration and the decision of the case was based on a majority opinion agreed upon by five or more of the nine justices. In this study opinions were grouped according to the individual justices who rendered them and were classified on the basis of consensus (agreement) with or dissent (disagreement) from the majority decision of the court. A consensus opinion was defined as one in which the justices responded in any of the following ways:

1. *Joined with the majority decision;*
2. *Agreed with the majority decision but without a separate opinion;*
3. *Agreed with the majority decision but with a separate opinion, showing that although a different line of reasoning was employed, the decision was the same.*

A dissenting opinion was defined as one in which the justice responded in either of the following ways:

1. *Dissented from the majority decision without a separate opinion;*
2. *Dissented from the majority decision with a separate opinion.*

Cases in which a justice neither dissented nor concurred, had no opinion, did not participate, or, in a complex case, dissented on one point and concurred on another, were considered to be neutral and classified as such.

As previously stated a clique herein is defined as a group consisting of two or more justices who tended to respond consistently together, that is concur or dissent, in opposition to the other members of the court.

A new justice was considered as such from the time he presented his first opinion to the court until another justice, newer than he, presented his first opinion.

The above grouping of opinions and classification according to consensus or dissent constituted the basis of analysis used in determining some of the group behaviors reflected by the Supreme Court from 1921 to 1953.

RESULTS

CLIQUES. The Supreme Court of the United States showed more agreement than disagreement in deciding the cases brought before it; however, when disagreement did occur, it consistently was displayed in given patterns of dissent by justices who tended to respond together to the exclusion of the other members of the court. These groupings of justices are herein viewed as constituting clique formations and the Supreme Court was found to contain some three cliques of justices. The first is here called "clique A" and the second, "clique B." Although these two cliques agreed on many decisions, when disagreement was displayed, these two cliques usually were in opposition. The third clique apparently did not have as fixed a point of view as either clique A or B, because this third clique acted in a pivotal manner, voting on some occasions with clique A, and on others with clique B. This clique is therefore called the "pivotal clique." A listing of the specific justices composing each of the cliques is presented in Table I.

CLIQUE FUNCTION. On the basis of the content of the opinions rendered by the cliques with respect to specific cases, it would have been acceptable twenty-five years ago to refer to clique A as the more "liberal" clique and to clique B as the more "conservative." However, since that time the implication of these terms has changed considerably, and thus, in order to eliminate difficulties of interpretation, these terms are operationally defined as follows:

Liberal: a state of *readiness* to accept "new" constitutional interpretations.

Conservative: A state of *reluctance* to accept "new" constitutional interpretations.

Thus, the clique A point of view tended to be the more dynamic and changing ideology, while the point of view of clique B tended to be more static and, to a great extent, the resistor of new ideology. In this sense, clique A functioned in such a manner as to facilitate the newer legislation, while clique B tended to act as a brake on current legislation. Here then are two opposing forces—one, using all of its power to pull ahead into newer judicial interpretations and the other, using all of its power to constrain and pull back from these new judicial interpretations.

PIVOTAL CLIQUE: A DECISIVE FACTOR. In this ideological tug of war, cliques A and B frequently tended to cancel each other's power. This increased the effect of the power of the pivotal clique, for what generally occurred was that the pivotal clique, by adding its weight to one of the other of the two opposing cliques, was able to break this ideological stalemate and give victory to that clique with which it aligned. Thus it is apparent that since the two cliques tended to commit themselves to mutually opposing points of view, the pivotal clique held the potentiality of determining the victor. Therefore, of the three cliques the pivotal clique was considered to have had the greatest amount of effective power.

CLIQUES AND POLITICS. It has often been feared that political affiliation might constitute a dangerous bias in this, the highest tribunal of the United States. However, the results of this study tend to dispel this fear, for there appeared to be no relationship between the membership of a clique and the political affiliation of the presidents who appointed the justices. It was noted, for example, that the well-known combination of Justices Holmes and Brandeis, who for a number of years were both members of clique A, reflects Republican and Democratic appointments, respectively. This fear is further disproved by the fact that, although the Supreme Court from 1946 to 1953 consisted of justices all of whom were appointed by Democratic presidents, the three cliques still were found to be very much in evidence.

CLIQUES AND PRESIDENTS. In 1937, President Franklin D. Roosevelt asked for authority to increase the number of judges in the Supreme Court. It was feared that this would enable Roosevelt to "pack" the court with men whose ideologies tended most to favor Roosevelt's own ideology and thus bias this important judicial body. However, in this study it was found that very little relationship existed between the cliques of justices and the particular ideologies of the appointing presidents. For example, Justices Brandeis, McReynolds, and Clarke were all appointed by President Wood row Wilson, yet Brandeis was more or less consistently found in clique A, McReynolds in clique B, and Clarke in the pivotal clique. Further, since 1940, when the Roosevelt appointees numerically predominated in the Supreme Court, at no time did they, as a group, tend to be members of any one clique. It is noted in Table I that, from 1940 to 1943, the Roosevelt appointees were found in two separate cliques, namely, the pivotal clique and clique A, and from 1943 to 1953, they were found to be members of all three cliques.

Therefore, although there were cliques of justices in the Supreme Court, these cliques apparently were not biased by the specific president appointing the justices. This, at least to some degree, would appear to dispel the fear that the appointment of a majority of the justices to the Supreme Court by one specific president would bias this high tribunal.

CLIQUE MEMBERSHIP. Since cliques of justices were found to exist in the Supreme Court, it is now the concern of this study to attempt to discern how changes in group alignments occur. It was observed that some justices, such as Justices Pitney, Taft, and Sanford, were more or less consistent members of the pivotal clique, while others were found in clique A or B during most of their terms on the bench. Justice Black, for example, was a member of clique A from 1938 to 1953 with the exception of 1945 to 1946, when he was a member of the pivotal clique. This implies that Justice Black, along with Justices Holmes, Douglas, Murphy, and Rutledge, who also displayed this type of alignment, was a relatively consistent member of that clique which sought to explore newer judicial interpretations. Justice McReynolds, on the other hand, from the time of the first group of justices covered in this study, which was in 1921, until he left the bench in 1941, was consistently found in clique B, with the exception of two occasions, namely in 1922-1923 and in 1925-1930 when he was found in the pivotal clique. This implies that Justice McReynolds, along with Justices Sutherland, Butler, and Burton, who also displayed this type of alignment, was a relatively consistent member of that clique which sought to act as a brake on the exploration of newer judicial interpretations.

Most justices were relatively consistent members of a specific clique. When a change in clique membership did occur it did not tend to be radical, for it is cited in Table I that most change was from the liberal or conservative cliques (i.e. A or B) to the pivotal clique, or vice versa, and not from the liberal clique directly to the conservative (i.e. A to B) or vice versa. In fact, in the 32 years covered by the study, only two radical changes in clique membership were noted. The one occurred when Justice Frankfurter, who in 1943-45 was a clique B member, directly moved to clique A in 1945-46. The second occurred when Justice Jackson, who in 1946-1949 was a member of clique B, moved directly to clique A in 1949-1953. These two justices, namely Frankfurter and Jackson, were the only justices who made such radical changes in group alignment.

Justices Frankfurter and Jackson were also found to be exceptional in two other respects. First, these two justices displayed the maximum amount of repeated clique fluctuation, and secondly, they represented the only

TABLE I. CLIQUE LISTINGS FOR EACH GROUP OF
JUSTICES FROM 1921 TO 1953*

Group	Clique A	Pivotal Clique	Clique B
1921–22	Holmes (R), Brandeis (D), McKenna (R)	Pitney (R), Clarke (D), Day (R), Taft (R)	Van Devanter (R), McReynolds (D)
1922–23	Brandeis (D)	Holmes (R), Van Devanter (R), Taft (R), McReynolds (D), *Sutherland (R)*, *McKenna (R)*, Pitney (R), Day (R)	
1923–25	Holmes (R), Brandeis (D)	Van Devanter (R), Taft (R), McKenna (R), *Sanford (R)*, *Butler (R)*	McReynolds (D), Sutherland (R)
1925–30	Brandeis (D), Holmes (R), Stone (R)	Sanford (R), McReynolds (D), Van Devanter (R), Taft (R)	Sutherland (R), Butler (R)
1930–32	Brandeis (D), Holmes (R), Stone (R)	*Roberts (R)*, *Hughes (R)*	Van Devanter (R), Butler (R), Sutherland (R), McReynolds (D)
1932–37	Brandeis (D), Stone (R), *Cardozo (R)*	Roberts (R), Hughes (R)	Van Devanter (R), Butler (R), Sutherland (R), McReynolds (D)
1937–38		Brandeis (D), Cardozo (R), Stone (R), Hughes (R), *Black (D)*	Roberts (R), Sutherland (R), McReynolds (D), Butler (R)
1938–39	Black (D)	Brandeis (D), Cardozo (R), Stone (R), Hughes (R), *Reed (D)*, Roberts (R)	Butler (R), McReynolds (D)
1939–39	Black (D), *Frankfurter (D)*	Brandeis (D), Stone (R), Hughes (R), Reed (D), Roberts (R)	Butler (R), McReynolds (D)
1939–40	Black (D)	Reed (D), Frankfurter (D), Stone (R), *Douglas (D)*	Hughes (R), McReynolds (D), Roberts (R), Butler (R)
1940–41	Black (D), Douglas (D), Murphy (D)	Stone (R), Frankfurter (D), Reed (D)	Hughes (R), Roberts (R), McReynolds (D)
1941–43	Black (D), Douglas (D), Murphy (D)	Reed (D), Frankfurter (D), Stone (R), *Byrnes (D)*, *Jackson (D)*	Roberts (R)
1943–45	Black (D), Douglas (D), Murphy (D), *Rutledge (D)*	Stone (R), Reed (D)	Jackson (D), Frankfurter (D), Roberts (R)

(Continued on next page)

TABLE I. CLIQUE LISTINGS FOR EACH GROUP OF
JUSTICES FROM 1921 TO 1953*   (CONTINUED)

Group	Clique A	Pivotal Clique	Clique B
1945–46	Murphy (D), Rutledge (D), Frankfurter (D)	Black (D), Douglas (D), Jackson (D)	Reed (D), Stone (R), Burton (D)
1946–49	Murphy (D), Rutledge (D), Douglas (D), Black (D)	Frankfurter (D)	Jackson (D), *Vinson (D)*, Reed (D), Burton (D)
1949–53	Black (D), Douglas (D), Frankfurter (D), Jackson (D)	Burton (D), *Clark (D)*, Vinson (D)	Minton (D), Reed (D)

*In this table, when the name of a justice appears in italics it means that he was a newly appointed justice on that court. The symbol (R) or (D) after the name of each justice means that he was appointed by a Republican or Democratic president, respectively.

changes in coalition membership which ran from clique B to clique A. This is to say that the direction of clique change generally was from clique A to clique B, that is from the more liberal to the more conservative clique, although it is important to note that when these changes did occur, in each case the justice spent an intervening period as a member of the pivotal clique prior to becoming a member of clique B. This seems to indicate that it apparently was easier for a justice to change from the liberal clique toward the conservative clique and relatively impossible to join the liberal ranks having once been a conservative.

These alignment changes from clique A toward clique B were exemplified by several justices such as Justice Brandeis who had been a clique A member for 16 years when he changed to pivotal clique membership for the remaining two years on the bench and also for Justice Hughes who had been a member of the pivotal clique for the first nine years of his term when he changed to clique B for the remaining two years of his term. Justice Reed also reflected this tendency. He, after seven years as a member of the pivotal clique, switched to clique B for the next eight years at which period this study concluded with Justice Reed still in clique B. Justice Stone probably presents the most pertinent example of this type of clique membership change, for Justice Stone began as a clique A member but after 12 years of membership, he joined the pivotal clique. However, he did not stop here, for after eight years in the pivotal clique, Justice Stone then moved on to clique B, where he remained for his final year with the Court.

This raises the serious question of why was it apparently easier for a justice to change from the liberal toward the conservative clique rather than vice versa? It may be that there is a tendency for one's viewpoint to become more conservative as one grows older. However, this was not found to be the case in this study for the justices' points of view, per se, reflected little change. Rather, the Supreme Court itself, as a collective body of justices, was found to reflect a highly dynamic conceptual framework. It appears that, with progressive changes in the personnel of the Court, the conceptual framework of this body changed so much that an opinion which was once considered a clique A point of view, without changing, suddenly was found to be a neutral or even a clique B point of view. This implies that an opinion which was considered "liberal" in 1930, might well have been considered "conservative" in 1945. In this sense, it appears that Justice Brandeis, without altering his views, became automatically realigned with the pivotal clique rather than with the liberal clique on the basis of the dynamics of the group itself. It is also conceivable that this dynamic element was so forceful by the 1945-1946 court that the responses of Justice Stone, previously a clique A member, were suddenly too conservative even for the pivotal clique and rather more consistent with clique B responses.

It was noted, however, that some justices did not find it necessary to give up their clique A membership, for such justices as Black and Douglas were relatively consistent clique A members along with Justices Murphy and Rutledge who never joined any other clique. This would seem to indicate that these justices were able to alter their views at the same rate of speed as the changing views of the Court itself, and thus by keeping pace with the Court's changing conceptual framework they were able to remain the liberal clique.

Having examined some of the group processes evident in the Supreme Court, it is now the concern of this study to examine how the Supreme Court assimilates new members and how these new members find their places in this already established and functioning group.

THE NEWLY APPOINTED JUSTICES. As previously stated, a justice was considered new from the time he presented his first opinion in the Court, until another justice, newer than he, presented his first opinion. There were 19 newly appointed justices on the courts covered by this study. Five of these new justices initiated their terms by aligning with clique A and three with clique B. The remaining 11 justices, however, aligned with the pivotal clique. This tendency for the newly appointed justice to initiate his term in the pivotal clique may have resulted from any or all of the following factors:

First, it may have been that the new justice, entering this already established body, lacked the assurance necessary to defend an extreme stand in constitutional interpretation and therefore found it more comfortable to respond as a member of that clique which reflected the more neutral point of view. It is true that some justices had previous judicial experience, but many did not. And in respect to those who had, few had ever served on a court of such high national esteem. In this respect it is not altogether inconceivable that the new justice to some degree might have experienced a lack of assurance and thus responded in a neutral manner.

Secondly, it may have been that the new justice entering this notable group of men was not immediately able to attain an "in-group" feeling, and, therefore, feeling like a "somewhat lesser member," he may have remained neutral rather than show any consistent identification with either of the two already established cliques.

Thirdly, it may have been that the new justice entered the Court without a fixed liberal or conservative point of view and thus was afforded the luxury of flexibility—that is, identifying on some occasions with clique A and on others with clique B.

Whatever the underlying factor, the new members of the Supreme Court were assimilated into the Court as members of the pivotal clique. This is important to the extent that it suggests that the men with the least amount of experience in the Supreme Court immediately tended to become members of that clique which, as has previously been pointed out, frequently held the potentiality of determining the victor, and, therefore, was viewed as having the greatest amount of effective power. This is clearly shown since the new justices apparently did not find it necessary to dissent as frequently as the older justices. In fact, the average number of dissents for the newly appointed justices was only 4.8 as compared with 7.3 for the older justices.

It was further noted that, although the new justices started their terms in the court by aligning with the pivotal clique, most of them, after a period of time, became members of clique A or clique B. Thus, after acquiring experience, these men tended to align with a clique which, as previously stated, was found to have a lesser amount of effective power.

In this respect it was noted that Justices Sutherland, Butler, and Roberts, after starting as pivotal clique members, finally joined clique B, while justices Black and Douglas joined clique A. Justice Jackson also began as a pivotal clique member and finally aligned with clique B and clique A at different times.

This tendency for a newly appointed justice to align with clique A or B after initiating his term with the Court as pivotal clique member may have reflected any or all of the following processes:

First, it may have been that, after gaining some experience with this, the highest decision-making body in the United States, the justice finally acquired an assurance which enable him to "take a stand" with one of the two cliques which reflected a more extreme point of view.

Secondly, it may have been that after functioning for a period of time with this notable group of men, the new justice finally identified with one of the two opposing cliques on the basis of personalities involved. In effect, he may have been influenced by a certain personality which tended to mold his thinking and thus enable him to align with that clique.

Thirdly, it may have been that the experience of functioning with the Supreme Court itself created in the justice an unassailable point of view so that the new justice ultimately may have found himself unable to respond in a manner which might have suggested a neutral point of view.

Whatever the underlying principles, the fact remains that the newly appointed justice tended to be "ingested" by the Supreme Court through the pivotal clique and then, after a period of functioning with the Court, found his place in the group by joining one of the two opposing cliques.

SUMMARY

This study was undertaken in an attempt to examine the Supreme Court as a small group. Certain patterns of behavior were noted as follows:

The Supreme Court contained three cliques of justices. The first, called clique A, was the more "liberal" and acted in such manner as to facilitate "newer" constitutional interpretations; the second, called clique B, was the more "conservative" and acted as a brake on "newer" interpretations; the third clique reflected a middle point of view, aligning with clique A on some occasions and with clique B on others, and thus was called the pivotal clique. Since cliques A and B were opposing forces, they tended to cancel each other's power which allowed the pivotal clique to break this ideological stalemate by aligning with one of them and in this manner determine the victor. The pivotal clique, therefore, was considered to have had the greatest amount of effective coalition power.

Membership in the cliques tended to be determined by ideological principles and not by political party considerations. This tends to dispel the fears that the political affiliation of the justices or the appointment of a majority of the justices by one specific president might bias this high tribunal. Both of these hypotheses were tested and found to be unsubstantiated.

Changes in clique membership did occur but these changes did not tend to be radical. Membership change appeared to run from the more "liberal" clique A to the "neutral" pivotal clique and in some cases even progressed to the more "conservative" clique B. The majority of these changes did not reflect a change in the justices particular point of view, per se, but rather were brought about by the dynamics of the Court itself. This dynamic element within the Supreme Court resulted from the progressive additions of new justices to the Court which tended to broaden the conceptual framework of the Supreme Court as a group to the extent that what was considered to have been a liberal view in 1921 might well have been considered conservative in 1953.

The Supreme Court tended to "absorb" or assimilate new members through the pivotal clique. However, after a period of functioning with the Court, the new justice found his place in the group by joining one of the two opposing cliques. This is important in that the new "inexperienced" justice tended to be a member of the clique which had the more effective clique power but, after acquiring experience with the Court, tended to become a member of a clique which had the less effective clique power. This is clearly shown in that the new justice did not find it necessary to dissent as frequently as the older member of the Court.

This article purports only to have examined some of the group behaviors reflected by the Supreme Court. Other important considerations such as the Court's response to superior and inferior litigant types, the Court's response to the decisions of the lower courts, and the "predictability" of the Supreme Court were analyzed and are to be reported in the future.

The Analysis of Behavior Patterns in the United States Supreme Court

S. SIDNEY ULMER

Those who write about the United States Supreme Court often find it convenient to speak of "blocs" on the Court. And since Herman Pritchett's work on the Roosevelt and Vinson Courts the existence of such blocs has been common knowledge. Yet we cannot assume that the number, size, composition and cohesion tendencies of blocs of justices are constant. We can identify and speak more meaningfully about change in such characteristics if we first devise adequate methods of measurement. Moreover the term "bloc" in its general sense is one of those words with many shades of meaning. A prime requisite to the growth of any social science is the development of precision in definition and communication.

Appropriate to these goals is the modified form of factor analysis developed by McQuitty. The method seeks to identify a "typical structure"

Reprinted from *The Journal of Politics,* vol. 22 (November 1960), pp. 629–53 by permission of the publisher.

which is a structure in which "every member of a type is more like some other member of that type (with respect to the data analyzed) than he is like any member of any other type." When the members of a type have been isolated, a prototype may be defined. The prototype is a composite of the characteristics possessed by members of the type and represents the characteristics which the members possess in common. It is in short the centroid of the characteristics common to the typal members. The relevancy which each member of the type has to the centroid or prototype may be computed by the method used to extract first factor loadings in factor analysis. The loadings are extracted, however, from sub-matrices rather than from the entire matrix.

The first step is to construct a matrix of correlation coefficients expressing the relations of the variables being analyzed. Table I is such a matrix. The coefficients reflect the tendency of pairs of justices to agree or disagree in responding to civil liberty cases. A linkage analysis of this matrix establishes the existence of types or sub-matrices. The analysis consists of the following steps: First the highest coefficient in each column of the primary matrix is underlined. The highest coefficient for the entire

TABLE I. CORRELATIONS* BETWEEN THE RESPONSES OF NINE SUPREME COURT JUSTICES IN FORTY-TWO CIVIL LIBERTY CASES**
1958 TERM

	DO	BL	WA	BR	WH	FR	HA	ST	CL
DO		708	843	706	−232	−296	−313	−172	−313
BL	708		713	593	−155	−259	−223	−223	−223
WA	843	713		882	−203	−183	−183	−151	−238
BR	706	593	882		−116	−179	−183	−064	−183
WH	−232	−155	−203	−116		795	670	180	263
FR	−296	−259	−183	−180	795		1000	448	480
HA	−313	−223	−183	−183	670	1000		414	392
ST	−172	−223	−151	−064	180	448	414		053
CL	−313	−223	−238	−183	263	480	392	053	

*Using the Phi Coefficient. Decimals are dropped and figures rounded for convenience. The responses were tallied as *pro* or *con* the civil liberty claim.

**One case is omitted due to a (4–4) split.

DO — Douglas
BL — Black
WA — Warren
BR — Brennan
WH — Whittaker
FR — Frankfurter
HA — Harlan
ST — Stewart
CL — Clark

matrix is then determined and the two variables involved constitute the core of the first type. The underlined coefficients in the row of each of the two variables are then used to link additional variables to the type. These are called "first cousin" variables. The same procedure is repeated for the rows of the "first cousin" variables and if additional linkage results the additions are called "second cousin" variables. This procedure is continued until all variables of one type have been identified. When one type has been established the procedure is applied to the remaining variables and so on until all variables have been classified. In the present case two types are identified. The first is composed of Frankfurter, Harlan, Whittaker, Stewart and Clark. The second consists of Warren, Douglas, Brennan and Black.

```
          CL                              DO
           ↙                               ↘
HA ⇄ FR ← WH              BR ⇄ WA
           ↖                               ↖
          ST                              BL
```

FIGURE 1. THE TYPES

Code:

⇄ means a reciprocal pair of variables.

⟶ means that the variable at the tail of the arrow is highest with the one at the head, but the one at the head is not highest with the one at the tail.

Table I shows that each member of a bloc correlated at a higher rate with each member of his own bloc than with any justice not a member of the bloc. Figure I indicates that the highest correlation within the two blocs was respectively between Harlan and Frankfurter and Warren and Brennan. Speculation concerning leadership within the blocs is promoted by the fact that each member of a type correlated at a higher rate with either Frankfurter or Warren, as the case may be, than with any other member of his respective type. This facet of the typal relationships may be measured by the extraction of typal relevancies using the method previously mentioned. The results reported in Table II indicate that Warren and Frankfurter have more of the characteristics common to the members of the type than other justices in the respective blocs. These two justices closely approximate the prototype. If a positive relationship between possession of characteristics common to a group and influence within the group may be assumed, Warren and Frankfurter may be suspected of being "leaders" of their respective blocs. This inference would not violate prevailing conceptions for the Court is generally considered to have Warren and Frankfurter wings.

TABLE II. TYPAL RELEVANCIES

	Type I	*Type II*
DO	.887	
BL	.780	
WA	.950	
BR	.876	
WH		.749
FR		1.000
HA		.956
ST		.424
CL		.464

In the Warren group Black, Douglas and Brennan all have a high loading on the prototype. In the Frankfurter group, however, we note that Stewart and Clark have relatively low loadings on the prototype. The inference is that were a third bloc to form in the Court, its most likely nucleus would be Stewart or Clark. We should not imply necessarily from this data that Frankfurter and Warren dominated their two reciprocating justices, Harlan and Brennan. The influence or status relationship between any pair of justices must be analyzed in a different manner. For while a correlation of the behavior of two justices may show that they tend to act together, it does not indicate who is leading and who is following. We shall return to this momentarily.

At this point we are concerned with leadership within a bloc. The suggestion is that where a justice more closely approximates the prototype than any other member of his own group, leadership ability on his part may be suspected. This may very well be, however, what is known as second order leadership. For example Frankfurter and Harlan have the highest reciprocating correlation in civil liberty cases in the 1958 term. Whittaker, Clark and Stewart correlate highest with Frankfurter, suggesting that he has influence within the group. But if Frankfurter tends to be influenced by Harlan then a tendency on the part of Whittaker, Clark and Stewart to follow Frankfurter would, in effect, result in leadership for Harlan. In other words, it is important to establish, if possible, the status relationship between the two highest reciprocating justices in each bloc. This obviously is not simple to achieve in view of the inability within the profession to agree upon such concepts as "leadership" or "status." This shortcoming is sometimes accepted as a justification for doing nothing. Yet, some insight may be gained by examining the inter-personal relationships varying at the same time the angles of observation.

One approach is through Solidarity Analysis. This furnishes us with an index based upon the ratio of supportive and non-supportive behavior directed by each justice to each other member of the Court. Support or non-support is conceptualized respectively as the agreement or disagreement of one judge with the written opinions of another. In a given case a justice has a number of choices about such things. He may, of course, be asked to write the opinion for the Court. If he does not write for the Court his area of choice is much larger. He may in such case behave in any of the following ways:

(1) He may concur in the result.
(2) He may write a concurring opinion.
(3) He may dissent.
(4) He may write a dissenting opinion.
(5) He may concur with a concurring opinion, with a dissenting opinion or with the opinion of the Court.

It is surmised that the way in which he makes this choice furnishes one *crude* indication of his relationship to his colleagues. This, of course, becomes even more significant if consistent patterns of behavior can be observed through time.

Table III contains data which bears upon the relationships between the two justices in each group who correlate at the highest level. The Solidarity Index shows that Brennan received almost twice the ratio of supportive acts from Warren that Warren received from Brennan. We infer that Bren-

TABLE III. INTERINDIVIDUAL SOLIDARITY INDEX:
CIVIL LIBERTY CASES—1958 TERM

Justices as targets	*Justices as Initiators*								
	DO	BL	WA	BR	CL	ST	WH	FR	HA
Douglas		.73	.53	.53	.20	.20	.20	.14	.13
Black	.58		.58	.42	.25	.08	.08	.09	.08
Warren	.88	.67		.56	.33	.25	.44	.33	.22
Brennan	.64	.88	1.00		.11	.15	.22	.22	.22
Clark	.00	.00	.00	.11		.44	.44	.44	.56
Stewart	.22	.11	.22	.33	.22		.44	.33	.44
Whittaker	.25	.75	.67	.75	.75	.75		.67	.75
Frankfurter	.00	.00	.09	.09	.67	.67	.67		.78
Harlan	.11	.22	.11	.11	.78	.44	.78	.78	

$ISI = \dfrac{aij}{aij + dij} \times 100$ where $aij =$ the number of supportive acts originated by the ith individual and directed toward the jth individual; $dij =$ the number of non-supportive or negative acts originated by the ith individual and directed toward the jth individual. Supportive and non-supportive acts in this case are represented by agreement or disagreement by the ith individual with an opinion written by the jth individual.

nan exerted strong influence upon the Chief Justice in the 1958 civil liberty cases. We note further that Brennan had the highest mean excess of support in his bloc. In comparing Frankfurter and Harlan we encounter a tie. It is notable, however, that Frankfurter's mean excess of support is more than double that of Harlan.

A third way of looking at the relationships on the Court is in terms of the relative exercise of power in civil liberty cases. For this purpose we may utilize the Shapely-Shubik power index,* which defines power as the probability of being pivotal in a majority decision. The index is a function, therefore, of both the frequency of participation in the majority and the size of the majority. Table IV gives the relative rankings for forty-three

TABLE IV. RELATIVE RANKING OF SUPREME COURT JUSTICES ON
SHAPELY-SHUBIK POWER INDEX—1958 TERM

Justice*	All Cases**		Civil Liberty Cases Only	
	Mean Coefficient	Rank	Mean Coefficient	Rank
Douglas	.0908	9	.0803	9
Black	.1012	8	.1004	7
Warren	.1084	7	.0898	8
Brennan	.1218	2	.1014	6
Clark	.1249	1	.1273	2
Stewart	.1122	6	.1227	4
Whittaker	.1135	5	.1316	1
Frankfurter	.1153	3	.1200	5
Harlan	.1148	4	.1246	3

*Burton is omitted for inadequate participation.
**121 opinion cases only.

civil liberty cases as well as for 121 opinion cases. On this index Brennan turns up as the most powerful member of his bloc while Warren ranks third within the bloc. Frankfurter ranks a poor fifth in his own bloc. The failure of Frankfurter and Warren to reflect in this index the roles indicated by the correlation analysis reveals the fact that much of the support they received came in cases decided by large rather than small majorities. The Shapely-Shubik power index places a premium on participation in marginal majorities.

In comparing the rank order of all cases with that of civil liberty cases only we find a correlation that is statistically significant at the .02 level. But the coefficient (.64) does not obscure the fact that as far as the full

* The index is explained on pp. 384–86.

Court is concerned Whittaker's role is more crucial and Brennan's less crucial in civil liberty decisions than in decision-making in general. In sum it would seem that firm conclusions about leadership on the Court must await more conclusive evidence although Warren, Brennan, Frankfurter and Harlan seem more likely candidates for this mantle than other members of the Court.

CHAPTER SIX

DECISION-MAKING

THE interactions continually occurring in a system, whether they are social, political, economic, or otherwise, may be classified as formal and informal. The former do not require specific affirmation or rejection, while the latter call for, and are the end product of, conscious decision-making processes. The more sensitive an ongoing system to changes in its internal and external environment, the more frequent the use of such processes. For basic system decisions are, in part, adaptations to environmental demands. They involve, primarily, the combining of values, attitudes, information, perception, and situation into a choice among alternative courses of action. The choices, once made, become the basis for multiple series of new interaction patterns.

Since a political system by its very nature must be hypersensitive to environmental change, decision-making looms large in the study of politics. Thus the science of politics is sometimes described as the science of making political decisions. This process may involve leaders of government, political party functionaries, or individual voters; the more democratic a political system, the greater the number of political decision-makers will be. In this section, however, the primary interest is not who makes decisions, but how decisions are made and how the process may be fruitfully studied. The answers which these questions solicit are apt to depend on the authority consulted; the psychiatrist, the economist, and the behavioral scientist bring to the subject varying vocabularies and concepts. The behavioralist's view may be distinguished by comparison with that of the management scientist in public administration. The latter group (which includes operations researchers, statistical decision theorists, and industrial engineers) adopts rationality as the keystone of its conceptions. The behavioralist, on the other hand, takes a less rigid view, believing that, although ends may or may not be the result of logical processes, decisions as to means involve logic, discrimination, analysis, and choice. Defects in the factual basis of such processes or in the reasoning therefrom do not alter the case. The response of a system to a demand situation is rarely rational in the primary sense, although such responses may partake of rationality in varying degrees.

Discussion of decision-making, therefore, tends to be complicated by considerations of rational versus nonrational decisions and conscious versus unconscious decisions. Yet, there is general recognition of something called the decision-making process; a recognition shared by sociologists, psychologists, economists, political scientists, and even by engineers who have increasingly devoted time and energy toward construction of thinking machines. Our modern computers are also based on decision theory and involve particular methods of choosing among alternatives. Sociologists and behavioral scientists, on the other hand, have observed decision-making processes in small face-to-face groups through controlled experiments, introducing such variables as uncertainty and learning opportunities. All of these activities concern processes of communication, information, and decision.

The readings in this section are designed to familiarize the student with some of the basic considerations in the study of political decision-making and to introduce him to a particularized method of analyzing decision processes which is known as *game theory*. It has drawn increasing attention since 1947, when Von Neumann and Morgenstern published their highly technical *The Theory of Games.*

The game theory model has two general uses: (1) Given the necessary assumptions, it enables a player (decision-maker) to get the highest possible minimum utility at the lowest possible maximum cost. (2) The model may be used in analysis to indicate the extent to which political decision-makers in fact depart from the game model. It is in the latter category that a great value of the model for the study of political processes is found.

The articles by Richard Snyder and Karl Deutsch furnish us with a basic outline of game theory and its possible uses and limitations. Glendon Schubert, on the other hand, presents several techniques he has found useful in analyzing judicial decision-making. Among these is a concrete use of the game theory model with empirical data. Robert Dahl's work is also in the area of judicial behavior. His analysis indicates that the function of the Court as a national policy-maker is intimately related to, and limited by, elements in its external environment—namely, the United States Congress and public opinion. This finding is highly consonant with the emphasis of systems theory on the interrelatedness of the parts of a political system. The same can be said for Anthony Downs' presentation on government decision-making. Focusing upon budget decisions, Downs argues that the voter-government relationship is basically that of mutual interdependence in a democratic system.

The Basic Logic of Government
Decision-Making

ANTHONY DOWNS

According to our hypothesis, governments continue spending until the marginal vote gain from expenditure equals the marginal vote loss from financing. The determinants of vote loss and vote gain are the utility incomes of all voters and the strategies of opposition parties. Thus governments are engaged in political warfare as well as maximization problems.

Under conditions of certainty, a government's best strategy is to adopt choices which are favored by a majority of voters. Before making any expenditure, it takes a hypothetical poll to see how voters' utility incomes are affected by the expenditure and the necessary financing. . . . In other words, when a newly elected (or reëlected) government sets up its plan of action, it asks about each expenditure, "Is it worth its cost in votes in terms of votes gained?" just as a profit-making firm asks about each of its expenditures, "Is it worth its cost in dollars in terms of added revenue?"

But the government takes over many of the activities of its predecessor without really considering doing away with them, although it may consider marginal alteration of their quantity or reorganization of their administration. Hence it starts out with a mass of essential activities which it knows by experience are worth their cost in votes. Also, there will probably exist a set of basic revenue-raising devices which the government knows cost less in votes than would cessation of those activities they support. Thus the crucial weighing of votes occurs at the margins of both expenditure and revenue patterns.

Most governments separate the early stages of expenditure-planning from the early stages of revenue-planning as a part of their internal division

Reprinted from *An Economic Theory of Democracy* (1957), pp. 69–73 by permission of the publisher. Copyright 1957 by Harper and Brothers.

of labor. Two sets of plans are drawn up and submitted to some central balancing agency, which must delimit the expenditure pattern and find some kind of financing, whether taxed, printed, or borrowed, for all of it. If a government is acting so as to maximize votes, these plans are rated by their additions to or subtractions from the individual utility incomes of every voter. The balancing agency weighs each additional act of spending against the additional financing needed for it and decides whether it will gain or lose votes, in light of the utility functions of all voters and the possible strategy of the opposition.

The government is likely to adopt any act of spending which, coupled with its financing, is a net addition of utility to more voters than it is a subtraction, i.e., it pleases more than it irritates. Otherwise the opposition may approve it and make an issue of it in the forthcoming campaign. Conversely, whenever a proposed expenditure irritates more voters than it pleases, the party in power will most likely refuse to carry it out. The government continues to weigh proposals in this manner long after its first plan is formulated, since conditions change and new possibilities must be considered.

Thus the pressure of competition motivates the government in the same way that it motivates private firms, though the number of competitors is much smaller, and the competition is for votes instead of dollars. This pressure even causes parties to innovate so as to meet new social needs and keep technically in step with their competition.

The preceding description of government budgeting applies when the government follows the majority principle, but it need not employ that principle under all conditions. As we have seen, whenever the opposition uses a coalition-of-minorities strategy or is kept from adopting an issue-matching strategy by uncertainty, the government is freed from the necessity of agreeing with the majority on every issue.

As a result, it is not interested in the net impact upon a voter's utility income of each action but of all its actions taken together. Upon occasion, it is willing to irritate more voters than it pleases, if subsequent actions will placate those irritated and yet not completely cancel the satisfaction of those pleased. This means the government can no longer weigh acts individually, but must look at the effect of all of them as a unit. Consequently its decisions become much more complex. . . .

As an example, let us say that the government is pondering some problem that has just arisen at T_n, which is any moment between T_b, the beginning of the election period, and T_e, the date of the election. All of its actions from T_b to T_n must be considered as given, since they are already affecting individual utility incomes. Also, a blueprint has previously been drawn up for the future acts from T_n to T_e, which were originally coördinated with the now-given acts into a single master plan covering the whole period. Unforeseen events cause constant deviations from this master plan, each of which is actually a reformulation of the whole plan from T_n to T_e, in the light of the acts already taken from T_b to T_n. Thus every single unforeseen decision involves a new prediction of every voter's net utility income position on election day.

In practice, no government actually carries out such elaborate calculations. Not only does it lack information about the shapes of individual utility functions, but also it cannot possibly make such staggering calculations for each decision. Nevertheless, the rudiments of this kind of thinking appear in the government's keeping an eye on various groups in society to see how they are doing and to discover what actions should be taken to appease them or ensnare their votes. By simplifying the millions of voters into a small number of blocs, and merging the thousands of acts into a few major policy groups, the government can actually make the kind of recalculations discussed. It can take into account how a given policy will affect farmers, labor, businessmen, etc., and how this policy will fit into the net effect that its whole program will have had on each of these homogeneous groups by election day, given the actions already taken.

We conclude that governments in our model world either (1) make each spending decision separately by means of the majority principle, or (2) fit each decision into the entire pattern and recalculate the whole impact of their spending program upon all voters. Which of the two methods they follow depends upon the degree of uncertainty in their knowledge of voters' utility functions, and the strategies adopted by opposition parties. . . .

Thus majority rule does not always prevail on specific issues, but it usually does in a two-party system whenever the majority strongly favors a certain policy. Such passionate majorities exist when citizens feel more strongly about the policy views most others share with them than about those regarding which they are in the minority. By encouraging specialization of viewpoint, the division of labor tends to break up passionate majorities and foster minority-coalition governments.

When government is following the majority principle, it plans its budget by taking a hypothetical poll on each decision. When it is using some other strategy, it judges every action as a part of its whole spending plan for the election period. Unforeseen events force it to recalculate the whole plan in the light of what it has already done.

Since governments plan their actions to please voters and voters decide how to vote on the basis of government actions, a circular relation of mutual interdependence underlies the functioning of government in a democracy.

Decision-Making in a Democracy: The Supreme Court as a National Policy-Maker

ROBERT A. DAHL

To consider the Supreme Court of the United States strictly as a legal institution is to underestimate its significance in the American political system. For it is also a political institution, an institution, that is to say, for arriving at decisions on controversial questions of national policy. As a political institution, the Court is highly unusual, not least because Americans are not quite willing to accept the fact that it *is* a political institution and not quite capable of denying it; so that frequently we take both positions at once. This is confusing to foreigners, amusing to logicians, and rewarding to ordinary Americans who thus manage to retain the best of both worlds.

I

A policy decision might be defined as an effective choice among alternatives about which there is, at least initially, some uncertainty. This uncertainty may arise because of inadequate information as to (a) the alternatives that are thought to be "open"; (b) the consequences that will probably ensue from choosing a given alternative; (c) the level of probability that these consequences will actually ensue; and (d) the relative value of the different alternatives, that is, an ordering of the alternatives from most preferable to least preferable, given the expected consequences and the expected probability of the consequences actually occurring. An *effective* choice is a selection of the most preferable alternative accompanied by measures to insure that the alternative selected will be acted upon.

No one, I imagine, will quarrel with the proposition that the Supreme Court, or indeed any court, must make and does make policy decisions in this sense. But such a proposition is not really useful to the question before us. What is critical is the extent to which a court can and does make policy decisions by going outside established "legal" criteria found in precedent, statute, and constitution. Now in this respect the Supreme Court occupies a most peculiar position, for it is an essential characteristic of the institution that from time to time its members decide cases where legal criteria are not in any realistic sense adequate to the task. . . .

Reprinted from *The Journal of Public Law*, vol. 6 (1957), pp. 279–95 by permission of the author and the publisher.

Very often the cases before the Court involve alternatives about which there is severe disagreement in the society, as in the case of segregation or economic regulation; that is, the setting of the case is "political." Moreover, they are usually cases where competent students of constitutional law, including the learned justices of the Supreme Court themselves, disagree; where the words of the Constitution are general, vague, ambiguous, or not clearly applicable; where precedent may be found on both sides; and where experts differ in predicting the consequences of the various alternatives or the degree of probability that the possible consequences will actually ensue. Typically, in other words, although there may be considerable agreement as to the alternatives thought to be open [(a)], there is very serious disagreement as to questions of fact bearing on consequences and probabilities [(b) and (c)], and as to questions of value, or the way in which different alternatives are to be ordered according to criteria establishing relative preferability [(d)].

If the Court were assumed to be a "political" institution, no particular problems would arise, for it would be taken for granted that the members of the Court would resolve questions of fact and value by introducing assumptions derived from their own predispositions or those of influential clienteles and constituents. But, since much of the legitimacy of the Court's decisions rests upon the fiction that it is not a political institution but exclusively a legal one, to accept the Court as a political institution would solve one set of problems at the price of creating another. Nonetheless, if it is true that the nature of the cases arriving before the Court is sometimes of the kind I have described, then the Court cannot act strictly as a legal institution. It must, that is to say, choose among controversial alternatives of public policy by appealing to at least some criteria of acceptability on questions of fact and value that cannot be found in or deduced from precedent, statute, and Constitution. It is in this sense that the Court is a national policy-maker, and it is this role that gives rise to the problem of the Court's existence in a political system ordinarily held to be democratic.

Now I take it that except for differences in emphasis and presentation, what I have said so far is today widely accepted by almost all American political scientists and by most lawyers. To anyone who believes that the Court is not, in at least some of its activities, a policy-making institution, the discussion that follows may seem irrelevant. But to anyone who holds that at least one role of the Court is as a policy-making institution in cases where strictly legal criteria are inadequate, then a serious and much debated question arises, to wit: Who gets what and why? Or in less elegant language: What groups are benefited or handicapped by the Court and how does the allocation by the Court of these rewards and penalties fit into our presumably democratic political system?

II

In determining and appraising the role of the Court, two different and conflicting criteria are sometimes employed. These are the majority criterion and the criterion of Right or Justice.

Every policy dispute can be tested, at least in principle, by the majority criterion, because (again: in principle) the dispute can be analyzed according to the numbers of people for and against the various alternatives at issue, and therefore according to the proportions of the citizens or eligible members who are for and against the alternatives. Logically speaking, except for a trivial case, every conflict within a given society must be a dispute between a majority of those eligible to participate and a minority or minorities; or else it must be a dispute between or among minorities only. Within certain limits, both possibilities are independent of the number of policy alternatives at issue, and since the argument is not significantly affected by the number of alternatives, it is convenient to assume that each policy dispute represents only two alternatives.

If everyone prefers one of two alternatives, then no significant problem arises. But a case will hardly come before the Supreme Court unless at least one person prefers an alternative that is opposed by another person. Strictly speaking, then, no matter how the Court acts in determining the legality or constitutionality of one alternative or the other, the outcome of the Court's decision must either (1) accord with the preferences of a minority of citizens and run counter to the preferences of a majority; (2) accord with the preferences of a majority and run counter to the preferences of a minority; or (3) accord with the preferences of one minority and run counter to the preferences of another minority, the rest being indifferent.

In a democratic system with a more or less representative legislature, it is unnecessary to maintain a special court to secure the second class of outcomes. A case might be made out that the Court protects the rights of national majorities against local interests in federal questions, but so far as I am aware, the role of the Court as a policy-maker is not usually defended in this fashion; in what follows, therefore, I propose to pass over the ticklish question of federalism and deal only with "national" majorities and minorities. The third kind of outcome, although relevant according to other criteria, is hardly relevant to the majority criterion, and may also be passed over for the moment.

One influential view of the Court, however, is that it stands in some special way as a protection of minorities against tyranny by majorities. In the course of its 167 years, in seventy-eight cases, the Court has struck down eighty-six different provisions of federal law as unconstitutional, and by interpretation it has modified a good many more. It might be argued, then, that in all or in a very large number of these cases the Court was, in fact, defending the rights of some minority against a "tyrannical" majority. There are, however, some exceedingly serious difficulties with this interpretation of the Court's activities.

III

One problem, which is essentially ideological in character, is the difficulty of reconciling such an interpretation with the existence of a democratic polity, for it is not at all difficult to show by appeals to authorities as various and imposing as Aristotle, Locke, Rousseau, Jefferson, and Lincoln that the term democracy means, among other things, that the power to rule resides in popular majorities and their representatives. Moreover, from entirely reasonable and traditional definitions of popular sovereignty and political equality, the principle of majority rule can be shown to follow by logical necessity. Thus to affirm that the Court supports minority preferences against majorities is to deny that popular sovereignty and political equality, at least in the traditional sense, exist in the United States; and to affirm that the Court *ought* to act in this way is to deny that popular sovereignty and political equality *ought* to prevail in this country. In a country that glories in its democratic tradition, this is not a happy state of affairs for the Court's defenders; and it is no wonder that a great deal of effort has gone into the enterprise of proving that, even if the Court consistently defends minorities against majorities, nonetheless it is a thoroughly "democratic" institution. But no amount of tampering with democratic theory can conceal the fact that a system in which the policy preferences of minorities prevail over majorities is at odds with the traditional criteria for distinguishing a democracy from other political systems.

Fortunately, however, we no not need to traverse this well-worn ground; for the view of the Court as a protector of the liberties of minorities against the tyranny of majorities is beset with other difficulties that are not so much ideological as matters of fact and logic. If one wishes to be at all rigorous about the question, it is probably impossible to demonstrate that any particular Court decisions have or have not been at odds with the preferences of a "national majority." It is clear that unless one makes *some* assumptions as to the kind of evidence one will require for the existence of a set of minority and majority preferences in the general population, the view under consideration is incapable of being proved at all. In any strict sense, no adequate evidence exists, for scientific opinion polls are of relatively recent origin, and national elections are little more than an indication of the first preferences of a number of citizens—in the United States the number ranges between about forty and sixty per cent of the adult population—for certain candidates for public office. I do not mean to say that there is no relation between preferences among candidates and preferences among alternative public policies, but the connection is a highly tenuous one, and on the basis of an election it is almost never possible to adduce whether a majority does or does not support one of two or more policy alternatives about which members of the political elite are divided. For the greater part of the Court's history, then, there is simply no way of establishing with any high degree of confidence whether a given alternative was or was not supported by a majority or a minority of adults or even of voters.

In the absence of relatively direct information, we are thrown back on indirect tests. The eighty-six provisions of federal law that have been declared unconstitutional were, of course, initially passed by majorities of those voting in the Senate and in the House. They also had the president's formal approval. We could, therefore, speak of a majority of those voting in the House and Senate, together with the president, as a "lawmaking majority." It is not easy to determine whether any such constellation of forces within the political elites actually coincides with the preferences of a majority of American adults or even with the preferences of a majority of that half of the adult population which, on the average, votes in congressional elections. Such evidence as we have from opinion polls suggests that Congress is not markedly out of line with public opinion, or at any rate with such public opinion as there is after one discards the answers of people who fall into the category, often large, labelled "no response" or "don't know." If we may, on these somewhat uncertain grounds, take a "lawmaking majority" as equivalent to a "national majority," then it is possible to test the hypothesis that the Supreme Court is shield and buckler for minorities against national majorities.

Under any reasonable assumptions about the nature of the political process, it would appear to be somewhat naive to assume that the Supreme Court either would or could play the role of Galahad. Over the whole history of the Court, on the average one new justice has been appointed every twenty-two months. Thus a president can expect to appoint about two new justices during one term of office; and if this were not enough to tip the balance on a normally divided Court, he is almost certain to succeed in two terms. Thus, Hoover had three appointments; Roosevelt, nine; Truman, four; and Eisenhower, so far, has had four. Presidents are not famous for appointing justices hostile to their own views on public policy nor could they expect to secure confirmation of a man whose stance on key questions was flagrantly at odds with that of the dominant majority in the Senate. Justices are typically men who, prior to appointment, have engaged in public life and have committed themselves publicly on the great questions of the day. As Mr. Justice Frankfurter has recently reminded us, a surprisingly large proportion of the justices, particularly of the great justices who have left their stamp upon the decisions of the Court, have had little or no prior judicial experience. Nor have the justices—certainly not the great justices—been timid men with a passion for anonymity. Indeed, it is not too much to say that if justices were appointed primarily for their "judicial" qualities without regard to their basic attitudes on fundamental questions of public policy, the Court could not play the influential role in the American political system that it does in reality play.

The fact is, then, that the policy views dominant on the Court are never for long out of line with the policy views dominant among the lawmaking majorities of the United States. Consequently it would be most unrealistic to suppose that the Court would, for more than a few years at most, stand against any major alternatives sought by a lawmaking majority. The judicial agonies of the New Deal will, of course, quickly come to mind; but Mr. Roosevelt's difficulties with the Court were truly exceptional. Generalizing over the whole history of the Court, the chances are about one out of five that a president will make one appointment to the Court in less than a year, better than one out of two that he will make one within two years, and three out of four that he will make one within three years. Mr. Roosevelt had unusually bad luck: he had to wait four years for his first appointment; the odds against this long an interval are four to one. With average luck, the battle with the Court would never have occurred; even as it was, although the "court-packing" proposal did formally fail, by the end

TABLE 1. THE INTERVAL BETWEEN APPOINTMENTS TO THE SUPREME COURT

Interval in Years	*Per Cent of Total Appointments*	*Cumulative Per Cent*
Less than 1	21	21
1	34	55
2	18	73
3	9	82
4	8	90
5	7	97
6	2	99
12	1	100
Total	100	100

Note: The table excludes the six appointments made in 1789. Except for the four most recent appointments, it is based on data in the Encyclopedia of American History 461–62 (Morris ed., 1953). It may be slightly inaccurate because the source shows only the year of appointment, not the month. The twelve-year interval was from 1811 to 1823.

of his second term Mr. Roosevelt had appointed five new justices and by 1941 Mr. Justice Roberts was the only remaining holdover from the Hoover era.

It is to be expected, then, that the Court is least likely to be successful in blocking a determined and persistent lawmaking majority on a major policy and most likely to succeed against a "weak" majority; e.g., a dead one, a transient one, a fragile one, or one weakly united upon a policy of subordinate importance.

IV

An examination of the cases in which the Court has held federal legislation unconstitutional confirms, on the whole, our expectations. Over the whole history of the Court, about half the decisions have been rendered more than four years after the legislation was passed.

TABLE 2. PERCENTAGE OF CASES HELD UNCONSTITUTIONAL ARRANGED BY TIME INTERVALS BETWEEN LEGISLATION AND DECISION

Number of Years	New Deal Legislation %	Other %	All Legislation %
2 or Less	92	19	30
3– 4	8	19	18
5– 8	0	28	24
9–12	0	13	11
13–16	0	8	6
17–20	0	1	1
21 or More	0	12	10
Total	100	100	100

Of the twenty-four laws held unconstitutional within two years, eleven were measures enacted in the early years of the New Deal. Indeed, New Deal measures comprise nearly a third of all the legislation that has ever been declared unconstitutional within four years after enactment.

TABLE 3. CASES HOLDING LEGISLATION UNCONSTITUTIONAL WITHIN FOUR YEARS AFTER ENACTMENT

Interval in Years	New Deal No.	New Deal %	Other No.	Other %	Total No.	Total %
2 or Less	11	29	13	34	24	63
3 to 4	1	3	13	34	14	37
Total	12	32	26	68	38	100

. . . . The entire record of the duel between the Court and the lawmaking majority, in cases where the Court has held legislation unconstitutional within four years after the enactment, is summerized in Table 4.

TABLE 4. TYPE OF CONGRESSIONAL ACTION AFTER SUPREME COURT DECISIONS HOLDING LEGISLATION UNCONSTITUTIONAL WITHIN FOUR YEARS AFTER ENACTMENT (INCLUDING NEW DEAL LEGISLATION)

Congressional Action	Major Policy	Minor Policy	Total
Reverses Court's Policy	17	2	19
None	0	12	12
Other	6	1	7
Total	23	15	38

Thus the application of the majority criterion seems to show the following: First, if the Court did in fact uphold minorities against national majorities, as both its supporters and critics often seem to believe, it would be an extremely anomalous institution from a democratic point of view. Second, the elaborate "democratic" rationalizations of the Court's defenders and the hostility of its "democratic" critics are largely irrelevant, for lawmaking majorities generally have had their way. Third, although the Court seems never to have succeeded in holding out indefinitely, in a very small number of important cases it has delayed the application of policy up to as much as twenty-five years.

V

How can we appraise decisions of the third kind just mentioned? Earlier I referred to the criterion of Right or Justice as a norm sometimes invoked to describe the role of the Court. In accordance with this norm, it might be argued that the most important policy function of the Court is to protect rights that are in some sense basic or fundamental. Thus (the argument might run) in a country where basic rights are, on the whole, respected, one should not expect more than a small number of cases where the Court has had to plant itself firmly against a lawmaking majority. But majorities may, on rare occasions, become "tyrannical"; and when they do, the Court intervenes; and although the constitutional issue may, strictly speaking, be technically open, the Constitution assumes an underlying fundamental body of rights and liberties which the Court guarantees by its decisions.

Here again, however, even without examining the actual cases, it would appear, on political grounds, somewhat unrealistic to suppose that a Court whose members are recruited in the fashion of Supreme Court justices would long hold to norms of Right or Justice substantially at odds with the rest of the political elite. Moreover, in an earlier day it was perhaps easier to believe that certain rights are so natural and self-evident that their fundamental validity is as much a matter of definite knowledge, at least to all reasonable creatures, as the color of a ripe apple. To say that this view is unlikely to find many articulate defenders today is, of course, not to disprove it; it is rather to suggest that we do not need to elaborate the case against it in this essay.

In any event the best rebuttal to the view of the Court suggested above will be found in the record of the Court's decisions. Surely the six cases where the policy consequences of the Court's decisions were overcome only after long battles, will not appeal to many contemporary minds as evidence for the proposition under examination. A natural right to employ child labor in mills and mines? To be free of income taxes by the federal government? To employ longshoremen and harbor workers without the protection of workmen's compensation? The Court itself did not rely upon such arguments in these cases, and it would be no credit to their opinions to reconstruct them along such lines.

So far, however, our evidence has been drawn from cases in which the Court has held legislation unconstitutional within four years after enactment. What of the other forty cases? Do we have evidence in these that the Court has protected fundamental or natural rights and liberties against the dead hand of some past tyranny by the lawmakers? The evidence is not impressive. In the entire history of the Court there is not one case arising under the First Amendment in which the Court has held federal legislation unconstitutional. If we turn from these fundamental liberties of religion, speech, press and assembly, we do find a handful of cases—something less than ten—arising under Amendments Four to Seven in which the Court has declared acts unconstitutional that might properly be regarded as involving rather basic liberties. An inspection of these cases leaves the impression that, in all of them, the lawmakers and the Court were not very far apart; moreover, it is doubtful that the fundamental conditions of liberty in this country have been altered by more than a hair's breadth as a result of these decisions. However, let us give the Court its due; it is little enough.

Over against these decisions we must put the fifteen or so cases in which the Court used the protections of the Fifth, Thirteenth, Fourteenth and Fifteenth Amendments to preserve the rights and liberties of a relatively privileged group at the expense of the rights and liberties of a submerged group: chiefly slaveholders at the expense of slaves, white people at the expense of colored people, and property holders at the expense of wage earners and other groups. These cases, unlike the relatively innocuous ones of the preceding set, all involved liberties of genuinely fundamental importance, where an opposite policy would have meant thoroughly basic shifts in the distribution of rights, liberties, and opportunities in the United States—where, moreover, the policies sustained by the Court's action have since been repudiated in every civilized nation of the Western world, including our own. Yet, if our earlier argument is correct, it is futile— precisely because the basic distribution of privilege *was* at issue—to suppose that the Court could have possibly acted much differently in these areas of policy from the way in which it did in fact act.

VI

Thus the role of the Court as a policy-making institution is not simple; and it is an error to suppose that its functions can be either described or appraised by means of simple concepts drawn from democratic or moral theory. It is possible, nonetheless, to derive a few general conclusions about the Court's role as a policy-making institution.

National politics in the United States, as in other stable democracies, is dominated by relatively cohesive alliances that endure for long periods of time. One recalls the Jeffersonian alliance, the Jacksonian, the extraordinarily long-lived Republican dominance of the post-Civil War years, and the New Deal alliance shaped by Franklin Roosevelt. Each is marked by a break with past policies, a period of intense struggle, followed by consolidation, and finally decay and disintegration of the alliance.

Except for short-lived transitional periods when the old alliance is disintegrating and the new one is struggling to take control of political institutions, the Supreme Court is inevitably a part of the dominant national alliance. As an element in the political leadership of the dominant alliance, the Court of course supports the major policies of the alliance. By itself, the Court is almost powerless to affect the course of national policy. In the absence of substantial agreement within the alliance, an attempt by the Court to make national policy is likely to lead to disaster, as the *Dred Scott* decision and the early New Deal cases demonstrate. Conceivably, the cases of the last three decades involving the freedom of Negroes, culminating in the now famous decision on school integration, are exceptions to this generalization; I shall have more to say about them in a moment.

The Supreme Court is not, however, simply an *agent* of the alliance. It is an essential part of the political leadership and possesses some bases of power of its own, the most important of which is the unique legitimacy attributed to its interpretations of the Constitution. This legitimacy the Court jeopardizes if it flagrantly opposes the major policies of the dominant alliance; such a course of action, as we have seen, is one in which the Court will not normally be tempted to engage.

It follows that within the somewhat narrow limits set by the basic policy goals of the dominant alliance, the Court *can* make national policy. Its discretion, then, is not unlike that of a powerful committee chairman in Congress who cannot, generally speaking, nullify the basic policies substantially agreed on by the rest of the dominant leadership, but who can, within these limits, often determine important questions of timing, effectiveness, and subordinate policy. Thus the Court is least effective against a current lawmaking majority—and evidently least inclined to act. It is most effective when it sets the bounds of policy for officials, agencies, state governments or even regions, a task that has come to occupy a very large part of the Court's business.

Few of the Court's policy decisions can be interpreted sensibly in terms of a "majority" versus a "minority." In this respect the Court is no different from the rest of the political leadership. Generally speaking, policy at the national level is the outcome of conflict, bargaining, and agreement among minorities, the process is neither minority rule nor majority rule but what might better be called *minorities* rule, where one aggregation of minorities achieves policies opposed by another aggregation.

The main objective of presidential leadership is to build a stable and dominant aggregation of minorities with a high probability of winning the presidency and one or both houses of Congress. The main task of the Court is to confer legitimacy on the fundamental policies of the successful coalition. There are times when the coalition is unstable with respect to certain key policies; at very great risk to its legitimacy powers, the Court can intervene in such cases and may even succeed in establishing policy. Probably in such cases it can succeed only if its action conforms to and reinforces a widespread set of explicit or implicit norms held by the political leadership: norms which are not strong enough or are not distributed in such a way as to insure the existence of an effective lawmaking majority but are, nonetheless, sufficiently powerful to prevent any successful attack on the legitimacy powers of the Court. This is probably the explanation for the relatively successful work of the Court in enlarging the freedom of Negroes to vote during the past three decades and in its famous school integration decisions.

Yet the Court is more than this. Considered as a political system, democracy is a set of basic procedures for arriving at decisions. The operation of these procedures presupposes the existence of certain rights, obligations, liberties and restraints; in short, certain patterns of behavior. The

existence of these patterns of behavior in turn presupposes widespread agreement (particularly among the politically active and influential segments of
the population) on the validity and propriety of the behavior. Although
its record is by no means lacking in serious blemishes, at its best the Court
operates to confer legitimacy, not simply on the particular and parochial
policies of the dominant political alliance, but upon the basic patterns of
behavior required for the operation of a democracy.

Game Theory and the Analysis of
Political Behavior

RICHARD C. SNYDER

The purpose of game theory is two-fold: to formulate mathematically
complete principles that will specify what is rational behavior in certain
kinds of social situations and, on the basis of such principles, to isolate
the general characteristics of such behavior. Thus it is a method of analysis
and a method of selecting the best courses of action. The social situations
are those that are goal-oriented—action is geared to accomplishment of
certain ends. These situations call for rational behavior, *i.e.,* behavior designed to produce decisions and courses of action embodying the least costly
way to achieve goals or to keep losses to a minimum given operating conditions. These situations are marked by conflict, competition, and often co-
operation. What action is rational when all relevant possibilities are known
and the outcome is not determined by any one participant? Game theory
attempts to answer this question by developing a mathematical theory for
choice-making among alternative courses of action when it is impossible
to control *all* the factors that govern outcomes because of the actions of
others. It is to be noted that the term rational applies only to action, not
goals, and that the theory does not ignore the possible impact of irrational
behavior. . . .

It must be emphasized that the "game" is an analytic device, a model
for describing and predicting behavior the properties of which are specified
by the model. Game theory is in essence a simplifying analytic scheme that
enables us to concentrate on crucial aspects of conflict situations. . . .

Reprinted from *Research Frontiers in Politics and Government: Brookings Lectures 1955,* pp. 76–95 by permission of the author and the publisher. Copyright 1955
by The Brookings Institution.

Game theory envisages several types of games. Perhaps the basic game, the one in which the most theoretical development has taken place, is the two-person, zero-sum game. In this game there are two players only, and the winnings and losses cancel out. A two candidate election race is an example. All votes that one wins, the other loses, and the results can be computed as a loss for one and a gain for the other. If the victory is computed as plus $(+1)$ and the defeat is computed as minus (-1), then the values of the game for each player are canceling. On the other hand, it must be emphasized that the two-person, non-zero-sum game is a basic political type—particularly in bilateral international relationships. The other major type of game is the n-person, non-zero-sum game in which there are more than two persons and in which the winnings and losses do not cancel out. For example, in a three-person election with one office open, the results will be plus one for the winning candidate, and minus one for each of the losers. It will be recognized that n-person, non-zero-sum games are the most complicated and also the most frequent.

MAJOR CONCEPTS OF THE THEORY

There are five concepts of game theory that must be mentioned. First is the concept of *strategy*. Ordinarily the word strategy means a skillful or an adroit plan. As employed by game theory it means a complete plan— so complete it cannot be upset by an opponent or by nature. Strategy refers to a previously decided upon set of moves that complete the game in such a way that at least a certain minimal outcome is guaranteed regardless of what an opponent does. Strategy takes into account the potential behavior of opponents and renders irrelevant the expectations of the latter concerning one's own behavior. The theory assumes that within the limits of particular situations, the range of strategies for any one player is usually not infinite and each player's strategies are known to the others. Rational behavior in a two-person-zero-sum game constitutes the selection of a strategy by each player that will either maximize the minimum he can obtain or will minimize the maximum loss he can sustain.

In these games, the theory yields a single strategy or a pattern of probabilities that indicate the frequency with which several alternative strategies should be used. Rational play is one or the other depending on circumstances. There is always an optimal strategy available for both players. If only a single strategy happens to be optimal for each player, it is called a *pure* strategy. If on successive plays, a different strategy is required to minimize loss and maximize gains, the strategy is said to be *mixed*. When each player chooses an optimal strategy, he can guarantee himself an expected value of the game. Minimax is a guaranteed value of the outcome of a game such that one player gains the largest plus-score he could gain in the face of his opponent's best play, and the other player will receive the smallest minus score. In simple games a minimum of two strategies will be available to the players. More complicated games may have a very large number of strategies.

The optimal strategy—whether pure or mixed—is chosen so as to protect the player against *anything* his opponent can do. Game theory assumes an opponent who is as wily as the rules permit and who is bent on pursuing an antithetical goal. If the opponent acts irrationally, naturally it may be possible to score added gains against him.

The *pay-off* refers to the value of the game to each player as pairs of strategies clash, a value that results when each person plays his optimum strategy. In brief, the pay-off is what the game is worth at the end in terms of probabilities fulfilled, in terms of winnings and losses, in terms of positive or negative progress toward avowed goals. For every pair of strategies in a two-person game, the rules of the game determine a value. If the players have five strategies each, then there will be twenty-five possible pairs of strategies and twenty-five different values depending on which pair is chosen. What is referred to as the pay-off matrix is calculated by plotting the strategies and their probabilities in box-fashion. To revert to the case of a two-man election, let us assume there are six campaign strategies open to each candidate, A and B. Thus there will be thirty-six numbers representing the values or outcomes of possible pairings of pure strategies used by each player. The theory says that for each player there will usually be one strategy—in the above example perhaps strategy number four for candidate A and strategy number two for candidate B—that will maximize minimum gains and minimize maximum losses regardless of what each does. Even for n-person games, pay-offs can be calculated by treating coalitions as single players.

In parlor games, there are well-known *"rules"* that govern play— instructions that clearly specify what is allowed and what is not allowed. In sociological conflict situations, the rules are different. The rules are the laws of nature and human nature—geographical, biological, sociological, and psychological factors. In other words, the rules are the limiting conditions under which the game takes place. The values in the pay-off are determined by the rules as are available strategies. In many communities the ethnic factor requires a slate of candidates commonly referred to as a balanced ticket, which then is a rule of the game. The absence of uranium deposits is a rule of the game. Human endurance is a rule of the game in air duels. Public apathy may be a rule of the game in certain situations. Any game or conflict situation will manifest a distribution of power to enforce choices. Voting procedures, for example, give each member of a committee leverage on the group decision. Much of the capabilities analysis dones by C.I.A. with respect to the "control over power factors" of the Soviet Union exemplified an attempt to illuminate one important aspect of the "rules of the game" for conflict situations involving the Soviet Union.

Another significant building-block of game theory is *information*. Presumably, every game will have a "structure" of information. Actually, the information state is included in the rules of the game, but it is worth pulling out for special emphasis. In some political games, spies and information agencies may be required to substitute for, say, the information carried by the informative bid in a bridge game. Signaling and bluff can be illustrated by parlor game analogies. Ordinarily in bridge, the players know the rules of the game but cannot see what cards opponents have—hence they do not have perfect information. If the bridge hand were played with all cards face up, every player would be completely informed about all previous plays and future possibilities. When incomplete information is the rule, signaling may be necessary. In poker it may be good strategy to misinform an opponent by bluff. Depending on the goals, the rules, the existence of coalitions, and so on, it may be part of the optimal strategy to reveal the grand design of moves one has selected, or it may be optimal strategy to let the opponent guess in the hope he will commit himself to a pattern of moves first. The concept of information suggests the great importance of timing of moves.

Coalitions are very important in n-person games. Two or more players may gain more as a unit. The pay-off is shared by the members of a coalition and may or may not be shared equally. Formation of coalitions will result from competitive bargaining. Coalitions may be held together by some formal enforcement device or by the price of double-crossing other members of the coalition. The price of violating a coalition agreement will depend on sanctions available to the members, on whether the game is a one-shot affair. One important aspect of over-all strategy is the discovery that the pay-off function can be measurably increased by forming a coalition and that losses can be minimized by joining forces with other players. Choice of strategy is governed first by a calculation of the pay-off to a coalition relative to the pay-off to a single player, and secondly by a decision that distributes the pay-off among the members of a coalition. At the moment, the first can be easily handled by game theory, but the second, as might be imagined, is troublesome—partly because so little is known about the formation and disruption of coalitions under actual conditions. The point to be stressed here is that games can be played co-operatively or non-co-operatively. Optimal strategy and the process of arriving at optimal strategy will be different in each case.

Now it is clear from the foregoing that game theory embraces both simple and very complex models. Perhaps the simplest is the two-person zero-sum, two-strategy game while the most complex is the n-person, non-zero-sum, co-operative games with many strategies. It is imperative not to assume automatically that politics in real life can only be represented adequately by the most complex games. For example, the purpose of many political coalitions is to maintain the status quo in which case there is no problem of determining how the pay-off is to be divided. . . . The reader who has waited patiently for concrete cases may feel let down, but the alternative is to say that there is nothing to game theory—which the author firmly does not believe—or to provide examples that the reader might accept on their merits without accepting their implications or general relevance. . . .

As in the case of analytic aids, an attempt will be made to suggest a range of applications. It is not necessary to assume that only complete solutions of problems would be useful to the practical policy-maker and politician. And it is more important to open some doors rather than to conclusively "prove" the case.

Viewing an election as a two-person, zero-sum game, political parties might get some help from a game theorist with respect to the expenditure of resources, stress on certain issues, and on secrecy of strategies to be employed. In many two-person zero-sum games, it pays to try to get your opponent to commit his strategy first. The strategy of the Republicans in maneuvering their 1956 national convention to come late in the summer *after* the Democrats have nominated their candidate seems to be a classic example of game theory intuitively applied to a practical problem. Simultaneous presidential nominating conventions might produce entirely different results than successive conventions in which one party must commit itself to a candidate and a campaign platform. Unpredictability (secrecy) may be indicated and the differences in pay-off can be clearly shown. . . .

One of the points in the American political structure where the choice of strategies is extremely significant and where the game situation often prevails is interaction between President and Congress. Assume a two-person, non-zero-sum game. The rules in this case state that there will be a bill passed—ruling out refusal by Congress to vote. The bill is divided into three sections valued differently by the President, but this is not known to Congress. Congress, on the other hand, is opposed to all three sections, but not in the same degree. Congress may propose substitutes for any of the three sections. It is not known to the President which of its sections Congress values most.

Four strategies are open to the President in presenting his bill. He may: (1) inform Congress ahead of time that he is proposing a bill and what is in it; (2) not inform Congress ahead of time; (3) let Congress advise on the bill in advance; and (4) let Congress participate in shaping the bill.

Congress thus has 16 strategies, four for each of the President's one: (1) concede the President one section, and propose two of their own; (2) concede the President two sections of his bill and one of its own sections; (3) concede the President's bill in entirety; (4) propose a bill containing three sections wanted by Congress.

This simplified game suggests a possible solution at some time in the future to the problem of optimal strategy for President and Congress. If—and again it is a big if—we knew the outcomes of these strategies, and if we knew the pay-off value attached by the two participants, we could solve mathematically for the minimax. Even if the President simply knew the number of pure or mixed strategies available to Congress and could assign pay-off values to various pairings of strategies, he would be well along in the solution to his problem. The fact that we do not have this kind of interaction data has enormous consequences for our political system. However, further studies might show that the system yields close to a minimax pay-off in zero-sum situations. Yet periodic instability in executive-legislative relations suggests that "stable sets" of co-operative solutions to the game have not been established.

The Study of Judicial Decision-Making as an Aspect of Political Behavior

GLENDON A. SCHUBERT

In a recent essay, Richard Snyder has stated that: "[A] paradox in political science is the lack . . . of any systematic attention to the analysis of the decision-making behavior of judges." It is not my purpose to argue either for or against the particular frame of reference for decision-making analysis advocated by Snyder. I do believe, however, that he has correctly identified the approach—the analysis of judicial decision-making as an aspect of political behavior—which is most likely to command the focus of interest and activity of the coming generation of political scientists whose substantive concern is with the study of political problems in the area of our discipline traditionally known as public law.

The concept "political behavior" remains sufficiently novel within the public law fraternity to impose something of an obligation to make clear

Reprinted from *The American Political Science Review*, vol. 52 (1958), pp. 1007–25 by permission of the author and the publisher. Copyright 1958 by The American Political Science Association.

what I have in mind in using the term. I shall borrow from David B. Truman who, in a Brookings Lecture not long ago, defined the "behavioral sciences" as "those bodies of knowledge, in whatever academic department they may be found, that provide or aspire to provide 'verified principles' of human behavior through the use of methods of inquiry similar to those of the natural sciences." Truman noted that the research techniques that have characterized developments in the behavioral sciences during the period since 1930 include . . . experimentation in group dynamics (and, in particular, sociometric analysis of interaction and influence structure in small groups) ; . . . and the theory of games. . . . I shall present some . . . questions about judicial behavior that can be investigated with the aid of these tools. . . .

I. BLOC ANALYSIS

We are all familiar with Pritchett's studies of dissenting votes and bloc affiliations on the Supreme Court. I shall not use the derisive term "box scores," which appears to be particularly popular among those political scientists whose research experience with quantitative methods begins and ends with the aphorism that "Thinkers don't count, and counters don't think." Although Pritchett's work is methodologically quite simple, he has done far more than merely to count heads. His quantitative studies have aided him in making highly perceptive and sophisticated interpretations of the voting behavior of the justices, and he has taken a long stride in the direction of a group dynamics approach to Supreme Court decision-making.

The surprising thing is that, in a profession of political "scientists," no one appears to have tried to replicate Pritchett's experiments. No one has criticized or suggested improvements in his methods, or applied them to study other periods in the Supreme Court's history, or to study the work of other courts.

I shall confine my remarks about bloc analysis to three points. In the first place, Pritchett has used two basic kinds of tables: those which analyze paired agreement in dissent (see, *e.g.*, Figure 1) ; and those which present paired agreement in both assent and dissent in divided decisions, expressed as a percentage of total paired participation (Figure 2). It is also possible to construct dissent tables which focus upon marginal decisions only (Figure 3), and to construct tables of paired agreement in assent in divided decisions (Figure 4). Tables of marginal dissents reveal significant patterns of voting behavior that would otherwise be missed. During the 1953–1956 Terms, for instance, Clark cast his dissenting votes about equally with the left and with the right wings of the Court (Figure 1) ; but he was definitely affiliated with the left bloc of Black-Douglas-Warren in marginal dissents (Figure 3). Assent tables help, in the interpretation of dissent

FIG. 1. DISSENTING BLOCS ON THE WARREN COURT, 1953-1956 TERMS

	Douglas	Black	Warren	Clark	Minton	Reed	Burton	Frankfurter	Harlan	
Douglas	(19)	72	37	13	11	6	11	12	4	
Black	72	(2)	37	10	6	2	2	13	2	
Warren	37	37		12	3	4	3	2		
Clark	13	10	12	(2)	7	13	16	4	3	INDEX OF COHESION
Minton	11	6	3	7		30	26	9	10	IC[Left] = .611
Reed	6	2	4	13	30	(5)	33	10	14	IC[Center] = .489
Burton	11	2	3	16	26	33	(3)	28	29	IC[Right] = .478
Frankfurter	12	13	2	4	9	10	28	(5)	41	
Harlan	4	2		3	10	14	29	41	(6)	
Total dissents:	113	82	44	41	52*	62*	79	76	61*	

* Minton, Reed, and Harlan each served for less than four complete terms of the Court. Jackson, Brennan, and Whittaker, each of whom served a single term or less during the period covered, have been deleted from this computation, and also from Figures 2-4 for the same reason. Numbers in parentheses denote instances in which the justice is in "paired agreement" with himself, viz., his solo dissents.

tables and tables of over-all interagreement, to determine the locus of decisive power within the Court. Libertarians may deride Clark, for instance, for the uninspired quality of his judicial writing—to say nothing of the content of his views—but bloc analysis of recent terms shows him to have been the most powerful justice on the Court—with the possible exception of the Chief Justices—in terms of participation in winning majority coalitions, and by no means a conservative in relation to his colleagues. Bloc analysis also confirms the journalistic observation that Clark votes as an acolyte to the Chief Justice on the far right of the Court under Vinson and slightly left of center under Warren and immediately to his right (Figures 1–4).

In the second place, bloc identification does not need to be intuitive, but can be placed upon an objective basis by the use of standard indices to denote the presence and composition of blocs. In my own experiments in the use of bloc analysis, I have developed three such indices, which I offer tentatively until someone else comes up with something better. For the analysis of dissent tables, I suggest an Index of Cohesion, which is the ratio of the mean of the included dissenting pairs, in a postulated bloc,

FIG. 2. INTERAGREEMENT IN SPLIT DECISIONS OF THE WARREN COURT, 1953-1956 TERMS, IN PERCENTAGES

	Douglas	Black	Warren	Clark	Minton	Reed	Burton	Frankfurter	Harlan
Douglas		80	67	50	34	30	31	34	30
Black	80		77	58	44	37	36	46	31
Warren	67	77	(76)	54	55	53	55	42
Clark	50	58	(76)		64	68	65	55	46
Minton	34	44	54	64		74	61	54	49
Reed	30	37	55	68	74		71	48	51
Burton	31	36	53	65	61	71		61	65
Frankfurter	34	46	55	55	54	48	61		80
Harlan	30	31	42	46	49	51	65	80	
% of assent:	70	78	88	89	81	80	79	80	71

INDEX OF INTERAGREEMENT

II[Left] = .747
II[Center] = .673
II[Right] = .687
II(Wa-C) = .760

to the mean of the total dissents (for the period of time under investigation) of the included justices. It is, in other words, a decimal fraction which results from dividing the average of the dissenting participation of the included justices into the average of agreement among the included pairs. This index assumes that a justice can affect the over-all cohesion of a dissenting bloc significantly only to the extent that both his rate of inter-agreement with other members of the bloc, and his volume of dissent, are high. On the basis of limited empirical application, I consider an Index of Cohesion of .50 or greater to be high; .40_.49 to be moderate; and less than .40 to be low. In Figure 1, for instance, the Index of Cohesion for the Left Bloc = 1/3 (146) ÷ 1/3 (239) = .611, which is quite high.

For the analysis of assent tables, one might consider an Index of Adhesion, defined as the ratio of the mean of the included pairs to the total number of split decisions under investigation. This index measures the extent to which the justices combine to form a dominant majority bloc. Because of the non-participants, the assent matrix which this index measures is not necessarily the converse of the dissent matrix for a given period. Apart from the difference in the matrices to which they apply, the Index of Adhesion differs from the Index of Cohesion in two respects: (1) the denominator of the IA is a constant for any measurement of a given matrix, while the denominator of the IC is a variable; and (2) the denominator of the IA is always much larger than the denominator of

FIG. 3. DISSENTING BLOCS IN MARGINAL DECISIONS OF THE WARREN COURT, 1953-1956 TERMS

	Douglas	Black	Warren	Clark	Minton	Reed	Burton	Frankfurter	Harlan	
Douglas		26	20	10	7	2	6	6	1	
Black	26		18	10	4	2	1	4		
Warren	20	18		12	2	3	3	2		INDEX OF
Clark	10	10	12			7	5	2		COHESION
Minton	7	4	2			9	15	5	7	IC[Left]=.610
Reed	2	2	3	7	9		15	4	5	IC[Center]=.557
Burton	6	1	3	5	15	15		13	14	IC[Right]=.587
Frankfurter	6	4	2	2	5	4	13		10	
Harlan	1				7	5	14	10		
Total dissents:	34	28	24	19	22*	19*	29	20	14*	

*See Figure 1.

the IC, since no justice dissents all the time. (The highest level of dissent on the Supreme Court during the past decade appears to be Douglas's 51 percent during the 1952 Term.) I consider an IA of .60 or more to be high; .50 to .59 to be moderate; and less than .50 to be low. An IA of less than .50 for a pair or bloc would signify that the justices concerned had participated together in the majority in less than half of the split decisions of the Court for the period under examination. The IA for the Left Bloc in Figure $4 = 1/3$ (401) $\div$ $256 = .522$, which is moderate.

For the tables of over-all interagreement, which are expressed in percentages, the average of the ratios of the included pairs can be used as an Index of Interagreement, with .70 or better considered high, .60–.69 moderate, and less than .60 low. For the Left Bloc in Figure 2, the Index of Interagreement$=1/3$ $(2.24)=.747$, which is high.

Although bloc analysis appears to have been applied only to the United States Supreme Court, I think that fruitful applications can be made to state courts. In order to test his notion, I have made a bloc analysis of four recent terms of the Michigan Supreme Court. The 1954-1957 Terms were chosen, because it was during this interval that Governor Williams, near the end of a decade in office, finally succeeded in placing on the Court a majority of like-minded Democrats. Bloc analysis of recent

FIG. 4. PARTICIPATION IN THE MAJORITY IN SPLIT DECISIONS OF THE WARREN COURT, 1953-1956 TERMS

	Douglas	Black	Warren	Clark	Frankfurter	Burton	Reed	Minton	Harlan
Douglas		122	130	109	73	67	52	46	42
Black	122		149	129	98	87	66	66	43
Warren	130	149		173	135	131	102	88	64
Clark	109	129	173		130	144	114	97	68
Frankfurter	73	98	135	130		124	83	80	79
Burton	67	87	131	144	124		107	90	70
Reed	52	66	102	114	83	107		92	36
Minton	46	66	88	97	80	90	92		23
Harlan	42	43	64	68	79	70	36	23	
Total assents:	141	163	209	204	176	176	135*	117*	93*

INDEX OF ADHESION

IA[Left]=.522

IA[Center]=.545

IA(Wa-C)=.676

TOTAL DECISIONS=256

*See Figure 1.

periods of the United States Supreme Court shows no relationship between partisan affiliation and bloc composition and voting behavior. In recent Terms, for instance, we find Democrat Black and Republican Warren on the left wing, and "Independent" Frankfurter and Republican Harlan on the right wing. The most interesting finding from bloc analysis of the Michigan Supreme Court was the perfect correlation between political party affiliation and bloc composition and voting behavior during the 1956 and 1957 Terms, after the Williams justices accrued in sufficient numbers to begin to take over control of the court (see Figure 5). This finding, in turn, raises interesting questions about the relative impact upon judicial behavior of appointment for life as compared with election for fixed terms.

II. SCALOGRAM ANALYSIS

Scalogram analysis, or cumulative scaling, offers probably the easiest research technique to use as well as the most widely applicable of those surveyed in this paper. The method for constructing scales of judicial cases can be stated in terms of fixed, objective procedures, too lengthy for development here. In essence, scale analysis measures the presence of a single dominant variable in a set of additional data. Assume, *e.g.*, that

FIG. 5. DISSENTING BLOCS ON THE MICHIGAN SUPREME COURT, 1957 TERM

		Smith	Black	Edwards	Voelker	Kelly	Dethmers	Carr	Sharpe	
Smith	(Dem.)		9	9	7			1	1	
Black	(Dem.)	9	(1)	9	8			1	1	
Edwards	(Dem.)	9	9		7	1	1	1		
Voelker	(Dem.)	7	8	7						INDEX OF COHESION
Kelly	(Rep.)			1		(1)	8	11	10	IC[Left] = .830
Dethmers	(Rep.)			1		8		12	12	IC[Right] = .675
Carr	(Rep.)	1	1	1		11	12		23	
Sharpe	*	1	1			10	12	23		
Total dissents:		8	12	10	10	12	13	25	25	

* Although Sharpe originally was elected to the court as a Democrat in 1933, he was not so regarded in the mid-fifties; nor did the Williams Administration consider that Justice Sharpe served in any sense as a spokesman for its views and policies.

several related cases decided on the merits by the Court have asked questions of the justices to which they should have responded consistently if they understood the questions to relate to a single basic issue. Scalogram analysis provides a technique for arranging both the cases and the respondent justices in uniquely determined rank orders. Moreover, it can tell us both how consistent and how intense the underlying attitudes of the respective individual justices, and of the Court as a collective group, have been.

It happens that the fifteen "right to counsel" cases decided by the Supreme Court from the 1940 Term through the end of the 1947 Term form that empirical rarity, a perfect scale, so I shall use it as an example (Figure 6). The cases can be arranged in an order such that, it is assumed, the cases to the left of the scale are most seriously damaging to the claimed rights and interests of the defendants, and those to the right of the scale least so. Here the question the justices are asked to answer is: "How sympathetic are you to claims of the right to counsel under the Fourteenth Amendment?" Or we can conceptualize the cases as raising a set of questions of this order: "Do you approve when a criminal defendant in a state court is denied counsel to the extent of X?" "Do you approve when he is denied counsel to the extent of $X+Y$?," "to the extent of $X+Y+Z$?"—and so on. In this particular example the cases ranged from several, to the left of the scale, in which the Court voted unanimously in favor of the de-

FIG. 6. A SCALOGRAM OF THE "RIGHT TO COUNSEL" CASES, 1940-1947

Scale Scores	Respondent's Name	Smith v. O'Grady, 312 U.S. 329 (1941)	White v. Ragen, 324 U.S. 760 (1945)*	Lutz v. Ragen, 324 U.S. 760 (1945)*	Hawk v. Olson, 326 U.S. 271 (1945)	DeMeerleer v. Mich., 329 U.S. 663 (1947)*	House v. Mayo, 324 U.S. 42 (1945)*	Williams v. Kaiser, 323 U.S. 471 (1945)	Tomkins v. Missouri, 323 U.S. 485 (1945)	Rice v. Olson, 324 U.S. 786 (1945)	Carter v. Illinois, 329 U.S. 173 (1946)	Foster v. Illinois, 332 U.S. 134 (1947)	Betts v. Brady, 316 U.S. 455 (1942)	Canizio v. New York, 327 U.S. 82 (1946)	Avery v. Alabama, 308 U.S. 444 (1940)	Total votes per justice	Total inconsistencies per justice
	Scale Position:	1	2	3	4	5	6	7	8	9	10	11	12	13	14		
13	Murphy	(+)	(+)	(+)	(+)	(+)	(+)	(+)	(+)	(+)	'+'	+)	+)	'+'		13	0
13	Rutledge		(+)	(+)	(+)	(+)	(+)	(+)	(+)	(+)	+)	'+'		'+'		11	0
12	Black	'+'	(+)	(+)	(+)	(+)	(+)	(+)	(+)	'+'	+)	'+'	'+'	'-'	'-'	14	0
12	Douglas	(+)	(+)	(+)	(+)	(+)	(+)	'+'	'+'	(+)	'+'	+)	+)	(-)	(-)	14	0
9	Reed	(+)	(+)	(+)	'+'	(+)	(+)	(+)	(+)	(+)	(-)	(-)	(-)	(-)	(-)	14	0
9	Stone	(+)	(+)	(+)	(+)		(+)	(+)	(+)	(+)			(-)	(-)	(-)	11	0
8	Jackson		(+)	(+)	Y	(+)	(+)	(+)	(+)	-	(-)	(-)	(-)	Y		10	0
6	Frankfurter	(+)	(+)	(+)	(+)	(+)	(+)	'-'	'-'	'-'	'-'	'-'	(-)	(-)	(-)	14	0
5	Vinson				(+)						(-)	(-)				3	0
5	Burton			(+)	(+)						(-)	(-)	(-)			5	0
3	Roberts	(+)	+	+			-	-)	-)	-)		'-'		(-)		9	0
1	Hughes	(+)												(-)		2	0
0	McReynolds														(-)	1	0
0	Byrnes												(-)			1	0
	Division of votes: +	8	9	9	8	9	8	7	7	6	4	4	3	2	0	122	
	−	0	0	0	0	0	1	2	2	3	5	5	6	6	8		
	Number of inconsistencies per case:	0	0	0	0	0	0	0	0	0	0	0	0	0	0		0

*Per curiam decision. $CR = 1 - \dfrac{0}{62} = 1.000$

fendants' claims, to the case at the right of the scale which found even Black and Douglas joining in a unanimous decision against the defendant. Murphy and Rutledge have the highest scale scores; neither of them ever voted against a right to counsel claim. Frankfurter voted, with perfect consistency, in favor of defendants in the first six cases along the scale, and against defendants in the remaining eight. We can readily rank, on the basis of their voting participation, all of the members of the Court during the eight-year period. But we can do more than this, we can also predict how they should have voted in the cases in which they did not participate.

In fact, scalogram theory postulates that, knowing the scale of cases and the scale scores of the justices, we should be able to predict all votes in all cases comprising the scale. If any justices voted inconsistently in some cases, the degree of their inconsistency can be measured by a Co-efficient of Reproducibility, which is the decimal fraction resulting from the subtraction, from unity, of the number of inconsistent votes divided by the total number of votes in all cases except those decided unanimously or with a single dissenting vote. It is conventional, based upon experience in analyzing other types of data, to consider a CR of .900 or better to be evidence of unidimensionality in a scale. I have followed the convention, although ultimately the question whether scales with CR's of .900 are acceptable for the analysis of Supreme Court decision-making must await considerably more experimentation than appears to have taken place to date. The CR for the right-to-counsel cases of our example was, of course, 1.000.

It may be either fool's or beginner's luck, but every hypothesis that I have tested thus far has resulted in an acceptable scale. The subject matter of these scales includes: (a) Federal Employers' Liability Act evidentiary cases since 1942; (b) aliens' claims since 1950; (c) all the split decisions of the 1936 Term—the term of the "Court-packing" controversy; (d) the right to counsel cases since 1940; and (e) the search and seizure cases, both federal and state, since 1937. On the other hand, it is easy to state inappropriate hypotheses which lead to unacceptable scales, as the report of the experiments of a sociologist demonstrates.

The matrix of the scalogram can readily include supplementary information of considerable value in the interpretation of the data. In addition to the votes of the justices, the scalogram can show who wrote, and who joined in the majority opinion; which justices concurred and/or wrote concurring opinions; and which justices dissented and/or wrote dissenting opinions.

Scalograms of judicial decisions focus attention upon the justices whose voting has been least, or most, consistent; and cases displaying inconsistent votes are pinpointed. Such clues may suggest, in the attitudes of inconsistent justices, the possible presence of a secondary variable and, as regards inconsistent cases, the additional possibility that a case has been misclassified.

I should like to offer just one more example of the kinds of hypotheses that can be tested by scalogram analysis. The Court's "official" doctrine in the right-to-counsel cases is familiar enough: that the Constitution unequivocally requires representation by counsel in state criminal trials only for capital offenses. Scalogram analysis demonstrates conclusively that the

Court has been just as consistent, and just as favorable, in non-capital as in capital cases. The Court has decided 66⅔ percent of the right to counsel cases involving non-capital offenses, and 62½ percent of the capital-offense cases, in favor of defendants, and the coefficients of reproducibility for the two subscales are both very high: .962 and .972. Which among the Court's many other doctrines may be confirmed, and which may be deflated by scalogram analysis, one cannot predict on *a priori* grounds; but I am confident that cumulative scaling offers a most powerful analytic tool for the study of the Supreme Court. . . .

III. GAME ANALYSIS

The judicial process is tailor-made for investigation by the theory of games. Whatever may be their obligations as officers of courts, attorneys frequently play the role of competing gamesmen, and the model of the two-person zero-sum game certainly can be applied to many trials. The two examples that I should like to describe briefly, however, involve the application of game theory to the analysis of the behavior of Supreme Court justices. I hope that I will be forgiven if I forego any attempt to explain game theory and its basic concepts, and simply describe the two games.

The first of these I shall call the Hughberts Game. During the 1936 Term, the Court was divided between a three-justice liberal bloc and a four-justice conservative bloc, with Hughberts (Hughes and Roberts) in the middle. If we assume that, in the face of Roosevelt's attack upon the Court, the Chief Justice—with the support of Roberts—wished to maximize both his own authority within the Court and the degree of unanimity in the Court's decisions, while at the same time directing the Court to as liberal a course of decision as possible in order to forestall the possibility of the more drastic reforms proposed by the President, game theory can tell us how Hughberts should vote if he—I shall consider Hughes and Roberts to be a single player from now on—were to behave rationally in order to realize these objectives. A game must have a payoff which can be expressed in numerical terms, and for this purpose I have used the Shapley-Shubik empirical power index in order to be able to compare the Court's actual voting behavior with the imputed utilities (*i.e.*, the payoff) postulated by the game model. Simply stated, the Shapley-Shubik index measures the extent to which each justice shared in the power of decision, which is defined as the probability of his having been pivotal in the winning coalition.

The left bloc and the right bloc are each defined as players in the game, which is three-person and zero-sum. Hughberts has a pure strategy, which in essence requires that he form a coalition with the Left when possible, that he form a coalition with the Right when splintering or nonparticipation makes it impossible for him to form a winning coalition with the Left, and that he always join the coalition of the Left and the Right when the other players do not choose to adopt conflicting strategies. In fact, the voting behavior of Hughes and Roberts conforms very closely to

The Left		Hughberts		The Right	
Brandeis	.1312	Hughes	.1600	VanDevanter	.0957
Cardozo	.1264	Roberts	.1536	Sutherland	.0864
Stone	.1054			Butler	.0742
				McReynolds	.0672
Totals	.3630		.3136		.3235
Expected power:	.3333		.3333		.3333
Difference:	+.0297		−.0197		−.0098

the prescriptions of the game model (Figure 9). In terms of the empirical payoff, the four-justice right bloc, the three-justice left bloc, and the two-justice center bloc are all approximately equal in power: It is easy to demonstrate that in a three-person simple majoritarian game, equality of power is imputed among the players. It is by no means a self-evident proposition, however, that among nine justices each casting a single and equal vote, two justices can be just as powerful as four justices.

I shall call the other example the Certiorari Game. Do Supreme Court justices combine into a bloc with the deliberate objective of forcing upon the rest of the Court the consideration of an issue which the bloc wants decided in a particular way? The data for the game consist of the decisions of the Supreme Court, both jurisdictional and on the merits, in Federal Employers' Liability Act evidentiary cases since 1942. The basic assumption is that a certiorari bloc was functioning throughout this period, although the number of justices affiliating with the bloc varied at different times and an antagonist player (Frankfurter) in opposition to the certiorari bloc entered the game (as such) only during the latter stages of the play. In order to simplify the discussion, let us confine our attention to the first period of the game, comprising the 1942-1948 Terms.

At that time, the certiorari bloc consisted of Murphy, Rutledge, Black, and Douglas. If we assume that the objective of the bloc was to maximize the number of decisions favorable to workmen's claims, game theory can prescribe how the bloc should behave rationally in order to accomplish this objective. Four justices are adequate to grant certiorari, but not (normally) to decide cases on the merits. It is assumed that, during this period, the remaining five justices had no fixed predisposition either towards or against the claimants. The only question in these cases is whether the trial court correctly evaluated the evidence; the cases turn, in other words, on questions of fact rather than law. Typically, they fall into two categories: (a) the trial court directs a judgment for the defendant railroad, on the ground that the evidence is insufficient for the case to go to a jury, or else the court directs a judgment for the defendant notwithstanding a jury verdict for the plaintiff; or (b) the trial judge enters a judgment for the

FIG. 9. PAYOFF MATRIX FOR THE HUGHBERTS GAME

HUGHBERTS
(2 votes)

		+	−		
	+	(3/9, 2/9, 4/9) [96] 2 (R) 1 (Bu, M) 1 (M) 1 (M)[St] 1 (Su)	(3/7, 0, 4/7) [0]	+	
THE LEFT (3 votes)	+	(3/5, 2/5, 0) [6] 1 [St, V]	(0, 1/3, 2/3) [4] 1 (H) 1 [St] 1 (R) 1 [Br, St]	−	THE RIGHT (4 votes)
	−	(0, 1/3, 2/3) [5] 3 [St] 1 (Br) 1 (H, Br)[St]	(3/5, 2/5, 0) [8] 1 (M) 1 (V)[St]	+	
	−	(3/7, 0, 4/7) [0]	(3/9, 2/9, 4/9) [76] 2 (Bu, M) 1 (Bu) 1 (Br, R) 1 (M) 1 (M)[St]	−	

Legend: The symbol + and − designate the players' strategies:
  + = voting for affirmance of the lower court's decision
  − = voting for reversal of the lower court's decision
The imputations for partitioning of the payoff among the players, according to the intersection of strategies, are given within parentheses at the top of each cell.
The number of decisions falling within each cell is given in brackets. The number of decisions, in each cell, in which there were deviations from the blocs, are itemized. Justices who defected from their respective blocs are shown in parentheses, and those who failed to participate in particular decisions are shown in brackets, according to the following key:

Br = Brandeis	H = Hughes	M = McReynolds
C = Cardozo	R = Roberts	Bu = Butler
St = Stone		Su = Sutherland
		V = VanDevanter

(Mr. Justice Cardozo did not deviate from the voting position attributed to the left bloc in any of the 195 decisions of the 1936 Term.)

plantiff on the basis of a jury verdict. In either event, the decision of the trial court has been affirmed or reversed by a court of appeals, and either the plaintiff workman or the defendant railroad has petitioned the Supreme Court for certiorari. It is assumed that, since these cases turn only on the evaluation of evidence, there is an equal chance that any of the five uncommitted justices will vote either for or against a claimant if the court of appeals has disagreed with the trial court. Therefore, since the certiorari bloc needs to pick up only one additional favorable vote on the merits, the chances of its doing so should be 31/32, for the only permutation of the five uncommitteed members on which the bloc could lose would be for all five of the other justices to vote against the claimant. The certiorari bloc has a pure strategy: never to vote in favor of petitions filed by railroads, always to vote to grant certiorari in cases in which review is sought by workers *and* in which an appellate court has reversed a judgement in favor of the plaintiff, and always to vote for the petitioner on the merits. *If* the certiorari bloc follows its pure strategy, the Court should decide 97 percent of the cases in favor of the claimants. If the bloc departs from its pure strategy, it can expect to win a smaller proportion of victories on the merits, because it has played irrationally.

As a matter of fact, the payoff to the certiorari bloc during this period was 92 percent (12 pro decisions and 1 con) in cases in which the bloc adhered to its pure strategy; of the 11 cases in which the bloc departed from its pure strategy by voting to grant certiorari for petitioners who had been two-time losers in the courts below, 8 were pro and 3 were con, for a payoff of only 73 percent. In later periods of the game, the bloc adhered much more closely to its pure strategy, and consequently enjoyed greater success. During the present period, the bloc consists of five justices, so the expected payoff is 100 percent. As a matter of fact, the bloc lost one of the fourteen cases decided on the merits during the 1956 and 1957 Terms, perhaps because the bloc, a little power drunk, became careless and granted certiorari in a case so frivolous that even the bloc members joined in the unanimous decision against the claimant. An alternative explanation for this deviant decision might be that the certiorari bloc was not being irrational, but rather that it *deliberately* accepted jurisdiction with the expectation that the decision would go unanimously against the workman, for the public relations objective of countering criticism that it *always* favored workmen.

IV. CONCLUSION

I hope that I may have succeeded in suggesting some of the kinds of hypotheses that may be worth looking into if we are willing to consider adding other strings to our bow, instead of limiting ourselves to the tradi-

tional workways in public law. In addition to the many political scientists
who will doubtless continue to pursue the legal, historical and philosophical
approaches to the study of public law, those who may have, or may develop,
an interest in the quantitative approach to the study of judicial behavior
will find a great deal of work awaiting their attention.

Game Theory and Politics: Some Problems
of Application

KARL W. DEUTSCH

Theory of Games and Economic Behavior by John von Neumann and
Oskar Morgenstern represents a new approach to the study of political and
social decisions and to the study of those decisions about other decisions
which we call strategies. Empirically the approach of the theory of games
is based on the existence of far-reaching similarities between certain conventionally standardized games and certain recurrent social situations.
Where such similarities exist, it is held to be more profitable to analyze
first the games rather than the far less sharply defined social situations.

The similarity of certain games and certain social situations is of
course not accidental. A considerable body of psychological research deals
with the transfer of patterns of social behavior into the play activity of
children and back from the play of children into social life. It seems
plausible that adults as well as children may tend to find those types of
games more interesting which permit them to adopt patterns of behavior
they can also apply to some social situation, or which permit them to act
out, as games, those patterns of behavior initiated in some experience of
social life but which only in the innocuous form of games can be carried to
completion. Though we cannot wage private war and kill our opponent,
we can play chess and checkmate the opponent's king; and the art of deceiving others profitably is more safely practiced first in the game of poker
than in politics or economic life.

Granting the potential relevance of games to the analysis of political
behavior, the approach of the theory consists first of all in analyzing
simplified prototypes of games such as chess, poker, and others; then, in
calculating as accurately as possible the winning chances for each player

Reprinted from *The Canadian Journal of Economics and Political Science*,
vol. 20 (February 1954), pp. 76–83 by permission of the author and the publisher.
Copyright 1954 by The University of Toronto Press. Footnotes omitted.

and each hand; and in determining the conditions under which advantageous coalitions can be made or alternative strategies can be evaluated for their chances of success.

Most of the decisions in games of this kind must be made under conditions of incomplete information. In a card game we may be ignorant of our opponent's hand or of the cards he or we may draw from the pile. In chess we know the position of the pieces of our opponent, and have theoretically "perfect information," at least so far as classical game theory is concerned; but even here we do not know his strategy, even though we do know that our decisions must depend on his and his on ours in turn. In sum, we know the limits in each game and characteristics of a smaller or larger ensemble of possibilities, and the theory assumes that these can be treated by a sophisticated application of the mathematics of probability and of the mathematical treatment of decision sequences.

Within certain limits, which will be discussed later, this assumption seems to be justified; and the relevance of this approach to certain problems of politics seems clear. In international as well as in domestic politics, coalitions are made and broken by decisions based on estimates of strength under conditions of incomplete information about the present and uncertainties about the future. If the concept of the balance of power, as developed by Machiavelli and his successors, has its place in the field of political science, then the theory of games cannot be denied a similar standing. To assess the probabilities of success of a political or military venture and to select a strategy most likely to insure it have long been major preoccupations of statesmen. Even more often, perhaps, statesmen have attempted to assess the strength of a political position or institution and the chances for its change or overthrow, in order to be able to select the safest course of action. In one form or another all these problems appear in the theory of games, and its eventual impact on political and social science should be considerable.

Already today some traces of this impact can be noticed. Interest in the theory of games has promoted a new style of thinking, in much the same manner as has the more general interest in the development of social science concepts that would be amenable to mathematical treatment. As a result, political and social theories are more frequently formulated in terms which are at least "conceptually quantifiable" and which are expected to lend themselves eventually to accurate mathematical representation. This has forced social scientists to seek a sharpness in the definition of their terms to which they had rarely been accustomed, and it has forced them to ask in the case of each concept whether there existed any practicable operations by which it could in fact be tested or measured. Some of these emphases on mathematical representability and operational definitions, in turn, may induce political scientists to realize more clearly the implications of familiar notions which previously had been taken for granted.

Thus the theory of games points out that the assumption of "transitivity" must be explicitly made for a game or a decision system. If in a card game a queen has a higher value than a jack and a king a higher value than a queen, we must stipulate that the king must also have a higher value than the jack. At first glance this seems logical, but it is quite possible to have games where this rule does not apply and where A takes B, B takes C, but C takes A. Such loop patterns of dominance have been observed by biologists in the peck order of chickens, and it may have its counterpart in the relationship of the British parliament to the Prime Minister, where the House of Commons can overthrow the Premier but the Premier can dissolve the House; or in the relationship of the British voters to their parliament, where the voters at election time can turn out the old Parliament, but where the Parliament can postpone the period of election and, at least in theory, could postpone such elections on the grounds of war or emergency for an indefinite period.

In contrast to this, the simple notion of sixteenth and seventeenth century lawyers, that there must always be one single supreme law-giver or sovereign in a country, contains the hidden assumption that the political decision system of each country must be transitive. This is an assumption which may correspond to the facts in some instances but not in others. In point of fact, it might be worth investigating whether any decision system that has autonomy, i.e., self-steering and self-control, can be completely transitive.

Again, much of our thinking about politics, economics, and social life is based on the tacit assumption that there is one "best" solution for any set of given conditions and desires. This leads often to heated argument about the presumed all-round "superiority" of this or that political or economic system or the counter-assertion that almost any system of solutions should be workable. The authors of *Theory of Games and Economic Behavior* deal explicitly with this problem of multiple solutions, and they go well beyond the classic emphasis of Montesquieu in suggesting that in general solutions are not unique. Indeed in most cases we shall observe a multiplicity of solutions. "Considering . . . solutions as stable 'standards of behavior' this . . . [means] that given the same physical background, different 'established orders of society' or 'accepted standards of behavior' can be built, all possessing . . . characteristics of inner stability. . . ."

In addition to emphasizing specificity of definitions, explicitness of assumptions, and limited ensembles of possible solutions, the approach of the theory of games tends to make explicit the contrast between strategies which are "objectively" promising or successful, that is, which have a high probability of being rewarded by the workings of the game which are not controlled by the player, and strategies which are "subjectively" convenient, that is, strategies which are expressive of some learned habits or felt needs and desires of the player, regardless of their likelihood of being rewarded or penalized by the impersonal biases and rules of the game. Explicitly, game theory deals only with objective strategies which it evaluates as good or bad, better or worse, regardless of the personality structure of the player or the cultural characteristics of the group of players who are to use them. Implicitly, however, it is precisely this identification of objectively good strategies which—as far as it is successful—makes it possible to disentangle impersonal probabilities from personal preferences and to determine the extent and direction of the mistakes of any player, i.e., his deviations from the theoretically best strategy. (Some limits upon this possibility of identifying "best" strategies will be discussed below.)

Despite these instances of potential usefulness to political science, most of the implications of game theory to politics lie in the future. If its potentialities are to be fulfilled, game theory must obtain from political scientists concepts and data which are sufficiently well defined and measured to be amenable to its treatment. On the other hand, however, political scientists may feel that many of the present restrictions of game theory reduce its ability of dealing with political problems.

Generally, present-day game theory assumes no change in the performance characteristics of the elements of the game during the time that the game is in progress. If kings are higher than jacks, they usually retain their higher value from the beginning to the end. Changes—even limited changes—in the behavior of the parts of the game are held to be exceptions, not the rule. In society and politics, however, limited changes of behavior may be the rule and exact repetition the exception. This possibility has perhaps found its classical expression in Lewis Carroll's image of the croquet game in *Alice in Wonderland*. In that game, as we all remember, the balls were live hedgehogs, the goals were doubled up soldiers, and the mallets were live flamingoes. The hedgehogs would crawl, the soldiers would stretch, and the flamingoes would squirm at every stage of the game. It was a very difficult game indeed, and it would perhaps have been not less difficult for the present theory of games, but it looks in some ways very much like the kind of game that political scientists are trying to describe.

Just as game theory ordinarily does not allow for changes in the performance characteristics of particular elements, so it does not provide ordinarily for changes in the rules of the game. Taken together these two restrictions seem to cut it off from the description of much of the process of learning.

In most conventional social games, moreover, all resources of the players are treated as given from the outside, either in their hands, or in some pool of cards, or the like, with limited probabilities of combinations given in advance. A typical question of present-day policy, such as whether to convert a thousand tons of steel into an end product, such as guns, or into capital goods, such as machine tools or mining equipment which will eventually increase the supply of steel, has found few close counterparts among the problems originally treated by the theory of games. The few comparable problems that do appear in conventional games, such as the queening of a pawn, occupy a minor position in the total ensemble of possible strategies of those games in which they are found and which are dominated primarily by quite different considerations.

More generally put, conventional games as well as much of game theory thus far have been apt to picture more nearly problems in the distribution of existing resources and to neglect relatively the problems of the growth of new resources from limited beginnings. In doing so game theory has not been able to cope with the problems of growth, novelty, and innovation.

This is not to say, however, that game theory as such ignores these problems. On the contrary, by stating its assumptions in an explicit and precise manner it highlights them and prepares the way for their solution. Thus the problem of the change in performance—though not the problem of learning—is being considered in some of the current work on linear programming and in Morgenstern's unpublished work on the "compressibility" of an economy, that is ability to provide substitutes for destroyed or otherwise eliminated products or services.

Von Neumann and Morgenstern are emphatic in admitting the limitations of the theory. They say:

We repeat most emphatically that our theory is thoroughly static. . . . A static theory deals with equilibria. The essential characteristic of an equilibrium is that it has no tendency to change. . . .

They add that such a static theory is a prerequisite for the later development of any sound dynamic theory. Physical theory advanced in this manner from statics to dynamics, and social science, the authors suggest, might likewise find a usable dynamic theory of games and social behavior at some time in the future. . . .

Finally, as game theory cannot deal with major changes over time, so it cannot deal with the problem of finding relevant solutions quickly enough to be of use. It cannot do so, it would seem, because thus far game theory has made no allowance for the time and cost needed for acquiring information. On the assumption that everybody can study quickly and easily all the probabilities relevant for any particular game situation, it has tended to favor the so-called minimax type of strategy, that is, the strategy that seeks to incur the least risks of loss, even at the price of accepting the smallest chance of gain. Under this strategy, a poker player will bluff from time to time, not in the expectation of deceiving his opponent, but merely in order to prevent him from relying on not being bluffed. Von Neumann and Morgenstern are careful to point out that:

. . . while our good strategies are perfect from the defensive point of view, the will (in general) not get the maximum out of the opponent's (possible) mistakes,—i.e., they are not calculated for the offensive. . . . [A] theory of the offensive in this sense, is not possible without essentially new ideas.

The assumption underlying the minimax strategy, that one may always be found out, is another form of the assumption that all relevant information about the game is freely and instantly available to all players. Von Neumann and Morgenstern say:

[We] cannot avoid the assumption that all subjects of the economy under consideration are completely informed about the physical characteristics of the situation in which they operate and are able to perform all statistical, mathematical, etc., operations which this knowledge makes possible. . . . *Our investigations . . . assume "complete information" without any further discussion . . . .*

The theory—as theory—assumes, in short, that thinking or calculating can be carried on without any limitation of time or cost.

This assumption seems unrealistic in politics. It seems even unrealistic in such cases as chess. According to an unpublished study by Dr. L. C. Haimson, Russian handbooks of championship chess have advised promising players since the 1930's not to follow a "strongest position" strategy, but rather to force their opponent to make some definite commitment on the board, even at the cost of some loss in position to themselves. Once the Russian player has induced his adversary to commit his pieces to a particular position on the board, and to commit his mind to working out the possibilities of a particular kind of strategy, he is then advised, according to this theory of chess, to make a radical switch in strategy and to confront his opponent with a new set of problems for which his pieces are not effectively disposed and for which his mind is not prepared.

In such situations the main attack may well be directed at first not so much against the principal material resources but rather against the decision-making capacity of the mind of the player. Through confronting his mind with a burden of decisions greater than he can manage within the limits of available time and intellectual resources, the efficiency of his decisions, and only subsequently his physical position, is to be disrupted.

Since the number of possible combinations in chess is very large, and becomes astronomical if the possible combinations for more than two moves ahead are to be considered, it is impossible for any chess player to consider all potentially relevant possibilities within any practical limit of time. In tournament chess, the time allowed each player for considering his next move is of the order of one hour. During that period he would have to consider all possible moves for, let us say, two moves ahead, then, on the basis of this preliminary scanning, to select the seemingly most promising strategies; and then to investigate each of these selected strategies intensively, by considering all or some of their possible consequences for another four or six moves ahead. Without the superficial scanning of all possibilities, the player could not be sure that he was not overlooking important strategic opportunities. Without adequate criteria of selection (where adequacy would have to be defined in terms of some probability considerations), he could not be sure that he had recognized the promising possibilities among the vast number of possible moves he had surveyed. And without the intensive investigation of all the possibilities selected as interesting, he could not know whether his tentative selections had in fact been good, or whether any one of the strategies selected as promising was any better than the others.

The player would thus have to perform four major operations: (1) broad provisional scanning; (2) highly restrictive selection of a few promising possibilities; (3) intensive development of the possible strategies selected; and (4) a decision as to which of the intensively investigated strategies to put into operation. In order to be completely effective, he would have to make sure that he had scanned superficially all relevant possibilities; recognized every single promising strategy among them; developed each of these strategies, together with all possible countermoves of his adversary, far enough ahead to establish a clear probability for the outcome; and chosen the strategy with the greatest probability of success. No human player, or any existing or realistically imaginable electronic calculator, could carry out completely these four operations in the time of an hour, of a day, or of a year.

The decisive weakness is in the second stage. There is no sure way of recognizing which of all the combinatorial possibilities studied in the first stage could be developed into winning strategies, just as there is no sure way to teach a million monkeys writing on a million typewriters how to select out of all the possible combinations of letters those sequences which will parallel the merit of the plays of Shakespeare. All that can be done in this selection stage is to fish with a very small net of criteria of interest in a very large ocean of superficially scanned possibilities. In any finite time, this search for interesting possibilities must be superficial rather than exhaustive. A combination of suitable criteria of interest with a broad process of statistical sampling could perhaps improve the efficiency of the process, but could not remove the basic uncertainty about its outcome.

It should now be clear that chess played with ordinary time limitations is not and cannot be a completely determinate game, at least for as long a period of the development of human brains and electronic calculators as we can now foresee. It should also be clear why similar considerations of uncertainty will apply to political or economic decisions which must be selected from large ensembles of possible decisions under definite limitations of time. And it should be clear what the Russian theory of chess playing, as described by Dr. Haimson, hopes to accomplish. It is aimed at overloading the second or selection stage in the strategic thinking of its opponent. Once this opponent has been forced into making a commitment that seems advantageous to him when considered in itself, then his material and intellectual capacity for responding to radically new changes may have been overburdened. From this point on, the player has two enemies against him: the radically changing strategies of his opponent and the ticking of the clock.

The fact that Russian players have prominently figured among recent chess champions may or may not be germane to this discussion. In any case, there is reason to expect that at some future time the world championship in chess, like so many other championships, may well be again in the hands of an American. What seems more likely to remain, however, regardless of the changing fortunes of chess competitions, is the introduction of *time* as an explicit variable in the planning of strategy, and the allowing for a specific time and *cost* element in the making of strategic decisions.

Since the original theory of von Neumann and Morgenstern assumed that all information was available to players who were under no limitation of time or cost in making up their minds, the explicit introduction of these limitations seems now to be leading into a "post-Neumannian" stage of the theory of games—a stage in which Professors von Neumann and Morgenstern themselves may well play a leading part. As this new stage in the theory of games develops, it should become increasingly applicable to problems of international as well as domestic politics.

Chapter Seven

COMMUNICATIONS

COMMUNICATIONS has been defined, in general, as the process of transmitting meaningful information between individuals. The importance of such processes for human society is not easily exaggerated. Indeed the survival of the individual and his social system depends on successful interchange of intentions, desires, needs, and knowledge. Yet, in spite of its great importance, communications has only recently become a subject of scientific inquiry. Contemporary research by political scientists, sociologists, psychologists, and others reflects the belated recognition by social scientists of the crucial role of communications and information in social interaction processes.

Communications research is many faceted. Some scholars take the view that the scope and direction of decision-making is determined in large part by access to relevant information. Thus, from this point of view, whoever controls the channels through which information passes possesses power in the full sense. Some recent research suggests that formal organizational structure may be modified by the location and control of communication channels. The fascinating word "cybernetics" has been adopted by Norbert Weiner and others to describe the study of society through its messages and communications facilities. For this school of thought, communications is viewed as vital in implementing man's control of his environment, and man and machine are viewed as systems which receive inputs (data introduced) and produce outputs (effects on the outer world). In human beings and complex machines, output may depend on any number of combinations of data from external and memory sources. A variation of the memory system introduces the concept of feedback by which man and machines take into consideration and adjust to variations in environment.

In all communications systems there is a certain amount of distortion or information loss. To study the effects of this distortion, a mathematical theory of information has been built around attempts to measure the transmission of information and its loss whatever the reason. As Anatol Rapoport shows, this loss may be due to redundancy or other factors. An understanding of such loss and its measurement is crucial for any science of communications.

Anthony Downs, S. I. Hayakawa, and Felix Cohen discuss other facets of the communications problem. Downs introduces the important concept of information cost by suggesting that, while access to relevant information is important for political behavior, it is likely to be affected by the varying cost of the information needed. Hayakawa, on the other hand, emphasizes the relationship of language to behavior and suggests the advantages of certain evaluative techniques. Finally, Felix Cohen argues that in the development of the law, legal concepts have not kept pace and that, as a result, many such concepts are now either meaningless or misleading. In addition, he urges a recognition of the fact that language should be functional.

Cybernetics

NORBERT WIENER

It is the thesis of this [paper] that society can only be understood through a study of the messages and the communication facilities which belong to it; and that in the future development of these messages and communication facilities, messages between man and machines, between machines and man, and between machine and machine, are destined to play an ever-increasing part.

When I give an order to a machine, the situation is not essentially different from that which arises when I give an order to a person. In other words, as far as my consciousness goes I am aware of the order that has gone out and of the signal of compliance that has come back. To me, personally, the fact that the signal in its intermediate stages has gone through a machine rather than through a person is irrelevant and does not in any

Reprinted from *The Human Use of Human Beings* (second edition revised), pp. 16–27 by permission of the publisher and the author. Copyright 1950, 1954 by Houghton Mifflin Company.

case greatly change my relation to the signal. Thus the theory of control in engineering, whether human or animal or mechanical, is a chapter in the theory of messages.

Naturally there are detailed differences in messages and in problems of control, not only between a living organism and a machine, but within each narrower class of beings. It is the purpose of Cybernetics to develop a language and techniques that will enable us indeed to attack the problem of control and communication in general, but also to find the proper repertory of ideas and techniques to classify their particular manifestations under certain concepts.

The commands through which we exercise our control over our environment are a kind of information which we impart to it. Like any form of information, these commands are subject to disorganization in transit. They generally come through in less coherent fashion and certainly not more coherently than they were sent. In control and communication we are always fighting nature's tendency to degrade the organized and to destroy the meaningful; the tendancy, as Gibbs has shown us, for entropy to increase.

Much of this [paper] concerns the limits of communication within and among individuals. Man is immersed in a world which he perceives through his sense organs. Information that he receives is co-ordinated through his brain and nervous system until, after the proper process of storage, collation, and selection, it emerges through effector organs, generally his muscles. These in turn act on the external world, and also react on the central nervous system through receptor organs such as the end organs of kinaesthesia; and the information received by the kinaesthetic organs is combined with his already accumulated store of information to influence future action.

Information is a name for the content of what is exchanged with the outer world as we adjust to it, and make our adjustment felt upon it. The process of receiving and of using information is the process of our adjusting to the contingencies of the outer environment, and of our living effectively within that environment. The needs and the complexity of modern life make greater demands on this process of information than ever before, and our press, our museums, our scientific laboratories, our universities, our libraries and textbooks, are obliged to meet the needs of this process or fail in their purpose. To live effectively is to live with adequate information. Thus, communication and control belong to the essence of man's inner life, even as they belong to his life in society.

The place of the study of communication in the history of science is neither trivial, fortuitous, nor new. Even before Newton such problems were current in physics, especially in the work of Fermat, Huygens, and Leibnitz, each of whom shared an interest in physics whose focus was not mechanics but optics, the communication of visual images.

Fermat furthered the study of optics with his principle of minimization which says that over any sufficiently short part of its course, light follows the path which it takes the least time to traverse. Huygens developed the primitive form of what is now known as "Huygens' Principle" by saying that light spreads from a source by forming around that source something like a small sphere consisting of secondary sources which in turn propagate light just as the primary sources do. Leibnitz, in the meantime, saw the whole world as a collection of beings called "monads" whose activity consisted in the perception of one another on the basis of a pre-established harmony laid down by God, and it is fairly clear that he thought of this interaction largely in optical terms. Apart from this perception, the monads had no "windows," so that in his view all mechanical interaction really becomes nothing more than a subtle consequence of optical interaction.

A preoccupation with optics and with message, which is apparent in this part of Leibnitz's philosophy, runs through its whole texture. It plays a large part in two of his most original ideas: that of the *Characteristica Universalis,* or universal scientific language, and that of the *Calculus Ratiocinator,* or calculus of logic. This Calculus Ratiocinator, imperfect as it was, was the direct ancestor of modern mathematical logic.

Leibnitz, dominated by ideas of communication, is, in more than one way, the intellectual ancestor of the ideas of this [paper], for he was also interested in machine computation and in automata. My views in this [paper] are very far from being Leibnitzian, but the problems with which I am concerned are most certainly Leibnitzian. Leibnitz's computing machines were only an offshoot of his interest in a computing language, a reasoning calculus which again was in his mind, merely an extension of his idea of a complete artificial language. Thus, even in his computing machine, Leibnitz's preoccupations were mostly linguistic and communicational.

Toward the middle of the last century, the work of Clerk Maxwell and of his precursor, Faraday, had attracted the attention of physicists once more to optics, the science of light, which was now regarded as a form of electricity that could be reduced to the mechanics of a curious, rigid, but invisible medium known as the ether, which, at the time, was supposed to permeate the atmosphere, interstellar space and all transparent materials. Clerk Maxwell's work on optics consisted in the mathematical development of ideas which had been previously expressed in a cogent but non-mathematical form by Faraday. The study of ether raised certain questions whose answers were obscure, as, for example, that of the motion of matter through the ether. The famous experiment of Michelson and Morley, in the nineties, was undertaken to resolve this problem, and it gave the entirely unexpected answer that there simply was no way to determine the motion of matter through the ether.

The first satisfactory solution to the problems aroused by this experiment was that of Lorentz, who pointed out that if the forces holding matter together were conceived as being themselves electrical or optical in nature, we should expect a negative result from the Michelson-Morley experiment. However, Einstein in 1905 translated these ideas of Lorentz into a form in which the unobservability of absolute motion was rather a postulate of physics than the result of any particular structure of matter. For our purposes, the important thing is that in Einstein's work, light and matter are on an equal basis, as they had been in the writings before Newton; without the Newtonian subordination of everything else to matter and mechanics.

In explaining his views, Einstein makes abundant use of the observer who may be at rest or may be moving. In his theory of relativity it is impossible to introduce the observer without also introducing the idea of message, and without, in fact, returning the emphasis of physics to a quasi-Leibnitzian state, whose tendency is once again optical. Einstein's theory of relativity and Gibbs' statistical mechanics are in sharp contrast, in that Einstein, like Newton, is still talking primarily in terms of an absolutely rigid dynamics not introducing the idea of probability. Gibbs' work, on the other hand, is probabilistic from the very start, yet both directions of work represent a shift in the point of view of physics in which the world as it actually exists is replaced in some sense or other by the world as it happens to be observed, and the old naïve realism of physics gives way to something on which Bishop Berkeley might have smiled with pleasure.

At this point it is appropriate for us to review certain notions pertaining to entropy which have already been presented in the introduction. As we have said, the idea of entropy represents several of the most important departures of Gibbsian mechanics from Newtonian mechanics. In Gibbs' view we have a physical quantity which belongs not to the outside world as such, but to certain sets of possible outside worlds, and therefore to the answer to certain specific questions which we can ask concerning the outside world. Physics now becomes not the discussion of an outside universe which may be regarded as the total answer to all the questions concerning it, but an account of the answers to much more limited questions. In fact, we are now no longer concerned with the study of all possible outgoing and incoming messages which we may send and receive, but with the theory of much more specific outgoing and incoming messages; and it involves a measurement of the no-longer infinite amount of information that they yield us.

Messages are themselves a form of pattern and organization. Indeed, it is possible to treat sets of messages as having an entropy like sets of states of the external world. Just as entropy is a measure of disorganization, the information carried by a set of messages is a measure of organization. In fact, it is possible to interpret the information carried by a message as essentially the negative of its entropy, and the negative logarithm of its probability. That is, the more probable the message, the less information it gives. Clichés, for example, are less illuminating than great poems.

I have already referred to Leibnitz's interest in automata, an interest incidentally shared by his contemporary, Pascal, who made real contributions to the development of what we now know as the desk adding machine. Leibnitz saw in the concordance of the time given by clocks set at the same time, the model for the pre-established harmony of his monads. For the technique embodied in the automata of his time was that of the clockmaker. Let us consider the activity of the little figures which dance on the top of a music box. They move in accordance with a pattern, but it is a pattern which is set in advance, and in which the past activity of the figures has practically nothing to do with the pattern of their future activity. The probability that they will diverge from this pattern is nil. There is a message, indeed; but it goes from the machinery of the music box to the figures, and stops there. The figures themselves have no trace of communication with the outer world, except this one-way stage of communication with the pre-established mechanism of the music box. They are blind, deaf, and dumb, and cannot vary their activity in the least from the conventionalized pattern.

Contrast with them the behavior of man, or indeed of any moderately intelligent animal such as a kitten. I call to the kitten and it looks up. I have sent it a message which it has received by its sensory organs, and which it registers in action. The kitten is hungry and lets out a pitiful wail. This time it is the sender of a message. The kitten bats at a swinging spool. The spool swings to its left, and the kitten catches it with its left paw. This time messages of a very complicated nature are both sent and received within the kitten's own nervous system through certain nerve end-bodies in its joints, muscles, and tendons; and by means of nervous messages sent by these organs, the animal is aware of the actual position and tensions of its tissues. It is only through these organs that anything like a manual skill is possible.

I have contrasted the prearranged behavior of the little figures on the music box on the one hand, and the contingent behavior of human beings and animals on the other. But we must not suppose that the music box is typical of all machine behavior.

The older machines, and in particular the older attempts to produce automata, did in fact function on a closed clockwork basis. But modern automatic machines such as the controlled missile, the proximity fuse, the automatic door opener, the control apparatus for a chemical factory, and the rest of the modern armory of automatic machines which perform military or industrial functions, possess sense organs; that is, receptors for messages coming from the outside. These may be as simple as photoelectric cells which change electrically when a light falls on them, and which can tell light from dark, or as complicated as a television set. They may measure a tension by the change it produces in the conductivity of a wire exposed to it, or they may measure temperature by means of a thermocouple, which is an instrument consisting of two distinct metals in contact with one another through which a current flows when one of the points of contact is heated. Every instrument in the repertory of the scientific-instrument maker is a possible sense organ, and may be made to record its reading remotely through the intervention of appropriate electrical apparatus. Thus the machine which is conditioned by its relation to the external world, and by the things happening in the external world, is with us and has been with us for some time.

The machine which acts on the external world by means of messages is also familiar. The automatic photoelectric door opener is known to every person who has passed through the Pennsylvania Station in New York, and is used in many other buildings as well. When a message consisting of the interception of a beam of light is sent to the apparatus, this message actuates the door, and opens it so that the passenger may go through.

The steps between the actuation of a machine of this type by sense organs and its performance of a task may be as simple as in the case of the electric door; or it may be in fact of any desired degree of complexity within the limits of our engineering techniques. A complex action is one in which the data introduced, which we call the *input,* to obtain an effect on the outer world, which we call the *output,* may involve a large number of combinations. These are combinations, both of the data put in at the moment and of the records taken from the past stored data which we call the *memory.* These are recorded in the machine. The most complicated machines yet made which transform input data into output data are the high-speed electrical computing machines, of which I shall speak later in more detail. The determination of the mode of conduct of these machines is given through a special sort of input, which frequently consists of punched cards or tapes or of magnetized wires, and which determines the way in which the machine is going to act in one operation, as distinct from the way in which it might have acted in another. Because of the frequent use of punched or magnetic tape in the control, the data which are fed in, and which indicate the mode of operation of one of these machines for combining information, are called the *taping.*

I have said that man and the animal have a kinaesthetic sense, by which they keep a record of the position and tensions of their muscles. For any machine subject to a varied external environment to act effectively it is necessary that information concerning the results of its own action be furnished to it as part of the information on which it must continue to act. For example, if we are running an elevator, it is not enough to open the outside door because the orders we have given should make the elevator be at that door at the time we open it. It is important that the release for opening the door be dependent on the fact that the elevator is actually at the door; otherwise something might have detained it, and the passenger might step into the empty shaft. This control of a machine on the basis of its *actual* performance rather than its *expected* performance is known as *feedback,* and involves sensory members which are actuated by motor members and perform the function of *tell-tales* or *monitors*—that is, of elements which indicate a performance. It is the function of these mechanisms to control the mechanical tendency toward disorganization; in other words, to produce a temporary and local reversal of the normal direction of entropy.

I have just mentioned the elevator as an example of feedback. There are other cases where the importance of feedback is even more apparent. For example, a gun-pointer takes information from his instruments of observation, and conveys it to the gun, so that the latter will point in such a direction that the missile will pass through the moving target at a certain time. Now, the gun itself must be used under all conditions of weather. In some of these the grease is warm, and the gun swings easily and rapidly. Under other conditions the grease is frozen or mixed with sand, and the gun is slow to answer the orders given to it. If these orders are reinforced by an extra push given when the gun fails to respond easily to the orders and lags behind them, then the error of the gun-pointer will be decreased. To obtain a performance as uniform as possible, it is customary to put into the gun a control feedback element which reads the lag of the gun behind the position it should have according to the orders given it, and which uses this difference to give the gun an extra push.

It is true that precautions must be taken so that the push is not too hard, for if it is, the gun will swing past its proper position, and will have to be pulled back in a series of oscillations, which may well become wider and wider, and lead to a disastrous instability. If the feedback system is itself controlled—if, in other words, its own entropic tendencies are checked by still other controlling mechanisms—and kept within limits sufficiently stringent, this will not occur, and the existence of the feedback will increase the stability of performance of the gun. In other words, the performance will become less dependent on the frictional load; or what is the same thing, on the drag created by the stiffness of the grease.

Something very similar to this occurs in human action. If I pick up my cigar, I do not will to move any specific muscles. Indeed in many cases, I do not know what those muscles are. What I do is to turn into action a certain feedback mechanism; namely, a reflex in which the amount by which I have yet failed to pick up the cigar is turned into a new and increased order to the lagging muscles, whichever they may be. In this way, a fairly uniform voluntary command will enable the same task to be performed from widely varying initial positions, and irrespective of the decrease of contraction due to fatigue of the muscles. Similarly, when I drive a car, I do not follow out a series of commands dependent simply on a mental image of the road and the task I am doing. If I find the car swerving too much to the right, that causes me to pull it to the left. This depends on the actual performance of the car, and not simply on the road; and it allows me to drive with nearly equal efficiency a light Austin or a heavy truck, without having formed separate habits for the driving of the two. I shall have more to say about this in the chapter in this book on special machines, where we shall discuss the service that can be done to neuropathology by the study of machines with defects in performance similar to those occurring in the human mechanism.

It is my thesis that the physical functioning of the living individual and the operation of some of the newer communication machines are precisely parallel in their analogous attempts to control entropy through feedback. Both of them have sensory receptors as one stage in their cycle of operation: that is, in both of them there exists a special apparatus for collecting information from the outer world at low energy levels, and for making it available in the operation of the individual or of the machine. In both cases these external messages are not taken *neat*, but through the internal transforming powers of the apparatus, whether it be alive or dead. The information is then turned into a new form available for the further stages of performance. In both the animal and the machine this performance is made to be effective on the outer world. In both of them, their *performed* action on the outer world, and not merely their *intended* action, is reported back to the central regulatory apparatus. This complex of behavior is ignored by the average man, and in particular does not play the role that it should in our habitual analysis of society; for just as individual physical responses may be seen from this point of view, so may the organic responses of society itself. I do not mean that the sociologist is unaware of the existence and complex nature of communications in society, but until recently he has tended to overlook the extent to which they are the cement which binds its fabric together.

We have seen in this [paper] the fundamental unity of a complex of ideas which until recently had not been sufficiently associated with one another, namely, the contingent view of physics that Gibbs introduced as a

modification of the traditional, Newtonian conventions, the Augustinian attitude toward order and conduct which is demanded by this view, and the
theory of the message among men, machines, and in society as a sequence
of events in time which, though it itself has a certain contingency, strives
to hold back nature's tendency toward disorder by adjusting its parts to
various purposive ends.

What is Information?

ANATOL RAPOPORT

Suppose someone tosses a penny, and you try to guess "heads" or "tails."
Every time you guess correctly you win the penny, and every time you guess
wrong you pay your opponent a penny. You have a fifty-fifty chance to win
on each throw. If you keep playing long enough, unless you are extremely
lucky or unlucky, your winnings will about equal your losses.

Now suppose some character comes along and tells you he has a crystal ball through which he can see how the penny falls, and that for a price,
he will signal this information to you, so that you can win every time. You
have no scruples about playing the game fairly (you are the "economic
man" that classical theoreticians of economics keep talking about). What
is the information offered worth to you?

A common sense argument shows that if the crystal ball really works,
the information is worth to you anywhere up to a penny a reading. If you
pay a whole penny, you will win all of your opponent's money and pay it
all to the crystal ball reader. Then you can expect to be no better or no
worse off than if you played the game trusting to your own guesses (or if
you didn't play the game at all: the fun of playing the game doesn't count
here, because the "economic man" doesn't have any fun anyway). It follows that if you pay your informant anything less than a penny a guess, you
are sure to be ahead in the long run.

Now suppose the man with the crystal ball is a charlatan. He can't
guess the throws any better than you can. He knows, of course, that very
soon he will give you wrong information and that when he does, you may
balk at paying him further "tip offs." So he proposes what seems like a
fair deal: you give him a percentage of your winnings *only* when you win
and pay him nothing if his information proves false. Is it now worthwhile
to employ him? This time a common sense argument says that it is worth

Reprinted from *Etc,* vol. X (1952–1953), pp. 247–60 by permission of the
publisher.

nothing to have him around. If he is no better guesser than you are, you may as well make the guesses yourself and not pay anything.

But now consider the intermediate case, where the crystal ball is good but not perfect. In other words, your informant can guess better than you, but he makes mistakes. Now is it worthwhile to pay him? Yes, it is worthwhile, and it is the more worthwhile the greater the *difference* between his guessing ability and yours. Certainly if you are as good as he is, there is no point in paying him. In other words, if your chances of guessing are as good as his, he is *giving you no information in the long run*. If he is better than you are, even if he is not a perfect guesser, your guessing record will be improved by the information he gives you, and the amount of improvement is, in a way, a measure of the information you receive from him. If he is a worse guesser than you are, you *lose* information if you follow his advice. This situation hints at a possibility of defining information *quantitatively* as the improvement of one's chances of making the right guess.

In *any* situation, information about something we already know is worthless as information. The keen competition among newspapers for "scoops" reflects this attitude. A "scoop" carries more information than a re-write story. Any kind of a message carries more or less information in it depending on the state of knowledge of the recipients. This much has been known ever since messages were invented. In our own day of precise formulation of problems, however, an altogether new way of measuring the amount of information in a message is being developed.

In the example just cited a measure of the amount of information contained in a message is indicated in terms of how much such information is worth in a gambling situation. It is not necessary, however, to measure information in terms of its monetary value any more than it is necessary to depict chance events in terms of gambling situations. Such examples are often chosen because gambling has long served as a link between commonplace situations and sophisticated probabilistic arguments. There is more to the mathematical theory of information than a computation of how much we are willing to pay for the privilege of cheating in games or how the novelty of stories is reflected in the circulation of the newspapers that print them.

THE MATHEMATICAL THEORY OF INFORMATION

The mathematical theory of information was born among communication engineers and is commanding ever greater attention among mathematically inclined biologists and semanticists. The reason for this increasing interest lies, I think, in the fact that the mathematical theory of information has been recognized as another successful instance of making *precise* and *quantitative* an extremely important concept which had been talked about only vaguely before. I believe that the notion of the "quantity of information" is a Big Idea in science, similar in scope to the precise definition of "the amount of matter" as registered on a balance or the "amount of energy" as derived from potentials, velocities, and heat, or the "amount of entropy" as derived from the probabilities of the states of a system. The vast importance of this new big idea is in its potential applications to the fundamental biological and general semantics problems. We will touch on some of these below. Let us first take a closer look at some basic notions contained in the definition of the "amount of information."

As Warren Weaver has remarked, the amount of information in your message is related not to what you are saying but to what you *could* say. This relation links the amount of information in a message with the amount of *pre-conceived* knowledge about its content (recall the intuitive relation between the amount of information and how much we already know or can guess).

Let us suppose that all you can say is "yes" and "no" (in other words, you are as either-or-ish as you can possibly be). Then all you are ever *expected* to say is "yes" or "no," so that one already has a 50% "knowledge" of your potential pronouncements. Thus, if you are entirely two-valued, you cannot give as much information in your one-word speeches as you could if you were "multi-valued." If you selected your messages from *ten* possible ones, all equally likely, then one could hope to guess what you are going to say only once in ten times, instead of every other time, and your information giving capacity would be considerably increased.

The "canned" messages offered by Western Union (birthday greetings, etc.) carry far less information (and therefore are cheaper to send) than individually composed messages, because there are far fewer canned messages to choose from.

In order to define the amount of information in a message, then, we must know the total number of messages in the *repertoire of the source* from which the message is chosen. Let us take a concrete case.

For simplicity, we will assume that all messages are in code and consist of combinations of two signals "1" and "0" (just as all Morse Code messages are combinations of two signals "dit" and "dah"). We ask: how many different messages can we send? Obviously if the length of the message is unlimited, we can send an unlimited number of messages. Let us, therefore, consider only messages of a certain length, say n signals long. We can easily see that there can be exactly 2^n distinct messages n signals long. This follows, because we have 2 choices for the first signal ("1" or "0"), 2 for the second, which makes $2^2 = 4$ choices for a message of two signals. To each of these, we can again add either of two signals to make a message three signals long, etc., so that to make a message n signals long, we have $2\times2\times2$ . . . 2 a product of n 2's or 2^n choices.

Therefore if you know that a certain message is n "binary" signals long, you know you have one chance in 2^n to guess its contents exactly, provided all the messages are equally likely. We could therefore take the number 2^n as a measure of the amount of information such a message carries. But we don't have to take 2^n. We can take some other number *derived* from 2^n, if it is more convenient to do so. The choice of a quantity with which we measure something is not unique. For example, to measure the "size" of a circle, we can take its diameter, but we are equally justified in taking its area, which is a quantity derived from the diameter in a certain way. There is good reason for taking as the measure of the amount of information, carried by a message n binary signals long, not 2^n (which is the reciprocal of the probability of guessing it, or, if you like, the "unlikelihood" of guessing it) but the *logarithm* of that number.

If you remember your high school algebra, you will recall that the logarithm of a number is the power to which a certain fixed number, called the "base" must be raised to get that number. If we conveniently take 2 as our base, then $\log_2(2^n)$ (read "the logarithm to the base two of two to the n-th) is just n. Thus, by the convention we have just established, a message n binary signals long contains n "binary units" of information, or one binary unit per signal. This binary unit is called a "bit" for short. Now we see the advantage of taking the logarithm of the unlikelihood of guessing (2^n) for our measure, since we can now say that a message twice as long (one $2n$ signals long) will contain just twice the amount of information. This is a very convenient way of talking.

It may have occurred to the reader that we have gone around in a circle. Would it not have been simpler to skip the argument about "probabilities of guessing" altogether and start out by a "natural" definition of the amount of information as simply a number proportional to the length of the message?

It would, if we confined ourselves to messages from a single source. However the interesting part of information theory deals with determining the amount of information in a message in terms of the character of its *source,* not merely in terms of its length (it isn't what you say; it's what you *could* say). It is the amount of information per *signal* that we are interested in, in other words, the rate at which information is coming at us as we are receiving the mesage. This rate is one bit per signal in the case of a source with two equally likely signals. Where there are more signals in the source, and especially where the signals are not equally likely or where they are not independent, the amount of information per signal is not nearly so easy to compute. For this purpose, the "round about" definition is necessary. Furthermore, the "round about" definition points up the connection between information theory and the possibility of mathematicizing psychological and semantic concepts, as we shall see.

Let us again suppose that we speak a language composed of two binary signals "1" and "0." But let us now suppose that the "1" occurs far more frequently that the "0." Such is actually the case with the symbols of the languages we ordinarily use. For example, good English can be written with some 30 symbols (the 26 letters, a "space" and some punctuation marks). We can say definitely that some signals occur in English far more frequently than others. Or suppose that "1" and "0" are signals given out by a machine which is inspecting mass-produced parts, where "1" means "O.K." and "0" means "reject." If on the average only one item in a hundred is defective, then the "1" will register ninety-nine times more frequently than the "0." How much information is now contained in a message n units long?

In view of what we said about the meaning of information, we must conclude that in this case the amount of information contained in a message n units long must be less than n bits, because we already have a good chance of guessing what a message will say. If n is, say, 10, we have better than nine chances out of ten to guess the message if we guess it to be all "1's." Since the message does not add as much to our knowledge as it would if the signals were equally likely, we must conclude that it carries less than n bits of information. But how much less?

Suppose a message n units long has n_1 "1's" and n_2 "0's," so that $n_1 + n_2 = n$. What is the probability of occurrence of such a message? If the occurrence of one signal does not influence that of another, it doesn't matter in what order the signals occur. Since in our example the probability of a "1" is .99, and that of a "0" is .01, the probability of n_1 "1's" and n_2 "0's" *arranged in a particular way* (that is, the probability of a particular message) will be $(.99)^{n_1} (.01)^{n_2}$. The logarithm of the reciprocal of this number to the base 2, as we have agreed, will be a measure of the amount of information in such a message. This logarithm is equal to $- n_1 \log_2(.99) - n_2 \log_2(.01)$.

Now we have the amount of information in a particular message with n_1 "1's" and n_2 "0's." But we don't want to measure the information of particular messages. We want to measure the information of an *average* message n signals long coming from the source we have described. We will get this average if we substitute for n_1 and n_2 their average values, averaged over a great many messages coming from the source. Since the frequencies of the "1's" and the "0's" are in the ratio of 99 to 1, it follows that the average value of n_1 will be 99 times than of n_2. Furthermore, $n_1 + n_2$ must equal n. Therefore $n_1 = .99n$ and $n_2 = .01n$ on the average. Then the amount of information in an average message n signals long will be $—.99n \log_2(.99) —.01n \log_2(.01)$. If we wish to express the amount of information per signal, we divide by n and get $—.99 \log (.99) —.01 \log (.01)$. If we calculate this number, we find it to be equal to about .11 bits or only one-ninth of what it would be if the "O.K." and "reject" signals were equally likely.

The method here described can be extended to compute the amount of information per signal from any source in which the occurrence of one signal does not influence the occurrence or non-occurrence of another. If the source has a repertoire of signals numbered 1 to N, and if they occur with relative frequencies (probabilities) p_1, p_2 . . . p_N, then the amount of information per signal, usually denoted by H, is expressed in the following formula:

$$H = —p_1 \log p_1 — p_2 \log p_2 — p_2 \log p_3 \ldots —p_N \log p_N$$

In the example we solved there were only two signals, whose p_1 and p_2 were respectively .99 and .01.

APPLICATIONS TO TECHNOLOGICAL COMMUNICATION THEORY

So far we really did nothing but define terms and draw consequences from our definitions. We said nothing concrete about why we should want to make these particular definitions or draw these particular consequences. We did mention the looming importance of the information concept in semantics, psychology, and biology, but to some one who encounters this concept for the first time, the connection between it and what is generally thought to be the subject matter of biology, etc., is anything but clear.

It is not easy to make such connections clear. In fact, the strenuous work of highly skilled specialists goes almost entirely into uncovering such connections. They cannot be therefore obvious or intuitively evident or even easy to understand when explained. All we can do within the scope of this article is give hints about the sort of reasoning which leads to uncovering the possibilities of applying the quantification of information to several scientific fields.

The first step in solving a problem is to state it. The statement usually involves a description of an existing state and a desirable state of affairs where the factors involved in the discrepancy are explicitly pointed out. The success with which any problem is solved depends to a great extent on the clarity with which it is stated. In fact, the solution of the problem is, in a sense, a clarification (or concretization) of the objectives. Take the problem of curing disease. For ages, it had been implicitly stated thus:

> A is sick.
> This is bad.
> Let us find ways to make A well.

Vague statements lead to vague methods, where success is erratic and questionable. With the classification of diseases (as initiated, say, by Hippocrates), the problem is re-stated:

> A has a fever.
> This is bad.
> Let us look for ways to rid A of fever.

Here there is more promise of success, because the events which make up sickness are somewhat extensionalized. Still further extensionalization appears with the discovery of events *concomitant* with the symptoms, for example the presence of micro-organisms. Now the problem is

> A is infected with tuberculosis bacilli.
> They make A sick.
> Let us find ways to get rid of the bacilli.

Further extensionalization could be, for example, a description of the biochemical processes characteristic of the tuberculosis bacilli which interfere with A's biochemical processes, etc. The more a given problem is extensionalized, the greater promise there is in finding a solution.

The problems of communication hygiene are now assuming an importance equal to those of physiological hygiene. A naive statement of a communication problem dates back to antiquity.

> A talks to B.
> B does not understand A.
> Let us explain to B what A means.

However "attempts to explain" *themselves* depend on the proper functioning of the communication process. If this process is not understood, attempts to explain cannot be expected to have more success than the original attempt to communicate. The first steps in communication hygiene are therefore aimed at the understanding of the communication process. Hence the emergence of communication science.

In examining instances of "failure to understand," we see that it can occur on different levels. A most obvious cause of such failure can be laid to the imperfect transmission of signals. B can fail to understand A simply because A talks with a heavy accent, or is a small child who has not learned to pronounce the words clearly or is talking over a telephone with a bad connection or over a radio with too much static.

Communication problems on this level may deal with acoustics or electronics but also with physiological functions such as hearing and sight and their psychological correlates, the perception of "gestalts" and recognition. Obviously no transmission and no reception of any signal is perfect. An important class of questions in communication theory concerns with the *thresholds* of intelligibility. One wishes to know, for example, how bad static has to be before it begins seriously to interfere with the transmission of spoken information over a radio channel of given characteristics. Evidently both the characteristics of transmission and reception and those of the subject matter broadcast are important in the problem. Information theory provides a measure of these variables. It provides, for example, a measure of the complexity involved in "fidelity" of reproduction. It provides a method of estimating quantitatively the effects of "noise" on reception, since the effects of noise are equivalent to loss of information. It provides theoretical limits for the performance of a channel of given characteristics, somewhat in the way thermodynamics indicates the limits of efficiency of a heat engine.

APPLICATIONS TO SEMANTICS

The semanticist is usually unconcerned with these purely "technical" problems of communication and leaves them to the communication engineer. Division of labor is entirely proper in approaching any complicated set of problems; but it is a mistake to take too seriously the dichotomies we set up in parceling out the jobs. These dichotomies lead not only to the persistence of elementalistic notions but also delay the discovery of analogous *methods* fruitful in the various aspects of the problem. It may be true that the technical problems of long range communication (radio, television, etc.) can be treated entirely independently of the semantic content of the messages or the semantic reactions of the audience. But it may also be true that the methods involved in treating those problems (for example, the mathematical theory of information) can be applied in the seemingly different context of the events which interest general semanticists, psychologists, and others.

Such possibilities are already apparent. To point them out, we will examine a little more closely the formula given above which describes the amount of information in terms of the repertoire of the source and the relative frequencies of the signals employed. As we said, the formula holds if the signals are independent of each other. But what if this is not the case? What if the occurrence of one signal influences the chances of the occurrence of another? This is certainly true in the case where the source is the English alphabet, and the messages consist of English sentences. In this case, it is almost certain that the letter q will be followed by a u (barring comparatively rare words like Iraqi). It is practically impossible for the letter z to be followed by a consonant, etc.

Under these conditions, the formula for the amount of information per signal must be modified. We will not go into the details of this modification here. We will only point out that the problem of computing the amount of information under various conditions of communication has led to a number of important *concepts,* in terms of which the technical problems of communication are described. One important characteristic of those concepts is that they are often stated in mathematical language *and therefore the techniques of mathematical deduction can be applied to them.* This circumstance makes the problems of communication much more explicit and the solutions to such problems easier to find.

Another important advantage of those concepts is that they give hints on how the precise methods of dealing with communication in the (comparatively) uncomplicated area of technology could be extended to the more complicated areas of psychology, semantics, and general semantics. For example, the modification of our formula on page 311 to take into account the interdependence of signals gives rise to the concept of "redundancy" of the source output, and if the source is an entire language, this concept can be extended to mean the "redundancy" of a language. In information theory, redundancy is a measure of the interdependence of the signals. But redundancy has also an intuitive component, and the precise defination makes possible the extensionalization of this intuitive component.

The connection between the precise and the intuitive notions of redundancy is dramatically illustrated in C. Shannon's monograph, *The Mathematical Theory of Communication.* Suppose we put all the letters of the English alphabet into a hat in equal amounts and pull them out one by one "at random." What would they spell? Here is a sample of such a "language."

XFOML RXKHRJFFJUJ ZLPWCFWKCYJ FFJEYVKCQSGHYD
QPAAMKBZAACIBZLHJQD

In any one's estimation this sample does not "make sense." Now suppose that instead of putting the letters into the hat in equal numbers, we put them in proportionally to the frequency with which they actually occur in English and again pull them out at random. The resulting sample now looks like this.

OCRO HLI RGWR NMIELWIS EU LL NBNESEBYA TH EEI
ALHENHTTPA OOBTTVA NAH BRL.

This still doesn't make "sense." But there is no question that it makes
somewhat more "sense" than before. It *looks* more like English. It does
not bristle quite so much with J's and Z's. Somehow we feel that a "gradation" of sense can be established even among random samples of letters.
The feeling is strengthened when we perform the next experiment. We now
put into our hat not single letters but *pairs,* taking care of keeping their
numbers proportional to their actual occurrence in English. Now we get the
following sample.

ON IE ANTSOUTINYS ARE T INCTORE ST BE S DEAMY
ACHIN D ILONASIVE TUCOOWE AT TEASONARE FUSO
TIZIN ANDY TOBE SEACE CTISBE.

Now there is no doubt that we are approaching "English." The sample
contains two or three real English words and several "near-words" like
DEAMY and TEASONARE. A sample of "triples" looks even better.

IN NO IST LAT WHEY CRATICT FROURE BIRS GROCID
PONDENOME OF DEMONSTURES OF THE REPTAGIN IS
REGOACTION OF CRE.

Perhaps this sample reminds us of Jabberwocky. It should, because
Jabberwocky too is an "approximation" to English, a very good approximation that almost makes real sense.
What can be done with letters can be done with words. Compare, for
example, the sample of randomly selected words,

REPRESENTING AND SPEEDILY IS AN GOOD APT OR COME
CAN DIFFERENT NATURAL HERE HE THE A IN CAME THE
TO OF TO EXPERT GRAY COME TO FURNISHES THE LINE
MESSAGE HAD BE THESE

with a sample of randomly selected *pairs* of words,

THE HEAD AND IN FRONTAL ATTACK ON AN ENGLISH
WRITER THAT THE CHARACTER OF THIS POINT IS
THEREFORE ANOTHER METHOD FOR THE LETTERS
THAT THE TIME OF WHO EVER TOLD THE PROBLEM
FOR AN UNEXPECTED,

and see how much more "sense" there is in the second, although it still doesn't "mean" anything.

These "approximations" to English are examples of how the intuitive feeling that one piece of gibberish is somehow closer to the English language than another is a reflection of a precisely and quantitatively defined situation. The situation has to do with the characteristic linkages used in English. The extent of these linkages is also a measure of the *redundancy* of the English language. Redundancy can also be taken as a measure of the fraction of letters which can be randomly deleted from a reasonably long message without making the message unintelligible. FR EXMPLE WENTYIVE PRCET OF HE LTTERS I TIS SENTENCE HVEBEN DLETED AT RANM. The redundancy of English is said to be over 50%.

Redundancy is thus both a linguistic and a mathematical term. The more redundancy there is in a source, the more tolerance there is for noise and other imperfections of transmission without serious interference with intelligibility. The importance of the redundancy concept in cryptogrophy is likewise apparent. The more redundant the source of messages, the easier it is to break a code. In stenography redundancy is a measure of the amount of drastic abbreviation that can be introduced without danger of confusion. All these linguistic matters are contiguous to the field of interest of semanticists and of general semanticists. A manner of expression full of clichés is, of course, high in redundancy. It turns out in the mathematical theory of information that messages from a cliché-ridden source (such as the oratorical repertoire of a run-of-the-mill politician) are also poor in information. This is something semanticists have known all along, but it is gratifying to have this knowledge formulated precisely. Precisely formulated knowledge is valuable not only for its own sake but also as a jumping-off place to new knowledge.

The Returns from Information and
Their Diminution

ANTHONY DOWNS

Political information is valuable because it helps citizens make the best possible decisions. Therefore the primary measure of its value is the margin of utility income by which the outcome of the best decision exceeds that

Reprinted from *An Economic Theory of Democracy* (1957), pp. 252–59 by permission of the publisher. Copyright 1957 by Harper and Brothers.

of the worst one. However, every rational citizen discounts this margin when deciding what data to acquire because his voice is only one among the many that make the decision.

For voting purposes, a citizen's basic return on information is his party differential.* From it he calculates the expected pay-offs of various sets of information bits. Before being compared with the cost of data, these returns must be drastically reduced to accord with the infinitesimal role which each citizen's vote plays in deciding the election. As a result, the returns are so low that many rational voters refrain from purchasing any political information *per se*. Instead they rely upon free data acquired accidentally.

In order to influence government policy-making in any arena of decision, a citizen must be continuously well-informed about events therein. Unlike a voter, he cannot deal merely with *post facto* differentials. The expense of such awareness is so great that no citizen can afford to bear it in every policy area, even if by doing so he could discover places where his intervention would reap large profits. If he is going to exercise any influence at all, he must limit his awareness to areas where intervention pays off most and information costs least. . . . These are the areas of his production specialization, since his income flows from them and he already knows a great deal about them.

A. THE COST OF COMMUNICATION

In spite of similarities, there are significant differences between acquiring information in order to vote and acquiring it in order to influence policy-making. In the first place, voters automatically communicate their decision to government in the act of voting, but influencers must transmit their opinions to government by specific act in order to get results. Like all acts, this one uses scarce resources; i.e., it is costly. The amount of this *cost of communication* depends upon the position of the citizen in society. If he happens to be Vice-President of the United States, it will be low; if he is a laborer in a mining town, it may be very high.

Whatever size this cost is, someone must pay it. However, the one who pays need not be the citizen himself. If his interest in a policy area stems from his business, he can charge the costs of transmitting his views to his firm, which will probably deduct them from its taxable income. Thus the firm and the government bear the cost, not the citizen. But no matter who pays, whatever part of the cost falls on the influencer must

* Party differential is defined as the difference between utility income received in a period *t* (adjusted for trends) and that which would have been received had the opposition been in power.

be counted as part of the marginal cost to be balanced against whatever marginal return there is from being informed. This cost varies depending upon to whom in the government a citizen communicates his views, because it is more expensive to reach some officials than to reach others. Of course, the opinion impact also depends upon whom the influencer contacts. Both these factors must be accounted for in deciding how much information to buy for purposes of influencing policy.

B. WHY INFLUENCERS ARE BETTER INFORMED THAN VOTERS

There is a second important distinction between the two types of return from information: almost everyone at least considers voting, but relatively few citizens ever consider exerting influence in any particular area of policy. As we have seen, a voter's party differential is subject to heavy discounting because of the great number of other voters. In contrast, an influencer's intervention value may suffer hardly any discount because only a small number of others are interested in the policy he wants to influence. Perhaps many people are affected by this policy, but since most of them do not realize in advance the source of these effects, they cannot seek to alter policy pursued at that source.

Such ignorance is not the result of mere apathy; rather it stems from the great cost af obtaining enough information to exert effective influence. Each influencer must be acquainted with the situation at least well enough to be in favor of a specific policy. True, many people voice strong policy preferences without benefit of much information, and the ballots these people cast are just as potent as those of the well-informed. Nevertheless, the government knows that its behavior in a given policy area will affect many people who show no immediate interest in that area. Consequently, it must be persuaded that these presently passive citizens will not react against whatever policy an influencer is promoting. A would-be influencer has to be knowledgeable enough to carry out this persuasion.

Thus formulation of policy requires more knowledge than choosing among alternatives which others have formulated. As a result, influencers need more information about the policy areas they operate in than even the most well-informed voters; hence their data costs are higher. The complexity of these areas often forces influencers to become experts before they can discover what policies best suit their own interests. And because many influencers with different goals are competing with each other for power, each must (1) produce arguments to counter any attacks upon him, (2) assault the others' contentions with data of his own, and (3) be informed enough to know what compromises are satisfactory to him.

In contrast, a voter need find only the differential impact on him of a few alternatives formulated by others. He does not have to examine all the possible alternatives, since not all are open to his choice—though all are open to the choice of a policy-maker. Also, a voter need not be well-informed enough to think of compromises, since either one party or the other will win (except in the case of coalition governments). In addition, unless he is trying to persuade others to vote his way, he does not have to argue with opposing forces, so he is under no competitive pressure to become informed.

The gist of this analysis is that influencers are specialists in whatever policy areas they wish to influence; whereas voters are generalizers trying to draw an overall comparison between parties. Specialization demands expert knowledge and information, especially if competition is keen, but most men cannot afford to become expert in many fields simultaneously. Therefore influencers usually operate in only one or two policy areas at once. This means that in each area, only a small number of specialists are trying to influence the government.

Naturally, the men who stand most to gain from exerting influence in a policy area are the ones who can best afford the expense of becoming expert about it. Their potential returns from influence are high enough to justify a large investment of information. In almost every policy area, those who stand the most to gain are the men who earn their incomes there. This is true because most men earn their incomes in one area but spend them in many; hence the area of earning is much more vital to them than any one area of spending. Furthermore, the cost of data purchased in order to influence government policy in an area of production can often be charged to a business firm or labor union. These corporate units can, in turn, deduct the cost from their taxable incomes. Also they may be large enough to gain economies of scale in data consumption through intensive specialization in relevant policy areas.

For all these reasons, producers are much more likely to become influencers than consumers. The former can better afford both to invest in the specialized information needed for influencing and to pay the cost of communicating their views to the government. This conclusion even applies to business firms, since their revenue nearly always comes from fewer policy areas than their cost inputs. However, almost every man is both a producer and a consumer at different moments of his life. Therefore we must rephrase the above conclusion as follows: men are more likely to exert political influence in their roles as income-receivers than in their roles as income-spenders, whether acting as private citizens or as members of a corporate entity.

This conclusion is of great importance because from it we can deduce (1) the pattern of information investment which any particular citizen is likely to make, (2) which citizens are likely to be well-informed on any given policy area, and (3) what pressures upon government are likely to be strongest in any area. Clearly, the cost of acquiring information and communicating opinions to government determines the structure of political influence. Only those who can afford to bear this cost are in a position to be influential. . . .

The foregoing analysis explains why only a few men try to exert influence in each area, even though many could actually gain by doing so. Most potential gainers cannot afford to discover where influence would profit them. They are forced to leave the field to a few specialists in each area; consequently each of the specialists need discount his intervention value relatively slightly when subtracting the influence of other men. As noted, this conclusion does not apply to voting. The cost of voting is so small that multitudes can rationally afford to do it; hence each voter must discount his own impact heavily to account for the huge number of his fellows.

In general, it is irrational to be politically well-informed because the low returns from data simply do not justify their cost in time and other scarce resources. Therefore many voters do not bother to discover their true views before voting, and most citizens are not well enough informed to influence directly the formulation of those policies that affect them. These results demonstrate that true political equality is impossible even in democracies as long as (1) uncertainty exists, (2) there is a division of labor, and (3) men act rationally.

Language and Behavior

S. I. HAYAKAWA

Many of the inquiries into language, thought, and behavior . . . would largely have remained hidden from public notice—indeed, would largely have remained isolated from each other—had it not been for "general semantics," a body of theory which was the direct inspiration of most of the popular educators and writers who from 1938 on made semantics a familiar term in the United States. General semantics was the name given by Alfred Korzybski (1879-1950), Polish-American scholar ond engineer, to a new educational discipline, the purpose of which, he said, was to train people in "proper evaluation." All day long, human beings have to "evaluate" (react to, think-and-feel about) events, words, and symbols in their environment. Korzybski found a sharp contrast to exist between evaluative

Reprinted from *Etc* (Summer 1952) pp. 26–31 by permission of the publisher and the author. Copyright 1952 by the International Society of General Semantics.

habits ("thinking habits") common in science and technology, in which progress has been rapid and has grown more rapid with each new success, and those common in other areas, such as philosophy, ethics, and politics, in which confusion has been rife and progress has often appeared impossible.

To Korzybski this contrast between progress and stalemate was crucial. He attributed this difference to the differing evaluative habits which people brought to bear on scientific and nonscientific problems. The unspoken assumptions about the relation of language to fact implicit in modern science Korzybski found to be radically different from those implicit in older Western philosophical (and therefore educational) tradition. If evaluative habits with respect to problems not yet regarded as scientific were revised so as to be consistent with the linguistic assumptions underlying modern science, social wisdom would have a chance of keeping up with the problems created by the rapid progress of technologies. Korzybski's proposal of general semantics as a discipline to attain this revision constituted, therefore, the manifesto of a cultural revolution—a proposal that the people of Western culture (and presumably of other cultures too) change radically their patterns of thinking with respect to human, social, philosophical, and ethical problems.

General semantics was based on an extraordinarily broad survey of diverse fields of knowledge, among them mathematics, mathematical logic, physics, biology, neurology, the various schools of psychology and psychiatry since Freud. In each of these Korzybski examined tendencies of thought, the evaluative habits, the ways of approaching problems. It should here be explained for the nonscientific reader that each of these fields was either new or had made revolutionary progress in the twentieth century. In each of them dogmas and assumptions which had been held unquestioned for centuries had been overthrown—in physics, such basic concepts as "time," "space," and "matter"; in psychology, the traditional notions of "mind"; in logic, the belief that propositions had to be either "true" or "false," etc.

Then Korzybski summarized, in a few simple and highly original formulations, what he felt to be the basic assumptions underlying the habits of evaluation common to the most advanced contemporary thinkers. The modern habits of evaluation appeared to rest, he said, on three fundamental non-Aristotelian premises. Comparing the relation of language (as well as of thought, memory, mental images) to reality with the relation of maps to the territory they represent, he laid down these premises: (1) a map *is not* the territory (words *are not* the things they represent); (2) a map *does not* represent *all* of a territory (words *cannot* say *all* about anything); (3) a map is *self-reflexive,* in the sense that an ideal map would have to include a map of the map, which in turn would have to include a map of the map of the map, etc. (it is possible to speak words about words, words about words about words, etc.; in terms of behavior this means that it is possible to react to our reactions, react to our reactions to our reactions, etc.). Evaluative habits based on these premises, Korzybski said, result in flexibility of mind, lack of dogmatism, emotional balance and maturity, such as characterize the best scientific minds—at least in their thought within their special fields.

But almost everywhere, evaluative rigidity prevailed. In Western culture, people were addicted, on all topics in which scientific orientations were not yet general, to rigid adherence to systems of dogma, "eternal verities," slogans and catchwords. Such evaluative habits Korzybski attributed to the *internalizing* of the basic Aristotelian assumptions: (1) A thing *is* what it *is* ("Pigs are pigs," "Acts of aggression should be called by their right name"); (2) Everything is *either* A *or* not-A ("You are either for us or against us; there is no middle ground"); (3) Nothing is *both* A and not-A ("You cannot be both a communist and not a communist"). In order to facilitate the transition from Aristotelian to non-Aristotelian orientations, he offered a set of rules by means of which individuals could *evaluate their own evaluative processes*. Among the rules were the following:

1. *Indexing*. Words lump together unique individuals under a common name. Names give a false impression of identity to non-identical objects and events; this impression when translated into behavior results in identical reactions to all individuals to which the same name can be given. For example, some persons have fixed reactions to "Republicans," "unions," "subsidies," etc. Hence the practice of adding index numbers to all our terms: Republican 1, Republican 2 . . . subsidy 1, subsidy 2 . . . etc., as reminders that there are differences as well as similarities among individuals of the same name.

2. *Dates*. Heraclitus said that you cannot step into the same river twice. The world and everything in it is in process of change. But many behavior patterns, opinions, beliefs, tend to remain fixed and static in spite of changes in circumstances. "Maps" of yesterday are used as guides to the "territories" of today. All terms, statements, opinions, and beliefs should therefore be dated: Supreme Court 1950, Supreme Court 1951 . . . John Smith Monday, John Smith Tuesday. . . . This principle also takes into account the fact that the same object or individual is different in different environments: e.g., violin 1 (rainy day) is not identical with violin 1 (dry day). The habit of dating all terms and statements, when translated into patterns of reaction, makes rigidity of attitudes impossible and a dynamic time-minded orientation habitual.

3. *Et cetera*. All statements should be accompanied by an implicit "et cetera," to remind one of the premise that "maps" do not represent all the "territory," that no statement about objects or events in the real world can ever be final.

4. *The "is" of identity.* The common injunction to "call a spade a spade" has the profoundly misleading implication that we call it a spade because that's what it *is*. ("Pigs are rightly called pigs because they are such dirty animals.") To be wary of the "is" of identity is to guard against confusing words and things, confusing verbal descriptions with actual events.

5. *Quotation marks.* Many terms in everyday language have prescientific metaphysical or structural implications. However, ordinary vocabulary often contains no better terms. Hence such terms ("mind," "race," "substance," "objective," "subjective," "same," etc.) should be used in quotation marks as a reminder that they are not to be trusted.

6. *Hyphens.* Traditional language separates verbally many things that cannot actually be separated. A revolution in physics was accomplished by Einstein's demonstration that space and time cannot be separately considered and that one should think in terms of space-time. Similarly, psychosomatic medicine does not separate physical and mental disorders; biophysics offers general methods for dealing at once with the living and the non-living. The use of such hyphenated terms (psycho-biological, socio-cultural, geo-political) sharpens the awareness of the interrelatedness of events which traditional language treated as unrelated.

Korzybski did not intend these rules merely to be said by rote. Each of them was intended to point beyond itself to subverbal levels—to observing and feeling and absorbing as directly perceived data the nonliguistic actualities distorted by language. The rules were intended as a discipline of, to use the prescientific terms, the "senses," the "emotions," and the "mind"— or to use modern terms, the "organism-as-a-whole." Continued application of the rules, Korzybski claimed, would gradually liberate the individual from his Aristotelian orientations and make a modern man of him—a non-Aristotelian.

A unique feature of general semantics was that it offered, for what its originator believed to be the first time in scientific history, a positive, functional theory of sanity. The rules of evaluation were purported to describe not only how the best scientific minds do work, but how all human minds ought to work. Here Korzybski made use of his study of the mentally ill, as well as of his studies of political controversy and philosophical disputation. In these areas he found lack of indexing (e.g., prejudice), lack of dating (inflexibility, adherence to outworn notions), reliance on word-magic and incantation, and other violations of his rules to be extremely common. To thinkers on social, political, and ethical problems, therefore, he urged the systematic application of his rules as a way of enabling them to escape the limitation placed upon their thought by outmoded evaluative habits and inadequate traditional language structures. To psychiatrists, furthermore, he offered general semantics as a theoretical basis for the re-education of patients towards greater maturity of evaluation.

Both psychiatrists and cultural anthropologists, finding certain patterns of behavior normal in one culture and abnormal in others, had long had difficulty in offering grounds for preferring, in any general sense, some behavior patterns over others. In the light of general semantics, however, any systematic failure of indexing (e.g., class and race barriers), any authoritarian system of dogma, any overvaluation of symbols at the expense of the realities symbolized (e.g., pre-occupation with money rather than with the economic actualities of goods and services), any rigid proscription of the communicative process (e.g., "thought control"), could be described as blocking the full utilization of the human resources of communication and cooperative interaction. As a theory of sanity, therefore, general semantics offered a basis upon which cultures and cultural institutions could be criticized. Societies are sane, according to this view, to the degree to which they permit and encourage the free exchange of communications and the fullest transmission into the future of the usable knowledge of the past, so that knowledge increases in accuracy and predictive value as time goes on. Time, said Korzybski, is the human dimension. This free exchange of communications is the basic process by which cultures are created; hence cultural institutions or evaluative habits which inhibit communications or cause communications to miscarry are subversions of the cultural process. An energetic restatement of this ethic from the point of view of a philosopher of science was made in 1950 by Rapoport in his *Science and the Goals of Man.*

Transcendental Nonsense and the
Functional Approach

FELIX S. COHEN

That something is radically wrong with our traditional legal thought-ways has long been recognized. Holmes, Gray, Pound, Brooks Adams, M. R. Cohen, T. R. Powell, Cook, Oliphant, Moore, Radin, Llewellyn, Yntema, Frank, and other leaders of modern legal thought in America, are in fundamental agreement in their disrespect for "mechanical jurisprudence," for legal magic and word-jugglery. But mutual agreement is less apparent when we come to the question of what to do: How are we going to get

Reprinted from *The Columbia Law Review,* vol. 35 (1935), pp. 809–34 by permission of the publisher. Copyright 1935 by the trustees of *The Columbia Law Review.*

out of this tangle? How are we going to substitute a realistic, rational, scientific account of legal happenings for the classical theological juris-prudence of concepts?

Attempts to answer this question have made persistent use of the phrase "functional approach." Unfortunately, this phrase has often been used with as little meaning as any of the magical legal concepts against which it is directed. Many who use the term "functional" intend no more than the vague connotation which the word "practical" conveys to the "practical" man. Again, the term "functional approach" is sometimes used to designate a modern form of animism, according to which every social institution or bi-ological organ has a "purpose" in life, and is to be judged good or bad as it achieves or fails to achieve this "purpose." I shall not attempt to be faith-ful to these vague usages in using the term "functional." I shall use the term rather to designate certain principles or tendencies which appear most clearly in modern physical and mathematical science and in modern phil-osophy. For it is well to note that the problem of eliminating supernatural terms and meaningless questions and redefining concepts and problems in terms of verifiable realities is not a problem peculiar to law. It is a problem which has been faced in the last two or three centuries, and more especially in the last four or five decades, by philosophy, mathematics, and physics, as well as by psychology, economics, anthropology, and doubtless other sciences as well. Functionalism, operationalism, pragmatism, logical positivism, all these and many other terms have been used in diverse fields, with differing overtones of meaning and emphasis, to designate a certain common ap-proach to this general task of redefining traditional concepts and tradi-tional problems.

It may perhaps clarify the significance of the functional approach in law to trace some of the basic contributions which the functional method has made in modern science and philosophy.

1. THE ERADICATION OF MEANINGLESS CONCEPTS

On its negative side (naturally of special prominence in a protestant movement), functionalism represents an assault upon all dogmas and de-vices that cannot be translated into terms of actual experience.

In physics, the functional or operational method is an assault upon such supernatural concepts as absolute space and absolute time; in mathe-matics, upon supernatural concepts of real and imaginary, rational and ir-rational, positive and negative numbers. In psychology, William James inaugurates the functional method (of which behaviorism is an extreme form) by asking the naive question: "Does consciousness exist?" Modern "functional grammar" is an assault upon grammatical theories and dis-

tinctions which, as applied to the English language, simply have no verifiable significance—such empty concepts, for instance, as that of noun
syntax, with its unverifiable distinction between a nominative, an objective,
and a possessive case. And passing to the field of art, we find that functional
architecture is likewise a repudiation of outworn symbols and functionless
forms that have no meaning,—hollow marble pillars that do not support,
fake buttresses, and false fronts.

So, too, in law. Our legal system is filled with supernatural concepts,
that is to say, concepts which cannot be defined in terms of experience, and
from which all sorts of empirical decisions are supposed to flow. Against
these unverifiable concepts modern jurisprudence presents an ultimatum.
Any word that cannot pay up in the currency of fact, upon demand, is to
be declared bankrupt, and we are to have no further dealings with it.
Llewellyn has filed an involuntary petition in bankruptcy against the concept Title, Oliphant against the concept Contract, Haines, Brown, T. R.
Powell, Finkelstein, and Cushman against Due Process, Police Power, and
similar word-charms of constitutional law, Hale, Richberg, Bonbright, and
others against the concept of Fair Value in rate regulation, Cook and
Yntema against the concept of Vested Rights in the conflict of laws. Each
of these men has tried to expose the confusions of current legal thinking
engendered by these concepts and to reformulate the problems in his field
in terms which show the concrete relevance of legal decisions to social facts.

2. THE ABATEMENT OF MEANINGLESS QUESTIONS

It is a consequence of the functional attack upon unverifiable concepts
that many of the traditional problems of science, law, and philosophy are
revealed as pseudo-problems devoid of meaning. As the protagonist of logical
positivism, Wittgenstein, says of the traditional problems of philosophy:

> *"Most propositions and questions, that have been written about philo-
> sophical matters, are not false, but senseless. We cannot, therefore, answer
> questions of this kind at all, but only state their senselessness. Most ques-
> tions and propositions of the philosophers result from the fact that we do
> not understand the logic of our language. (They are of the same kind as
> the question whether the Good is more or less identical than the Beautiful.)
> And so it is not to be wondered at that the deepest problems are really
> no problems."*

The same thing may be said of the problems of traditional jurisprudence. As commonly formulated, such "problems" as, "What is the holding
or *ratio decidendi* of a case?" or "Which came first,—the law or the state?"

or "What is the essential distinction between a crime and a tort?" or "Where is a corporation?" are in fact meaningless, and can serve only as invitations to equally meaningless displays of conceptual acrobatics.

Fundamentally there are only two significant questions in the field of law. One is, "How do courts actually decide cases of a given kind?" The other is, "How ought they to decide cases of a given kind?" Unless a legal "problem" can be subsumed under one of these forms, it is not a meaningful question and any answer to it must be nonsense.

It is often easier to distinguish a school of thought by asking not, "What basic theory does it defend?" but rather, "What basic question does it propound?"

A failure to recognize that the law is a vast field in which different students are interested in diverse problems has the unfortunate effect of making every school of legal thought an *ex officio* antagonist of every other school. Dean Pound's classification of jurists into mutually exclusive "analytical," "historical," "philosophical," and "sociological" schools, with subspecies too numerous to mention, has given a good deal of prestige to the idea that a new school of jurisprudence must offer a revolutionary threat to all existing schools. It would be unfortunate to regard functionalism in law as a substitute for all other isms. Rather, we must regard functionalism, in law as in anthropology, economics, and other fields, as a call for the study of problems which have been neglected by other scientific methods of investigation.

In general, when one comes upon a strange fact and seeks to understand it, there are four inquiries he can pursue.

In the first place, our investigator can *classify* the fact—either by putting an arbitrary label upon it or by discerning in the fact to be explained the significant similarities and differences which relate it to other facts.

Again, one may seek to discover the *genesis* of the fact in question, to trace its historical antecedents.

In the third place, one may inquire into the *nature* of the fact presented, endeavoring by logical analysis to resolve it into simpler elements.

A fourth possible approach seeks to discover the *significance* of the fact through a determination of its implications or consequences in a given mathematical, physical or social context.

It is this last approach to which the term "functional" has been applied. Obviously, it is not the *only* way of gathering useful information, and, obviously, it is largely dependent upon the results of classificatory or taxonomic investigation, genetic or historical research, and analytical inquiries. Finally, it must be remarked that the functional method is not a recent invention. Plato's attempt to define justice by assessing the activities of a just state, and Aristotle's conception of the soul as the way a living body behaves are illustrious examples of functional analysis. So, too, Hume's analysis of causation in terms of uniformity of succession, and Berkeley's analysis of matter in terms of its appearances, are significant attempts to redefine supernatural concepts in natural terms, to wash ideas in cynical acid (borrowing Holmes' suggestive phrase).

If functional analysis seems novel in the law, this is perhaps traceable to the general backwardness of legal science, which is the product of social factors that cannot be exorcized by new slogans.

With these caveats against the notion that the functional approach is a new intellectual invention which will solve all the problems of law (or of anthropology, economics, or any other science), we may turn to the significant question: "What are the new directions which the functional method will give to our scientific research?"

In attempting to answer this question for the field of law we may find suggestive precedents in other social sciences.

Applied to the study of religion, for instance, the functional approach has meant a shift of emphasis away from the attempt to systematize and compare religious beliefs, away from concern with the genesis and evolution of religions, and towards a study of the consequences of various religious beliefs in terms of human motivation and social structure. Outstanding examples of this focus are Weber's and Tawney's studies of the influence of Protestantism in the development of modern capitalism, and James' essays on the psychological significance for the individual of various religious beliefs. The functional approach asks of every religious dogma or ritual: How does it work? How does it serve to mould men's lives, to deter from certain avenues of conduct and expression, to sanction accepted patterns of behavior, to produce or alleviate certain emotional stresses, to induce social solidarity, to lay a basis for culture accumulation by giving life after death to the visions, thoughts and achievements of mortal men? The significance of a religious dogma is found not in a system of theological propositions but in a mode of human conduct. The functional approach demands objective description of this conduct, in which the empirical significance of the religious belief is embodied. Just so, the functional approach in physics captures the significance of a physical concept in the actual processes and operations of the physicist, rather than in the theological or metaphysical interpretations which physicists put upon their own activities. It is an application of this same approach that discovers the significance of a legal principle in the actual behavior of judges, sheriffs, and litigants rather than in conventional accounts of the principles that judges, sheriffs, and litigants are supposed to follow.

In anthropology, the functional method represents a movement away from two types of study: the naïve reporting and classification of striking human peculiarities; and the more sophisticated attempt to trace the historical origin, evolution, and diffusion of complexes. Those who have embraced the functional approach (not all of whom have invoked the word "functional") have been primarily concerned to trace the social consequences of diverse customs, beliefs, rituals, social arrangements, and patterns of human conduct. This approach has led to fertile fields that most earlier investigators missed. In the study of primitive art, the new focus has brought into the foreground the question of the craftsman's motivations and purposes, the significance of art as an individualizing or socializing force, the whole problem of interplay between materials, techniques, and social needs. The study of primitive social organization comes increasingly to deal with the functional significance of family, clan, and tribal groupings as social determinants in the production, distribution, and use of property, as well as in the noneconomic human relationships of education, religion, play, sex, and companionship. In the study of primitive law, the functional approach raises to the fore the problem of incentives to obedience and the efficacy of these incentives, the techniques of law enforcement, and the relations of rivalry or supplementation between legal sanctions and other social forces.

A similar use of the functional approach is characteristic of modern political science, in which revolt against the classical supernatural conception of sovereignty is a point of agreement uniting the most diverse schools of contemporary thought. Typical is the following statement:

By institutions we merely mean collective behavior patterns, the ways in which a community carries on the innumerable activities of social life. . . . Society achieves certain results through collective political actions. The means that it uses are the behavior patterns which we call courts, legislative bodies, commissions, electorates, administration. We idealize these institutions collectively and personify them in the State. But this idealization is pure fancy. The State as a juristic or ideal person is the veriest fiction. It is real only as a collective name for governmental institutions.

Under the influence of the functional approach political theory ceases to be a science of pure forms, and comes increasingly to grips with the psychological motives and technological forces that function through political instruments.

In economics we have witnessed a similar shift of research from the taxonomic or systematic analysis of economic norms to the study of the actual economic behavior of men and nations. Veblen's indictment of classical economic theory may be applied word for word to classical jurisprudence, if we merely substitute for the terms "economic" and "economist" the terms "legal" and "jurist":

The standpoint of the classical economists *in their higher or definitive, syntheses and generalizations, may not inaptly be called the standpoint of ceremonial adequacy. . . . In effect, this preconception imputes to things a tendency to work out what the instructed common sense of the time accepts as the adequate or worthy end of human effort. . . . This ideal of conduct is made to serve as a canon of truth. . . .*

The metaphors are effective, both in their homiletical use are as a laborsaving device—more effective than their user designs them to be. By their use the theorist is enabled serenely to enjoin himself from following out an elusive train of causal sequence. . . . The scheme so arrived at is spiritually binding on the behavior of the phenomena contemplated. . . . Features of the process that do not lend themselves to interpretation or terms of the formula are abnormal cases and are due to disturbing cause. In all this the agencies or forces causally at work in the economic *life process are neatly avoided. The outcome of the method, at its best, is a body of logically consistent propositions concerning the normal relations of things—a system of* economic *taxonomy.*

The same "standpoint of ceremonial adequacy" has to some extent characterized the works of our classical jurists—such masters of the law as Beale, Williston, and even Wigmore. For them, as for the classical economists, it was easy to avoid "an elusive train of causal sequence." Principles, conceived as "spiritually binding on the behavior of the phenomena contemplated," diverted their attention from the hard facts of the legal world —the human motivations and social prejudices of judges, the stretching or shrinking of precedents in every washing, the calculations of juries, and the fact of legislation—and at the same time diverted attention from the task of legal criticism.

The age of the classical jurists is over, I think. The "Restatement of the Law" by the American Law Institute is the last long-drawn-out gasp of a dying tradition. The more intelligent of our younger law teachers and students are not interested in restating the dogmas of legal theology. There will, of course, be imitators and followers of the classical jurists in the years ahead. But I think that the really creative legal thinkers of the future will not devote themselves, in the manner of Williston, Wigmore, and their fellow masters, to the taxonomy of legal concepts and to the systematic explication of principles of justice and reason, buttressed by "correct" cases. Creative legal thought will more and more look behind the pretty array of correct cases to the actual facts of judicial behavior, will make increasing use of statistical methods in the scientific description and prediction of judicial behavior, will more and more seek to map the hidden springs of judicial decision and to weigh the social forces which are represented on the bench. And on the critical side, I think that creative legal thought will more and more look behind the traditionally accepted principles of justice and reason to appraise in ethical terms the social values at stake in any choice between two precedents.

"Social policy" will be comprehended not as an emergency factor in legal argument but rather as the gravitational field that gives weight to any rule or precedent, whether it be in constitutional law, in the law of trade-marks, or in the most technical details of legal procedure.

There is implied in this shifting of the paths of legal research a change in the equipment needs of the student of law. Familiarity with the words of past judicial opinions and skill in the manipulation of legal concepts are not enough for the student who seeks to understand the social forces that control judicial behavior, nor for the lawyer who seeks to use these forces.

The vested interests of our law schools in an independent science of law are undermined by every advance in our knowledge of the social antecedents and consequences of judicial decision. It becomes the part of discretion, in law schools aware of such advances, to admit that legal science necessarily involves us in psychology, economics, and political theory. Courses in our more progressive law schools are beginning to treat, most gingerly, of the psychological doctrines embedded in our rules of evidence, the sociological theories assumed in our criminal law, the economic assumptions embalmed in our doctrines of constitutional law, and the psychological, sociological, and economic *facts* which give force and significance to rules and decisions in these and other fields of law. The first steps taken are clumsy and evoke smiles of sympathy or roars of laughter from critics of diverse temperaments. The will to walk persists.

For the lawyer, no less than for the legal scholar, handling of materials hitherto considered nonlegal assumes increasing importance. And courts that shut their doors to such nonlegal materials, laying the taboos of evidence law upon facts and arguments that reveal the functional social significance of a legal claim or a legal precedent, will eventually learn that society has other organs—legislatures and legislative committees and administrative commissions of many sorts—that are willing to handle, in straightforward fashion, the materials, statistical and descriptive, that a too finicky judiciary disdains.

CHAPTER EIGHT

POWER

OF all the social sciences, none has been more concerned with the concept of power than political science. A content analysis of the political writings from Aristotle to the present would no doubt reveal power as the central concept around which attempts to explain politics have revolved. Thus, Professor Morgenthau's suggestion in 1957 that we make power the "central concept" in political science is little more than recognition of what has generally been the case. But to build a theory of politics around the concept, as Morgenthau suggests, remains to be done. Such a theory would not presume that all political action is controlled by power relations. It would assume, however, that the student possessed a full understanding of the concept. The fact that we are scarcely closer to a general theory of power than we are to a general theory of politics suggests that such an assumption is somewhat less than valid.

Robert Dahl surmises that our difficulty may be that power is many things. This observation points up the first major problem confronting anyone who ventures down this precarious path and is verified by the examinations of the various ramifications of power undertaken by Goldhamer and Shils on the one hand, and Maurice Ash on the other.

For while political scientists can agree that the power process is a vital adjunct to the total political process, they have not yet agreed on a general definition of power. The significance of this failure lies in the possible inference that the power vineyard is barren of fruit. An alternative view recognizes the improbability of developing a satisfactory general theory, but suggests the possibility of a number of theories more limited in scope. Such theories may have applicability in specific subject matter areas or in particular research efforts.

The use of limiting definitions of power presents no insuperable obstacles as long as care is exercised in their formulation. Unless we are to be satisfied with intuitive generalizations, we must establish as a minimal requirement that definitions of power be operational. An operational definition is one whose applicability may be determined by performing certain operations on the data which have been identified as relevant. The operational definition must enable us to measure and compare in some meaningful way that which we have defined. The importance of measuring has been recognized by several of those utilizing the power concept in its limited sense. Examples may be found in the work of Dahl, Simon, and Shapley and Shubik.

Dahl defines power as the difference between the probability that an act of an inducer will produce a particular response on the part of an inducee, and the probability that the same response will be forthcoming if the inducer changes his behavior. Shapley and Shubik focus on the decision-making control possessed by members of a group operating under majority rule. They define the power of a member of a group making decisions by majority rule as the probability that the member is critical to the successful coalition. For example, in Supreme Court cases decided by a full Court, the fifth vote is always pivotal since at least five votes are necessary to make a majority. Given adequate information, Shapley and Shubik would assign the total power involved in making a decision to the pivotal member. Lacking such information, the power assignment can only be made on a probability basis. The probability that any member of a majority is pivotal may be derived by taking the reciprocal of the size of the majority. Thus, in a five-man majority, the probability that any one member is pivotal is .200. For a series of decisions, the power allotments may be summed and averaged using the total number of decisions as the divisor. Through this procedure then, we may derive a numerical expression of certain relationships (labeled *power* by Shapley and Shubik) for one or a series of decisions. The usefulness of this measure in systems analysis has been illustrated in an earlier paper in this volume.

While Dahl centers his attention on the power of one actor to control the behavior of another and Shapley and Shubik concentrate on the power of A, B, C, . . . N members of a decision-making group to determine decisions, Simon's focus is on power as an influence process. The latter defines the power of A over B as the ratio of the limit of B's zone of acceptable behavior induced by A to the total possible behavior of B. Simon makes a positive contribution in his penetrating analysis of the problems associated with defining and measuring power. On balance, the work of the above writers makes it clear that power in the complete sense is impossible to pin down and measure at the present stage of methodological development. Yet the work of the power theorists has not been in vain. Shapley and Shubik, in particular, have shown that certain relationships defined as power in the nominal sense or aspects of power in the real sense may be observed, quantified, and measured. This is important in building toward definition and measurement of power in a more absolute sense.

Types of Power and Status

HERBERT GOLDHAMER AND EDWARD A. SHILS

A person may be said to have *power* to the extent that he influences the behavior of others in accordance with his own intentions. Three major forms of power may be distinguished in terms of the type of influence brought to bear upon the subordinated individual. The power-holder exercises *force* when he influences behavior by a physical manipulation of the subordinated individual (assault, confinement, etc.) ; *domination* when he influences behavior by making explicit to others what he wants them to do (command, request, etc.) ; and *manipulation* when he influences the behavior of others without making explicit the behavior which he thereby wants them to perform. Manipulation may be exercised by utilizing symbols or performing acts. Propaganda is a major form of manipulation by symbols. The undermining of confidence in an enterprise by sabotaging its activities may be taken as an example of manipulation by acts.

Most power-holders claim legitimacy for their acts, i.e., they claim the "right to rule" as they do. If the legitimacy of the exercise of power is acknowledged by the subordinated individuals we speak of *legitimate power;* if it is not recognized we call it *coercion* (provided, of course, that the intention of the power-holder is realized). There are three major forms of legitimate power. Legitimate power is regarded as *legal* when the recognition of legitimacy rests on a belief by the subordinated individuals in the legality of the laws, decrees, and directives promulgated by the power-holder; *traditional* when the recognition of legitimacy rests on a belief in

Reprinted from *The American Journal of Sociology*, vol. 45 (1939), pp. 171–82 by permission of The University of Chicago Press. Copyright 1939 by The University of Chicago.

the sanctity of traditions by virtue of which the power-holder exercises his power and in the traditional sanctity of the orders which he issues; and *charismatic* when the recognition of legitimacy rests on a devotion to personal qualities of the power-holder. Usually, of course, these personal qualities are, or appear to the followers to be, extraordinary qualities such as sanctity and heroism.

A person whose general position as a power-holder is recognized as legitimate may exercise force, domination, or manipulation. But, as far as the recognition of the legitimacy of individual acts of power is concerned, it is clear that manipulation cannot be legitimate power, since in the case of manipulation there is no recognition by the subordinated individual that an act of power has been effected. Persons who are subject to force (especially as an initial form of influencing behavior and not as a sanction) frequently do not recognize the legitimacy of such acts of power. Generally, therefore, the recognition of a power-holder as a legitimate exerciser of power rests on the recognition of the legitimacy of his acts of domination. However, this need not mean that he may not also exercise force or manipulation.

Attempted domination may meet with obedience or disobedience. The motivation for obedience and disobedience is *instrumental* to the extent that it is based on an anticipation of losses and gains, and *noninstrumental* to the extent that it is based on ethical or affective imperatives of conduct dictating obedience or disobedience to the command. In the case of obedience these imperatives may derive either (*a*) from a belief that the recognition of power as legitimate, i.e., as legal, traditional, or charismatic, imposes obedience as a norm of conduct or (*b*) from norms of conduct (e.g., the mores) which dictate, not obedience to the power-holder but the performance of the particular acts commanded. In the case of disobedience the imperatives will likewise derive either (*a*) from a belief that the recognition of power as nonlegitimate, i.e., coercive, imposes disobedience as a norm of conduct or (*b*) from norms of conduct which dictate not disobedience to the power-holder but the nonperformance of the particular acts commanded. Although one may recognize the legitimacy of power, yet one may also obey or disobey out of instrumental considerations. This signifies in the case of disobedience that the instrumental considerations outweigh the motivation toward conformity arising from the recognition of legitimacy.

If the attempt of a person to exercise power fails, the power act may be followed either by a substitute power act or by a sanction. A *substitute power act* is intended primarily to attain the original aim of the first act. Substitution may take place both within or between types of power. Thus a command may be substituted for a polite request (both forms of attempted domination), or unsuccessful propaganda may be succeeded by an outright command (manipulation and domination). A *sanction* is a power act initiated primarily as a reprisal for nonconformity with a prior act of power; its intent is punitive and not primarily directed toward achieving the goal of the prior unsuccessful power act. Since persons who are subjected to attempted exercise of force or manipulation do not—unlike persons subjected to commands—either obey or disobey, sanctions may most properly be spoken of as a reprisal for disobedience to a command (domination) rather than as nonconformity to other types of power. However, it may be true that an unsuccessful propagandist or unsuccessful exerciser of force may (irrationally) take actions with punitive intent against persons who fail to succumb to his propaganda or to his attempt to exercise force.

A sanction may be either a deprivation of values already possessed or an obstruction to the attainment of values which would have been realized were it not for the punitive intervention of the power-holder. A sanction may be either a physical loss (beating, confinement, etc.) or a nonphysical loss (fining, confiscation, removal from office, ridicule, etc.).

Disobedience to the command of a power-holder may result not only in consciously intended sanctions but also in unintended penalizations (such as guilt feelings, loss of prestige, etc.), the anticipation of which may motivate the individual to conform. Market operations afford an important case of unintended penalizations. The demands of buyers and sellers upon each other produce a collective compromise expressed in the price level. Intransigent buyers and sellers are not necessarily subject to intended losses, but their intransigence is, in fact, likely to squeeze them out of the market. The conformity of the buyers or sellers to the imperatives of market conditions involves, in this case, conformity not only to the immediate demands of those with whom they have direct relations but through them, indirectly, with all other persons in the market. Unintended consequences may also be derivative penalizations, i.e., they may be unintended results from the infliction of an intended sanction. Thus imprisonment may (even after release) result in the loss of job, prestige, and associations.

Sanctions may be exercised either directly by the power-holder himself or indirectly through others in official or nonofficial positions. Most power-holders of any consequence possess a staff of officials to whom the exercise of sanctions is delegated. Although power-holders may instigate persons without official position (mobs, the public, "the consumer," etc.) to take reprisals against nonconformists, the exercise of sanctions by nonofficials is perhaps most important in the case of unintended and derivative penalizations and in the case of intended sanctions without instigation from official power-holders.

A power relation is *unilateral* if only one party to the relationship exercises power over the other and *bilateral* if both parties exercise power over each other. The power relationships between officers and privates in an army are typically unilateral. A major form of bilateral power relation is the case of bargaining power, to the extent that each party influences the behavior of the other in the intended direction. In bargaining each party attempts to influence the behavior of the other either by depriving him of values already possessed or by obstructing the attainment of values not yet possessed but desired. Bilateral power relations exist not only in the case of domination (as when each party is able to make demands on the other) but also in the case of manipulation. That is, each party may influence the behavior of the other party without making explicit what behavior is desired. Thus parties may mutually influence each other's behavior in a desired direction by propaganda or by acts. The outcome of attempted bilateral domination or manipulation may be complete fulfilment of the intentions of both parties (provided they are not incompatible) or a compromise, i.e., a partial success by both parties or the fulfilment (partially or fully) of the intention of only one party or, finally, modes of behavior completely different from the intention of either party.

The exercise of power is *direct* when the power-holder alters the behavior of others without utilizing an intermediary and *indirect* when a chain of direct power acts is initiated by a power-holder who utilizes one or more subordinate power-holders. The control of an army by a general or of factory workers by a large-scale entrepreneur is largely by means of indirect power. The chain of direct power acts constituting the exercise of indirect power may be composed of different types of direct power acts. Thus the initial act may be a command (domination) to a subordinate power-holder who may alter the behavior of others by propaganda (manipulation) in order to instigate mob violence (force) against certain groups, thus attaining the intention of the initiating power-holder. The personnel utilized in the sequence of direct power acts composing indirect power may be both official and nonofficial.

The amount of power exercised by an individual may be measured either by the ratio of his successful power acts to all of his attempted power acts or by certain criteria specified below. These measures may be used as a basis of comparison between different power-holders. The two "amounts" represent not alternative techniques of measurement but differences in what is measured. Amount in these cases does not mean the same thing. Most investigations of power, in so far as they deal with the amount of power, utilize "amount" in the second sense.

Two principal criteria may be used to measure the amount of power exercised by a power-holder: the number of actions of any given person, in each of any number of selected types of behavior, over which control is realized (or potential) ; and the number of persons so controlled. The definition of dictatorship as "a form of government where everything that is not forbidden is obligatory" indicates complete power in terms of the spheres of behavior over which control is exercised.

Concentration of power is not diminished if the power-holder acts through many subordinates, provided he is able to exercise control over them. In fact, however, the utilization of a large subordinate staff is very likely to diffuse power, since the chief power-holder is rarely able to control fully the actions of his subordinates who may therefore exercise a certain amount of independent or initiatory, rather than dependent, power. Further the impossibility of maintaining complete control over the subordinate staff and the reliance which the power-holder must place on them tends to set up a bilateral power relation between the chief power-holder and his subordinates, giving the latter power over the chief power-holder in addition to any independent power they may exercise over the mass. Subordinate power-holders, to the extent that they exercise independent power in the sphere claimed by the chief power-holder, will limit the power of the latter, and to that extent lose their character of subordinates. On the other hand, a plurality of independent power-holders (whether partially or completely independent) may not only limit but also reinforce or not at all affect one another's exercise of power. This will be true only to the extent that the power-holders influence the behavior of others in a manner which does not obstruct the intentions of their co-power-holders. With the growing interdependence of all aspects of social life, however, and consequently the increased probabilities that any act will have more extensive repercussions throughout the society than formerly, it becomes more essential for a power-holder both to control many aspects of behavior that formerly might have seemed quite unnecessary for carrying out his intentions and to prevent others from exercising powers that formerly might not have interfered with his intention. Although one finds in contemporary society, both in public and in private spheres, an increasing concentration of power, the necessity, as enterprises increase in size, of exercising power through the utilization of many subordinate power-holders tends to limit the actual if not the formal concentration of power.

The amount and stability of power exercised will be limited by the means which the power-holder has available for influencing the behavior of others by making them want to do what he wants them to do or by the sanctions which they anticipate that he can bring to bear upon them. Large amounts of power cannot be exercised in a purely coercive fashion, for even though the mass of subordinated individuals do not recognize the power-holder as exercising legitimate power, the necessity of utilizing a large staff would introduce other than purely coercive power into the total power system; for the subordinate power-holders, who exercise dependent power and carry out sanctions for cases of nonconformity among the mass, cannot themselves be controlled by coercion alone. The greater the amount of coercive power exercised, the greater is the dependence of the chief power-holder on his staff. For this reason and because the possible supervision over, and sanctions against, the mass often fall short of the requirements for the exercise of coercive power, the latter frequently has to be augmented and supported by manipulation. This may serve the purpose not only of getting people to act in a desired manner without exercising coercion but also of developing a belief in the legitimacy of the power exercised and thereby also limiting the need for coercive action.

It is sometimes assumed that a person who uses force or is in a position to impose very drastic sanctions in the event of nonconformity with his commands is somehow more powerful than one who exercises power without the use of these means. But, the amount of power exercised by a legitimate power-holder may be as great as, or greater than, the amount exercised by a coercive power-holder. If, however, we restrict comparison only to coercive power-holders, then it is true, all other things being equal, that power varies directly with the severity of the sanctions that the power-holder can impose.

Men evaluate the objects, acts, and human attributes with which they come into contact. These evaluations may become systematized into a hierarchy of values. The individual makes judgments of others and ranks them on the basis of his hierarchy of values and his knowledge concerning what characteristics these other persons possess. Such a judgment of rank made about either the total person or relatively stable segments of the person constitutes the *social status* of that person (for the individual making the judgment). Societies and individuals use different gestures to express degrees of deference which they accord to varying ranks of social status. These gestures expressing the status of an individual may be called *deference gestures* or more simply, *deference*.

The deference gestures which a person directs toward or about another person are *genuine* when the deferrer holds them appropriate for expressing the status he ascribes to that other individual, and *spurious* when they are not those which he holds as appropriate for expressing the status he ascribes to the other individual. Spurious deference may be the giving of a deference either higher or lower than that which the deferrer considers appropriate for the status in question (or higher or lower than the deferrer customarily gives to a person with the status in question). The first of these two types of spurious deference constitutes a frequent form of manipulation, the spurious deference being intended to induce a desired form of behavior.

Status judgments are *total* when the evaluation is made of the person as a whole and not of any particular role which he performs or any particular attribute which he possesses and *segmental* when the evaluation is made of the person in terms of a particular role which he performs or of a particular attribute which he possesses.

Deference gestures are *specialized* when they are utilized only toward persons performing certain roles (such as saluting in the case of the army); and *nonspecialized* when they are used equally toward persons of the same status irrespective of their roles (as general terms of respect such as "sir"). People often accord generalized deference gestures to persons to whom they accord segmental status because specialized gestures exist only for a very limited number of roles (such as military or ecclesiastical roles). The use of a nonspecialized deference gesture, such as "sir," does not signify, therefore, that the individual using it necessarily does so because he accords high total status. Persons may, however, intentionally use certain nonspecialized deference gestures in order to create a definite impression that a high total status is being accorded when in fact the status actually accorded is only high segmental status. To the extent that this is successfully used to influence behavior it constitutes manipulation.

Deference gestures frequently become highly conventionalized and hence uniform throughout a society or segments of a society. There may, however, be considerable individuation of deference gestures, i.e., a considerable deviation from the conventional forms. Clearly the more individuated such gestures become, the less they will serve to convey to others the deference being accorded by the person making the gestures. Deference gestures vary not only in their degree of individuation but also in the degree to which they discriminate differences in status. Thus in eighteenth-century Germany *Fräulein* as a mode of address was a highly discriminatory deference gesture, as it was used only in addressing young women of the upper classes.

In some periods societies or special groups within societies have attempted to level status and deference distinctions, even though they have found it impossible to erase differences in those objective characteristics of persons which usually give rise to status and deference distinctions. Such attempts are often found in the early stages of religious sectarian movements (for the members are equal before God and should therefore be equal before one another) and in the early periods of egalitarian revolutions. It would seem that the attempt to level deference distinctions is usually more successful than the attempt to level status distinctions. Thus leveling terms such as *citoyen* are universally applied to all members of the society, and various honorific terms if retained are universally applied and thus lose their discriminatory value. Because of this one finds that in time new deference gestures are evolved to permit expressions of the different degrees of status developed on the basis of the new revolutionary value system.

The status accorded to a person depends on the value hierarchy held by the individual making the status judgment and the individual's knowledge of the characteristics of the person judged. A status judgment that a person makes of another is *true* if based on an accurate knowledge of the characteristics of the person judged, and *false* if based on an incorrect knowledge of the characteristics of the person judged. Thus if a person ranks wealth very high in his hierarchy of values and if he believes another person to be very wealthy, he will rank the latter high in the status scale. If, in fact, the person judged is wealthy, the status accorded him by the person making the judgment is a true status; but if, in fact, the person judged is poor, then the judgment is a false status. To say that a status judgment concerning an individual is "true" does not imply an objectively true status judgment in the sense that any status judgment deviating from it is false. If persons have different value hierarchies and all have approximately the same correct knowledge of the characteristics of the individual being judged, the various different status judgments will all be true status judgments. As long as the value hierarchies of the persons making the judgments differ, the status judgments must differ if they are true.

The status judgments referred to in this article are privately or subjectively made status judgments. A person may make true status judgments but publicly may state that the individual in question has in his opinion a higher or lower status than he privately judges him to have. Such falsifications may be termed spurious status to distinguish them from status judgments based on incorrect knowledge, i.e., false status judgments. Status judgments are often given expression through deference gestures, and falsification of these constitutes, of course, spurious deference.

The present discussion of status might seem to impute to individuals a high degree of awareness of their own value systems and considerable conscious analysis in the process of assigning status to an individual and according him the appropriate deference gestures. Status judgments and deference gestures are, of course, not usually arrived at in such a fashion, although such a process is likely to occur in the case of some types of persons, such as religious and political sectarian leaders who make all evaluations in terms of a few clearly and fervently held principles. Again, it is possible that an individual may apply different value hierarchies in making status judgments of different types of individuals. The possession of a plurality of value hierarchies is perhaps most likely to exhibit itself in making status judgments of the self and of others with the same objective characteristics. To what extent, however, individuals may have more than one independent value hierarchy is difficult to say. Furthermore, for the entire discussion of social values and social status it is of the highest importance to realize that for some individuals and in some periods for a considerable proportion of the population the value hierarchies may be in a condition of great flux resulting in both ambiguity and ambivalence of status judgments. No investigation of status and deference could afford to ignore the complications mentioned above, but the present discussion does not attempt either to analyze the psychological processes by which status judgments and deference gestures are made or to deal with the manifold consequences resulting from ambiguous and ambivalent value systems.

The Concept of Power

ROBERT A. DAHL

That some people have more power than others is one of the most palpable facts of human existence. Because of this, the concept of power is as ancient and ubiquitous as any that social theory can boast. If these assertions needed any documentation, one could set up an endless parade of great names from Plato and Aristotle through Machiavelli and Hobbes to Pareto and Weber to demonstrate that a large number of seminal social theorists have devoted a good deal of attention to power and the phenomena associated with it. Doubtless it would be easy to show, too, how the word and its synonyms are everywhere embedded in the language of civilized peoples, often in subtly different ways: power, influence, control, pouvoir, puissance, Macht, Herrschaft, Gewalt, imperium, potestas, auctoritas, potentia, etc.

I shall spare the reader the fruits and myself the labor of such a demonstration. Reflecting on the appeal to authority that might be made does, however, arouse two suspicions: First (following the axiom that where there is smoke there is fire), if so many people at so many different times have felt the need to attach the label power, or something like it, to

Reprinted from *Behavorial Science,* vol. 2 (July 1957), pp. 201–15 by permission of the author and the publisher.

some Thing they believe they have observed, one is tempted to suppose that the Thing must exist; and not only exist, but exist in a form capable of being studied more or less systematically. The second and more cynical suspicion is that a Thing to which people attach many labels with subtly or grossly different meanings in many different cultures and times is probably not a Thing at all but many Things; there are students of the subject, although I do not recall any who have had the temerity to say so in print, who think that because of this the whole study of "power" is a bottomless swamp.

Paradoxical as it may sound, it is probably too early to know whether these critics are right. For, curiously enough, the systematic study of power is very recent, precisely because it is only lately that serious attempts have been made to formulate the concept rigorously enough for systematic study. If we take as our criterion for the efficiency of a scientific concept its usability in a theoretical system that possesses a high degree of systematic and empirical import, then we simply cannot say whether rigorous definitions of the concept of power are likely to be useful in theoretical systems with a relatively large pay-off in the hard coin of scientific understanding. The evidence is not yet in.

I think it can be shown, however, that to define the concept "power" in a way that seems to catch the central intuitively understood meaning of the word must inevitably result in a formal definition that is not easy to apply in concrete research problems; and therefore, operational equivalents of the formal definition, designed to meet the needs of a particular research problem, are likely to diverge from one another in important ways. Thus we are not likely to produce—certainly not for some considerable time to come—anything like a single, consistent, coherent "Theory of Power." We are much more likely to produce a variety of theories of limited scope, each of which employs some definition of power that is useful in the context of the particular piece of research or theory but different in important respects from the definitions of other studies. Thus we may never get through the swamp. But it looks as if we might someday get around it.

With this in mind, I propose first to essay a formal definition of power that will, I hope, catch something of one's intuitive notions as to what the Thing is. By "formal" I mean that the definition will presuppose the existence of observations of a kind that may not always or even frequently be possible. Second, I should like to indicate how operational definitions have been or might be modelled on the formal one for some specific purposes, and the actual or possible results of these operational definitions.

I should like to be permitted one liberty. There is a long and honorable history attached to such words as power, influence, control, and authority.

For a great many purposes, it is highly important that a distinction should be made among them; thus to Max Weber, *"Herrschaft ist . . . ein Sonderfall von Macht,"* Authority is a special case of the first, and Legitimate Authority a subtype of cardinal significance. In this essay I am seeking to explicate the primitive notion that seems to lie behind *all* of these concepts. Some of my readers would doubtless prefer the term "influence," while others may insist that I am talking about control. I should like to be permitted to use these terms interchangeably when it is convenient to do so, without denying or seeming to deny that for many other purposes distinctions are necessary and useful. Unfortunately, in the English language power is an awkward word, for unlike "influence" and "control" it has no convenient verb form, nor can the subject and object of the relation be supplied with noun forms without resort to barbaric neologisms.

POWER AS A RELATION AMONG PEOPLE

What is the intuitive idea we are trying to capture? Suppose I stand on a street corner and say to myself, "I command all automobile drivers on this street to drive on the right side of the road"; suppose further that all the drivers actually do as I "command" them to do; still, most people will regard me as mentally ill if I insist that I have enough power over automobile drivers to compel them to use the right side of the road. On the other hand, suppose a policeman is standing in the middle of an intersection at which most traffic ordinarily moves ahead; he orders all traffic to turn right or left; the traffic moves as he orders it to do. Then it accords with what I conceive to be the bedrock idea of power to say that the policeman acting in this particular role evidently has the power to make automobile drivers turn right or left rather than go ahead. My intuitive idea of power, then, is something like this: *A* has power over *B* to the extent that he can get *B* to do something that *B* would not otherwise do.

If Hume and his intellectual successors had never existed, the distinction between the two events above might be firmer than it is. But anyone who sees in the two cases the need to distinguish mere "association" from "cause" will realize that the attempt to define power could push us into some messy epistemological problems that do not seem to have any generally accepted solutions at the moment. I shall therefore quite deliberately steer clear of the possible identity of "power" with "cause," and the host of problems this identity might give rise to.

Let us proceed in a different way. First, let us agree that power is a relation, and that it is a relation among people. Although in common speech the term encompasses relations among people and other animate or inanimate objects, we shall have our hands full if we confine the relationship to human beings. All of the social theory I mentioned earlier is interesting only when it deals with this limited kind of relationship. Let us call the objects in the relationship of power, actors. Actors may be individuals, groups, roles, offices, governments, nation-states, or other human aggregates.

To specify the actors in a power relation—*A* has power over *B*—is not very interesting, informative, or even accurate. Although the statement that the President has (some) power over Congress is not empty, neither is it very useful. A much more complete statement would include references to *(a)* the source, domain, or *base* of the President's power over Congress; *(b)* the *means* or instruments used by the President to exert power over Congress; *(c)* the *amount* or extent of his power over Congress; and *(d)* the range or *scope* of his power over Congress. The base of an actor's power consists of all the resources—opportunities, acts, objects, etc.—that he can exploit in order to effect the behavior of another. Much of the best writing on power—Bertrand Russell is a good example—consists of an examination of the possible bases of power. A study of the war potential of nations is also a study of the bases of power. Some of the possible bases of a President's power over a Senator are his patronage, his constitutional veto, the possibility of calling White House conferences, his influence with the national electorate, his charisma, his charm, and the like.

In a sense, the base is inert, passive. It must be exploited in some fashion if the behavior of others is to be altered. The *means* or instruments of such exploitation are numerous, often they involve threats or promises to employ the base in some way and they may involve actual use of the base. In the case of the President, the means would include the *promise* of patronage, the *threat* of veto, the *holding* of a conference, the *threat* of appeal to the electorate, the *exercise* of charm and charisma, etc.

Thus the means is a mediating activity by *A* between *A*'s base and *B*'s response. The *scope* consists of *B*'s responses. The scope of the President's power might therefore include such Congressional actions as passing or killing a bill, failing to override a veto, holding hearings, etc.

The *amount* of an actor's power can be represented by a probability statement: e.g., "the chances are 9 out of 10 that if the President promises a judgeship to five key Senators, the Senate will not override his veto," etc. Clearly the amount can only be specified in conjunction with the means and scope.

Suppose now we should wish to make a relatively complete and concise statement about the power of individual *A* over individual *a* (whom I shall call the respondent) with respect to some given scope of responses. In order to introduce the basic ideas involved, let us restrict ourselves to the

2 by 2 case, where the actor A does or does not perform some act and the respondent a does or does not "respond." Let us employ the following symbols:

(A, w) = A does w. For example, the President makes a nation-wide television appeal for tax increases.

$(A, \overline{w})$ = A does not do w.

(a, x) = a, the respondent, does x. For example, the Senate votes to increase taxes.

$(a, \overline{x})$ = a does not do x.

$P(u|v)$ = Probability that u happens when v happens.

Then a relatively complete and concise statement would be symbolized:

$$P(a, x | A, w) = p_1$$
$$P(a, x | A, w) = p_2$$

Suppose now, that $p_1 = 0.4$ and $p_2 = 0.1$. Then one interpretation might be: "The probability that the Senate will vote to increase taxes if the President makes a nationwide television appeal for a tax increase is 0.4. The probability that the Senate will vote to increase taxes if the President does not make such an appeal is 0.1."

PROPERTIES OF THE POWER RELATION

Now let us specify some properties of the power relation.

1. A necessary condition for the power relation is that there exists a time lag, however small, from the actions of the actor who is said to exert power to the responses of the respondent. This requirement merely accords with one's intuitive belief that A can hardly be said to have power over a unless A's power attempts precede a's responses. The condition, obvious as it is, is critically important in the actual study of power relations. Who runs the XYZ Corporation? Whenever the president announces a new policy, he immediately secures the compliance of the top officials. But upon investigation it turns out that every new policy he announces has first been put to him by the head of the sales department. Or again, suppose we had a full record of the times at which each one of the top Soviet leaders revealed his positions on various issues; we could then deduce a great deal about who is running the show and who is not. A good bit of the mystery surrounding the role of White House figures like Sherman Adams and Harry Hopkins would also be clarified by a record of this kind.

2. A second necessary condition is, like the first, obvious and nonethe-

less important in research: there is no "action at a distance." Unless there is some "connection" between A and a, then no power relation can be said to exist. I shall leave the concept of "connection" undefined, for I wish only to call attention to the practical significance of this second condition. In looking for a flow of influence, control, or power from A to a, one must always find out whether there is a connection, or an opportunity for a connection, and if there is not, then one need proceed no further. The condition, obvious as it is, thus has considerable practical importance for it enables one to screen out many possible relations quite early in an inquiry.

3. In examining the intuitive view of the power relation, I suggested that it seemed to involve a successful attempt by A to get a to do something he would not otherwise do. This hints at a way of stating a third necessary condition for the power relation. Suppose the chances are about one out of a hundred that one of my students, Jones, will read *The Great Transformation* during the holidays even if I do not mention the book to him. Suppose that if I mention the book to him and ask him to read it, the chances that he will do so are still only one out of a hundred. Then it accords with my intuitive notions of power to say that evidently I have no power over Jones with respect to his reading *The Great Transformation* during the holidays—at least not if I restrict the basis of my action to mentioning the book and asking him (politely) to read it. Guessing this to be the case, I tell Jones that if he does not read the book over the holidays I shall fail him in my course. Suppose now that the chances he will read the book are about 99 out of 100. Assume further that nothing else in Jones's environment has changed, at least nothing relevant to his reading or not reading the book. Then it fully accords with my intuitive notions of power to say that I have some power over Jones's holiday reading habits. The basis of my power is the right to fail him in his course with me, and the means I employ is to invoke this threat.

Let me now set down symbolically what I have just said. Let

$=$	$(x \, {}^{\prime}f)$	my threat to fail Jones if he does not read *The Great*
$=$	$(\underline{m} \, {}^{\prime}a)$	*Transformation* during the holidays.
		no action on my part.
$=$	$(m \, {}^{\prime}a)$	Jones reads *The Great Transformation* during the holidays.

Further, let

$p_1 = P(J, \, x | D, \, w)$ the probability that Jones will read *The Great Transformation* if I threaten to fail him.

$p_2 = P(J, x|D, \overline{w})$ the probability that Jones will read the book
if I do not threaten to fail him.

Now let us define the *amount of power*. To avoid the confusion that might arise from the letter p, let us use the symbol M (from *Macht*) to designate the amount of power. Then, in accordance with the ideas set out in the illustration above, we define A's power over a, with respect to the response x, by means of w, as M, or, more fully:

$$M\left(\frac{A}{a}:w, x\right) = P(a, x|A, w)$$
$$- P(a, x|A, \overline{w}) = p_1 - p_2$$

Thus in the case of myself and Jones, M, my power over Jones, with respect to reading a book during the holidays, is 0.98.

We can now specify some additional properties of the power relation in terms of M:

a. If $p_1 = p_2$, then $M = 0$ and no power relation exists. The absence of power is thus equivalent to statistical independence.

b. M is at a maximum when $p_1 = 1$ and $p_2 = 0$. This is roughly equivalent to saying that A unfailingly gets B to do something B would never do otherwise.

c. M is at a minimum when $p_1 = 0$ and $p_2 = 1$. If negative values of M are to be included in the power relation at all—and some readers might object to the idea—then we shall have a concept of "negative power." This is not as foolish as it may seem, although one must admit that negative control of this kind is not ordinarily conceived of as power. If, whenever I ask my son to stay home on Saturday morning to mow the lawn, my request has the inevitable effect of inducing him to go swimming, when he would otherwise have stayed home, I do have a curious kind of negative power over him. The Legion of Decency sometimes seems to have this kind of power over moviegoers. Stalin was often said to wield negative power over the actions on appropriations for foreign aid by the American Congress. A study of the Senate that will be discussed later suggested that at least one Senator had this kind of effect on the Senate on some kinds of issues.

Note that the concept of negative power, and M as a measure, are both independent of the *intent* of A. The measure does, to be sure, require one to assign a positive and negative *direction* to the responses of the respondent; what one chooses as a criterion of direction will depend upon his research purposes and doubtless these will often include some idea as to the intent of the actors in a power relation. To take a specific case, p_1 *could* mean "the probability that Congress will defeat a bill if it is contained in the President's legislative program," and p_2 could mean "the probability that Congress will defeat such a bill if it is not contained in the President's legislative program." By assigning direction in this way, positive values of M would be associated with what ordinarily would be interpreted as meaning a "negative" influence of the President over Congress. The point of the example is to show that while the measure does require that direction be specified, the intent of A is not the only criterion for assigning direction.

POWER COMPARABILITY

The main problem, however, is not to determine the existence of power but to make comparisons. Doubtless we are all agreed that Stalin was more powerful than Roosevelt in a great many ways, that McCarthy was less powerful after his censure by the Senate than before, etc. But what, precisely, do we mean? Evidently we need to define the concepts "more power than," "less power than," and "equal power."

Suppose we wish to compare the power of two different individuals. We have at least five factors that might be included in a comparison: (1) differences in the basis of their power, (2) differences in means of employing the basis, (3) differences in the scope of their power, i.e., in type of response evoked, (4) differences in the number of comparable respondents, and (5) differences in the change in probabilities, or M.

The first two of these may be conveniently thought of as differences in properties of the actors exercising power, and the last three may be thought of as differences in the responses of the respondents. Now it is clear that the pay-off lies in the last three—the responses. When we examine the first two in order to compare the power of individuals, rulers, or states, we do so on the supposition that differences in bases and means of actors are very likely to produce differences in the responses of those they seek to control.

As I have already indicated, much of the most important and useful research and analysis on the subject of power concerns the first two items, the properties of the actors exercising power, and there is good reason to suppose that studies of this kind will be as indispensable in the future as they have been in the past. But since we are concerned at the moment with a formal explication of the concept of power, and not with an investigation of research problems, (some of these will be taken up later on) it is important to make clear that analysis of the first two items does not, strictly speaking, provide us with a comparison of the power of two or more actors, except insofar as it permits us to make inferences about the last three items. If we could make these inferences more directly, we should not be particularly interested in the first two items—at least not for purposes of making comparisons of power. On the other hand, given information about the responses, we may be interested in comparing the efficiency of different bases or means; in this case, evidently, we can make a comparison only by holding one or both of the first two factors constant, so to speak. In general, the properties of the power wielder that we bring into the problem are determined by the goals of one's specific research. For example, one might be interested in the relative power of different state governors to secure favorable legislative action on their proposals by means of patronage; or alternatively, one might be interested in the relative effectiveness of the threat of veto employed by different governors.

In whatever fashion one chooses to define the relevant properties of the actors whose power he wishes to compare, strictly speaking one must compare them with respect to the responses they are capable of evoking. Ideally, it would be desirable to have a single measure combining differences in scope, number of comparable respondents controlled, and change in probabilities. But there seems to exist no intuitively satisfying method for doing so. With an average probability approaching one, I can induce each of 10 students to come to class for an examination on a Friday afternoon when they would otherwise prefer to make off for New York or Northampton. With its existing resources and techniques, the New Haven Police Department can prevent about half the students who park along the streets near my office from staying beyond the legal time limit. Which of us has the more power? The question is, I believe, incapable of being answered unless we are ready to treat my relationships with my students as in some sense comparable with the relations of the Police Department to another group of students. Otherwise any answer would be arbitrary, because there is no valid way of combining the three variables—scope, number of respondents, and change in probabilities—into a single scale.

Let us suppose, for a moment, that with respect to two of the three variables the responses associated with the actions of two (or more) actors we wish to compare are identical. Then it is reasonable to define the power of A as greater than the power of B if, with respect to the remaining variable, the responses associated with A's acts are greater than the responses associated with B's acts. It will be readily seen, however, that we may have jumped from the frying pan into the fire, for the term "greater than" is still to be defined. Let us take up our variables one by one.

To begin with, we may suppose that the probability of evoking the response being the same for two actors and the numbers of comparable persons in whom they can evoke the response also being the same, then if the scope of responses evoked by A is greater than evoked by B, A's power is greater than B's. But how can we decide whether one scope is larger than another? Suppose that I could induce my son to bathe every evening and to brush his teeth before going to bed and that my neighbor could induce his son to serve him breakfast in bed every morning. Are the two responses I can control to be counted as greater than the one response my neighbor can control? Evidently what we are willing to regard as a "greater" or "lesser" scope of responses will be dictated by the particular piece of research at hand; it seems fruitless to attempt to devise any single scale. At one extreme we may wish to say that A's scope is greater than B's only if A's scope contains in it every response in B's and at least one more; this would appear to be the narrowest definition. At the other extreme, we may be prepared to treat a broad category of responses as comparable, and A's scope is then said to be greater than B's if the number of comparable responses in his scope is larger than the number in B's. There are other possible definitions. The important point is that the particular definition one chooses will evidently have to merge from considerations of the substance and objectives of a specific piece of research, and not from general theoretical considerations.

Much the same argument applies to the second variable. It is clear, I think, that we cannot compare A's power with respect to the respondents $a_1, a_2, \ldots a_n$ and B's power with respect to the respondents $b_1, b_2 \ldots b_n$ unless we are prepared to regard the two sets of individuals as comparable. This is a disagreeable requirement, but obviously a sensible one. If I can induce 49 undergraduates to support or oppose federal aid to education, you will scarcely regard this as equivalent to the power I would have if I could induce 49 Senators to support or oppose federal aid. Again, whether or not we wish to treat Senators as comparable to students, rich men as comparable to poor men, soldiers as comparable to civilians, enlisted men as comparable to officers, military officers as comparable to civil servants, etc., is a matter that can be determined only in view of the nature and aims of the research at hand.

The third variable is the only one of the three without this inherent limitation. If scope and numbers are identical, then there can be no doubt, I think, that it fully accords with our intuitive and common-sense notions of the meaning of power to say that the actor with the highest probability of securing the response is the more powerful. Take the set of Democratic Senators in the United States Senate. Suppose that the chance that at least two-thirds of them will support the President's proposals on federal aid to education is 0.6. It is fair to say that no matter what I may do in behalf of federal aid to education, if there are no other changes in the situation except those brought about by my efforts the probability that two-thirds of them will support federal aid will remain virtually at 0.6. If, on the other hand, Senator Johnson, as majority leader, lends his full support and all his skill of maneuver to the measure the probability may rise, let us say, to 0.8. We may then conclude (what we already virtually know is the case, of course) that Senator Johnson has more power over Democratic Senators with respect to federal aid to education than I have.

Earlier in defining the amount of power by the measure, M, I had already anticipated this conclusion. What I have just said is precisely equivalent to saying that the power of A with respect to some set of respondents and responses is greater than the power of B with respect to an equivalent set if and only if the measure M associated with A is greater than the measure M associated with B. To recapitulate:

$$M\left(\frac{A}{a}:w,\ x\right)\ =\ p_1 - p_2,\ \textit{where}\ p_1 = P(a,\ x|A,\ w)$$

the probability that a will do x, given action w by A

$$p_2 = P(a,\ x|A,\ \bar{w})$$

the probability that a will do x, given no action w by A.

$$M\left(\frac{B}{b}:y,\ z\right)\ =\ p_1{}^* - p_2{}^*,\ \text{where}$$
$$p_1{}^* = P(b,\ z/B,\ y)$$
$$p_2{}^* = P(b,\ z/B,\ y).$$

Now if these two situations are *power comparable* (a notion we shall examine in a moment) then A's power is greater than B's if and only if

$$M\left(\frac{A}{a}:w,\ x\right) > M\left(\frac{B}{b}:y,\ z\right).$$

In principle, then, whenever there are two actors, A and B, provided only that they are power comparable, they can be ranked according to the amount of power they possess, or M. But if it is possible to rank A and B, it is possible to rank any number of pairs. And it is obvious from the nature of M that this ranking must be transitive, i.e.,

$$\text{if } M\left(\frac{A}{a}:w,\ x\right) > M\left(\frac{B}{b}:y,\ z\right), \text{ and}$$
$$M\left(\frac{B}{b}:y,\ z\right) > M\left(\frac{C}{c}:u,\ v\right), \text{ then}$$
$$M\left(\frac{A}{a}:w,\ x\right) > M\left(\frac{C}{c}:u,\ v\right).$$

In principle, then, where any number of actors are in some relation to any number of equivalent subjects, and these relations are regarded as power comparable, then all the actors can be unambiguously ranked according to their power with respect to these subjects.

There is, as everyone knows, many a slip 'twixt principle and practice. How can one convert the theoretical measure, M, into a measure usable in practical research? Specifically, suppose one wishes to examine the power relations among some group of people—a city council, legislature, community, faculty, trade union. One wants to rank the individuals in the group according to their power. How can one do so?

The first problem to be faced is whether given the aims, substance, and possible theoretical import of his study, one does in fact have *power comparability*. One of the most important existing studies of the power structure of a community has been criticized because of what appears to have been a failure to observe this requirement. A number of leaders in a large Southern city were asked, "If a project were before the community that required *decision* by a group of leaders—leaders that nearly everyone would accept—which *ten* on the list of forty would you choose?" On the basis of the answers, individuals were ranked in such a way that a "pyramidal" power structure was inferred to exist in the city, i.e., one consisting of a small number of top leaders who made the key decisions, which were then executed by a larger middle-group of subordinate leaders. The significance of this conclusion is considerably weakened, however, if we consider whether the question did in fact discriminate among different kinds of responses. Specifically, suppose the leaders had been asked to distinguish between decisions over local taxes, decisions on schools, and efforts to bring a new industry to the community: would there be significant differences in the rankings according to these three different kinds of issues? Because the study does not provide an answer to this question, we do not know how to interpret the significance of the "pyramidal" power structure that assertedly exists. Are we to conclude that in "Regional City" there is a small determinate group of leaders whose power significantly exceeds that of all other members of the community on all or nearly all key issues that arise? Or are we to conclude, at the other extreme, that some leaders are relatively powerful on some issues and not on others, and that no leaders are relatively powerful on all issues? We have no way of choosing between these two interpretations or indeed among many others that might be formulated.

Let us define A and B as formally power comparable (in the sense that the relative magnitudes of the measure M are held to order the power of A and B correctly) if and only if the actors, the means, the respondents and the responses or scopes are comparable. That is,

the actor	A is comparable to the actor,	B;
A's respondent,	a " " " B's respondent,	b;
A's means,	w " " " B's means,	y; and
a's response,	x " " " b's response,	z.

But this is not a very helpful definition. For the important question is whether we can specify some properties that will insure comparability among actors, respondents, means, and scopes. The answer, alas, is no. So far as an explication of the term "power" is concerned, power comparability must be taken as an undefined term. That is, power comparability will have to be interpreted in the light of the specific requirements of research and theory, in the same way that the decision as to whether to regard any two objects—animals, plants, atoms, or whatnot—as comparable depends upon general considerations of classification and theoretical import. To this extent, and to this extent only, the decision is "arbitrary"; but it is not more "arbitrary" than other decisions that establish the criteria for a class of objects.

To political scientists it might seem farfetched to compare the power of a British prime minister over tax legislation in the House of Commons with the power of the President of the United States over foreign policy decisions in the Senate. It would seem farfetched because the theoretical advantages of such a comparison are not at all clear. On the other hand, it would not seem quite so farfetched to compare the two institutional positions with respect to the "same" kind of policy—say tax legislation or foreign policy; indeed, political scientists do make comparisons of this kind. Yet the decision to regard tax legislation in the House of Commons as comparable in some sense to tax legislation in the Senate is "arbitrary." Even the decision to treat as comparable two revenue measures passed at different times in the United States Senate is "arbitrary." What saves a comparison from being genuinely arbitrary is, in the end, its scientific utility. Some kinds of comparisons will seem more artificial than others; some will be theoretically more interesting and more productive than others. But these are criteria derived from theoretical and empirical considerations independent of the fundamental meaning of the term power.

On what grounds, then, can one criticize the study mentioned a moment ago? Because the use of undiscriminating questions produced results of very limited theoretical significance. By choosing a relatively weak criterion of power comparability, the author inevitably robbed his inquiry of much of its potential richness. Considerations of comparability are, therefore, critical. But the criteria employed depend upon the problem at hand and the general state of relevant theory. The only way to avoid an arbitrary and useless definition of "power comparability" is to consider carefully the goals and substance of a particular piece of research in view of the theoretical constructs one has in mind. Thus in the case of the Senate, it may be satisfactory for one piece of research to define all Senate roll-call votes on all issues as comparable; for another, only votes on foreign policy issues will be comparable; and for still another, only votes on foreign policy issues involving large appropriations; etc. In a word, the researcher himself must define what he means by comparability and he must do so in view of the purpose of the ranking he is seeking to arrive at, the information available, and the relevant theoretical constructs governing the research.

APPLICATIONS OF THE CONCEPT OF POWER COMPARABILITY

Assuming that one has power comparability, the next problem is to rank every actor whose rank is relevant to the research. Here we run into practical problems of great magnitude.

Suppose we wish to rank a number of Senators with respect to their influence over the Senate on questions of foreign affairs. Specifically, the respondent and response are defined as "all Senate roll-call votes on measures that have been referred to the Foreign Relations Committee." To begin with, let us take two Senators. What we wish to find out is the relative influence on the Senate vote of the activities of the two Senators for or against a measure prior to the roll call. "For" and "against" must be defined by reference to some standard "direction." Passage of the measure is one possible "direction" in the sense that a Senator can be for passing the measure, against it, or without a position for or against passage. This is not, however, a particularly significant or meaningful direction, and one might wish to determine the direction of a measure by reference to the President's position, or by content, or by some other standard. For this discussion, I shall assume that "for" and "against" are defined by reference to the first standard, i.e., passing the measure.

Let us now assume that a Senator does one of three things prior to a roll-call vote. He works for the measure, he works against it, or he does nothing. (The assumption, although a simplification of reality, is by no means an unreasonable simplification). Let us further assume (what is generally true) that the Senate either passes the measure or defeats it. With respect to a particular Senator, we have the following conditional probabilities:

	The Senator		
	Works For	Works Against	Does Nothing
Passes	p_1	p_2	p_3
The Senate Defeats	$1 - p_1$	$1 - p_2$	$1 - p_3$

Since the bottom row provides no additional information we shall, in future, ignore it. Following the earlier discussion of the concept M, the measure of power, it is reasonable to define

$$M_1 = p_1 - p_3$$
$$M_2 = p_3 - p_2$$

M_1 is a measure of the Senator's power when he works for a measure and M_2 a measure of his power when he works against a measure; in both cases a comparison is made with how the Senate will act if the Senator does nothing. There are various ways in which we might combine M_1 and M_2 into a single measure, but the most useful would appear to be simply the sum of M_1 and M_2. To avoid confusion with the earlier and slightly different measure which we are now approximating, let us call the sum of M_1 and M_2, M^*. Like M, it is at a maximum of 1 when the Senate always passes the bills a given Senator works for and always defeats the bills he works against; it is at a minimum of -1 when the Senate always defeats the bills he works for and always passes the bills he works against; and it is at 0 when there is no change in the outcome, no matter what he does.

In addition, there is one clear advantage to M^*. It is easily shown that it reduces to

$$M^* = p_1 - p_2.$$

In a moment we shall see how advantageous such a simple measure is.

The theoretical problem, then, is clear-cut and a solution seems reasonably well defined. It is at this point, however, that practical research procedures begin to alter the significance of a solution, for the particular operational means selected to breathe life into the relatively simple formal concepts outlined so far can produce rather different and even conflicting results.

Let me illustrate this point by drawing on a paper by Dahl, March, and Nasatir on influence ranking in the United States Senate. The aim of the authors was to rank thirty-four Senators according to their influence on the Senate with respect to two different areas, foreign policy and tax and economic policy. The 34 Senators were all those who had held office continuously from early 1946 through late 1954, a long enough period, it was thought, to insure a reasonably large number of roll-call votes. The classification of measures to the two areas was taken from the *Congressional Quarterly Almanac,* as were the votes themselves. Thus the subject was well defined and the necessary data were available.

No such systematic record is maintained of course, for the positions or activities of Senators prior to a roll-call vote, and what is more it would be exceptionally difficult to reconstruct the historical record even over one session, not to say over an eight year period. Faced with this apparently insuperable obstacle, it was necessary to adopt a rather drastic alternative, namely to take the recorded roll-call vote of a Senator as an indication of his position and activities *prior to* the roll-call. While this is not unreasonable, it does pose one major difficulty: a vote is necessarily cast either for or against a measure and hence the roll-call provides no way of determining when a Senator does nothing prior to the roll-call. But the very essence of the formal concept of power outlined earlier hinges on a comparison of the difference between what the Senate will do when a Senator takes a given position and what it does when he takes no position.

It is at this point that the advantages of the measure M^* reveal themselves. For provided only that one is prepared to take the Senator's recorded vote as a fair indication of his prior position and activities, the data permit us to estimate the following probabilities, and hence M^*

		The Senator	
		Works For	Works Against
The Senate	Passes	p_1	p_2

One could, therefore, estimate M^* for each of the 34 Senators and rank all of them.

The validity of this method ranking would appear to be greatest, however, when all Senators are ranked on precisely the same set of bills before the Senate. To the extent that they vote on different (although mostly overlapping) sets of bills, the comparability of M^* from one Senator to another will be reduced, conceivably to the vanishing point.

For a number of reasons, including a slightly different interpretation of the characteristics of an ideal measure, the authors chose a rather different approach. They decided to pair every Senator against every other Senator in the following way. The number in each cell is an estimate of the probability that the Senate will pass a proposal, given the positions of the two Senators as indicated; the number is in fact the proportion of times that the Senate passed a foreign policy (or tax) measure in the period 1946–54, given the recorded votes of the two Senators as indicated.

		S_1	
		Favors the motion	Opposes the motion
S_2	Favors the motion	p_{11}	p_{12}
	Opposes the motion	p_{21}	p_{22}

With 34 Senators, 561 possible pairs of this kind exist; but only 158 pairs were tabulated for foreign policy and 206 for tax and economic policy over the whole period. The measure used to enable comparisons to be made between the two Senators in each pair might be regarded as an alternative to $M*$. This measure—let us call it M''—rests upon the same basic assumption, namely that we can measure a Senator's influence by the difference between the probability that the Senate will pass a measure the Senator opposes and the probability that it will pass a measure he supports. However, there are two important differences. First, the authors decided not to distinguish between "negative" and "positive" power; consequently they used absolute values only. Second, in estimating the probability of a measure passing the Senate, the positions of two Senators were simultaneously compared in the manner shown in the table. Thus the influence of S_1 over the Senate was measured as the difference between the probability that a bill will pass the Senate when S_1 favors it and the probability that it will pass when S_1 opposes it. However, this difference in probabilities was measured twice: (1) when S_2 favors the motions before the Senate; and (2) when S_2 opposes the motions. In the same way, S_2's influence was measured twice. Thus:

$$M_1''(S_1) = |p_{11} - p_{12}|,$$

that is, the change in probabilities, given S_2 in favor of the bill.

$$M_2''(S_1) = |p_{21} - p_{22}|,$$

that is, the change in probabilities, given S_2 in opposition to the bill. Likewise,

$$M_1''(S_2) = |p_{11} - p_{21}|$$
$$M_2''(S_2) = |p_{12} - p_{22}|.$$

The influence of S_1 was said to be greater than the influence of S_2 only if $M_1''(S_1) > M_1''(S_2)$ and $M_2''(S_1) > M_2''(S_2)$. That is, if

$$|p_{11} - p_{12}| > |p_{11} - p_{21}| \text{ and}$$
$$|p_{21} - p_{22}| > |p_{12} - p_{22}|.$$

Except for the rare case of what would ordinarily be regarded as "negative" power which, as I have already said, this particular measure was not intended to distinguish from "positive" power—the absolute values are the same as the algebraic ones. Where the algebraic differences can be taken, and this will normally be the case, both inequalities reduce to

$$p_{21} > p_{12}.$$

In the ordinary case, then, using the measure M'' we can say that the power of Senator George is greater than that of Senator Knowland if the probability that the Senate will pass a measure is greater when Senator George favors a bill and Senator Knowland opposes it than when Senator Knowland favors a bill and Senator George opposes it.

The results, some of which are shown in Tables 1 to 3, are roughly consistent with expectations based on general knowledge.

TABLE I. THIRTY-FOUR U.S. SENATORS RANKED ACCORDING TO "POWER" OVER SENATE DECISIONS ON FOREIGN POLICY, 1946–54	TABLE 2. THIRTY-FOUR U.S. SENATORS RANKED ACCORDING TO "POWER" OVER SENATE DECISIONS ON TAX AND ECONOMIC POLICY, 1946–54

	HIGH		*HIGH*
Hayden	(tie) Magnuson		George††
	Chavez		Millikin††
	Smith (N. J.)**		Ellender
	George**		Byrd††
	Maybank		Saltonstall†
	Green**		Cordon
	Hill*		McCarran
Aiken	(tie) Wiley**		Young
	Hoey		Hoey††
	Kilgore		Maybank
	Ferguson*	Johnson (Colo.)	††(tie) McClellan
	Murray*		Hickenlooper
	Knowland*		Eastland
	Morse		Russell
Fulbright**	(tie) Saltonstall		Smith (N. J.)
	Johnston		Knowland
	Cordon		Aiken
	Hickenlooper**		Capehart
	Ellender		Johnston
Millikin	(tie) McClellan		Bridges
	Eastland		Hayden (tie) Chavez
	Russell		Butler (Nebr.)†† (tie) Wiley (tie) Ferguson
	Bridges*		Langer (tie) Hill (tie) Murray (tie) Magnuson
	Johnson (Colo.)		(tie) Fulbright (tie) Green
	Byrd		Morse (tie) Kilgore
	Butler (Nebr.)		
	Langer*		*LOW*
	Young		
	Capehart*		†† member of Finance Committee five or more years
	McCarran		† member of Finance Committee one to four years

LOW

**member of Foreign Relations Committee five or more years

*member of Foreign Relations Committee one to four years

		Foreign Policy		
		High influence	Medium influence	Low influence
	High influence	George**†† Hoey†† Maybank	Ellender Saltonstall† Cordon	Millikin†† Byrd†† McCarran Young Johnson (Colo.)†† McClellan
Tax and Economic Policy	Medium influence	Smith (N.J.)** Aiken* Hayden Chavez	Hickenlooper** Knowland* Johnston	Eastland Russell Capehart* Bridges*
	Low influence	Wiley** Hill* Magnuson Green**	Ferguson* Murray* Fulbright** Morse Kilgore	Butler (Nebr.)†† Langer*

** member of Foreign Relations Committee five or more years
 * member of Foreign Relations Committee one to four years
†† member of Finance Committee five or more years
 † member of Finance Committee one to four years

Note how the formal concept of power has been subtly altered in the process of research; it has been altered, moreover, not arbitrarily or accidentally but because of the limitations of the data available, limitations that appear to be well-nigh inescapable even in the case of the United States Senate, a body whose operations are relatively visible and well recorded over long period of time.

The most important and a first glance the most innocent change has been to accept the roll-call position of a Senator as an indication of his position prior to the roll-call vote. This change is for most practical purposes unavoidable, and yet it generates a serious consequence which I propose to call the problem of the chameleon. Suppose a Senator takes no prior position on any bill and always decides how to vote by guessing how the Senate majority will vote; then, if he is a perfect guesser, according to the ranking method used he will be placed in the highest rank. Our common sense tells us, however, that in this case it is the Senate that has power over the Senator, whereas the Senator has no influence on the votes of other Senators.

If the reader will tolerate an unnatural compounding of biological and celestial metaphors, a special case of the chameleon might be called the satellite. Although I have no evidence that this was so, let us suppose that Senator Hoey took no prior positions on issues and always followed the lead of Senator George (Table 3). Let us assume that on foreign policy and tax policy, Senator George was the most powerful man in the Senate—as indeed nearly every seasoned observer of the Senate does believe. By following George, Hoey would rank as high as George; yet, according to our hypothetical assumptions, he had no influence at all on George or any other Senator.

The problem of the chameleon (and the satellite) is not simply an artifact created by the method of paired comparisons employed. It is easy to see that ranking according to the measure M^* would be subject to the same difficulties *given the same data*. The formal concept of power, that is to say, presupposes the existence of data that in this case do not seem to be available—certainly not readily available. If one had the kinds of observations that permitted him to identify the behavior of the chameleon or satellite then no serious problem would arise. One could treat chameleon activity as equivalent to "doing nothing" to influence the passage or defeat of a measure. Since, as we have seen, under the measure M^* the column "does nothing" is superfluous, the effect would be to ignore all cases of chameleon or satellite behavior and make estimates only from the instances where a Senator actually works for or works against various bills.

Thus the conceptual problem is easily solved. But the research problem remains. In order to identify chameleon behavior and separate it from actual attempts at influence, one cannot rely on roll-calls. One needs observations of the behavior of Senators prior to the roll-calls. But if it is true, as I have been arguing, that observations of this kind are available only with great difficulty, rarely for past sessions, and probably never in large numbers, then in fact the data needed are not likely to exist. But if they do not exist for the Senate, for what institutions are they likely to exist?

CONCLUSIONS: A DIALOGUE BETWEEN A "CONCEPTUAL" THEORETICIAN AND AN "OPERATIONALIST"

The conclusions can perhaps best be stated in the form of a dialogue between a "conceptual" theoretician and a strict "operationalist." I shall call them C and O.

C. The power of an actor, A, would seem to be adequately defined by the measure M which is the difference in the probability of an event, given certain action by A, and the probability of the event given no such action by A. Because the power of any actor may be estimated in this way, at least in principle, then different actors can be ranked according to power, provided only that there exists a set of comparable subjects for the actors who are to be ranked.

O. What you say may be true in principle, but that phrase "in principle" covers up a host of practical difficulties. In fact, of course, the necessary data may not exist.

C. That is, of course, quite possible. When I say "in principle" I mean only that no data are demanded by the definition that we cannot imagine securing with combinations of known techniques of observation and measurement. The observations may be exceedingly difficult but they are not inherently impossible: they don't defy the laws of nature as we understand them.

O. True. But the probability that we can actually make these observations on, say, the U.S. Senate is so low as to be negligible, at least if we want relatively large numbers of decisions. It seems to me that from a strict operational point of view, your concept of power is not a single concept, as you have implied; operationally, power would appear to be many different concepts, depending on the kinds of data available. The way in which the researcher must adapt to the almost inevitable limitations of his data means that we shall have to make do with a great many different and not strictly comparable concepts of power.

C. I agree with all you have said. In practice, the concept of power will have to be defined by operational criteria that will undoubtedly modify its pure meaning.

O. In that case, it seems wiser to dispense with the concept entirely. Why pretend that power, in the social sense, is a concept that is conceptually clear-cut and capable of relatively unambiguous operational definitions like mass, say, in physics? Indeed, why not abandon the concept of power altogether, and admit that all we have or can have is a great variety of operational concepts, no one of which is strictly comparable with another? Perhaps we should label them: Power 1, Power 2, etc.; or better, let's abandon single, simple, misleading words like "power" and "influence", except when these are clearly understood to be a part of a special operational definition explicitly defined in the particular piece of research.

C. I'm afraid that I must disagree with your conclusion. You have not shown that the concept of power as defined by the measure M is inherently defective or that it is never capable of being used. It is true, of course, that we cannot always make the observations we need in order to measure power; perhaps we can do so only infrequently. But the concept provides us with a standard against which to compare the operational alternatives we actually employ. In this way it helps us to specify the defects of the operational definitions as measures of power. To be sure, we may have to use defective measures; but at least we shall know that they are defective and in what ways. More than that, to explicate the concept of power and to pin-point the deficiencies of the operational concepts actually employed may often help us to invent alternative concepts and research methods that produce a much closer approximation in practice to the theoretical concept itself.

Notes on the Observation and Measurement of Political Power

HERBERT SIMON

If political power is taken as one of the central phenomena to be explained by political science, then the propositions of political science will necessarily contain sentences and phrases like "the power of A is greater than the power of B," "an increase (or decrease) in the power of A," "the distribution of political power," and the like. And if the empirical truth or falsity of such propositions is to be tested, there must be agreement as to the operational definition of the term "power" and the operational means that are to be used to determine the degree of its presence or absence in any situation.

All of this is elementary enough—but how far has the task been carried out; to what extent have the operational tools of observation and measurement been provided us? That a great deal remains to be done can be made clear, I think, by an outrageous example. Suppose that, in the presence of a boorishly critical skeptic, we were to assert: "Peron holds a monopoly of power in Argentina." Suppose that our skeptic were to rely: "Prove it." We could, of course, adopt the tactics of Dr. Johnson who, when asked to prove the existence of the table at which he was sitting, suggested that his disputant kick it. While this reply has never been adjudged entirely adequate by metaphysicians, kicking a table would certainly settle the question of its existence to the satisfaction of most empirical scientists. But how, precisely, does one "kick" a dictatorship to find out if it exists? If I kicked Peron, I would go to jail; but I would also if I kicked the King of England, who is not usually regarded as a dictator.

Now I do not doubt that Peron is dictator of Argentina; nor (a slightly more difficult point to establish) that the King is not dictator of England; nor (an even more subtle point) that Stalin was dictator of Russia at a time when he held no official governmental position whatsoever. Nor will

Reprinted from *The Journal of Politics*, vol. 15 (1953), pp. 500–516 by permission of the publisher. Copyright 1953 by The Southern Political Science Association.

I ask the reader to doubt these propositions. I will ask the reader, however, to join me in an inquiry into the meanings of propositions like those just stated, and into the means for establishing the truth of such propositions— which truth, in spite of the appearance of self-evidence, can certainly be confirmed only by empirical data. In general, our inquiry may be regarded as a series of footnotes on the analysis of influence and power by Lasswell and Kaplan in *Power and Society,* which we will take as the starting point.

SKETCH OF A DEFINITION OF THE TERM "POWER"

Like Humpty Dumpty, we will insist that a word means what we want it to mean. But if our aim is to construct a body of science, and if we already have in view the general range of phenomena to be explained, our definitions may be willful, but they must not be arbitrary. If we were to say that we would measure a man's power by his height, this would be an internally consistent definition, but one hardly useful in exploring the phenomena referred to in common speech as the phenomena of power. If we were to say that we would measure a man's power by his wealth *or* his ability to influence the behavior of others, the definition would not even be internally consistent, for these two criteria might in fact be only imperfectly correlated.

POWER AND VALUE POSITION. I think that definitions which equate influence or power with the values an individual possesses are unsuitable for political science. The difficulty is revealed when we try to state what we mean by a "value." If we list specific values—wealth, wisdom, or what not —then the statement that "A possesses certain of these values" is not what we *mean* when we say "A has power." For if these two statements are regarded as identical by definition, then a proposition like "the wealthy are the powerful"—dear to Marxists and anti-Marxists alike—ceases to be an empirical proposition in political science, and becomes true simply by definition.

A second defect of such definitions is that they confront us with the necessity of inventing new values to account for persons whom we wish to regard as powerful, but whose values lie outside the usual lists—Gandhi is a good example.

The situation becomes even worse if we admit power into the list of social values that define power. That power is a value, i.e., something desired and valued, is generally admitted; but if so, to define power as value position renders meaningless propositions like: "We can measure a person's power by his ability to acquire power."

To summarize, I propose to define power and influence in such a way as to distinguish these concepts from value position. In doing so, I believe I am conforming to common usage, because (a) propositions, intended to be empirical, are often asserted with respect to the relation between power and value position, and (b) power is often asserted to be a value (but not the only value) that is desired.

If, having made a distinction between power and value position, we are able to establish an empirical relationship between the two, we can then use value position as an *index* of power—which is something quite different from using it as the defining operation. I think that we can conjecture what the relationship is likely to be. When a society is in a state of stable equilibrium, there is likely to be a close correspondence between the distribution of power and the distribution of value. If this is so, then *in equilibrium situations,* we can use the value distribution as an index of the power distribution when the latter is difficult to ascertain directly.

POWER AND VALUE POTENTIAL. Objections similar to those just mentioned can be raised against defining power or influence as synonymous with value potential. Value potential (see Lasswell and Kaplan, p. 58) is simply value position referred to some future date. As before, such a definition would transform from empirical propositions to definitional identities such statements as: "Those who have power will employ it to improve their value position"—which is roughly equivalent to: "Those who have power have high value potential."

In fact, the two definitional proposals examined thus far—relating power to value position and value potential, respectively—reveal that even at the empirical level we are not certain as to the relationship between the possession of values and of power. Does possession of power imply high value position or high potentiality of improving value position? In the previous section I suggested that, in equilibrium situations, we assume an empirical relationship to exist between value *position* and power in order to predict the latter from the former. In non-equilibrium situations, we often employ an assumed relationship between power and value *potential* to predict the latter from the former. These empirical dynamic relations may be represented diagrammatically thus:

Value Position —> Power —> Value Potential (Future Value Position).

AN ALTERNATIVE DEFINITION. As an alternative to the definitions just discarded, we propose the definition of "influence process" employed by Lasswell and Kaplan: "The *exercise of influence* (influence process) consists in affecting policies of others than the self."

This definition involves an asymmetrical relation between influencer and influencee. Now we are wary, in the social sciences, of asymmetrical relations. They remind us of pre-Humeian and pre-Newtonian notions of causality. By whip and sword we have been converted to the doctrine that there is no causation, only functional interrelation, and that functional relations are perfectly symmetrical. We may even have taken over, as a very persuasive analogy, the proposition that "for every action, there is an equal and opposite reaction." If, in spite of this, we persist in thinking that there is something asymmetrical about the influence (or power) relation, it may be reassuring that quite similar relations can be introduced into the most respectable of physical systems.

It should be noticed also that the Lasswell-Kaplan definition refers to processes of change rather than to a state of equilibrium. Presumably, we observe the influence of A over B by noting the differences between the way B actually behaves and the way he *would* behave if A were not present (or if A's desires changed). Influence belongs to the theory of dynamics, or of comparative statics, rather than to the theory of equilibrium.

ASYMMETRY OF THE POWER RELATION

The notion that the power or influence relation of A to B is asymmetrical carries with it some implication as to how the phenomenon of power can be observed and measured. Let us first consider the case where the asymmetry is supposed to be complete; i.e., A influences B, but B does not influence A at all. Then, if we are dealing with a determinate system, the behavior of A can be predicted without any reference to his relation to B, while the behavior of B follows once we know the behavior of A. Stated otherwise, the social system as a whole must contain a subsystem, that determines the behavior of A, but in which B does not appear (or at least B's reactions to A's behavior do not appear).

Now to determine the influence of A upon B, we simply observe a number of situations in which the behavior of A varies, and note what is the concomitant variation in B's behavior. As a concrete example, let us suppose that a dictator is "unilaterally coupled" to his subjects—his decisions determine their behavior, but there is no "feedback" from their behavior to his. Then, if by manipulating the variables that determine his own expectations or desires we can change his decisions, we can also observe what changes this brings about in the behavior of the subjects.

POWER IN THE PRESENCE OF FEEDBACK. It will immediately be objected that we are never faced with a situation involving unilateral coupling in this extreme sense—that there is always some feedback from the influencee to the influencer. This difficulty can be handled in either of two ways: (1) we can give up the idea that the relation is asymmetrical; or (2) we can add an asymmetrical relation operating in the opposite direction from the first. *If the processes of influence take time,* and particularly if the time lags associated with the two asymmetrical relations are different, there is at least the possibility that we can make separate empirical observations of the two relations.

If, in our previous example, our dictator makes a decision, and if he is sensitive to public approval and disapproval, then we will observe in sequence: (1) the decision, (2) subsequent changes in behavior of the subjects, (3) expressions of approval or disapproval by the subjects, and (4) modifications in the decision if it proves to be unpopular. In favorable cases, the feedback may involve large time lags. If, instead of a dictator, we have an elected president, the feedback might take the form of a change in the holder of the office at the next election.

Now, if there is any feedback at all, measurement of influence requires the observation of disequilibrium as well as equilibrium. In a state of equilibrium in the case of the elected president, the last previous election would have already put in office a president whose decisions would be acceptable to the citizens—it would be impossible to determine whether the chicken was mother or daughter of the egg.

THE RULE OF ANTICIPATED REACTIONS. But an even graver difficulty must be admitted. Because of the phenomenon that Friedrich has christened "the rule of anticipated reactions" and that the servomechanism engineer calls "anticipatory control," the time lags upon which we depend for measurement may be destroyed. If the President is elected, his decisions may be affected not only by what the citizens did in the last election, but also by his expectations of what they will do in the next.

I think it can be seen that the possibility of measuring the separate links in the chain of influence depend, in this instance, on the presence of some ignorance in the system. So long as the President is able to form exact expectations of the citizens' reactions, and they of what a candidate will do if elected, his influence on them cannot be distinguished from their influence on him, but let his or their forecasts be in error and the possibilities of disentangling the relations are re-established.

Fortunately for political scientists—who would otherwise be largely debarred from observation of the central phenomenon of their science—the members of the body politic are often far from accurate in their predictions. If President Roosevelt had foreseen the outcome of the 1938 "purges" he might not have undertaken them, and we should have been deprived of valuable information about influences on voting behavior. If the assassination of Lincoln had been anticipated, we would have lost instructive insights into the relative powers of President and Congress provided by the administration of Andrew Johnson. The unpredicted and the unexpected provide a break in the usual chain of intended connections and, serving as something of a substitute for controlled experimentation, permit us to observe the construction of the separate links.

IMPLICATIONS OF THE DEFINITION. Apart from the question of measurement, the habit of viewing a social structure as a network of (generally) asymmetrical relationships can help to clarify some of the ambiguities that are commonly found in statements of power relationships. This formulation teaches us that, when we wish to speak of the influence of a particular element in a social system upon that system, we must specify whether we mean the influence of the element considered as independent, with all the reverse feedback relations ignored, or whether we mean the net influence of the element, taking into account all the reciprocal influences of other elements upon it. Concretely, how powerful we consider the President to be depends on whether we ignore, or take into consideration, the fact that he is an elected official, and the fact that he is advised by a corps of permanent civil servants.

If we regard the President as an "independent variable," then we arrive at one assessment of his influence. If we add to our system the environmental influences created by the administrative bureaucracy, which greatly restrict the variability that differences in personal qualities and beliefs would otherwise produce in the behavior of different presidents, we arrive at a smaller estimate of the influence of those personal qualities and beliefs.

As an exercise for developing his skill in handling both this distinction and the rule of anticipated reactions, the reader may like to test his wits on the proposition: "The power of the President can be measured by the number of bills he vetoes where the veto is not overridden."

The interpretation of influence as unilateral coupling corresponds reasonably well with our everyday intuitive notions. We would ordinarily argue that it makes a greater difference to events in the United States if a Justice of the Supreme Court or a United States Senator is replaced than if John Jones, an Idaho potato farmer, retires and turns over his farm to his son. What we are saying here is that the personal characteristics of the individual occupying a particular position (a judgeship or a senatorial seat) constitutes a variable upon which other variables in the system depend. The influence of any position, according to this notion, is proportional to the amount of change induced throughout the system by a change in the characteristics of the individual occupying the position in question.

THE EXERCISE OF INFLUENCE AND THE INFLUENCE BASE

Direct measurements of influence are obtained when we can observe the ratio of change in behavior of influencee to change in behavior of influencer. If, starting with such measurements, we are able to determine empirically the conditions that make for influence—the characteristics of individuals and situations that permit us to predict that the influence of a particular individual will be large—then we can derive from these empirical relationships additional indirect measurements of influence. In particular, if we can measure the magnitude of the influence *base,* we can infer from this the magnitude of the influence. (E.g., if wealth is the principal influence base in a particular situation—the principal means for exercising influence—then in that situation we may measure influence indirectly by wealth.)

DYNAMIC RELATIONSHIPS. Now there are generally intricate relationships among the bases of influence and the values that are sought. In the first place, influence is the means, in rational social behavior, of securing the values that are desired. Hence, influence itself, and consequently the bases of influence also become something valued as means to other values. Moreover, many of the bases of influence may be valued *both* as means for the exercise of influence and for other reasons as well.

Wealth will serve as an example. Wealth, in most societies, is a base of influence, hence, a means for securing values. But wealth is also valued for the consumption it permits and the deference it commands. Now consider the extreme case of a society in which wealth is the only influence base, and where consumption and deference are the only values. In such a society, *investment* is the use of influence to augment the influence base, *consumption* is the use of influence to augment other values without increase in the influence base.

Similar dynamic relationships apply to influence bases other than wealth. Political power, too, can be "invested"—control of a legislature may be employed to gerrymander legislative districts in order to ensure continued control. It can also be consumed, to obtain desired legislation, sometimes at the expense of future power.

I have spelled out these dynamic relationships to emphasize the point made earlier that it is essential to distinguish between the operations that measure influence directly, and the indirect estimates of influence that can be inferred from measurements of the influence base. It is often true that influence is used to obtain value. (This accounts for the relationship between influence and value potential.) It is often true that value position provides the influence base. (This accounts for the relationship between influence and value position.) It is often true that influence is employed to augment future influence. In the scheme proposed here, these are all empirical relationships that should not be confused with definitional identities.

COMMENTS ON THE NATURE OF THE INFLUENCE BASE.   The term "influence base" has been used here to refer to the conditions for the exercise of influence. The influence base is by no means synonymous with the value position, although there are two significant connections between them. First, when values are exchangeable, they can be given to others in return for desired behavior. It is in this sense that values provide a base for influence. Second, any condition that gives its possessor influence is likely to become a desideratum—a value. It is not because being a Supreme Court Justice is valued that such a Justice has influence; but, conversely, it is because he has influence that the position is valued.

Because the connection between influence base and value is not always the same, a classification of influence bases in terms of the values related to them is rather superficial. A more fundamental basis for classification is with respect to the motivation of the influencee that leads him to accept influence. On this basis, Lasswell and Kaplan define three successively narrower terms: (a) influence (encompassing all motivations for acceptance); (b) power (acceptance motivated by sanctions); and (c) authority (acceptance motivated by attitudes toward legitimacy).

There has been some tendency in the literature of political science to regard ordinary sanctions, like money and physical force, as the bases of "effective" power; and legitimacy as the base of "formal" power. The implication of this kind of language is that "effective" power is what determines actual behavior, while "formal" power is some kind of epiphenomenal rationalization of the power structure—window-dressing, so to speak. Some political scientists, however, Charles Merriam being a notable example, insist on legitimacy as an important independent motivation for the acceptance of power.

Which of these viewpoints is correct—and to what extent—is an empirical question. The definitions we have thus far constructed indicate, at least schematically, what kinds of data would be needed to answer the question. What is required is a situation in which we can observe: (a) the distribution of power as indicated by behavior changes of influencees as a function of behavior changes of influencers; (b) the distribution of monetary, physical, and similar sanctions among the influencers; and (c) the attitudes of influencees toward legitimacy, and their beliefs as to where legitimate power lies. Situations where there is the greatest possible discrepancy between the possession of sanctions and the possession of legitimacy would be the most rewarding. Many clearcut examples of the discrepancy between power bases can be found, of course, in revolutions. An example of a more subtle situation that could profitably be examined from this viewpoint is the behavior of the United States Senate in the 1937 fight over the Supreme Court bill. I will not try to prejudge the evidence except to state my personal conviction that legitimacy will turn out to be a far from epiphenomenal aspect of the power structure.

EXPECTATIONS AND THE POWER BASE.   An empirical study of this problem will not proceed very far without disclosing another crucial behavioral variable: the *expectation* of each of the participants about the behavior of the others. I refer not merely to the obscuring effects of the rule of anticipated reactions, discussed earlier, but to the fact that the consequences an individual thinks will follow on his actions depend on what action he thinks other individuals will take.

A political régime prescribes appropriate behavior rôles to its participants; these rôles include appropriate actions to constrain any particular participant (or small group of participants) who departs from his rôle. But the constraints will be applied only if the remaining participants (or most of them) continue to play their rôles. Hence, most of the sanctions a political régime has at its disposal—whether they consist of money, force, attitudes toward legitimacy, or what not—disappear at once when a large number of the participants act in concert to depart from their rôles.

To each individual in a political régime, consequently, the régime looks exceedingly stable so long as he expects the other individuals to support it; it looks exceedingly unstable when he pictures himself as acting in concert with a large number of others to overthrow it. Hence, estimates of the stability of a political structure depends not only on observation of the distribution of actual power, or of the distribution of the power base; but equally upon estimates of the capacity of subgroups for co-ordinated action.

It follows from this that power and influence, measured in terms of the definitions we have proposed, are not additive quantities. Every observation of a power relationship makes an assumption, whether explicit or implicit, as to the pattern of expectation and of group co-ordination. Such an observation will have predictive value, in general, only so long as this assumption holds.

To take a specific example, if we were to make some observations as to the power of a political party to discipline an individual member, we would probably reach conclusions that would be completely inapplicable to the question of the party's power to discipline an organized dissenting clique.

EXPECTATIONS AS A MEANS OF MEASURING POWER.   At this point we might revert to a point raised at the beginning of this paper: how do we know that Peron is dictator of Argentina? If we accept the proposition we have just been urging, that expectations of consequences are a major determinant of behavior, then we can use such expectations, so long as the situation remains stable, to estimate where power lies.

We are faced here with an example of a self-confirming prophecy. Suppose we are able to ascertain that the people of Argentina really believe that Peron is dictator. It follows that they will expect sanctions to be applied to themselves if they do not accept the decisions of the Peron régime. Hence, so long as these expectations remain, they will behave as if Peron *were* dictator, and indeed, he will be.

It seems to me that this is the valid core of the naive method we commonly employ as political scientists when, seeking to determine the power structure in a particular situation, we ask the participants what the power structure is. This procedure is valid to the extent that the expectations of the participants constitute the power base. It gives us, in fact, an indirect measure of influence in the same way that data on wealth, or on attitudes of legitimacy, give us indirect measures of influence.

Now if this technique of observation is to be used sophisticatedly, certain cautions must be observed. First, such observations fail to reveal wheels within wheels in the power mechanism. Peron decides for Argentina, but who decides for Peron? Second, when expectations diverge from the other elements in the power base, they may conceal the fragility of the power structure. We have seen that revolution involves, above all, a change in the expectations, and this will be revealed only at the moment of revolution.

Both of these points can be illuminated by looking at the phenomenon of the "figurehead." The holder of power begins to move toward the status of figurehead when his behavior is no longer an "independent variable" but is itself determined by his submission to power. This can take place in at least two ways. First, he may be aware of sanctions to which he is subject that are not apparent to others (if he makes the wrong decision, the secret police will assassinate him, or his mistress will refuse to sleep with him). In this case, he becomes a figurehead when the existence of these sanctions becomes known, for this knowledge will alter the expectations to conform to the "real" power structure. (Of course, other power bases enter to modify the course of events—he may continue to wield power because feelings of legitimacy attach to him.)

Second, the power holder may sense that the system of expectations is fragile—that revolution is imminent unless he anticipates the reactions to his exercise of power and restrains it within limits. Again, when awareness develops of his self-restraint, expectations will begin to change and he will begin to lose his power. It can hardly be doubted that this was a central process in the movement of England from a monarchical to a democratic government.

With this we may close our comments on the influence base—the conditions for the exercise of influence. We have seen that influence and the bases of influence are distinct and separately observable concepts; and that independent observation of them is required to assess the relative effectiveness of various influence bases in the influence process. Finally, we have seen that observations of the exercise of influence must, to be meaningful, be accompanied by observations of the expectations and capacities for cooperative action of the various subgroups acting in the power arena.

THE UNITS OF OBSERVATION

Our definition of influence leaves quite ambiguous the kinds of units in which degrees of influence might be expressed. The quantities with which we are most familiar are those measured in *cardinal numbers:* A weighs 200 pounds; he weighs twice as much as B. Sometimes we deal with a "weaker" kind of number, the *ordinal number,* which permits us to say that: "A is cleverer than B," but not: "A is twice as clever as B." We may also be aware of quantities that are not single numbers but pairs, triples, or n-tuples of numbers (usually called *vectors*). If A has five oranges and three apples, we may denote his possessions by the vector (5,3). We can say that A has more than B, who has (4,2); but we cannot compare A with C, who has (4,5). We cannot say that D has twice as many as A unless he has exactly twice as many apples *and* twice as many oranges.

All of these kinds of quantities, and others as well, occur in the physical sciences. Mass is a cardinal number, hardness an ordinal number, and force a vector. We should expect to find at least as rich a variety of quantities in the social sciences. Hence, we must ask ourselves what "kind" of a quantity best represents influence and power.

I do not propose to tackle the problem in all its generality, but will, instead, examine one broad class of situations that I think is of significance. The particular class of power relations with which I shall be concerned is usually denoted by the term "authority," and I shall retain that term although it is used in a very different sense by Lasswell and Kaplan.

We will say that an individual accepts *authority* when his choice among alternative behaviors is determined by the communicated decision of another. The acceptance of authority may stem from any combination whatsoever of the bases of power—monetary inducements, force, legitimacy, or any others. Authority is never unlimited—the range of alternative behaviors from which the superior may select the particular choice he desires of the subordinate is a finite range. The limits within which authority will be accepted we will call the *zone of acceptance.*

It is clear from the definition that authority is a form of influence: when A exercises authority over B, he exercises influence over B. Hence, a measurement of authority will be a measurement of at least one form of influence.

Let us regard each possible behavior that B can perform as an element in a set, and let us designate the set of all such possible behaviors by V. The set of behaviors that B will perform at A's command (the subset of V corresponding to B's zone of acceptance) we will designate by S. Then we can use the size of the set S as a measure of A's authority over B.

But what kind of a quantity is the size of S? Suppose that at one time B will accept any order in the set S, but at some later time he will only accept orders in S', which is a part of S. Then we are surely justified in saying that A's authority has decreased. Under such circumstances, comparisons of "greater" and "less" are possible. But it may happen that the zone of acceptance changes from S' to S'' where these are intersecting (overlapping) sets neither of which entirely includes the other. In this case we cannot say that A's authority has increased or that it has decreased—our sets are not completely ordered. The kind of quantity that appears most suitable for measuring the degree of authority of A over B is what the mathematician would call a "partial ordering."

Now this may seem a disappointing result—we started off with brave talk about "measuring" and have ended with some statements about more or less inclusive sets. The point is that whatever quantities we construct must reflect the characteristics of the phenomena we propose to measure with them. Ordinary cardinal (or even ordinal) numbers possess the property that they are completely ordered. If power relations are only partially ordered, then we shall certainly end up by talking nonsense about them if we insist that they should be represented by cardinal numbers, or that we should always be able to predicate "greater" or "less" of them. If we feel disappointment, it should be directed at the phenomena with which we are confronted rather than at the kind of quantity that appears to represent them.

I must hasten to point out that the above discussion does not in any sense prove that it is impossible to associate cardinal numbers with authority relations. It often happens that, starting with sets of elements, we can associate a cardinal number with each set in such a way that the resulting complete ordering is consistent with the partial ordering defined by the sets themselves. (The cardinal number associated with each set measures, in some sense, its "size.") This is precisely what the tax assessor does when he associates with Jones' set of tangible possessions a number that represents the (presumed) amount of money for which these possessions could be exchanged in the market.

Putting aside the question of using cardinal numbers to measure the "sizes" of different zones of acceptance, we may ask how the sets themselves may be observed and measured. The procedure is relatively straightforward; we observe what kinds of decisions are accepted and what kinds are not. If His Majesty's first minister decides that several hundred additional lords shall be created to establish the supremacy of the House of Commons, will His Majesty accede to the request? The observation falls within our general definition of influence: how does the behavior of the influencee vary with the behavior (in this case the decision) of the influencer?

The difficulties that are generally involved in the observation of influence are present here also. Because of the rule of anticipated reactions, the influencee may behave in accordance with the anticipated decision, never expressed, of the influencer; and the influencer will seldom issue commands that he knows in advance lie outside the zone of acceptance of the influencee—the limits will seldom be observed except when predictions are faulty. Because of the effect of expectations, the zone of acceptance may be suddenly narrowed when the influencee judges that he will be joined in resistance to authority by others.

To pursue these matters further would carry us rapidly into some rather difficult mathematical questions. If we attempted to construct mathematical models for formulating and analyzing authority relations we would be led, I think, to models resembling very closely those employed by von Neumann and Morgenstern in their *Theory of Games and Economic Behavior*. I will not undertake such an analysis here, but will simply refer to some essays in this direction that have been published elsewhere.

CONCLUSION

Let us now draw together the threads of our discussion. The problem posed at the outset was how we can make observations and measurements of the distribution of influence and power. The definition of the key terms —"influence" and "power"—is the first step toward an answer. The position taken here is that the phenomenon we wish to measure is an asymmetrical relation between the behavior of two persons. We wish to observe how a change in the behavior of one (the influencer) alters the behavior of the other (the influencee).

We have seen that in most situations, all sorts of reciprocal power relations are present, and that their observation is complicated by the anticipation of reactions. The more accurate the predictions of participants in the system of the reactions of others, the more difficult it becomes to observe influence. Our main hope must be that human beings will remain fallible in their predictions.

To the extent that we can establish empirically the conditions for the exercise of power, these conditions, or influence bases, provide an indirect means for measurement. Observations of the distribution of values and of attitudes regarding legitimacy constitute two significant kinds of indirect evidence about the distribution of power. A third, of critical significance, are the expectations of the participants in the power situation.

In a final section we examined the types of units in terms of which measurement might be expressed. Our principal conclusion here is that we must be prepared to admit into our measurement schemes many other kinds of units besides cardinal numbers. In particular, certain notions from set theory, such as the concept of partial ordering among sets, may be suggestive of fruitful schemes of measurement.

An Analysis of Power, with Special Reference to International Politics

MAURICE A. ASH

It is possible to contend that in political science today, and particularly with regard to international politics, there is a significant trend towards interpreting events in terms of "power." . . . This paper . . . is based squarely on the supposition that power does constitute the generalized end of politics, an end which is basic as a means to other innumerable and variegated ultimate ends. Granted this supposition, however, it is contended that there does not yet exist a structure of analysis dealing with the processes involved in the attainment of this generalized end—a conceptual structure comparable to that of economics, which deals with the attainment of the generalized end of wealth. The purpose of this paper, then, is to propose a skeleton upon which a formal body of political theory might be constructed. . . .

It may be said that international relations, "world politics," form an excellent field in which to carry out our purpose, which might be considered as the construction of a "power model." For such a model is, of course, an abstraction, and in international politics there are prima facie grounds for thinking that situations are most simplfied in terms of those elements that must be abstracted for a power model. In relations between states a certain amount of the complexities of municipal life, or even of interpersonal relations, is missing. The opposing entities are more clearly defined, and their coercion of each other is more pronounced and accepted. At the same time, it must never be forgotten that these are only relative differences,

Reprinted from *World Politics,* vol. 3 (1951), pp. 218–32 by permission of the author and the publisher.

and that our model is essentially an abstraction from the full realities even of international relations.

Two points about the analysis may be stressed before it is begun. First, it will proceed from the particular to the general. Starting from the most simple case of one state in relation to one other, it will be built up by addition of increasing complexities. . . . Second, the analysis is to be one of relationships, not of absolutes. Thus, it will not be concerned with showing what "power" in some sense essentially is. Rather, it will be interested in how relationships vary and how power plays a part in such variations: how it functions, not what it is. Likewise, as a further example, peace and war will be considered not as idealized states, but as conditions of relationships.

I

The first step in the analysis is to clarify the concepts with which we shall work. . . . The main concepts are three in number: Power; the Group (in this case the State); and Force (in this case Armaments).

Power is to be conceived of as a product of relationships. That is to say, the phenomenon of relationship, of any two groups being in relationship with one another, implicitly involves the phenomenon of power. It is not possible for a relationship to exist without the factor of power being considered therein. It follows, firstly, that power is a subjective factor; that being induced by the fact of relationship, it is rather connected with the state of mind than with the objective conditions thereof. Power, then, is for us the sense of satisfaction felt with a relationship by one of the parties thereto. It is the subjective assessment of the condition of a relationship. Secondly, it also follows that power is conceived here as being relative. The power that one group has, or senses, is power relative to some other group. "Absolute power" can strictly have no meaning in this analysis. In sum, then, in the concept of it used here, power is both subjective and relative.

It is probably unnecessary, for the purposes of this analysis, to define the State as anything more than a type of social group. For we are not interested in it in itself, but only in its relationships with its kind. If it is desired to be a little more precise, however, it might be suggested that a State is a complex of relationships able to maintain itself externally against other such complexes. . . .

The last concept we come to is that of Armaments (or, in general, Force). This, as opposed to Power, is a concept of objectivity. Within the category of Armaments are included all those forms of force, all the means, with which states coerce each other, with which they exert coercive pressures. About this concept, certain implications must be noted.

First, it is implied that one state, merely by being in possession of armaments, is exerting pressure on another, or other states. A state, we have seen, is only meaningful in terms of its relationships with other states; and in such relationships the possession of armed forces cannot but be taken into account. . . .

Second, the objective character of this concept of Armaments consists not in anything physically immutable but rather in its contradistinction to the subjectivity of the Power concept. That is to say, Armaments are objective in that they are the objects of subjective perceptions. They constitute the situation which must be subjectively considered, both for what it is and for how it might be changed.

Third, the objective character of the concept of Armaments implies that some objective measure of these might be devised for the purposes of the analysis. . . . It remains, then, to determine what the unit of measurement of Armaments should be. And here the unit which suggests itself, and which will be used in this analysis, is that of monetary value: the pound, or the dollar, etc. The use of this unit does not indicate that the effect attained by a given amount of coercive force could also be achieved by an equivalent economic effort. Some things, for instance, are proverbially not for sale at any price. But the measurement suggested provides a guide to the expenditure of coercive effort, in so far as the ingredients of a state's armaments, their raw materials, as such, have market values. . . .

II

Armed, now, with these main concepts, the analysis can proceed with the construction of a model of inter-state relationships. And following the principle already mentioned, of starting with the simplest case, we shall begin by considering the position of one single state in its relationship with only one other state.

A state exerting force upon another and having force exerted upon itself will, as a consequence, experience a certain sense of power (or security). Now this degree of power, the resultant of the relationship of given levels of opposing forces, could conceivably be maintained constant at other levels of these forces, provided the latter varied in some sort of direct proportion to each other. . . .

This point can quite simply be illustrated in a diagram, a diagram giving a map of the subjective condition of the state being considered, showing its attitudes. (Chart I.)

It will be seen that what has been done here is to provide the basis for a measurement of Power. Such a measurement must be a subjective one. That is, it must deal in degrees of Power, of more or less or constant

CHART I

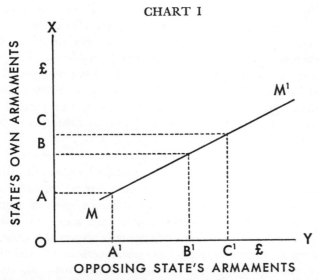

In this diagram, along the X axis are measured the armaments exerted by the state itself, measured in £ units, and along the Y axis is a similar measure of the force exerted upon the state by another. Then, at various coordinates of opposing forces, say *AA'*, *BB'*, *CC'*, it can be imagined that the power experienced by the state whose attitudes are here being illustrated will remain constant. Hence, the line *MM'* joining these points will be designated a Constant Power Curve.

Power. It will be seen then that any number of combinations of opposing forces can be imagined and that each one will result in a level of Power greater or less or equal to all the others. Thus, our "Power map" could be built up to show a schedule of Constant Power Curves, and thus to indicate which combinations of forces would give a state more power than others, etc. . . .

On the surface, it might seem reasonable to suppose that a given level of power would be maintained by a state if the ratio of opposing forces remained the same, no matter what were the absolute amounts of these. This supposition, however, would be based on the very simple conditions which alone have so far been admitted in the analysis—namely, of one to one relationships of states. The usefulness of this abstraction has now been exhausted, and it is time to enlarge the scope of the investigation of any one state's power attitudes by recognizing that it will be in relationship not with one but with several other states at the same time. . . .

. . . What is of major concern for this analysis is not simply the fact that any one state must face several neighbors, but rather a phenomenon arising from this, namely, that any one state will also maintain forces that are not specifically directed against any of its neighbors—that is, a general reserve. . . . The point which it is vital to note about a reserve is that it is a force not allotted to any particular front. No front can call the reserve, nor even any proportion of it, its own. Every front, of course, has its own reserves; but it does not, in any such sense, have the general reserve of the state at its disposal. . . . It can be imagined that the existence of a greater or lesser general reserve behind the armaments exerted by one state upon another will affect the power and security contingent upon that relationship.

From this it is not hard to deduce what must be the effect on the power felt by a state, as against another, of mutual increases of armaments in a constant ratio—or, alternatively, what must happen in order to keep that state's power at some constant level for different levels of armaments. Supposing the pressure maintained by one state upon another remains constant—that is, the ratio of opposing armaments is always the same. Then, the greater becomes the general level of armaments in this relationship, the less power will each additional increment of its armaments confer on the state whose attitudes we are considering. For, the greater the force the state exerts upon this one opponent, the greater will become the ratio of those forces to the state's general reserve; and therefore the less efficacious will that reserve become as a support for that front, the less security will it provide. What does this mean in terms of a state maintaining some constant level of power against another? It means that, to match every equal increment to the force exerted upon it by the latter, a state must increase its own armaments by ever greater amounts.

This indicates the general principle of the relation of Power to the forces exerted in a relationship. A little more can still be said, however, about the actual rate at which a state must increase its armaments to keep its power constant—as to whether this rate be a slightly or a sharply increasing one.

In the event of a state exerting but little force upon another—little, that is, in proportion to the size of its general reserve—the degree of power which it experiences in this relationship will to a great extent be accounted for by its dependence upon that reserve. Hence, the influence of such armaments as are directly exerting pressure will be disproportionately large. If, then, the opposing state increases its armaments by some amount, only a proportionately smaller increment of the forces directly exerted by our state may be necessary to keep its power constant, so valuable will an increase of such forces be felt to be in the circumstances. Consequently, when the general level of armaments in a particular relationship is very low, the rate at which a state must increase its forces against increments of its opponents in order to keep its power constant, this rate will be a very small one: every successive increment need be only slightly greater than the previous one. Were, in fact, a state in these circumstances to increase its own forces as much as proportionately to its opponent's, it would do more than keep its power constant thereby: it would increase its power. For this act would decrease the ratio of the general reserve to the directly employed armaments, reducing the former's importance but increasing the latter's by a greater amount.

However, as is known, the rate at which a state must augment its forces to keep its power constant is an increasing one. The higher the general level of armaments in a relationship, the more rapid will this rate of increase become. For, as the ratio of a state's general reserve to its forces deployed on any front becomes small, so will the former's influence decline and the security which springs from its support will diminish. Consequently, to keep its power constant against an opponent making equal increments to its armaments, a state must eventually make very large and ever larger additions to its own forces directly employed against that opponent. After a certain point these increments will certainly become proportionately greater than its opponent's. . . .

The core of this phase of the analysis is given by the term "armaments potential." The notion of a potential implies something that is being drawn upon, and which thus may exhibit a great variety and gradation of values. Obviously, a state has an armaments potential in this sense: it is able to exert either more or less force upon its neighbors, and it has some sort of a reservoir upon which it can draw. But the further question must be asked, as to how a state will, in fact, draw upon its resources. For, assuming that this is not fortuitously determined, what does limit the extent to which an armaments potential is drawn upon at any given moment?

The most obvious consideration in this respect would seem to be the relativity of a state's exertion of force. The force which a state exerts is limited by what will be exerted upon itself in return. It is not possible for it to exert pressure without an answering resistance being called into play, and this fact will somehow condition the amount of its own force that a state uses. This amount, in fact, will be conditioned by the pressure which the state thinks it can maintain upon another. And this pressure will be determined by the relative armament potentials of a relationship between two states. This pressure constitutes a ratio of armaments that will be constant for all and every different absolute level of these.

To this statement of the basic principles concerning the objective phenomena of the analysis, one note of explanation must be added. When it is stated that the pressure exerted by one state on another is determined by their relative armament potentials, it is not meant that this ratio is determined by the total armaments which, at any given moment, each possesses. Rather, it is assumed that each state simultaneously maintains pressures on its other neighbors so that the ratio of armaments between one state and another is dependent on this. The maintenance by states of pressures on each other, then, presupposes a certain mutual interdependence. The tenability of the pressure in any one relationship is based upon assurance of the pressures in other relationships also being maintained. And it can be assumed that this assurance will exist, for otherwise no ratio between two states' armaments could ever even be established, and the ratio between armaments would only be fortuitously determined.

The same form of diagram can be used to illustrate the principles governing the objective phenomena as was used for the subjective phenomena. (Chart II).

CHART II

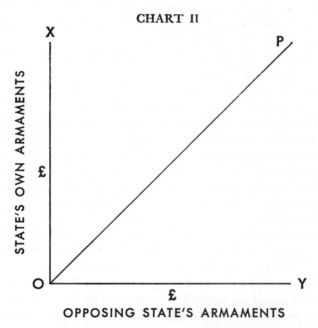

In this diagram the line *OP* indicates a ratio between the armaments potentials of two states. This ratio is constant for all absolute levels of armaments.

III

. . . . It should now be possible to answer the crucial question of this analysis: what determines, at any given moment, the exact amount of force that one state is exerting upon another? Any analysis of power, of the forces of coercion, of politics, which cannot answer or attempt to answer this question must abandon all pretensions to being scientific and be recognized as, in fact, merely speculative.

The two parts of the analysis have so far shown, firstly, how a state reacts to hypothetical situations in its relations with another state, situations compounded of opposing exertions of force; and secondly, how the pressure exerted by one state on another, the ratio of their armaments, is determined. To discover the exact absolute amount of force exerted by one state on another involves putting these two parts of the analysis together. This will indicate the reactions of the state to the concrete situation given by the pressure it maintains upon another state.

One may begin by assuming that the amounts of armaments used by two states on each other, in whatever ratio is determined by their potentials, is "very small." In these circumstances, the attitude of a state will be that it can increase its power (or security) by increasing its own forces, even though this involves a proportionate increase in those of its opponent. For at such a very low level of armaments the state in question will be inordinately dependent, for its power against the other, upon its general reserve of forces. Thus a proportionate increase in armaments between these two would increase the satisfaction derived by the state from the forces directly used by it in this relationship. However, if the general level of armaments were "very large," a mutual and proportionate reduction of armaments would presumably be beneficial. For in these circumstances the general reserve of forces supporting the state's armaments on that front would have become relatively so small as gravely to jeopardize security there. It follows that there must be some point intermediate between the "very small" and the "very large" levels of armaments at which the power of a state will be maximized. At this point either a small proportionate, mutual increase or a decrease of armaments would result in a loss of power to the state. . . .

To this analysis of how one state establishes its power equilibrium with another must be added the proviso that such equilibrium will not be stable unless its opponent also finds itself in equilibrium in these circumstances. However, there will be a tendency towards this more general equilibrium. For if the equilibrium position of one state should prove unsatisfactory to the other, so that the latter makes an adjustment, the resulting dislocation of the former's equilibrium will induce it to reassess the component elements of its provenly untenable position. Hence, it may be said that, in some degree, an armaments potential ratio and a state's power attitudes are functions of a satisfactory, stable relationship between states. . . .

A Method for Evaluating the Distribution of Power in a Committee System

L. S. SHAPLEY AND MARTIN SHUBIK

In the following paper we offer a method for the *a priori* evaluation of the division of power among the various bodies and members of a legislature or committee system. The method is based on a technique of the mathematical theory of games, applied to what are known there as "simple games" and "weighted majority games." We apply it here to a number of illustrative cases, including the United States Congress, and discuss some of its formal properties.

The designing of the size and type of a legislative body is a process that may continue for many years, with frequent revisions and modifications aimed at reflecting changes in the social structure of the country; we may cite the role of the House of Lords in England as an example. The effect of a revision usually cannot be gauged in advance except in the roughest terms; it can easily happen that the mathematical structure of a voting system conceals a bias in power distribution unsuspected and unintended by the authors of the revision. How, for example, is one to predict the degree of protection which a proposed system affords to minority interests? Can a consistent criterion for "fair representation" be found? It is difficult even, to *describe* the net effect of a double representation system such as is found in the U.S. Congress (i.e., by states and by population), without attempting to deduce it *a priori*. The method of measuring "power" which we present in this paper is intended as a first step in the attack on these problems.

Our definition of the power of an individual member depends on the chance he has of being critical to the success of a winning coalition. It is easy to see, for example, that the chairman of a board consisting of an even number of members (including himself) has no power if he is allowed to vote only to break ties. Of course he may have prestige and moral influence and will even probably get to vote when someone is not present. However, in the narrow and abstract model of the board he is without power. If the board consists of an odd number of members, then he has exactly as much power as any ordinary member because his vote is "pivotal" —i.e., turns a possible defeat into a success—as often as the vote of any other member. Admittedly he may not cast his vote as often as the others, but much of the voting done by them is not necessary to ensure victory (though perhaps useful for publicity or other purposes). If a coalition has a majority, then extra votes do not change the outcome. For any vote, only a minimal winning coalition is necessary.

Put in crude economic terms, the above implies that if votes of senators were for sale, it might be worth while buying forty-nine of them, but the market value of the fiftieth (to the same customer) would be zero. It is possible to buy votes in most corporations by purchasing common stock. If their policies are entirely controlled by simple majority votes, then there is no more power to be gained after one share more than 50% has been acquired.

Let us consider the following scheme: There is a group of individuals all willing to vote for some bill. They vote in order. As soon as a majority has voted for it, it is declared passed, and the member who voted last is given credit for having passed it. Let us choose the voting order of the members randomly. Then we may compute the frequency with which an individual belongs to the group whose votes are used and, of more importance, we may compute how often he is *pivotal*. This latter number serves to give us our index. It measures the number of times that the action of the individual actually changes the state of affairs. A simple consequence of this formal scheme is that where all voters have the same number of votes, they will each be credited with $1/n$th of the power, there being n participants. If they have different numbers of votes (as in the case of stockholders of a corporation), the result is more complicated; more votes mean more power, as measured by our index, but not in direct proportion (see below).

Of course, the actual balloting procedure used will in all probability be quite different from the above. The "voting" of the formal scheme might better be thought of as declarations of support for the bill, and the randomly chosen order of voting as an indication of the relative degrees of support by the different members, with the most enthusiastic members "voting" first, etc. The *pivot* is then the last member whose support is needed in order for passage of the bill to be assured.

Analyzing a committee chairman's tie-breaking function in this light, we see that in an *odd* committee he is pivotal as often as an ordinary member, but in an *even* committee he is never pivotal. However, when the number of members is large, it may sometimes be better to modify the strict interpretation of the formal system, and say that the number of members in attendance is about as likely to be even as odd. The chairman's index would then be just half that of an ordinary member. Thus, in the U.S. Senate the power index of the presiding officer is—strictly—equal to $1/97$.

Under the modified scheme it is 1/193. (But it is zero under either interpretation when we are considering decisions requiring a two-thirds majority, since ties cannot occur on such votes.) Recent history shows that the "strict" model may sometimes be the more realistic: in the present Senate (1953-54) the tie-breaking power of the Vice President, stemming from the fact that 96 is an even number, has been a very significant factor. However, in the passage of ordinary legislation, where perfect attendance is unlikely even for important issues, the modified scheme is probably more appropriate. . . .

The values given above do not take into account any of the sociological or political superstructure that almost invariably exists in a legislature or policy board. They were not intended to be a representation of present day "reality." It would be foolish to expect to be able to catch all the subtle shades and nuances of custom and procedure that are to be found in most real decision-making bodies. Nevertheless, the power index computations may be useful in the setting up of norms or standards, the departure from which will serve as a measure of, for example, political solidarity, or regional or sociological factionalism, in an assembly. To do this we need an empirical power index, to compare with the theoretical. One possibility is as follows: The voting record of an individual is taken. He is given no credit for being on the losing side of a vote. If he is on the winning side, when n others voted with him, then he is awarded the probability of his having been the pivot (or blocker, in the case of a defeated motion), which is $1/n+1$. His probabilities are then averaged over all votes. It can be shown that this measure gives more weight than the norm does to uncommitted members who hold the "balance of power" between extreme factions. For example, in a nine-man committee which contains two four-man factions which always oppose each other, the lone uncommitted member will always be on the winning side, and will have an observed index of 1/5, compared to the theoretical value of 1/9.

A difficulty in the application of the above measure is the problem of finding the correct weights to attach to the different issues. Obviously it would not be proper to take a uniform average over all votes, since there is bound to be a wide disparity in the importance of issues brought to a vote. Again, in a multicameral legislature (or in any more complicated system), many important issues may be decided without every member having had an opportunity to go on record with his stand. There are many other practical difficulties in the way of direct applications of the type mentioned. Yet the power index appears to offer useful information concerning the basic design of legislative assemblies and policy-making boards. . . .

CHAPTER NINE

ROLES

THE process by which man progresses from the animal to a civilized state is sometimes referred to as socialization. This development for an individual consists essentially of internalizing the attitudes of others and relating his responses to these attitudes. While this takes place in the total society, it also occurs in the various subsystems of which the social system is composed. Thus, when one becomes a member of a new social grouping, one goes through a process of learning what is expected of him within the group, and also, what is expected of others. By virtue of this learning process, one comes to recognize that social groupings define a number of statuses (collections of rights and duties), and roles (patterns of behavior corresponding to the system of status). The role of an individual, therefore, is defined not only by the system of which he is a part, but also by the status which he occupies in the system structure.

A social system or subsystem is merely a network of interacting roles. Systems theory teaches that the functionalism of a system in terms of goal attainment is related to the articulation of system roles. Three major dysfunctional factors may be identified. The first of these is role-incongruence (disagreement concerning the behaviors associated with given roles). A subsystem can tolerate a limited amount of such disagreement if it is to survive as a system. For example, in a classroom situation there may be an absence of consensus on role definitions and a lack of congruency between role definitions and role behaviors. Such disagreements would be so disrupting that the class as a system would cease to exist. It would be replaced by the class as a collection of individuals.

The degree of role consensus that characterizes any social grouping depends upon a number of disparate variables. For example, Edwin J. Thomas shows that workers' conceptions of their roles are apt to differ according to the size of the organization of which they are a part. In his study of a Michigan welfare department, he found that in the smaller bureaus there was greater role-consensus between workers and supervisors as to workers' roles. In a similar vein, John C. Wahlke and his associates reveal the impact of role conceptions on legislative behavior. The Wahlke article points up particularly the importance of role relations between an individual and a "generalized other," in this case, the pressure group. The way in which the legislator defines his role as legislator is crucial for such a relationship.

A second dysfunctional element is personality. Social research shows that role recruitment and role performance cannot be safely predicted from extrinsic examination of system structure and status. The personality of the individual occupying a status in a system has a crucial effect on role behavior. Thus, nurses aides in a mental hospital were found to play "custodial" or "humanistic" roles in the treatment of patients. A very high correlation was found between custodialism in patient treatment and authoritarianism in the personality as measured by the F scale.

The third factor considered disruptive for a system is role conflict. Since an individual may belong to many social groupings and possess a number of different statuses, he may play any number of related and non-related roles. Role play in one system is not always compatible with the role behavior dictated by status in a different system. A president of the United States, for example, may find various degrees of conflict in his roles as party leader, church member, statesman, or member of a golf club.

Role conflict for the American elected public official is discussed by William C. Mitchell. He raises the question: Under what conditions are role conflicts likely to occur? The importance of seeking an answer to this question is clear when we note that systems of interacting roles cannot avoid being fundamentally affected by such conflicts. Oscar Grusky raises a similar question in a different setting and finds that role conflict is closely related to goal conflict. The four articles in this section clearly point to role as a major concept for political analysis. It is this concept which serves to distinguish various social groupings from each other. Yet it links the various behavior patterns in the society into a meaningful whole and is therefore central to the analysis of a social system or its parts.

American State Legislators' Role Orientations
Toward Pressure Groups

JOHN C. WAHLKE, WILLIAM BUCHANAN,
HEINZ EULAU, LeROY C. FERGUSON

I

In modern pluralistic political systems, the legislature is a central forum where organized interest groups articulate and express their views and press for public action favorable to their concerns. . . . It seems obvious that legislators' *perceptions* of pressure groups—or of any other factor, for that matter—will vitally affect the part played by that factor in the legislative process. More particularly, legislators' perceptions of what constitutes legitimate or desirable or harmful activity by pressure groups or other factors, as well as their perceptions of the supposedly objective "facts" about such activity, are not random or idiosyncratic opinions held independently by each legislator individually, but are opinions intimately associated with what Truman has called the "influence of office" and Latham has called "officiality." Membership in the legislature constitutes a *status* or *position* in society. This means that people in the society *expect* certain behaviors by incumbents of that position. Legislators have similar expectations toward each other, and they all have expectations with respect to other classes of actors they encounter in doing their legislative business. The key concept to refer to these patterns of behavior associated with a given position or status in the expectations and orientations of people is *role*.

From the abstract and general principles of role theory we take the working hypothesis that legislators' conceptions of their role as legislators will be a crucial factor governing their legislative behavior and thereby affecting the access, influence or power of all groups, as well as differentiating among groups. General role theory suggests that legislators' role conceptions constitute a determining factor in pressure politics at least as important as the number, size, strategy, skill or other characteristics of pressure groups themselves, the individual group affiliations and identifications of legislators, or the peculiarities of personality and personal whim of those legislators. These role conceptions can usefully be made the focal point of comparative and analytical study. . . .

Among questions asked of some 474 legislators in four states during

Reprinted from *The Journal of Politics*, vol. 22 (1960), pp. 203–27 by permission of the publisher. Copyright 1960 by The Southern Political Science Association.

the 1957 legislative sessions were several which make it possible to explore legislators' role orientations toward pressure groups and their agents.

(1) A TYPOLOGY OF ROLE ORIENTATIONS TOWARD PRESSURE GROUPS. Several cautionary remarks should be made here. We are concerned with the functioning of the legislative *institution* in general, rather than with unique historical events or outcomes in the states studied. Similarly, the concern here is not with the *particular* group affiliations and identifications of individual legislators or their relative friendship or hostility toward specific groups but rather with their orientations toward pressure groups as a *generic* class of "significant others." The typology which follows has been constructed and used to suit this ultimate theoretical concern. . . .

Political scientists are familiar with the doctrinal disagreement about the value of pressure politics. One view holds, as did Rousseau, that expression and promotion of conflicting private interests is inimical to discovery and promotion of the public interest; an opposing view, that of many "pluralist" theorists, holds that what is called "the public interest" is never more than the harmonization of just such partial and private interests and that organized interest groups, therefore, play an indispensable part in defining and legislating in the public interest. Legislators' views on the subject likewise differ widely. Some agree with the member who said, "Hell! We wouldn't have a government if there were no interest groups. It would be a form of anarchy if groups and parties didn't do their job." Or, as another said, when asked about the desirability of having the individual citizen participate in government directly, rather than through interest groups, "How's he going to do it 'directly'? You have to organize or go into an organization to do anything." But others agree with the legislator who said in response to the same question, "Stop there (after the word 'directly') and you've got the whole story about our citizens and what they should do." Many legislators share the suspicion of interest groups in general expressed by the member who said, "I've heard of them all my life, but I didn't aim to fool with that, and I don't know anything about it."

It seems obvious that a legislator's reaction to the activities of pressure groups and lobbyists will vary according to such differences in evaluation of pressure politics. Legislators' generalized attitudes of friendliness, neutrality or hostility to pressure politics were therefore measured by a four-item Likert scale utilizing replies to the questions shown in Table 1. Their attitudes were found to vary as indicated in that table.

It likewise seems obvious that legislators' reactions to pressure groups or lobbyists will vary with their different degrees of knowledge or awareness of group activity. The legislator who knows what the Municipal League is,

TABLE 1. ATTITUDE OF STATE LEGISLATORS
TOWARD PRESSURE POLITICS

Question	Attitude* Friendly ↔ Hostile				
	1	2	3	4	5
1. Would you say that, on the whole, the legislature would work [better or worse] if there were no interest groups or lobbies trying to influence legislation? (N = 452)	41%	34%	12%	7%	6% = 100%
2. [Do you agree that] the job of the legislator is to work out compromises among conflicting interests? (N = 462)	31%	42%	2%	12%	13% = 100%
3. [Do you agree that] lobbyists and special interests have entirely too much influence in American state legislatures? (N = 464)	26%	34%	1%	22%	17% = 100%
4. [Do you agree that] under our form of government, every individual should take an interest in government directly, not through interest-group organizations? (N = 458)	19%	24%	3%	19%	35% = 100%

*Response categories to Question 1 were "much worse," "somewhat worse," "about the same," "somewhat better" and "much better"; to Questions 2–4, "agree," "tend to agree," "undecided," "tend to disagree" and "disagree." The most friendly responses are (1) "much worse," (2) "agree," (3) "disagree," and (4) "disagree."

what it wants, who speaks for it and when, will react differently to cues from the League than the legislator who never heard of it and doesn't identify anyone as its spokesman. Legislators' awareness of lobbying activities was therefore measured by asking them to identify a list of lobbyists more or less active in their state legislatures during the time of interviewing.

It is almost universally assumed that one important factor determining the representativeness, legitimacy and authority of any given legislature is the extent and manner of its taking into account the demands of significant interest groups in its social environment. This, in turn, is no more than a reflection of the behavior of the legislators. Some members, by their behavior toward lobbyists and other group representational agents or activity, will serve to accommodate the demands of organized interest groups in the legislative process. Others will serve to resist consideration or accommodation of these demands in any form. And still others, presumably attuned to other persons or factors, will play a neutral role toward such group demands.

Assuming, then, that any given legislator's behavior in this respect will depend to a considerable extent upon his general affective orientation toward pressure politics as a mode of political activity and his awareness of such activity when it occurs around him, one can construct the following very simple typology of legislators' role orientations toward pressure groups:

Facilitators: *Have a friendly attitude toward group activity and relatively much knowledge about it.*

Resisters: *Have a hostile attitude toward group activity and relatively much knowledge about it.*

Neutrals: *Either, (1) Have no strong attitude of favor or disfavor with respect to group activity (regardless of their knowledge of it),*

Or,   (2) Have very little knowledge about it (regardless of their friendliness or hostility toward it),

Or,   (3) Both (1) and (2).

By the measures of tolerance and awareness already described each of the legislators interviewed was classified under one of these three headings. They are distributed in the four states as shown in Table 2.

TABLE 2. DISTRIBUTION OF ROLE-ORIENTATIONS
TOWARD PRESSURE GROUPS IN FOUR STATE LEGISLATURES

Role Orientation	California N = 97	New Jersey N = 78	Ohio N = 157	Tennessee N = 116	Total N = 448
Facilitators	38%	41%	43%	23%	37%
Neutrals	42	32	35	37	37
Resisters	20	27	22	40	26
	100%	100%	100%	100%	100%

The reasons given by legislators for their varying opinions about groups further describe the differences among them. When legislators were asked why they thought the legislature would work better or worse in the absence of pressure group activity, most of their responses could be coded into a comparatively few categories. These have been arranged in the order of decreasing friendliness toward group activity in Table 3. When respondents made more than one comment, only the most favorable (highest in the table) was coded. The table shows that almost two-thirds of the Facilitators think the legislature could not get along without pressure group activity,

TABLE 3. ATTITUDE-DIFFERENCE AMONG FACILITATORS, NEUTRALS
AND RESISTERS AS SHOWN BY THEIR APPRAISALS OF
PRESSURE-GROUP ACTIVITY

Most Favorable Opinion Expressed	Role Orientation*		
	Facilitator N = 124	Neutral N = 105	Resister N = 76
1. Groups are indispensable.	63%	39%	14%
2. Group activity is in general good, though certain "bad practices" of groups are undesirable.	23	41	46
3. Other less favorable opinions: *e.g.*, group activity may be objectionable but one ought not interfere with the democratic right to be heard; group influence is overrated, it is not an important factor; group activity is a wholly disruptive force which ought to be eliminated.	14	20	40
	100%	100%	100%

*Total is only 305 because some legislators failed to give reasons when answering the question and others expressed appraisals not codable in these categories.

whereas a substantial number of Resisters (40%) expressed much less favorable opinions. The differences are of extreme statistical significance.

In spite of these very striking and consistent differences, however, it should not be overlooked that even the Resisters express fairly tolerant appraisals of group activity, some 60% venturing opinions (numbers 1 and 2 in Table 3) which are quite favorable. We must, in other words, recognize the fact that pressure politics has become rather widely accepted among legislators in American states.

Legislators' differences in perception of groups are not simple quantitative differences of more or less, as the initial measure of lobbyist-recognition might suggest. In responding to a question asking them to name the most powerful groups in their own state, 56% of the Facilitators but only 36% of the Resisters named only or mainly *specific organizations* or lobbyists; similarly, only 36% of the Facilitators but 58% of the Resisters referred to *broad interest aggregations* ("labor," "farmers," *etc.*). In other words, Facilitators, significantly more than either Neutrals or Resisters, tend to see groups and group activities in concrete and specific terms. That Facilitators are more alert to perceive groups and group cues is strikingly indicated by the fact that, even though interviewers sought, by probing, to have all respondents uniformly name six groups in response to the question. Facilitators nevertheless named significantly more groups than either Neutrals or Resisters.

Some of the grosser behavioral characteristics of the three types of legislator being described can also be explored. To begin with, assuming the validity of the role-orientation typology, one should expect to find Facilitators more ready than either Neutrals or Resisters to listen to the exhortations of pressure groups. This hypothesis is supported by the finding (see Table 4) that Facilitators named significantly more groups than did either Neutrals or Resisters when asked the question,

TABLE 4. FACILITATORS THINK MORE GROUPS WORTH
LISTENING TO THAN DO NEUTRALS OR RESISTERS

Number of Groups Named	*Role Orientation*		
	Facilitators N = 141	Neutrals N = 134	Resisters N = 108
0–1	11%	17%	20%
2–3	24	34	37
4 or more	29	27	23
"All are worth listening to"*	36	22	20
	100%	100%	100%
Mean number of groups named	4.17	3.50	3.35

*This response counted only if no more precise answer given (*i.e.*, no group named).

We've been told that there are always some groups whose advice ought to be considered, whether they happen to be powerful or not. Would you name some of these groups here in [state]?

Not only do Facilitators think more groups are worth listening to than do Neutrals or Resisters; they apparently tend also to give more weight to what they hear from group representatives. At least on the problem of school needs, which was selected as a typical issue, when legislators were asked to rate the influence of several factors—committee recommendations, advice of party leaders, views of constituents, *etc.*—on their own thinking, Facilitators attributed more importance to the "views of interest groups or lobbies" than did Neutrals or Resisters (See Table 5). Finally, the data provide internal evidence that at least two of the legislative behaviors one would expect to find associated with the accommodation of group interest and demands do indeed appear more characteristic of Facilitators than of

Neutrals or Resisters. Tables 6 and 7 show the former to be more ready to use, or at least to admit to using, the aid of lobbyists both in drafting bills and in lining up support for bills.

TABLE 5. FACILITATORS RATE IMPORTANCE OF PRESSURE GROUPS ON OWN VIEWS OF "SCHOOL NEEDS" PROBLEM HIGHER THAN DO NEUTRALS OR RESISTERS

Importance Attributed to Views of Pressure Groups	Role Orientation		
	Facilitators N = 146	Neutrals N = 137	Resisters N = 101
Very important or important	70%	57%	40%
Not very or not at all important	30	43	60
	100%	100%	100%

TABLE 6. MORE FACILITATORS THAN NEUTRALS OR RESISTERS AGREE LOBBYISTS GIVE THEM VALUABLE HELP IN DRAFTING BILLS

Answer to Statement that Lobbyists Give Valuable Help in Bill-Drafting	Role Orientation		
	Facilitators N = 163	Neutrals N = 160	Resisters N = 120
Agree or tend to agree	63%	52%	52%
Tend to disagree or disagree	37	48	48
	100%	100%	100%

TABLE 7. MORE FACILITATORS THAN NEUTRALS OR RESISTERS AGREE LOBBYISTS GIVE THEM VALUABLE HELP IN LINING UP SUPPORT FOR THE LEGISLATOR'S OWN BILLS

Answer to Statement that Lobbyists Give Valuable Help in Lining Up Support	Role Orientation		
	Facilitators N = 159	Neutrals N = 157	Resisters N = 115
Agree or tend to agree	78%	67%	61%
Tend to disagree or disagree	22	33	39
	100%	100%	100%

There is ample justification, then, for the conclusion that there are significant differences among legislators in their role orientations toward pressure groups and group agents. It is not just that they differ in tolerance and awareness of group activity—that, indeed, was assumed in constructing the typology of Facilitators, Neutrals and Resisters. The point is, important tendencies toward different patterns of behavior are associated with these basic differences in affect and cognition. The patterns are sharper for the Facilitators and Resisters, since they are attuned, favorably or unfavorably, to group behavior, and perceive, understand and react in characteristic fashion. The Neutrals, a category consisting of those who apparently fail to perceive, understand or formulate a coherent standard for judging groups-in-general, demonstrate, as one might expect, a more erratic, less distinct and consistent pattern. It is possible that each individual Neutral, at his own level of awareness or concern, behaves toward some or all group representatives in a manner that could be characterized as "role behavior," but that these patterns cancel each other out in the statistical treatment of responses. In any case, Facilitators are more likely to be aware of the nature of group demands and respond to them; Resisters to be aware of them but deliberately fail to respond; Neutrals to respond or resist, but for assorted other reasons, without caring or without knowing that a demand has been made by a group. It should be clear that these role categories do no more than classify one aspect of legislators' attitudes and behavior: they are not fixed categories of types-of-person, nor will they by any means describe all aspects of legislators' behavior. They are constructs, devised to help us explore further the working of the legislative system and, ultimately, the larger political system. . . .

Role Conceptions and Organizational Size

EDWIN J. THOMAS

The growth of organizations from modest-sized structures; often housed under one roof, to bureaucratic giants has brought a proliferation of administrative units and their dispersion over wide geographical areas. Although the units of these bureaucracies are generally part of the same organizational structure and are committed to achieving common objectives by means of uniformly applied operating procedures, the physical separation of bureaus and offices allows differences among them to germinate and grow. An important source of such differences is the number of persons in the local administrative units. These different sized units are a promising site for research on large-scale organizations because some of the characteristics that would normally vary freely in unrelated organizations are held equal.

Reprinted from *The American Sociological Review*, vol. 24 (February 1959), pp. 30–37 by permission of the author and the publisher. Copyright 1959 by The American Sociological Society.

Much still remains to be learned about the relations between the size of an organization and the behavior of its members. A central question of practical and theoretical significance is the extent to which an organization's size facilitates or impedes efforts to attain its formally stated objectives. To answer this question research must be focused upon two related problems: delineation of the differences in behavior of members in organizations varying in size; and consideration of how these behavioral correlates of size affect the organization's capacity to achieve its goals. Such research should add to the further understanding of those non-formal characteristics of large organizations that affect organizational behavior.

This study compares the role conceptions, the degree of role consensus, and the quality of work of welfare workers in different sized organizational units of a state welfare department. The objectives of the welfare program and the formal requirements for the performance of roles were the same throughout the organization. In comparing small and large units in the department many formal characteristics of the welfare bureaus were thus held constant. Of course, not all of the possibly influential variables were controlled because of differences in history and location of the bureaus.

Attention in the presentation of findings is given to the relationship of the variables to organizational size and, in the discussion of results, to interpretation of why the variables were associated with size and to the relationship of the size of the welfare bureau and their effectiveness in the attainment of one of the organizational goals.

THE ORGANIZATION

The Michigan State Department of Social Welfare administers a program of public assistance through bureaus located in 83 counties. Bureaus range in size from those of one person, who makes investigations and serves as bureau supervisor, to one with hundreds of employees. If sufficiently large, a bureau includes public assistance workers who investigate applications for financial assistance, case and bureau supervisors, and clerical personnel. Within a bureau the chain of authority runs from bureau supervisor to case supervisor and from case supervisor to public assistance worker, with each case supervisor generally supervising six to seven workers.

As noted earlier, the formal requirements of the role of public assistance worker are uniform throughout the organization. All workers have met the same minimal requirements for the job, all perform the same types of functions, and all follow the same rules and procedures as set forth in the manual of operation for the investigation of applications for assistance. At the same time, however, the role can be conceived and performed in different ways because of certain ambiguities in how it is defined (apart from other reasons). Consider, for example, the role of workers who handle cases in the Aid to Dependent Children program (these are the workers studied in this investigation). The federal laws define the ADC task too generally to be of much help in determining many concrete decisions. In contrast, the manual of operation, while very specific with respect to conditions of eligibility for financial assistance, does not cover numerous service problems met by the worker. Thus there is latitude for individual variability in performance and for different conceptions of the role.

PROCEDURE AND FINDINGS

The sample of 109 public assistance workers who handled ADC cases consisted largely of females, and most were married. A majority had worked in public assistance for less than four years, 22 per cent for less than a year. While three-quarters of the workers had college degrees, only nine per cent had specialized in social work and none had obtained a Master's degree in social work.

The sample was drawn from small, medium, and large administrative units. The "small" bureaus were those in which there were at least two but no more than five workers, and no more than a two-level hierarchy. A random sample of six small bureaus was drawn containing a total of 18 workers, all of whom participated in the study. The "medium-sized" bureaus were those that had six or more workers or a three-level hierarchy, but no more than three such levels. Five medium-sized bureaus were selected on a non-random basis, contributing 59 workers who handled ADC cases. The offices ranged in size from six to 22 workers and tended to be located in the more highly industrialized, urban counties. There was only one large bureau, Wayne County; it had a five-level hierarchy, with the positions of ADC division head and director above the level of case supervisor and below the level of bureau director. Thirty-two workers were selected from a pool of 96 ADC workers assigned to two different divisions by choosing four supervisory units at random. The mean number of workers in the small offices was 3.8; comparable figures for medium and large size were 17.4 and 45.5, respectively.

There was a direct relationship between the size of the bureaus and the number of hierarchically ordered strata, since bureaus in the sample were selected by criteria of size and number of strata. For the 83 bureaus in the state there was also a marked positive relationship between the number of employees and the number of strata.

The amount of specialization of function for the worker increased with size. Specialization for three of the four categories of cases was found in the largest bureau in the sample. In the two next largest ones, only a few of the workers had caseloads made up exclusively of ADC recipients, and for the remaining bureaus specialization by type of case was not found.

Characteristics of the workers in the units also differed by size. In the smaller administrative units there were found more older workers, more workers without college degrees, more who had married, more having children, and more workers with long experience in public assistance. The workers in the smaller units, as compared with the larger ones, moreover, lived in a more rural environment.

The personal characteristics of the workers were the only correlates that could be controlled statistically in the analysis of results reported below. There was no satisfactory way to separate the effects of specialization, degree of stratification, and population setting from those of the numbers of workers. Hence, even when the effects of personal characteristics were controlled, there was no way to determine whether it was the number of workers or some other factor that produced the effects. The results presented below were analyzed first without controls for variables operating concomitantly with size and, subsequently, with controls for the personal attributes of the workers. The different sized bureaus are labeled "small" or "large" as a matter of convenience; it should be understood that not merely the number of workers differentiates the offices.

Questionnaires were administered to the participating workers and to their case supervisors in the 12 administrative units. The questions referred to a wide range of variables. One of these, termed *role consensus,* is indicated by the degree of agreement between the public assistance worker and his supervisor about the importance of functions performed by workers. The amount of agreement was assumed to reflect the degree to which workers and supervisors shared a frame of reference regarding the importance of workers' functions. Eleven areas of knowledge and skill (for example, determining financial eligibility, job mechanics, and case-work methods) relevant to performance of the role of the public assistance worker were rated for importance on a seven-point scale by workers and supervisors and discrepancy scores were computed.

Another variable, termed *breadth of role conception,* refers to the number of activities or functions conceived as part of the role. In the questionnaire the workers were presented with nine activities (for example, budgeting and referral for vocational counselling) and were asked to indicate for each function whether they "always," "sometimes," or "never" performed it in cases for which that activity, as a type of service, *was needed.* Numerical values were assigned to responses and total scores were computed. The higher the score, the more broadly the role is conceived.

Another aspect of role, often implicit rather than formally defined, is the ethical commitment that it requires of individuals. In public welfare,

as well as in other service fields, those responsible for giving the services
are guided by ethical precepts. A test of *ethical commitment* was devised
to measure some of these, more exactly termed a test of commitment to
the ethics of professional social work, since it consists of items relating
to seven ethical areas highly endorsed by a sample of 75 professionally
trained social workers. The content of the items, given in Table 1, may be

TABLE 1. PERCENTAGES OF WORKERS, SUPERVISORS, AND MEMBERS OF PROFESSIONAL
ASSOCIATION SELECTING "CORRECT" ALTERNATIVES FOR ITEMS OF THE TEST OF
COMMITMENT TO THE ETHICS OF PROFESSIONAL SOCIAL WORK

Content of Item*	Inferred Underlying Value**	Group		
		Workers (N = 109)	Supervisors (N = 26)	Members of Professional Group (N = 75)
1. In interviewing, sacrifice directness *versus* ask direct questions	humanitarian *versus* utilitarian	49	54	63
2. Motivate by offering information *versus* urge directly	non-coercive *versus* coercive	72	88	97
3. When client is upset, discuss feelings *versus* ignore them	concern *versus* nonconcern for client's feelings	83	88	92
4. When client makes you angry, analyze your anger *versus* ignore it	awareness *versus* non-awareness of self as an instrument of change	72	92	97
5. Financial aid given to all *versus* to those who use it wisely	help universally *versus* help selectively	38	68	69
6. Illegitimacy demands focus on helping individual adjust *versus* changing individual	acceptance *versus* non-acceptance of deviance	28	38	74
7. Client making curtains in messy house, compliment *versus* mention housecleaning	positive *versus* negative methods to motivate	60	75	96

*The first of the alternatives for each item is the "correct" one.
**The first of the polarities of underlying values is the one matched to the "correct"
alternative for its corresponding item.

clustered into two categories: (a) how the worker should behave with a client, and (b) who should receive the benefits of social work services and under what conditions. To complete the validation, the responses of the professionally trained social workers were compared with those of the sample of public assistance supervisors and workers drawn in this study. In contrast to the professionally trained group, the majority of whom had obtained Master's degrees in social work, the public assistance workers generally had little such specialized training. Table 1 shows that the "correct" alternatives are most highly endorsed by the professional group and least highly endorsed by the workers, with the supervisors' responses falling between these extremes.

A final set of measures is related to the quality of the worker's performance on the job. It was possible to learn about the cognitive aspect of performance through indications of the analytic skill of workers as indicated by their ability, first, to identify the problems of families and, second, to propose appropriate treatment plans. To measure the first item, the workers were asked to describe the problems they noted for the members of a family depicted in a case vignette; responses were transformed into a numerical score of diagnostic acuity. To measure the second aspect of analytic skill, the workers were asked to describe what they would do for the individuals described in the case if they had the required time; responses were coded and scores were obtained for *appropriateness of treatment plans*. A motivational aspect of performance was inferred from responses to a question about how much the worker would like to work on the case described in the vignette.

RESULTS

Workers' conceptions of their roles differed according to the size of the welfare office. In the smaller bureaus there was found to be greater *role consensus* between the worker and his supervisor about the importance of functions that workers perform (Table 2), greater *breadth of role conception* (Table 3), and higher *ethical commitment* (Table 4).

QUALITY OF PERFORMANCE. The size of the administrative unit was found to be associated with all indicators of the quality of the worker's performance. Those workers scoring high on the three measures are much more likely to be in the small bureaus than in the larger ones (Table 5).

THE EFFECTS OF PERSONAL BACKGROUND FACTORS. Analyses were made with controls for age, education, experience on the job, marital status, and number of children. This procedure involved the relationship between organizational size and a dependent variable, holding constant the control

TABLE 2. NUMBER OF WORKERS HAVING LARGE AND SMALL
DISCREPANCY SCORES IN ROLE CONSENSUS, BY
SIZE OF ADMINISTRATIVE UNIT

Size of Administrative Unit	Discrepancy Score	
	Small (0–1)	Large (2–3)
Small	14	0
Medium	54	4
Large	21	11
	$X^2 = 15.00, p < .01$	

TABLE 3. NUMBER OF WORKERS CONCEIVING THEIR ROLES NARROWLY
AND BROADLY, BY SIZE OF ADMINISTRATIVE UNIT

Size of Administrative Unit	Breadth of Role Conception	
	Narrow (0–4)	Broad (5–8)
Small	4	14
Medium	20	37
Large	18	14
	$X^2 = 6.48, p < .05$	

TABLE 4. NUMBER OF WORKERS SCORING HIGH AND LOW ON ETHICAL COMMITMENT,
BY SIZE OF ADMINISTRATIVE UNIT

Size of Administrative Unit	Scores on Ethical Commitment	
	Low (1–4)	High (5–7)
Small	3	15
Medium	35	23
Large	26	6
	$X^2 = 20.04, p < .001$	

TABLE 5. NUMBER OF WORKERS SCORING HIGH AND LOW ON MEASURES OF THE
QUALITY OF PERFORMANCE, BY SIZE OF ADMINISTRATIVE UNIT

Size of Administrative Unit	Scores on Diagnostic Acuity		Scores on Appropriateness of Treatment Plan		Motivation to Help Recipients	
	High (4–8)	Low (0–3)	High (5–7)	Low (0–4)	High (3–7)	Low (1, 2)
Small	13	5	14	4	15	3
Medium	23	36	21	38	21	38
Large	6	25	10	20	12	19
	$X^2 = 13.46, p < .01$		$X^2 = 11.26, p < .01$		$X^2 = 13.30, p < .01$	

factor whenever it was found that the control characteristic was associated with the dependent variable. The .05 level of significance was used as a choice point.

Using this technique, age is the only control factor related both to the size of bureaus and the magnitude of discrepany of *role consensus*. Although the smaller bureaus had more older workers and more workers with small discrepancy scores, the effects of size remained with age held constant.

Two of the control factors are closely associated with the *breadth of role conception*. Broadly conceived roles were found more often for older workers and for those with lengthy experience in public assistance; the first relationship yields a X^2 of 17.73, the second a X^2 of 16.21, both giving p values of less than .001. When age and experience are controlled, size is no longer related to the *breadth of role conception*. Since there were more older workers and workers with longer experience in the smaller units, age and experience, and not other factors associated with size, account for the breadth of conception of roles.

Both the education and experience of workers are related to scores of *ethical commitment*. The less well educated and those with longer experience on the job most frequently show high as opposed to low scores on ethical commitment; the X^2 is 8.51 for the former ($p < .01$) and 4.05 for the latter ($p < .05$). The effects of size remain, however, when education and experience are each held constant.

The only control variable found to be related to any of the three indicators of the quality of the worker's performance was the number of children the workers had; those workers having children had higher scores on motivation to help recipients than did those having no children ($X^2 = 5.40$, $p < .05$). The effects of size remained for workers with or without children.

DISCUSSION AND CONCLUSIONS

Why should the variables examined here be associated with organizational size? Like many others, size is not a "pure" variable—a single unitary phenomenon. Size is more like an index because of its relationship to a complement of variables associated with the number of persons in the organization. The findings of this study provide suggestions about these variables, but offer few clues about *why* they are associated with size or about their interrelationships. We now turn to these questions.

Most of our results may be accounted for plausibly in terms of the population and the community setting of the county in which the welfare bureau was located. The size of the bureau itself depends largely upon the population size of a county, since the more populous counties are likely to contain more individuals in need of welfare assistance. Although organizational size bears no necessary relationship to the population of the area in which the organization is located, one may be an index of the other to the extent that (a) the organizational unit serves a portion of the population, as does a welfare bureau, and (b) the unit is located by such arbitrary geographical criteria as county, state, or region.

The association of the workers' personal characteristics with the size of welfare bureaus probably indicates that the pool of potential employees in the counties with large populations differs from those with small populations. Available information indicates that some of the contrasts between workers in the smaller and the larger bureaus parallel those between rural residents and residents of cities. This study provides no information about whether or not there is also selective retention of workers as a consequence of bureau size.

Roles were found to be more broadly conceived by workers in the smaller bureaus. The control analysis shows that age and experience account for the breadth of conception of roles. Welfare workers in rural areas change jobs less often than their urban counterparts, partly because there are fewer occupational alternatives and fewer welfare jobs from which to choose that pay as well or better than public assistance. Rural welfare workers therefore would be expected to be older and more experienced than urban ones. Furthermore, rural areas contain fewer specialized social services, making it necessary for the welfare worker in the rural area to take over informally more functions as part of her role than her urban colleagues.

Another correlate of organizational size is the ethical commitment of workers. Differences in ethical commitment can not be attributed to variations of professionalization, for none of the workers had had professional training in social work. The community setting of the welfare offices and the rural background of the workers account for the workers' ethical orientation most adequately. High scores on the test indicate a generally more positive approach to recipients—an approach probably growing out of a more intimate relationship with recipients in the smaller communities. The writer has been told by experienced welfare workers of the differences between working in the smaller and the larger urban communities. In the small community they note that there is more frequent community contact with recipients; perception of recipients as individuals more often than as "clients"; less social distance between worker and recipient, due in part to similarity of ethnic background; and greater need to attend to more of the recipients' problems. Consequently, the worker in the small bureau is more likely to be willing to assume greater personal responsibility for the recipient and to have more compassion for the recipient as a person than the worker in an urban bureau.

The attitude of helpfulness toward others and the "positive" approach to recipients engendered by the small community probably explain why workers in the small bureaus evidenced performance of higher quality than those in the larger ones. The measures of quality of performance were skill in analyzing problems of recipients, appropriateness of treatment plans, and motivation to help recipients—all of which reflect the extent of the worker's willingness to do a complete and adequate job of helping recipients. That the rural workers are more willing than those in urban settings to help recipients and to put forth the extra effort needed to analyze thoroughly the recipients' problems and to propose suitable treatment is consistent with the earlier observations about the small community.

The community setting of the bureaus does not readily explain why size is related to role consensus. Past theoretical and empirical work indicates that consensus is likely to be greater in small then in large groups. In this study, size alone is probably not the only organizational characteristic contributing to role consensus.

Another correlate of organizational size is the extent to which there was vertical and horizontal differentiation. Size enables differentiation to occur by providing a larger number of persons over whom functions may be distributed and by increasing the range of individual skill and ability needed to give feasibly different assignments to persons. In the organizational units studied here, differentiation in the larger bureaus was further facilitated by administrative policy stipulating the proportion of supervisory personnel required for a given number of workers and by the belief that specialized handling of cases is efficient only in the largest bureaus.

This discussion of the correlates of organizational size suggests that the number of workers may be a less potent variable in affecting the behavior of members than the community setting of the organizational unit. Studies of organizational units of an extended bureaucracy differing in size should be undertaken where it is possible to differentiate them in terms of the population size and type of community in which the units are located.

From another viewpoint, some of the variables used in this study can be said to reflect organizational effectiveness in providing services to families. These variables include the measures of the quality of work, ethical commitment, and breadth of role conception signified by the number of different services workers would perform for families were they needed. These three indications of service are negatively associated with the size of the organizational unit: the smaller bureaus show greater commitment to the ethics of professional social work, greater breadth of role conception, and better quality of work. To the extent that these variables reflect differences in performance of workers, the results indicate that the organizational goal of providing services to recipients was more effectively attained in the smaller welfare bureaus.

The findings of the study do not help to answer the question of how effectively the bureaus attained the organizational goal of determining eligibility for financial assistance.

Why were the small bureaus better able than the larger ones to provide services to families? If the interpretations of the findings presented above are correct, it is largely because the influences of the small community encourage a service orientation toward recipients. The impact of community setting thus may be viewed as reaffirming the significance of the secondary organizational goal, that of providing services, through orienting workers more toward the service aspects of their roles. The part played by the actual size of the welfare bureau is probably minimal, except in so far as it serves to mediate, through primary relationships, the service goal. The fact that role consensus was greater in the smaller bureaus may indicate greater cohesion of the primary groups and readier acceptance of the goal to provide service.

Role Conflict in Organization: A Study of Prison Camp Officials

OSCAR GRUSKY

The official goals of an organization determine in large part the types of role expectations associated with the positions that make up the social structure of the system. If an organization is assigned a new major goal, and if this goal is in conflict with what formerly was the only primary goal of the system, then we would expect that conflict between the goals would create new stresses for many members of the organization. These two or more sets of conflicting role expectations, defined by the organization as legitimate by the fact that they are derived from an official goal, create role conflict.

The increasing emphasis on quasi-environmental, rehabilitation or "milieu" treatment programs in organizations such as prisons and mental hospitals, which formerly have had primarily custodial goals, presents a

Reprinted from *The Administrative Science Quarterly,* vol. 3 (March 1959), pp. 452–72 by permission of the publisher.

situation containing the necessary ingredients for such role conflict. In this paper we are primarily concerned with the effect of the conflicting goals of custody and quasi-milieu treatment in a small midwestern prison camp (Camp Davis) on role conflict among the officers and staff.

Associated with the goal of custody in a prison or mental-hospital setting are staff role expectations that typically involve a general distrust and suspicion of inmate or patient behavior. Consequently in traditional custodial prisons, for example, the officials and inmates are characteristically hostile to one another and show a relatively low level of interaction. On the other hand, associated with the goal of quasi-milieu treatment is a distinctly opposite set of role expectations for officials. The guard or the attendant in a treatment-oriented setting is encouraged to trust the inmate or patient, to interact often with him, and in general to be emotionally supportive. The two goals, then, prescribe conflicting expectations for guard or attendant behavior. The assumption implicit in the custodial goal affirms that the function of the organization is to protect the community by keeping the prisoner in the organization. He is correspondingly labeled as "dangerous," deserving of punishment, and unfit for the "outside world." In contrast, the assumption implicit in the treatment goal affirms that the function of the organization is to protect the community by "rehabilitating" the prisoner. He is correspondingly seen as "mentally ill" or "neurotic" and hence to a considerable extent not really responsible for his past actions. He is deserving of "individual treatment" by which his personal needs can be cared for and his ego healed. . . .

Although conflict between an organization's basic objectives may create the underlying conditions necessary for role conflict, other factors will be instrumental in determining both the essential nature of the conflict for the role occupant and the type of adaptation to the role conflict that is possible. Formal position in the hierarchy of the organization is of fundamental importance in determining the extent of the conflict experienced. The occupants of the elite authority roles in most organizations are expected to demonstrate greater loyalty to the organization's goals (be they incompatible or not) than are other staff members. Moreover, the elite are commonly responsible for maintaining the integration of the organization and hence are likely to be subjected to a greater variety of internal pressures than are the nonelite. Finally, the elite are more likely to be responsible for negotiations with other social systems which impinge on their organization and thus are more exposed to forces from these systems than are the other officials.

With respect to the prison system that was the object of our research, we hypothesized as follows:

1) Role conflict among the prison camp officials stemmed directly

from the conflict between the organization's formal goals of custody and treatment.

2) The differences in the formal hierarchical position of the supervisor and the other staff members should produce different types of role conflict and correspondingly different types of adaptation to the conflict.

THE SUPERVISOR

The chief administrator of a prison organization is traditionally granted extensive independent authority. At Camp Davis the supervisor was at all times the center of a highly centralized authority system. No guard or other officer was permitted to make a policy decision without first consulting him. And in time of an emergency, such as an escape, his immediate notification was required even if he was not on duty.

The formal responsibilities of the supervisor involved policy making with respect to both of the camp's two major goals—custody (maintaining discipline and control over the inmates) and treatment ("rehabilitating" them). During any given time the supervisor's decisions played a crucial role in creating conditions consistent with one goal or the other. If he stressed discipline by establishing new restrictive rules and hence curtailing the inmates' freedom, he would be seen as decreasing the probability of achieving the quasi-milieu treatment goal, since such a policy would serve to increase inmate resentment toward the officials. On the other hand, if he was overly permissive in his policies, discipline and control would break down and he would not be able to sustain the custodial goal.

The mutual interdependence and the contradictions implicit in the camp's goals served both to create and to intensify three major problems confronting the supervisor. First, the guards were differentially committed to the two goals: some preferred emphasizing their custodial duties at the expense of their treatment responsibilities; others preferred emphasizing treatment and neglecting discipline. The problem for the supervisor was to maintain an integrated staff in the face of the divisive pressures generated by the two conflicting goals. The supervisor himself considered this to be his most pressing problem.

Well, strangely enough the biggest problem I've had is not with the inmates but with people that work for you. [What do you mean?] Well, it's kind of a long story. I've had trouble from the officers—not so much from their using poor judgment on handling something in camp, although that has come up, but more from personality traits. Some are intolerant and show it. They use poor discretion—talking about other officers in front of inmates. They've been either too lax or too custodially-minded. [And that's not what you want?] I want somebody who strikes a happy medium. ——— is a good example. ——— [the counselor] is the opposite. He's too treatment-minded and overlooks custodial affairs. The camp has overlooked relations with the community. For the sake of the whole program you've got to be custodially minded. You've got to show concern for protecting the people around here. We've had officers that have taken things home from the camp —which is strictly against the rules. Likewise they've brought things in to inmates that they shouldn't.

The two goals, moreover, helped to set the conditions for the creation of an informal system of social relationships among the guards, which in turn reinforced their incompatibility and increased the supervisor's integrative problems.

The second problem was that of reconciling the conflicting demands made by officials of the State Corrections Agency—demands which were often incompatible, though authoritative:

A good example would be that the Prison Camp Division [of the State Agency] demands that you must "shake down" inmates [search their person and their belongings] a few times a year while the Treatment Division feels you shouldn't disturb an inmate's personal belongings.

The position of the camp in the formal organizational structure of the State Corrections Agency was such that the supervisor was administratively responsible to separate divisions of the Agency for each of the camp's goals. Thus we see that conflict in the organizational goals, abetted by the organizational structure, created a situation where mutually conflicting demands were continually made on the supervisor on the policy-making level. Whereas in a typical prison camp it is perfectly in keeping with the supervisor's role to favor policies such as shaking down inmates, using inmate informants, and watching the inmates' behavior very closely, the same policies automatically became a source of potential strain in this treatment-oriented setting. . . .

THE GUARDS

Associated with role conflict is a lack of consensus in the organization concerning approved behavior in situations that are morally conflicting. In Camp Davis, as we have indicated, this lack of consensus lay in the conflict between the goal of custody and of treatment. For the guards the conflict stemmed principally from the fact that the objectives of quasi-milieu treatment required a different set of decision-making criteria than did the custodial objectives. If an inmate in a traditional prison system violates the rules, the guard simply writes up a "ticket" and the inmate is punished by a central disciplinary court or a disciplinary officer. However, if the same violation occurs in a treatment-oriented prison organization, it complicates the guard's response and creates conflict, for he must decide whether he ought to write up a ticket or whether, for treatment reasons, he ought to let the inmate "express his emotions." The directive to use the latter criterion is contained in this policy statement by the supervisor:

And you can, of course, be stern or security-minded and still keep the respect of the men. If you bear in mind to be fair—don't tell them one thing and do something else. And, uh, let them blow their top off once in awhile—if a man says s.o.b. to you, let him, but don't overdo it.

The nucleus of the conflict lies in the obvious ambiguity of the phrases "once in a while" and "but don't overdo it." Each situation then must be judged uniquely by the particular guard, and a precarious balance must be maintained with regard to the treatment and custodial expectations associated with the guard's role. The very vagueness and impreciseness of the expectations associated with the goal of quasi-milieu therapy heightens the guard's dilemma.

Two modes of adaptation to the situation were found among the four guards. Two of the guards (to be called "custodially oriented guards") responded by emphasizing the application of custodial criteria, and two (to be called "treatment-oriented guards") responded by emphasizing the application of treatment criteria. Hence, the opposite goals and the ambiguity of expectations derived from them created a corresponding bifurcation in the orientation of the guards.

Even the terminology of the custodially oriented guards reflected their orientation. The camp was a "penitentiary" and the offenders were labeled "inmates" or "cons." The treatment-oriented guards, in contrast, referred to the inmates as "men," "campers," or occasionally "boys." Both of the custodially oriented guards decried the lack of discipline in the camp.

I think discipline is necessary; possibly something similar to military discipline would help. [Do you think there's enough discipline here now?] Possibly enough if it was enforced strictly as it should be.

Off the cuff, [he] told me that everyone has his own idea about how a penitentiary [he used this word] should be run. He feels one should make an example of the inmate who disobeys the regulations by destroying state property or by lack of personal hygiene. He thinks more military-like inspections should be held—giving punishments and rewards to the inmates periodically. He says he'd be stricter now with the inmates except that the camp supervisor is against it. [Notes on a postinterview conversation.]

Not only did they recommend greater discipline in order to decrease the influence of treatment criteria, and thus decrease the ambiguity of their role expectations, but they believed that the inmates agreed with their orientation in this regard:

Most inmates would rather have a strict discipline. They know where they stand—don't like one officer writing up one thing and another officer overlooking the same thing.

All of the ambiguity implicit in their role, however, could not be resolved simply by stressing custodial criteria. Although the two guards could and did avoid participating in the formal aspects of the treatment program, and did interact less with the treatment-oriented guards, they could not completely reject the treatment goals, for to do so would have resulted in sanctions against them. Moreover, although this adaptation involved, at the least, latent resistance to the treatment aims, the very existence in the camp of a treatment program provided them with a distinct source of gratification. Unlike the guards in many prisons, all the guards in the camp had a considerable number of friendly associations with the inmates. Since it was the treatment program that helped facilitate such associations, even the custodially oriented guards experienced these rewards, as this guard noted:

Well, there's a whole lot of satisfaction in keeping this many unstable characters in line. [Uh huh] And, well, after a man's been here six months, having him come to you and tell you you've helped him and helped straighten him out—that happens quite often.

Naturally such personally satisfying events only complicated the problem for the custodially oriented guards. Committed as they were to a strong emphasis on discipline, an ambivalent orientation toward the treatment program could serve only to intensify their role conflict.

On the other hand, the treatment-oriented guards were faced with stresses of a different sort. The role of one of them was formally defined as having both counseling and guard functions attached to it. He was responsible for organizing and maintaining the treatment program and for providing individual counseling to the inmates. At the same time he was responsible for performing strictly custodial functions such as making a periodic count of the inmates. The former duties were the most time consuming; hence this role, more than any other, officially represented the treatment goals of the camp.

The counselor guard, being overcommitted to the treatment aspects of his role, saw the other duties as hindering his effectiveness.

The number one problem is the dual role of counselor and guard that I play. This is in terms of getting a positive feeling toward me so they [the inmates] will upon their own choosing come to see me.

The tireless efforts of the counselor guard and his almost missionary-like zeal enabled him to expand the treatment program to new areas of camp life. A sizable part of his efforts was devoted to gratifying the inmates by being extremely permissive. This policy on occasion included overt rejection of certain custodial requirements and did not increase his popularity among the custodially oriented staff, though it did make him popular with the inmates.

I try not to let them see that this is a rigid bureaucracy;—I try to let them see it as a flexible community. That is why on these rules I do very little on strictness; for example, I don't just tell them there are yard limits, period. I tell them about them and say if you want to go beyond the yard limits, see me and we'll see what we can do. [Have you ever let anybody go beyond the yard limits?] Sure, plenty of times, but if _____ [the head of the Prison Camp Division] saw me he'd have my neck. Sometimes the rules are so rigid in these places that it hampers us in helping these guys.

The other treatment-oriented guard, though somewhat less committed to the treatment aspects of his role than the counselor guard (he had no formal counseling functions) demonstrated a similar pattern. Only the two treatment-oriented guards on the staff, for example, led any group therapy sessions and, correspondingly, they tended to have much closer relations with the inmates than did the other guards.

The adaptation of the treatment-oriented guards like that of the custodially oriented guards could not entirely alleviate the ambiguity implicit in their role. The former could not fully reject the custodial expectations associated with their role just as the latter could not completely reject the treatment expectations. Thus both were left with strong feelings of ambivalence.

THE EFFECTS OF ADMINISTRATIVE SUCCESSION

Role adaptations which are appropriate at one period of time in an organization's history may not be appropriate at another time. One important source of change in an organization is succession, the process of replacement of key officials in the formal or informal network of relationships in the organization. Succession is a vital organizational phenomenon because it is inevitably disruptive, that is, it always creates some temporary disequilibrium in the organization. The effects of succession are, of course, variable. The more highly bureaucratized an organization is, for example, the less severe the consequences of succession are likely to be.

We have seen how the position of the supervisor and the guards helped promote their particular type of adaptation to the problems largely created by the incompatibility of the organizational objectives, custody and treatment. Now let us examine the impact of succession on these adaptations to role conflict.

The administrative changes that occurred consisted of the replacement of the camp supervisor and one of the custodially oriented guards. There is evidence that suggests that these personnel changes were related to a power struggle in the upper echelons of the Correction Agency between the faction representing custody and that representing treatment. The new supervisor was selected by the faction favoring custodial treatment and was therefore committed to its point of view. An adaptation of administrative neutrality was therefore not structured as a potential response for him. The new supervisor, confronted with a role in which he had had no previous experience and being relatively uncommitted to the quasi-milieu treatment goal, responded by formalizing relationships in the organization. The most important changes which he instituted involved the substitution of formal rules for informal ones. After being in charge of the camp for about a month, he inaugurated a list of fifty-two rules that the inmates were instructed to abide by rigorously. It was, of course, not the great number of rules themselves (for very few of the rules were new) but the rigidity implicit in the nature of the rules which became symptomatic of the development of a new type of relationship between the staff and the inmates. Under the administration of the former supervisor there had been relatively few standardized rules, thereby legitimating relatively individualized and informal relationships between the guards and the inmates. With the appointment of the new supervisor this informality was replaced by impersonal and formalistic relationships between the inmates and the staff promoted by this set of rules. Hand in hand with this policy went an increasing emphasis on closer supervision and stronger security controls. Policies which were consistent with the ideology of custody quickly supplanted the earlier pattern, in which both treatment goals and custodial objectives had had equally important roles in guiding decision making.

The hostility of the inmates to the new policies culminated in a crisis two weeks after the new rules were initiated, when a group of inmates perpetrated damage amounting to $400 to two Conservation Department trucks. The escape rate shortly thereafter rose to its highest point in the two-and-one-half-year history of the camp, as did the number of inmates who were voluntarily and involuntarily transferred out of the institution.

Three general factors within the camp's staff contributed to the organizational strain: (1) the decline of the old informal groups among the staff, (2) the inability of the new supervisor to enlist the staff's co-operation in enforcing the new policies because of his overcommitment to the custodial goal, and (3) the lack of direct communication channels from the inmates to the guards to the supervisor, resulting in a lack of immediate knowledge by the chief policy maker of the impact of his decisions.

The fact that new personnel were replacing key staff officials in a small, highly integrated social structure meant that new informal alignments had to be made among the staff. The addition of both a new custodially oriented guard and a new custodially oriented supervisor upset the previous balance. The treatment-oriented guards responded to this minority position by becoming more cohesive and remaining apart from the other officials. As a result the supervisor found it difficult to implement his policies. The treatment-oriented guards often did not enforce the new rules, whereas the custodially oriented guards did enforce them, as this incident illustrates:

[A treatment-oriented guard] is griping about the rules, suggesting that they just can't be followed in a place like Davis. He recounts the time last night when he saw three guys playing cards [Only two are allowed to play at one game]. He knew he was supposed to write them up for it, but he didn't. Instead he just told them to break it up [Notes, Sept. 17, 1956].

The inconsistencies in the administration of the new policies naturally produced anxiety, puzzlement, and concern on the part of the inmates with regard to their expected orientation toward the new regulations, as indicated in this exchange between an inmate leader and a treatment-oriented guard:

Inmate: *Now what about this visiting rule that cuts down visiting hours, is that gonna be enforced?*
Guard: *No.*
Inmate: *[Puzzled] Well, how do we know which rules are gonna be enforced and which are not? Why you may not write us a ticket and someone else will—how are we going to know what to do? Like going into the kitchen for coffee—it's against the rules now, but some guys do it and get away with it. . . .*
Y [a custodially oriented guard] just doesn't come around unless to catch somebody and write him a ticket—now how will he stand on the rule?"

The newness of the supervisor—the fact that he had not been acquainted either with the staff or with the inmates—resulted in his lacking any emotional ties to past staff policies that had become traditional in the camp. Moreover, once the supervisor had initiated his strongly custodially oriented policies, little informal interaction occurred between him and the treatment-oriented guards. This in turn resulted in an even greater decrease in the influence of treatment criteria on camp policies and also promoted a general lack of substantive knowledge on the part of the supervisor as to the impact of his policies on the inmates. Since the treatment-oriented guards had interacted more often with the inmates, they had functioned as a major source of information—information to which the former supervisor, because of his neutrality, had had access but which was unavailable to the new man because of his custodial orientation.

In summary, the process of succession intensified the role conflict of the staff members. The new supervisor's strong commitment to custody made it more difficult for him to implement the treatment expectations which were still defined as legitimate, though deemphasized informally, in the organization. The treatment-oriented guards, feeling compelled to go so far as to promote rule violations because of their strong commitment to the milieu-treatment goal, became extremely insecure. And, finally, the custodially oriented guards found themselves in a situation that minimized the possibility of maintaining friendly relations with the inmates, relations which had been defined as an important part of the treatment goal and which in the past had been a source of gratification for the guards themselves.

Occupational Role Strains: The American Elective Public Official

WILLIAM C. MITCHELL

An important subject for behavorial research is the interplay between organizational structure and personality, between the peculiar conditions or demands of given occupations and the kinds of accommodations that individuals make to them. This analysis is concerned with the strains and conflicts associated with elected political office in the United States. . . .

I shall consider seven general sources of strain for the elected public

Reprinted from *The Administrative Science Quarterly*, vol. 3 (1958), pp. 210–28 by permission of the publisher.

official. The categories used are by no means exhaustive, but they are primary in the sense that any other role strains are products of those selected for discussion. In the order in which they will be analyzed they are (1) insecurity of tenure; (2) conflict among public roles; (3) conflict of private and public roles; (4) ambiguities in political situations; (5) diffused responsibility and limited control of situations; (6) time and pressure of demands; (7) and status insecurity. Finally, it should be clear that I am writing not as a psychologist, but as a political sociologist. No attempt will be made, therefore, to analyze the effects of role strains upon the personality. My concern is solely with sources.

SOURCES OF STRAIN

INSECURITY OF TENURE.   No occupational role guarantees perfect security of tenure, least of all, perhaps, that of the politician. The turnover in the ranks of elected public officials is very great as the investigations of Charles S. Hyneman have demonstrated. His findings respecting tenure in ten state legislatures over a period of ten years (1925-1935) indicate that in only four of the twenty chambers studied had as many as 50 per cent of the members completed three sessions. And in seven chambers less than 25 per cent could show experience in three previous sessions. In "Tribulations of a State Senator" Duane Lockard claimed that "roughly half of the six thousand legislators you are going to elect will be entering the legislature for the first time. Most legislators cannot afford to serve more than one term." Regardless of the reason fragmentary evidence indicates that tenure is far from being guaranteed in politics.

Although the insecurity of public office is a fact, it does, however, require an explanation. Whenever an occupational role is part of a competitive situation—as it normally is in politics—insecurity of tenure is bound to be felt. Tenure, of course, refers to the role itself and not to any other roles the person may occupy. A politician may have a guaranteed income from other sources so that his economic anxieties are allayed; yet his insecurity as a politician will force him to reduce the tensions of the political role. And this will not necessarily be done for selfish reasons. The reduction of tension will be an indicator of success as a politician, meaning that his work is being done more effectively. A person who has to devote considerable time and energy to the security of his tenure will be more responsive, both consciously and subconsciously, to the wishes of those governing his tenure than one who does not. The politician is in this position because he is elected. He is therefore peculiarly sensitive to the currents of public opinion in his constituency. The fickle nature of the crosscurrents of opinion adds to his insecurity, for the number of issues on which the constituency can be unified into significant, clear-cut majorities is rather small. The politician's mandate, then, is ambiguous on most issues and his insecurity heightened for that reason. No politician can ignore public opinion. Even when he feels it to be wrong, it is still a fact that he has to calculate when attempting to rule.

The strains of insecurity then stem from the periodic, usually rather short, terms of office that a politician can attain only by winning elections. Much of what a politician does can be viewed as varying forms of response to political insecurity. The very fact that American politicians respond more quickly and willingly to the demands of their constituencies than to those of their parties is a recognition, by them, of the source of the insecurity. In devoting their attentions to the constituencies, they are hoping to relieve tension and its consequencs.

Increases in salary and pension plans are also means of coping with the problem. Control over elections—ranging from the purely legal ones of intense campaigning and gerrymandering to the illegal buying of votes— are additional responses. Among the better-known means of control has been the resistance of politicians to the adoption of open primaries. Since the primary adds another hurdle, many politicians obviously opposed it; when they could no longer prevent its development, they then moved to minimize its effects. They were aided in this by an indifferent electorate. No politician encourages competition, and certainly not at the primaries. There the effort is to eliminate as many potential competitors as possible before the formal election and to reduce the effectiveness of those who escape during the campaign.

Democratic forms of procedure, however, are designed to promote competition so that the politician can never be said to have complete control over his fate. And, as stated above, forces from without the constituency can and do affect tenure. Great social forces—and such well-known phenomenon as the "coattail" effect—all impinge upon the politician's tenure of office. They are, almost of necessity, imponderable forces and difficult for the practical politician to control.

ROLE CONFLICTS. The fact that most politicians serve in more than one role as elective public officials guarantees conflicts among norms of performance. Expectations emanating from a variety of sources impinge upon the politician every time he is to make a decision. Various persons and groups constantly attempt to influence the decisions and the premises of the politician so that the actual decision will satisfy the interests of the persons specifying the premises or decisions.

Talcott Parsons' pattern-variable scheme enables us to categorize the premises of decisions in terms of five dichotomous choices on the part of the actor in orienting himself to his situation. Different orientations mean different decisions on the part of the politician—hence the great concern in shaping the politicians' orientation by other persons. If a politician chooses to accept or be guided in his decision making by one role in preference to another, he is forced to de-emphasize other roles he might be expected by some to perform. This matter of choosing certain premises rather than others brings out the problem of role conflict.

We can illustrate the point by characterizing two roles, the administrative and the partisan. When these roles are analyzed in terms of the pattern variables, one can readily see that the expectations concerning performances are contrary at every relevant choice point. The premises of action in each role are opposed. Whereas the administrator is expected to be affectively neutral, the partisan is expected to be affectively involved in the situation. Whereas the administrator's role is functionally specific, the partisan's is diffused. The administrator is expected to employ universalistic standards; the partisan, to employ particularistic criteria. Whereas administrators are expected to be achievement-oriented, the partisan has to be ascriptively oriented. And, finally, partisans are expected to be self-oriented, while administrators are expected to be collectivity-oriented.

The norms or premises of action expected by others of the politician are not always in conflict. At some of the relevant junctures in decision making, the premises may be the same so that no role conflict ensues. We know that administrative and the judicial roles have much in common. The one role which, perhaps, conflicts the most with each of the other roles is that of the partisan. One should not deduce, therefore, that the partisan role is dysfunctional and to be suppressed. Whether it ought to be is a value judgment and not a scientific one.

The conflicts that theoretically exist among the four roles of the polity can be simply presented in tabular form. This means of presentation has the merit of bringing out the relationships among the norms in a clearer fashion. Table 1 illustrates the role structure and possible areas of conflict. Read horizontally, Table 1 describes in terms of the pattern variables the premises or norms of each of the four possible roles constituting an office. If instead of the rows the columns are read, we are presented with the points at which conflicts among the norms or premises of decisions are found. Thus in the first column the conflicts are found between the administrative role and both the executive and partisan roles. Again, the executive role conflicts with the judicial. In total there are four possible conflicts at this juncture in the decision-making process. One can proceed down the other columns in the same way and list the conflicts.

A fruitful question to pose at this time is: Under what conditions are role conflicts most likely to occur? On an impressionistic basis alone the

TABLE 1. THE PATTERN-VARIABLES AND ROLE CONFLICT

Role	*1*	*2*	*3*	*4*	*5*
Administrative	Specific	Affective neutrality	Universalistic	Collectivity orientation	Achievement
Executive	Diffuse	Affective neutrality	Universalistic	Collectivity	Achievement
Partisan	Diffuse	Affective	Particularistic	Self-orientation	Ascription
Judicial	Specific	Affective neutrality	Universalistic	Collectivity	Ascription

answer suggests that the major variables are the office, the structure of the constituency, and the incumbent of the office.

Obviously those offices which combine the greater number of roles will engender the most conflicts, whereas the offices with the fewest number of roles develop the fewest conflicts. Offices such as the presidency, governorships, and mayoralties of the large cities are likely to be the source of more conflicts than both legislative and judicial offices. In the latter case litigants and interested persons or groups have conflicting expectations about the outcome of a particular trial or decision, but the role of the justice is so clear-cut, so isolated from the other role, and so protected from the public and retribution that role conflicts are minimized. The legislative and executive offices are not so protected; but since the legislator generally has fewer roles to play, he has fewer conflicts. His conflicts are of another type involving the same role, usually the partisan, in conflict with other partisans rather than with other roles. Republican and Democratic congressmen apply the same premises of action but come out with opposing decisions on a particular piece of legislation. One votes "yes" and the other "no."

It stands to reason that in the matter of constituencies, those districts which have the greatest heterogeneity in the voting population will cause the greatest number of conflicts for their elective public officials to resolve. Some voters will expect their office-holders to act as executives, and others will emphasize other roles. Generally speaking, the larger the constituency in terms of population, the greater will be the heterogeneity and the subsequent number of conflicts. Senators probably face more role conflicts than do congressmen, assuming other factors are constant. Because of the districting process some congressmen have larger constituencies than do many senators, so the former's problems may be magnified as a result. Congressman Celler is a good example, as he has more constituents than many western senators do. Among the executive offices role conflicts are greater on the national level than on the state and local levels. . . .

AMBIGUITIES IN POLITICAL SITUATIONS. Lest the discussion suggest that most political situations are characterized by clear-cut conflicting expectations, let me emphasize the fact that as many or even more are dominated by ambiguity. Instead of being pulled in opposite directions by well-known forces, the elected official is often in the position of a lost hunter seeking direction.

Both the administrative and partisan roles share in the ambiguity, but the latter experiences a somewhat different type. The ambiguities of the administrative role stem from a lack of knowledge concerning means, and the partisan has difficulty defining the goals of the community. . . .

Politicians react to ambiguity by attempting to reduce it. Public opinion polls, newspaper commentary, personal contact with constituents, reports from advisers, research bureaus, investigating committees, and "trial balloons" are a few of the methods used to counteract uncertainty. But while politicians are utilizing more scientific processes to gather factual data for the structuring of situations, in the final analysis the data is never complete, nor can it resolve value questions, because logically an "ought" statement cannot be deduced from an "is" statement. The politician's responsibility to define system goals will always be fraught with ambiguity. . . . In a democracy diffused responsibility and limited controls over the situation are built into the situation of the leader. While the politician is often held responsible by someone for practically everything, he cannot control many of the variables that affect the outcome of the situation and its demands. This is, of course, more true of the executive role than of any other, and of national than of state and local offices. But politicians from all levels complain about the limited control they have to effectuate goals.

Most of the strain that comes from this disparity of responsibility and control relates to the structure of government in the United States. The American polity disperses power to such an extent that no one official is able to accomplish a task without the co-operation of several other officials, who may have different values and goals and may, in addition, belong to a different party. Because the formal means for securing co-operation are not always sufficient, many informal means have grown up. I need not specify these means here, but merely indicate that role strains have encouraged them. . . .

TIME AND THE PRESSURE OF DEMANDS. A persistent complaint of politicians at all levels is related to the number of demands being made on their time and influence. Voters commonly overestimate the influence of politicians;

consequently they ask them to do the impossible. More burdensome are their time-consuming requests; the politician often feels this time could better be devoted to more important matters. Local politicians expect to perform chores and usually do not complain to the same extent as do politicians who are concerned with more significant policy matters. Senator Downey of California gives a vivid portrait of the burdens of a senator, burdens which, incidentally, are increasing:

Each day Senators have matters come before them which could, if they could spare the time, occupy their attentions for months . . . yet here we are compelled to dispose of weighty and complicated matters after being able to listen to arguments only for perhaps an hour or two. . . . Observe for a moment the volume of business that is done in my office alone. It is so great as almost to break me and my whole staff down. In mail alone we receive from 200 to 300 letters every 24 hours. And this in addition to telegrams and long-distance calls and personal visits. . . .

Senator Fulbright adds his lament in the following words:

But the fact is that the multitude of requests for minor personal services comes close to destroying the effectiveness of a great many capable representatives. The legislator finds himself in a dilemma. If he refuses to see the constant stress of visitors or to give personal attention to their requests, they may become offended and withdraw their support. In addition, it is personally gratifying to be able to be of help to one's friends. On the other hand, if he does give his attentions to these matters, he literally has no time left for the intelligent study and reflection that sound legislation requires.

The senator further states that voters often will not accept the services of secretaries but insist on the personal attention of the politician. "They [the voters] feel that they elected the Senator and they are, therefore, entitled to his personal attention." Senator Kennedy adds:

If we tell our constituents frankly that we can do nothing, they feel we are unsympathetic or inadequate. If we try and fail—usually meeting a counteraction from other Senators representing other interests—they say we are like all the rest of the politicians. All we can do is retreat into the cloakroom and weep on the shoulder of a sympathetic colleague—or go home and snarl at our wives.

Several of the quotations just given suggest rather strongly that politicians, at least those on the congressional level, feel frustrated in their mission by the press of time and conflicting demands in their situation. The politician often feels that he has a job of considerable responsibility and that petty demands prevent him from making the contribution which he was elected to do and ought to do. Young politicians are frequently disillusioned about politics in this respect. Senator Neuberger, then a newly elected state legislator in Oregon, wrote: "I arrived at our new marble Capitol expecting to spend most of my time considering momentous issues —social security, taxes, conservation, civil liberties. Instead, we have devoted long hours to the discussions of regulations for the labeling of eggs."

STATUS INSECURITIES.   Adequate performance on the part of role incumbents requires some form of compensation or appreciation for the services rendered. Most men like to believe that what they are doing is a contribution to others and that the relevant others know this and are grateful. Politicians are no different in this respect than are other people; if anything, they are even more sensitive to opinion about their work than are many other groups in the community. Although politicians occasionally voice dissatisfaction with their monetary rewards, more often the complaint is about an assumed low social status. According to T. V. Smith and L. D. White, "The politician's faith in himself has been impaired by the people's distrust of him." I have some doubts about the assumption of a low status for the politician, but the important point is the assumption in the case of the politicians themselves. If they feel they are appreciated, they may act accordingly. "If he [the politician] believes in himself he'll devote himself to his high mission," Smith and White conclude.

Senator Robert La Follette, Jr., voiced a common complaint in respect to the status of Congressmen:

Congress has been a favorite target for the disgruntled, the disappointed, the intellectual snobs, and the doubters of democracy alike. But most of this criticism is not constructive. It springs from personal prejudice, political bias, and above all from an utter lack of knowledge of the workaday problems with which a great legislative body must deal. . . .

Status insecurities thus grow out of the ambivalent status accorded the politician by the voters. The politician is never quite certain whether he has a position of respect or not. If he is convinced that he has, he is still unsure about the reason for it. The reasons may not be particularly admirable ones, for the politician is subject to much selfish flattery. Some he can recognize, but not all. As a result many politicians are likely to manifest forms of behavior that indicate doubt about their prestige.

The foregoing quotations indicate some of the responses of the politician to his status insecurity. The first response is to give verbal expression to the fact, writing articles about the plight of the public official. Note, too, that the writers assert vigorously that the politician is mistakenly abused and that he serves a vital function in society. Typical in this respect is an article by Governor Bradford of Massachusetts entitled, "Politicians Are Necessary Too." A congressman and scholar has written an article on "The Magnitude of the Task of the Politician" to prove that the politician deserves better treatment. In *Profiles in Courage* a well-known present-day senator, John Kennedy, has defended the politician by citing historical examples of great politicians who lived up to their principles. There is a certain defensiveness about such articles and books, indicating that the politician is not only interested in correcting the public's view of him but in sustaining his own conception of himself as a useful member of society.

Status insecurity can take other forms. One of the more obvious is for the politician simply to leave the realm of active politics. As noted earlier, Senator Kefauver believes some excellent congressmen are leaving government for precisely this reason. I have no statistics on the matter, but it seems certain that status insecurity does lead some men to leave politics. The writer knows of two individuals who participated in local politics but decided, with the approval of their wives, that they had taken enough abuse from unappreciative voters. Their resentment is considerable, even though other politicians have taken more abuse during the same period and in the same area.

Politicians form a sort of informal mutual admiration society to compensate for their insecurities. The often exaggerated deference that politicians show for one another, in spite of party affiliations, suggests a latent function in terms of maintaining morale. The politicians who appear on television and radio to debate various issues always pay high tributes to their opponents and colleagues. The same is true of much of the debate that takes place in legislative assemblies. The contributions of one politician are always cited by other politicians in their public appearances. Incidentally the politician generally refers to his colleagues as "statesmen," and seldom, except during a campaign and only in regard to the opposition, as "politicians."

Still another means of coping with status insecurity is for the politician to adopt a cynical attitude toward those who are responsible for his situation, the voters. Not infrequently, the politician becomes tough-minded and cynical. By distrusting other people and their motives, he immunizes himself from criticism and disappointment. The politician may attempt to convince himself that he is uninterested in the attitudes of others. In fact, he cannot be, but the delusion is comforting.

Some politicians adopt a stoic view to handle their status problems.

Presidents Roosevelt, Truman, and Eisenhower have all been known to say that the varying degrees of abuse to which each has been subjected is petty and unimportant compared to the criticism suffered by some of the greatest of American Presidents. The detractors are, so Truman is reported to have once said, soon forgotten. The historical-minded politician is more concerned with what future generations will think of him than what his contemporaries do. The conviction that what one is doing will be of lasting importance sustains the politician through the rocky present.

The role of humor ought not to be underestimated as a means for handling the strains of politics, including that of status insecurity. Politicians like the late Senator Barkley were not only renowned for their gift of humor but also honored for the use which they made of it during times of great stress. The politician, as Senator Wiley has shown, is quite capable of laughing at himself. The fact that he can and does may constitute an effort to minimize the difficulties of political life.

CONCLUSION

I have indicated some of the major sources of strain in the occupation of the elected public official. Instead of summarizing them, I want, now, to list a few propositions or, better, hypotheses about role strains in the hope that others may be stimulated to further research. The hypotheses are stated in an unqualified manner and without supporting evidence.

Hypothesis 1. The more complex the social system, the more numerous are the possible sources of role strains.

Hypothesis 2. The more sharply roles are defined in a system the more intense will be the resultant strains where role conflict occurs.

Hypothesis 3. In the American polity executive offices are subject to more role strains than are legislative and judicial offices.

Hypothesis 4. Legislative offices are subject to more role strains than are judicial offices.

Hypothesis 5. The higher the office, i.e., in terms of the local, state, and national division, the more numerous the role strains. . . .

CHAPTER TEN

ELITES

IN his *Politics: Who Gets What, When, How,* Harold Lasswell views man in society as belonging to either the *elite* or the *mass.* The elite are the influentials who get the most of what there is to get; the rest are the mass. The study of politics, Lasswell suggests, is little more than the study of influence and the influentials. Thus in the Lasswellian scheme *elite* becomes a central concept of political science. From this point of view, identification of an elite must be preceded by determination of "what there is to get" and "who gets the most." What there is to get, of course, may differ from one social system to the other, as may the desires and needs of disparate elites. Most identifiable elites, however, seem to have one thing in common: the pursuit of power. Thus Lasswell, in another work, has defined "the elite" as those with most power in a group; "the mid-elite" as those with less power, and "the mass" as those with least power. In the selection incorporated in this book, Lasswell and his colleagues suggest that "the political elite" is the top power class.

Other writers are also concerned with the identification of the power elite. C. Wright Mills defines the power elite as those who are able to realize their will even if others resist it. In practical terms the power elite for Mills consists of the political, economic, and military circle which share, through overlapping cliques, control over decisions having at least national consequences. On the other hand, Lasswell believes that the elite concept is not necessarily incompatible with democratic processes.

The second basic distinction between the work of Lasswell and Mills is the position approach. Mills identifies what appears to be an irresponsible elite based upon institutional *position*. Lasswell's concept is sufficiently flexible to allow for consideration of *reputation* as well as *position* in the identification of elites. The work of Mills, therefore, is much closer to the traditional notion of a relatively unchecked ruling class governing in its own interests and perpetuating itself in spite of episodic changes in the more superficial social institutions.

The identification of a power elite on a national scale such as Mills attempts is, of course, a large order. Work of this nature has in general lacked a sharpness of attention to detail and adequacy of research design. The authors of the remaining articles in this section are clearly sensitive to both of these problems. This is recognized by Schulze and Blumberg in their focus on the local community as a universe of study. In the "Determination of Local Power Elites," the authors examine the problems involved in elite identification at the community level. One of the methods investigated is that used by Mills—identification by *position*. The other is the *panel technique* whereby the "knowledgeables" are queried as to elite structure In comparing the two approaches, Schulze and Blumberg discover that determination of elite composition depends significantly on the method used to make the identification.

Lewis Edinger, in a provocative bit of research which uses the position approach, finds that in complex and pluralistic societies the simplistic assumptions concerning the circulation of elites are questionable. Evidence from the denazification programs in postwar Germany suggests that a political elite may be replaced (or circulated) with less cost than a technical or managerial elite. Confirmation of Edinger's findings in subsequent research would, however, entail some modifications in elite theory.

Finally, in a summary view of approaches to leadership, Alvin Gouldner pinpoints some of the major analytical problems encountered by those working in this area.

The Elite Concept

HAROLD D. LASSWELL, DANIEL LERNER, AND C. EASTON ROTHWELL

The search for the political elite may well begin with what is conventionally known as the government. *Conventionally* speaking, government is the

Reprinted from *The Comparative Study of Elites* (1952), pp. 8–13 by permission of the publisher. Copyright 1952 by the Board of Trustees of Leland Stanford Junior University.

institution which is so named by the members of the community in question. *Functionally,* however, only the institution which makes the severely sanctioned choices can qualify. Since the true decision-makers are not necessarily known at the beginning of research the investigator can select government in the conventional sense as a convenient starting point.

The first research operation is to identify the individuals who have held a given position during a selected period. It is then possible to calculate the rate of *personal circulation,* which is the number of individuals occupying the post per unit of time.

The second problem is to determine the rate of *social circulation,* which refers to the social and personal characteristics of those passing through a specified position during a given interval. We are interested in the continuity (or discontinuity) of the social circulation. If everybody moves up a notch when his superior dies, the continuity of recruitment is complete. It is attained by providing for immediate succession. Continuity can also be realized by modes of recruitment which prescribe more remote succession, as when a process of election picks individuals outside the immediate and formal hierarchy. Discontinuity occurs when the method of replacing personnel is changed, or when it yields a personnel with novel traits.

In deciding whether new types of leaders are appearing we look into social class characteristics. An analysis of the House of Commons which included seven general elections, for example, showed that the percentage of members coming from titled families was high and stable (40 per cent). Other ties with the social structure are examined, such as wealth, occupation, and enlightenment (to mention only a few possibilities). We also consider the types of personality from which generals, legislators, judges, and other political personnel are recruited.

Having found the social circulation we can determine the *representativeness* of community leadership. During the past sixty years, for instance, over half of the presidents' cabinets have been lawyers (55 per cent). However, less than 1 per cent of the gainfully employed in the general population are lawyers and judges. It is typical for the parliaments of Western powers to underrepresent certain elements in the population, such as manual workers, clerks, farmers, women, and young people.

We also consider the *flexibility* with which a given leadership adapts to the changing composition of the community, or to varying levels of social crisis. From an analysis of social circulation through important governmental posts in New York, we know that during such crises as wars, officeholders are recruited to an increasing degree from among the wealthy. During intercrisis periods the wealthy return to private life, leaving the field clear to persons originating in lower income groups.

Further insight into the elite comes with the calculation of *interlocking* among positions. During the Fascist period in Italy it made sense to pay particular attention to the interlocking of various organs of government with the Fascist party, since it was possible to explain which agencies were rising or falling in influence on this basis. (When persons or positions are described as rising or falling in influence, it is a matter of specifying the amount of *vertical mobility* involved.)

Which time periods are the most suitable for elite studies? Even though no consensus exists, it is often assumed that "about a generation" is meant. But the boundaries of a generation are not fixed. We might arbitrarily choose a year to mark "coming of age." If we take the twentieth or twenty-first year, a century divides conveniently into five generations. This pace is perhaps too fast, since the oncoming wave of twenty-year-olds does not press upon or begin seriously to displace the elder generation until after more age and experience have been acquired. By the mid-thirties enough influence has been amassed to penetrate some important posts. Hence the convention of counting three generations per century has sometimes been adhered to. In crises, however, old ways of doing things rapidly grow obsolete, and leaders are superannuated at a faster rate than usual. During quiet times, on the contrary, a given personnel persists longer than usual.

No one clock serves the multifarious purposes of research on elites. Some inquiries are better served by gathering data by regular intervals of time and studying "chronological generations." For other research tasks a "functional generation" is more illuminating, since it is described according to varying phases of social adjustment. A functional example is the "revolutionary generation" of 1917, meaning the leaders who appeared during the first seizure and defense of power, and under whose direction the initial steps were taken toward industrializing Russia. The "Stalinist generation" is another functional case, referring to those in top positions after Stalin entrenched himself in command of the Party.

Among the personal and social characteristics of an elite which are worthy of separate examination must be included the means by which the *active* members of a ruling class reach the very top positions, or, contrariwise, fail. Not all members of a ruling class, as implied before, take an active role, or even an interest in politics. The point comes out plainly if we inspect a sample of 100 families of the British peerage in which the title has descended without interruption between 1800 and 1900. No less than thirty-one of these elite families were without known political activity. This was counterbalanced by the thirty-four families, two-thirds or more of whose members were active in politics. Since this sample was confined to the peers themselves, it is reasonable to assume that the degree of political interest has been understated rather than overstated. . . .

Because of the stress so often put upon the social origins of an elite, and upon the path by which active members of an elite rise to the top, it is sometimes lost sight of that origins are no infallible guide to eliteship. The essential condition to be fulfilled is *accountability*. To be accountable is to be influenced. We are acquainted with the wide range of devices evolved by representative governments in their long struggle to control the executive, and to keep all members of the active elite accountable to the passive elements of the ruling class. The devices include popular election of officials at frequent intervals; short official terms; initiative, referendum, recall; freedom of press; freedom to organize opposing (loyal) parties; freedom from coercion during campaigns and at the ballot box; separation of authority between branches of government; federation and devolution; substantive and procedural protections of the individual and of private associations from executive arbitrariness.

There is no body politic in which the active elite is wholly unaccountable to large circles within the community, and even to the community as a whole. Where means of peaceful influencing are not at hand, and deprivations are widespread, attempts at enforcing accountability are likely to end in coercion, whether in the form of assassination, uprising, sabotage, or civil disobedience. . . .

What has been said about the concept of the political elite can be summed up as follows: *The political elite comprises the power holders of a body politic. The power holders include the leadership and the social formations from which leaders typically come, and to which accountability is maintained, during a given generation. In other words, the political elite is the top power class.* Obviously it does not include all members of the body politic unless everyone shares equally in the decision process. The extent of power sharing must be determined in every situation by research, since there is no universal pattern of power. We speak of an *open elite* when all or a very considerable number of the members of a body politic are included. A *closed elite*, on the other hand, embraces only a few. A ruling caste is a ruling class closed to all save certain families.

The Power Elite

C. WRIGHT MILLS

The power elite are composed of men whose positions enable them to transcend the ordinary environments of ordinary men and women; they are in positions to make decisions having major consequences. Whether

Reprinted from *The Power Elite* (1956), pp. 3–4, 228–31 by permission of the publisher. Copyright 1956 by The Oxford University Press.

they do or do not make such decisions is less important than the fact that they do occupy such pivotal positions: their failure to act, their failure to make decisions, is itself an act that is often of greater consequence than the decisions they do make. For they are in command of the major hierarchies and organizations of modern society. They rule the big corporations. They run the machinery of the state and claim its prerogatives. They direct the military establishment. They occupy the strategic command posts of the social structure, in which are now centered the effective means of the power and the wealth and the celebrity which they enjoy.

The power elite are not solitary rulers. Advisers and consultants, spokesmen and opinion-makers are often the captains of their higher thought and decision. Immediately below the elite are the professional politicians of the middle levels of power, in the Congress and in the pressure groups, as well as among the new and old upper classes of town and city and region. . . .

As types, party politicians and political bureaucrats are the professionals of modern government, if only in the sense that their careers are spent mainly within the political orbit. But not all men who are in politics are professional politicians either in the party sense or in the bureaucratic sense: in fact, today the men at the political top are much less likely to be bureaucrats, and rather less likely to be party politicians than political outsiders.

The political outsider is a man who has spent the major part of his working life outside strictly political organizations, and who—as the case may be—is brought into them, or who forces his way in, or who comes and goes in the political order. He is occupationally formed by nonpolitical experience, his career and his connections have been in other than political circles, and as a psychological type, he is anchored in other institutional areas. In fact, he is usually considered by the professionals as a representative or as an agent within the government of some non-governmental interest or group. The political outsider is by no means confined to the Republican party. Under the Democrats, he is more likely to be on the make, striving to become acceptable to the corporate chieftains; whereas, under the Republicans, he is more usually a man already acceptable and therefore surer of himself and of how his decisions will be interpreted by those who count. A further consequence is that under the Republicans he can be less hypocritical.

Such outsiders, of course, may become bureaucratic experts by spending much time in administrative work, and thus linking their careers and their expectations to government; they may become party politicians by cultivating their role inside a political party, and coming to base their power and their career upon their party connections. But they need not make either transition; they may simply move into an inner circle, as an appointed consultant or adviser having intimate and trusted access to an official power-holder, to whom they are beholden for such political power as they possess.

There are, to be sure, other ways of classifying men as political animals, but these types—the party politician, the professional administrator, the political outsider—are quite serviceable in understanding the social make-up and psychological complexion of the political visage of present-day America.

Within American political institutions, the center of initiative and decision has shifted from the Congress to the executive; the executive branch of the state has not only expanded mightily but has come to centralize and to use the very party which puts it into power. It has taken over more initiative in legislative matters not only by its veto but by its expert counsel and advice. Accordingly, it is in the executive chambers, and in the agencies and authorities and commissions and departments that stretch out beneath them, that many conflicts of interests and contests of power have come to a head—rather than in the open arena of politics of an older style.

These institutional changes in the shape of the political pyramid have made the new political command posts worthy of being struggled for. They have also made for changes in the career of the type of political man who is ascendant. They have meant that it is now more possible for the political career to lead directly to the top, thus by-passing local political life. In the middle of the nineteenth century—between 1865 and 1881—only 19 per cent of the men at the top of the government began their political career on the national level; but from 1901 to 1953, about one-third of the political elite began there, and, in the Eisenhower administration, some 42 per cent started in politics at the national level—a high for the entire political history of the United States.*

From 1789 right up to 1921, generation after generation, the proportion of the political elite which has *ever* held local or state offices decreased from 93 to 69 per cent. In the Eisenhower administration, it fell to 57 per cent. Moreover, only 14 per cent of this current group—and only about one-quarter of earlier twentieth-century politicians—have ever served in any *state legislature*. In the Founding Fathers' generation of 1789-1801, 81 per cent of the higher politicians had done so. There has also been a definite decline in the proportions of higher politicians who have ever sat in the United States House of Representatives or in the Senate.*

*Only about 20 per cent of the political elite of 1789–1825 had done so; the historical average as a whole is about 25 per cent.

*In 1801–25, 63 per cent of the political elite had been politicians in the House, 39 per cent in the Senate; from 1865–1901, the proportions were 32 and 29 per cent; but during the 1933–53 era, only 23 per cent had ever been members of the House of Representatives, 18 per cent of the Senate. For the visible government of the Eisenhower administration, the proportions were 14 and 7 per cent.

The decline in state and local apprenticeships before entering national positions, as well as the lack of legislative experience, tie in with another characteristic trend. Since there are so many more elected positions on the lower and legislative levels and relatively few on the national, the more recent members of the political elite are likely to have reached their position through appointments rather than elections. Once, most of the men who reached the political top got there because people elected them up the hierarchy of offices. Until 1901, well over one-half, and usually more than two-thirds, of the political elite had been elected to all or most of their positions before reaching their highest national office. But of late, in a more administrative age, men become big politically because small groups of men, themselves elected, appoint them: only 28 per cent of the higher politicians in 1933–1953 rose largely by means of elective offices; 9 per cent held as many appointed as elected offices, and 62 per cent were appointed to all or most of their political jobs before reaching top position; 1 per cent had held no previous political position. Among the Eisenhower group, 36 per cent were elected to the top; 50 per cent had been appointed more than elected, and 14 per cent had never before held any political office.

For the American statesmen as a group, the median number of years spent in politics was 22.4; in non-political activities, 22.3. Thus, these top members of government have spent about the same time working in politics as in other professions. (For some of these years, of course, they were working at both at the same time.) But this over-all fact is somewhat misleading, for there is a definite historical trend: until the Civil War, the top men spent more time in politics than in non-political pursuits. Since the Civil War, the typical member of the political elite has spent more years working outside of politics than in it. Strictly political careers reached a peak in the generation of 1801–25, with 65 per cent of the total working life spent in politics. Outside activities reached their peak in the Progressive Era, 1901–21: at that time, professionals and reformers seem briefly to have entered high political positions, 72 per cent of this generation's active working time being taken up by non-political activities. It is not possible to make this calculation for politicians since 1933 for their careers are not yet over.

All these tendencies—(i) for the political elite to begin on the national level and thus to by-pass local and state offices, (ii) never to serve in national legislative bodies, (iii) to have more of an appointed than an elected career, and (iv) to spend less proportions of their total working life in politics—these tendencies point to the decline of the legislative body and to the by-passing of elective offices in the higher political career. They signify the bureaucratization of politics and the decline at the political top of men who are professional politicians in the simple, old-fashioned sense of being elected up the political hierarchy and experienced in electoral politics. They point, in short, to the political outsider. Although this type has prevailed in previous periods, in our time he flourishes, and in the Eisenhower administration he has become ascendant. This administration, in fact, is largely an inner circle of political outsiders who have taken over the key executive posts of administrative command; it is composed of members and agents of the corporate rich and of the high military in an uneasy alliance with selected professional party politicians seated primarily in the Congress, whose interests and associations are spread over a variety of local societies.

The Determination of Local Power Elites

R. O. SCHULZE AND L. U. BLUMBERG

We have witnessed lately a significant reawakening of interest in American sociologists and political scientists in the study of community power structures and decision-making. Although an earlier impetus was provided by the work of the Lynds and Mills, the fund of relevant research remained meager until the publication of Hunter's study of Regional City in 1953. Since that date a growing number of empirical studies have appeared. In fact, sufficient research has now been completed to warrant some initial stocktaking—as evidenced by the recent appearance of Peter Rossi's suggestive summing-up and critique of the relevant literature. Utilizing findings from two recent studies of a midwestern community, we propose, in this paper, to take a further second look at two of the central methodological problems which confront students of community power: the techniques for determining community power elites and some consequences of different operations in doing so.

Most students concerned with the structure and dynamics of community decision-making have initially assumed that a theoretically fruitful and empirically tenable distinction can be made between the most powerful persons and units in a community and those having lesser degrees of power. To make this assumption is not to deny that power relations in the modern urban community are "unneat," nor is it to argue that community power can necessarily be conceived in the form of either a single or a simple pyramid; neither is it inconsistent with Simmel's long-recognized thesis that dominance is always a two-way street. One can acknowledge that all per-

Reprinted from *The American Journal of Sociology,* vol. 63 (1957–58), pp. 290–96 by permission of the publisher. Copyright 1958 by The University of Chicago.

sons and units in the community exercise certain measures of influence and control without rejecting the proposition that some can mobilize such considerable resources—organizational, economic, psychological—that they have relatively most power over crucial community decisions and actions. Even C. Wright Mills, who in 1951 asserted that in contemporary America the "engineering of consent to authority has moved into the realm of manipulation where the powerful are anonymous," has since been moved to write a detailed and stimulating volume which suggests that the powerful may not, in fact, have become so very anonymous and that power relations may not have grown so nebulous, ill-defined, mercurial, and diffuse that they cannot be charted at all. So we begin by assuming that communities and societies contain power elites which are somehow delineable.

The next and crucial question is this: How do we proceed to determine "the most powerful and influential" in American communities? In general, sociologists and political scientists have employed one or the other of two techniques: one based on position and the other on reputation.

The method based on position involves selecting certain persons as most powerful and influential on the basis of their official status in the community's institutionalized economic, political, and/or civic structures. Thus both Lynd and Mills—following Marx—have contended that crucial power decisions are the province of individuals holding the top positions in the major industrial, credit, and business units in the community. And although Stouffer utilized top political and civic (rather than economic) status, he likewise employed this in identifying community elites.

A more prevalent technique has been to allow certain members of the community under study to do the determining. Based on local reputation and derived from theoretical formulations of Weber and Lasswell, with a debt to Warner, this method has been used most notably by Hunter and Angell. However, most students who have relied on local nominations have made use of a technique based on position as an intervening step. Thus the persons whose perceptions of community influence were utilized by both Hunter and Angell did not consist of randomly selected cross-sections of the local populations; they were, rather, individuals presumed to be knowledgeable because of their formal local social positions.

In this paper we ask the following questions:

1. To what extent do the methods based on reputation and on position yield similar or compatible answers to the question Who are the most powerful and influential in the community?

2. Considering only the approach based on reputation, what is the effect of using different panels of presumably knowledgeable persons?

The subject community—which we shall call Cibola—is a midwestern industrial city of some 20,000 inhabitants, located approximately 30 miles from one of the largest metropolitan centers in the United States. Over the past several decades and especially since World War II, Cibola has become increasingly involved in the industrial and social complex of this giant neighbor, Metro City.

In attempting to determine Cibola's power elite(s), we used both techniques. With regard to that centered on reputation, we initially designated as our "nominating panel" the formal heads of the local (white) voluntary associations. They were selected on the assumption that they were most representative of the broad, "grassroots" base of local organized power. Each was asked five questions. Although a total of 271 persons was named by at least one association head in response to at least one of the "perception of influence" questions, the 18 persons most frequently named accounted for the majority of all nominations. Accordingly, these 18 persons were designated as the public leaders of Cibola.

How did the composition of the public leadership category, as thus defined by reputation, compare with that of community elites determined on the basis of their positions in the economic or the political and civic organizations in Cibola?

Persons occupying the top formal status in the major local industrial and credit units were designated as the "economic dominants." They included the heads of all industries employing 75 or more workers, the heads of all banks with total assets in excess of one million dollars, and, in addition, persons who were members of the boards of directors of two or more of these industries and/or banks and who thus served in the formal "interlocking" of the dominant economic units. By this definition, a total of 17 persons was named as the economic dominants of Cibola.

There was almost no overlap between the public leaders and the economic dominants; specifically, the 17 economic dominants included but 2 of the 18 public leaders in the community.

A second method of employing criteria of position involves selecting persons filling the top political and civic status in the community. In his study, Stouffer selected as civic leaders fourteen objectively defined public statuses: mayor, president of the chamber of commerce, chairman of the Community Chest, president of the largest labor union, county chairmen of the Republican and Democratic parties, commander of the largest American Legion post, regent of the DAR, president of the women's club, chairmen of the library and the school boards, the parent-teachers' association, the bar association, and the publisher of the largest locally owned newspaper. Applying this definition of civic leaders in Cibola, *only 4* of the 18 public leaders were found to occupy any of the fourteen top civic statuses in Stouffer's list. Various other objective criteria for selecting the political-civic elite of Cibola were considered (e.g., selecting the members of the city council and the school board and the top lay officers in the largest churches and in the businessmen's luncheon clubs), and the results were compared with the leaders as defined on the basis of reputation. In no instance did the persons categorized as top political-civic leaders by any of these definitions include more than 4 of the 18 public leaders.

We may say, therefore, that the heads of voluntary associations definitely make a distinction between those persons who occupied the top formal political and civic offices and those who, in their opinion, wielded the most influence and exerted the greatest public leadership in the community. The fact that the association heads selected so few of the nominal leaders of Cibola as the "real" influential public leaders attests to a considerable degree of sophistication on their part.

On the other hand, that the heads of voluntary associations perceived so few of Cibola's economic dominants as community influentials may be due to the considerable social distance which perhaps separated most of them from the "real" centers of local power and influence. Our research design made it possible to test this possibility, for we asked the public leaders and the economic dominants the same "perception of influence" questions which we had previously addressed to the heads of associations and on the basis of which we had made our initial designation of public leaders. The over-all selections of the three panels—the heads of voluntary associations, the public leaders, and the economic dominants—are compared in Table 1.

While it is apparent that a nice similarity in rank orders did not obtain, Table 1 nonetheless reveals a high degree of consensus among all three categories interviewed as to the over-all composition of the local elite of power and influence. Thus the public leaders themselves specified 72 per cent (13 out of 18) of those defined as public leaders on the basis of nomination by the heads of associations. Likewise, the top group in influence as perceived by the economic dominants included 72 per cent of the men already categorized as public leaders. Only 3 of the 18 classified as public leaders failed to be included in the group selected by either the economic dominants or the public leaders.

Even more significant was the degree of agreement among the three panels with regard to the uppermost range of community power: of the 10 persons most frequently considered influential by the public leaders, 9 had, in fact, been operationally defined as public leaders; likewise, of the 10 most frequently regarded as influential by the economic dominants, 9 had been categorized as public leaders. Furthermore, 7 persons (Houston, Drew, Milan, Moseley III, Rush, Ford, and Chapman) are included among the top 9 in all three lists. And, finally, it is apparent that none of the panels discerned those of dominant economic status as an appreciable segment of public leadership. Like the heads of associations, the public leaders them-

TABLE 1. RANK ORDERS OF PUBLIC LEADERS AS PERCEIVED BY
ASSOCIATION HEADS, PUBLIC LEADERS, AND ECONOMIC DOMINANTS*

Association Heads' Selections	Public Leaders' Selections	Economic Dominants' Selections
1. HOUSTON	1. HOUSTON	1. HOUSTON
2. DREW	2. FORME	2. MOSELEY III
3. MILAN	3. MOSELEY III	3. FORD
4. MOSELEY III	4. FORD	4. DREW
5. RUSH	5. DREW	5.5. RUSH
6. FORME	6. RUSH	5.5. PETERS
7. FORD	7. CHAPMAN	7.5. CHAPMAN
8. JOHNS	8.5. MILAN	7.5. MILAN
9. CHAPMAN	8.5. Thomas	9.5. TAYLOR
10. SCHLAFF	10. TAYLOR	9.5. Staley
11. BERNARD	11. PETERS	11. Fielding, Sr.
12. WARNE	12. JOHNS	12. ROGERS
13. TAYLOR	13. Staley	12. FORME
14. MOSELEY II	14. HAAS	12. Fischer
15. PETERS	17. WARNE	15. MOSELEY II
16. GUYER	17. Lee	16. WARNE
17. HAAS	17. Smith	17.5. Kingsley
18. ROGERS	17. Arthur	17.5. Lake
	17. Lake	

*These rank orderings are based on total frequency of "nominations" by the 143
association heads, the 18 public leaders, and the 17 economic dominants, respectively,
in answer to the five "perception of influence" questions. Those defined as public
leaders (the top 18 in the association heads' list) are indicated in CAPITALS; those
defined as economic dominants are *underlined*. The public leaders' positions in the
rank orders are connected by solid lines; the positions of others are connected by
broken lines.

selves included but two economic dominants in the top group, while the
economic dominants themselves regarded an only somewhat greater number
of their fellow dominants as among Cibola's most influential—4 out of
the top 18, or 22 per cent.

These data show that, despite the fact that the heads of voluntary
associations, the public leaders, and the economic dominants occupied different positions and played dissimilar roles in the local social structure,
each category perceived substantially the same set of persons as most influential in the affairs of the community.

A question remains: If Cibola's most influential by reputation—its
public leaders—were neither the community's economic dominants nor the
current occupants of either its top political or civic offices, where did they
fit into the local social structure? All were white males. Their median age
was fifty-three; their median number of years' residence in Cibola was

thirty. In occupation they represented only the business and professional classes in the city, albeit a fairly wide range of positions within these broad categories. In general, it may be said that the public leaders were drawn almost wholly from the old middle-class segment. Only one, to be sure, was an official in any of the "big-business" firms. (And he resigned and opened an insurance office in partnership with a local politician during the course of our research.)

It cannot be assumed, however, that the public leaders constituted a representative cross-section of Cibola's small-business and professional men. They were, rather, persons intimately involved in the community's voluntary associations who, in earlier years, had occupied responsible positions in local civic and political units. For example, the median number of memberships currently held by the public leaders in voluntary associations was 9 (compared with a median of three for the economic dominants); each public leader was a member of at least one of the three most prominent civic luncheon clubs (Rotary, Kiwanis, Lions), and 14 were members of the Chamber of Commerce. Furthermore, 89 per cent of the public leaders (16 out of 18) had, at one time, served as president of at least one local voluntary association, and 61 per cent (11 out of 18) as president of at least one of the five associations regarded by all three basic categories of power figures—the association heads, the economic dominants, and the public leaders themselves—as most influential in the community. Finally, while not more than one of the public leaders could have been regarded as a professional politician, fully 89 per cent (all but 2) had occupied elective or appointive office in at least one of the local units of government: For example, 3 had served as mayor, 6 as city councilmen, 3 as school-board members, and 9 as appointive members of one or more of the several municipal boards and commissions.

We find, therefore, that, while a considerable majority of the local public leaders were businessmen, they were not the top businessmen, the economic dominants. Likewise, while almost all had held responsible civic and political positions in Cibola, they were not, with minor exceptions, among the community's formal civic and political leaders at the time of our study. Considering what we know about the power structures of other middle-sized American communities, it seems apparent that Cibola's public leaders were of the age, sex, race, length of residence, business and civic experience, and connections appropriate to community influence and leadership. And it became abundantly apparent, subsequently, that the public leaders did in fact constitute a closely knit friendship group which exercised substantial—if not always decisive—control over the community's decisions. Yet this important category of elites could not have been revealed had we relied solely on one of the usual methods based on position.

The two questions raised earlier in this paper may now be answered as follows:

The composition of the community's power elite, as defined by reputation, differs significantly from that defined on the basis of superordinate positions in *either* the local economic *or* the political-civic institutions.

However, the use of different panels of persons who may be assumed to be reasonably (although not similarly) knowledgeable does not produce significantly different results.

Generalizations based on the study of but a single community, as this is, are obviously provisional. Nevertheless, they strongly suggest the advisability of studying a community's power structures from at least two methodological perspectives—that based on position and that on reputation. It is not a question of whether one or the other is "right." Rather, by using both and by determining the nature and degree of similarity between the two resulting lists, valuable leads are found as to the structure and dynamics of local power. In Cibola, for example, the marked disparity between the categories of public leader and of economic dominant suggested —and further research confirmed—a widespread and growing reluctance on the part of the economic dominants to become involved in the initiation and determination of local political decisions. And this, in turn, raised the larger question of the changing role of major economic units—especially absentee-owned corporations—in the local power structures of American communities.

Post-Totalitarian Leadership: Elites in the German Federal Republic

LEWIS J. EDINGER

A good deal has been heard in recent years concerning the "liberation" of peoples living under totalitarian rule, but the question of who are the men who succeed to the leadership of a state after the fall of its totalitarian rulers has received relatively little attention. Such observations as have been made on the subject, whether by political opponents of a totalitarian regime or by professional social scientists, have tended to follow implicitly—if not

Reprinted from *The American Political Science Review,* vol. 54 (March 1960), pp. 58–82 by permission of the author and the publisher. Copyright 1960 by The American Political Science Association. Footnotes have been omitted as have several charts and other supporting data.

explicitly—the theory of alternating elites. There is assumed to be, on the one hand, a more or less homogeneous totalitarian elite, and, on the other, an actual or potential counter-elite, representing the political antithesis to the totalitarian elite. The stability of the rule of the former is said to vary inversely with the degree of organization of the latter. The totalitarian elite is variously identified with the holders of high positions in the totalitarian system, with the "responsible leaders," with an entire ruling class, or simply with those individuals who are said to be influential in the determination of national policy. The counter-elite is identified with the active overt and covert opponents of the totalitarian elite—resistance leaders, the "vanguard of the proletariat," prominent exiles, and "men on whose backs in concentration camps the lash has written the new gospel in blood and tears." Both elite and counter-elite are thus seen as directly, actively involved in the totalitarian system, either as its leaders or as its opponents.

Revolution, in this schema, is identified with the destruction of the totalitarian elite and its replacement by the counter-elite. Or, conversely, the destruction of the totalitarian elite is an act of revolution and will result in the emergence of the counter-elite to power. It is an attractively simple thesis, and it warrants investigation. . . . .

I. THE ELITE SAMPLE

The term elite needs to be used with caution, for its usage has unfortunately caused as much confusion as enlightenment. On the one hand, it has been employed in what might be termed the ascriptive-qualitative sense to identify groups who are said to be entitled to rule by virtue of racial, moral, intellectual or some other type of superiority. On the other hand, it has also been used in what might be called the descriptive-functional sense to identify the most powerful and influential groups in a community. The latter rather than the former definition seems implicit in the denazification directives of 1945–1946. Therefore, for the purpose of this analysis, the various elites in the contemporary pluralistic society of the German Federal Republic are said to consist of the present incumbents of "public and semi-public" national offices and "positions of responsibility in important private undertakings." It is assumed, as it was in the denazification directives, that these formal positions of leadership endow the incumbents not only with actual decision-making authority within the politically important groups which they head, but with influence far out of proportion to their number in the making of policy and decisions in the various branches of the German Federal Government.

The analysis that follows is based on an inventory of the incumbents of key positions in the formal structure of the German Federal Republic and not on a random sample of members of an assumed power elite. This has the advantage of establishing clearly who is included and why. It has the disadvantage of equating formal position with actual influence and power. The purpose of the investigation, the nature of the available data, and the apparent shortcomings of random samples in studies of this type seem to justify the use of such a selection. Like Gabriel Almond, in his *The American People and Foreign Policy*, I distinguish four categories of elites in a pluralistic, democratic society: political, administrative, interest, and communications. However, I have varied slightly from Almond's subcategories— designed for an analysis of American foreign policy-making—by including the clergy in the interest elite, rather than in the communications elite. This appears warranted in view of the rather different role which the leaders of the major churches have played and continue to play in Germany.

The sample consists of 529 individuals listed in four standard reference works as incumbents of leading public and semi-public positions in the German Federal Republic during the last quarter of 1956. The sample includes all the individuals listed who had volunteered at least some information for standard biographical works of the *Who's Who* type—84 per cent of the total number of incumbents listed. These individuals occupied leading positions in the four basic elites, and in fourteen sub-elites, as follows:

1. POLITICAL ELITE *(35 per cent of sample):*
   Federal Cabinet, Federal legislative leadership, the nine State Cabinets (the Saar not yet listed as a constituent state), the national leadership of the ruling Christian Democratic Union and its Bavarian branch, the Christian Social Union (CDU/CSU), (as represented by its Chairman, vice chairmen and its leading representatives in the executive and legislative branches of the Federal Government), and the Executive Committee of the Social Democratic Party, the chief opposition party.

2. ADMINISTRATIVE ELITE *(31 per cent of sample):*
   The Senior Civil Service of the Federal Government (defined as Division Chief, State Secretaries, and leading officers of the Federal Bank), the Senior Foreign Service (chiefs of missions abroad), and the leadership of the Armed Forces.

3. INTEREST GROUP ELITE *(20 per cent of sample):*
   Principal officers of the leading national employers' associations, principal officers of the three major trade unions, the Fulda Bishops Conference of the Roman Catholic Church (which includes all bishops and archbishops), and the leaders of the German Evangelical Church.

4. COMMUNICATIONS ELITE *(15 per cent of sample):*
   The press and radio elite, including the editors or publishers of leading dailies, of weeklies and politico-cultural periodicals, the

directors of the various radio and television networks, and the educational elite, which in Germany consists of the Rektors *of the institutions of higher learning.* . . . .

II. DENAZIFICATION REASSESSED: THE IMAGE AND THE REALITY

The Allied denazification plans at the Potsdam Conference in 1945, and the Control Council directives spelling out these plans in detail, proposed to impose a revolution on Germany. In particular, it was proposed to effect a genuine "revolutionary" change in the composition of the elite in contrast to what was generally believed to have been a counterfeit German revolution after the First World War, in the sense of no sufficient transformation in the composition of the elite. This time it was proposed to make drastic changes.

The new elites were to be recruited primarily from members of the anti-Nazi counter-elite. It was recognized that minor Nazis and Nazi collaborators, as well as others who had been ambivalent or neutral toward the totalitarian regime would have to be employed in certain elite positions requiring special skills. However, as far as possible, they were to be excluded from policy-making positions in the new Germany.

How did the reality of 1956 compare with the image of 1946? There were no major Nazi leaders in an elite position in 1956. Most of them were dead, imprisoned, or living in obscurity. About 7 per cent of the 1956 elites had held positions in the Nazi era non-political elite. That is, they had occupied positions of authority in its administration, armed forces, business organizations and communications media which, according to the denazification directives, implied major involvement in the operation of the totalitarian state. Fifteen members of the 1956 military elite had been senior officers of admiral or general rank. At least 12 of the senior civil servants and three of the senior diplomats of 1956 had held similar positions in the administrative elite of the Nazi era and three of the business leaders and one or more of the press-radio leaders of 1956 were also incumbents of elite positions in their respective occupations in the totalitarian era.

No more than about 11 per cent of the members of the 1956 elites could be classified as having belonged to an anti-Nazi counter-elite, in the sense of the denazification directives. They were concentrated mostly in the groups with the least influence over national policy-making, such as the Social Democratic, the Protestant and the trade union leadership. At least half of them Social Democrats, these individuals had been major opponents of the totalitarian regime as members of resistance groups in Germany and abroad; many of them had spent long periods in Nazi prisons and concentration camps or as exiles in foreign lands. Another 8 per cent, while they may also be considered former opponents of the regime, laid no claim to active and sustained participation in the anti-Nazi resistance movement, nor to the more serious forms of political persecution. At best, their involvement with the active opposition and its members was peripheral and not sustained. Many of them had been placed in opposition by the actions of the Nazi regime, rather than by their own acts, and had been victims of relatively mild forms of persecution, such as brief arrests, loss of jobs, police harassment, loss of pensions, denial of promotions, and punitive transfers.

Most members of the 1956 elites were recruited from the ranks of those Germans who had belonged neither to the Nazi elite nor to the counter-elite, who had neither been strong opponents nor strong supporters of the totalitarian regime, neither strongly involved in running that regime nor in fighting it. Perhaps one-quarter had been supporters, but only in relatively minor capacities. Former Nazi party members and minor Nazi leaders —like three of the Federal Ministers—and loyal members of the higher civil and foreign service, these men, in the words of the denazification directive, may be said to have "voluntarily given moral and material support or political assistance to the Nazi regime." However, unlike the former members of the non-political elite of the Nazi system, they were involved in the direction of that system in only a minor way. Not quite a tenth, as indicated above, had been minor anti-Nazis, in the same sense that members of the former group had been minor Nazis and collaborators. About half the incumbents of 1956 elite positions belonged to that large group of civil servants, professional men, military officers, educators, technicians, and clergy whose contemporary attitude toward the totalitarian regime could be called ambivalent and even neutral, in so far as that was possible. For some this meant an oscillating position between latent support and latent opposition, for others a conscious aloofness or studied indifference toward the regime, for still others a retreat into an "Inner Emigration."

In short, we find that only about 18 per cent of the contemporary German elite members were in any major way involved in the totalitarian regime, most of them as its opponents and victims. The other 82 per cent were involved in only a minor way or not at all, in so far as the totalitarian system permitted this. Or, looking at the elite members in terms of their known or conjectured attitudes toward the totalitarian regime (for example, loyal Nazi party members and military officers), we find that about 24 per cent may be considered to have been supporters of the regime, 57 per cent to have been ambivalent, neutral, or oscillating during the 12 years of Nazi rule, and no more than 19 per cent to have been more or less consistently opposed. Either way, the bulk of the post-totalitarian elite membership was recruited from the ranks of the Germans who, while old enough to care, were ambivalent or neutral toward the regime and were neither among its leaders nor among its major opponents. Most members of the 1956 elites belonged to that large number of Germans who had wavered in their attitude and behavior toward the totalitarian system in accordance with its fortunes and their own. They were neither rabid Nazis in the pre-war days when most Germans applauded Hitler's foreign policy successes, nor major anti-Nazis when the tide turned against Nazi Germany.

Obviously the image of 1946 and the reality of 1956 vary considerably. No anti-Nazi counter-elite is ruling today in the Federal Republic. However, neither can it be maintained that the Nazi elite has returned. Nor can we entirely agree with John Montgomery* that what took place between 1946 and 1956 was a restoration of the pre-totalitarian elites, which "resembled more a delayed counterrevolution to nazism than either a natural or a permanent revolution pointing in new directions." Our data do not bear out the theory implied in the denazification thesis and still current in much of the literature on post-totalitarian leadership. In the German Federal Republic the totalitarian elite was not succeeded by a counter-elite, but rather by a coalition of elites whose members were drawn largely from the ranks of those individuals who had been neither strong and consistent proponents nor opponents of the totalitarian regime.

Criticism of the denazification program of 1945-46 is not new. Many German critics have labeled it both morally and legally unjust. They claim that it deprived individuals innocent of any crimes of their jobs, income, and property without due process of law. Other critics have approved the principles of the program, but charge that it was improperly executed, or even sabotaged. While little fish were punished, the big fish escaped, it is said, and many a Nazi era "big shot" was permitted to retain his ill-gotten gains.

A third group also approves the program and its elitist assumptions in principle, but argues that it failed because it was at the same time too ambitious and not thorough enough. Thus, according to Montgomery, a "realistic . . . purge should be limited in dimensions and time," for "only a small number of leaders can be successfully purged and punished in the limited time available in a military occupation." On the other hand, Montgomery claims, the denazification purge was not sufficiently thorough in the removal of military and civilian officials of the Nazi era, as distinguished from the political leaders. Thus, for example, "the political purge had little effect against technical and economic elites," because the political potential of the bureaucracy was not adequately recognized.

A rather different reason for criticizing the denazification program is suggested by our data: the fallacious assumption that the purge of an elite, arbitrarily defined in terms of positions in the totalitarian regime, would

*Forced to Be Free (1957).

result more or less automatically in the emergence of a counter-elite to fill the places vacated. At least in the case of Western Germany, this thesis of the counter-elite proved to be a myth.

III. SOME CONCLUDING OBSERVATIONS

The concept elite, as used in this article and implied in the denazification directives, designates "the holders of high positions in a given society." The drafters of the allied denazification directives assumed that Nazi Germany had been ruled by a coalition of elites. The political elite, the Nazi party leaders, had been dominant, but by no means in exclusive control of the state. The leaders of large industrial enterprises, the principal administrative officials, diplomats, and military men were believed to have participated, directly or indirectly, in the decisions of the totalitarian state to a far greater extent than in the Soviet Union, though far less than in the pluralistic political communities of the Western democratic states. The professed object of denazification was to banish all such from positions of influence. . . . .
However, while Nazi political leaders could be replaced by a new political elite which met the criteria of the purge directives, it was a different matter when it came to finding replacements for skilled administrators and technical experts who had served the totalitarian state, let alone the leaders of religious groups.

Once the Western powers had decided to push the rapid recovery of German governmental and economic institutions and to let the Germans themselves do the job, the denazification directives were found to be "the most serious" obstacles to such a course, according to Harold Zink:*

Many mayors, county managers, department heads and other officials and employees had to be fired, despite the good work which they seemed to be doing, because their Nazi records were regarded as disqualifying. Efforts to obtain replacements brought forth few who could meet the denazification tests and these tended to be too old, too infirm, or too embittered as a result of their sojourn in concentration camps to be very satisfactory in the arduous job of reconstructing. . . .

As more and more authority for promoting rapid economic and political recovery was turned over to Germans by the occupying powers—culminating in the reestablishment of a central government, a diplomatic service, military establishment, and large industrial and banking combines—the demand for skilled experts was paced by the rapidity of recovery. There simply was no counter-elite source of qualified people to assume these tasks.

*The United States in Germany 1944–1955 (1957).

Western plans to use "reeducated" and anti-Nazi former prisoners-of-war apparently came to naught. Only a few proven anti-Nazis had some of the required skills and most of these were indeed either too old or infirm or politically unacceptable to the Western powers. They soon died or retired, worn out by their jobs, or were dismissed for political reasons. The groups with the strongest claim to membership in an anti-Nazi counter-elite consisted mostly of intellectuals, professional party functionaries, and resistance fighters who lacked the qualities required for reconstruction of the Federal Republic. Some of the anti-Nazi political leaders initially proposed a more monolithic organization of German society than the occupation powers were willing to sanction. Only thus, they argued, would the political leadership in post-Nazi Germany be able to dominate the non-political positions of authority. These ideas found favor neither with the occupation powers nor with most Germans. In the pluralist society which was preferred, major anti-Nazis proved to be in a minority even in the political elite.

Intensive and extensive socio-economic dislocation or intensive and extensive military occupation—or both—was a price which the Western powers were unwilling or unable to pay to "denazify" all the German elites. Realistic political flexibility or opportunism enabled minor Nazis and collaborators to overcome such denazification obstacles as remained on the road to non-political elite positions. The more extensive the training, skill, and technical "know-how" demanded by such a position, the more difficult it was to find an incumbent uncompromised by Nazi associations. Or, to put it another way, the more sharply defined an elite occupation in terms of skill and career qualifications, the less susceptible it was to a literal application of the denazification criteria. Thus, politics was a career occupation which demanded relatively little technical training, experience, or "know-how" in post-war Germany. The large number of newcomers to politics who achieved elite positions within a few years contrasts sharply with the even larger number of old-timers in non-political elite positions that called for extensive training and skill. Most administrative, diplomatic, military, and big business leaders were individuals who had acquired the skills required by their elite occupations over many years. Their career backgrounds extended well back into the totalitarian era—and frequently beyond.

It therefore seems that the assumptions underlying the denazification program are invalid for a complex and pluralistic society such as post-war Western Germany. Influence and high position are largely the reward of managerial and technical "know-how" in occupations required for the effective functioning of such a society. It follows that to carry through a post-totalitarian political purge demands either the replacement of the native elites by foreigners or extensive socio-economic dislocation. The more extensive the purge the more it will cost, one way or another. On the other hand, the less the victor is willing to pay one or the other price, the more difficult it will be to carry through such a purge. Simplistic assumptions concerning the circulation of elites, in any case, are out of place. . . .

Approaches to Leadership

ALVIN W. GOULDNER

In the past, the conditions which permitted an individual to become or remain a leader were often assumed to be *qualities* of the individual. These were in some way believed to be *located in* the leader. It was postulated that leadership could be explained in terms of the "traits" possessed by the leader. Thus a multitude of studies were made which purported to characterize leaders' traits—i.e., those of their distinctive ways of acting, or personality characteristics, which tended to recur.

Since the trait approach has in many ways exercised an important influence on thinking about leadership, examination of some of its findings and assumptions will further serve to orient this work. Trait studies of leadership can be classified in many ways. Two that seem most useful from the present point of view are: (1) classification of trait analyses of leadership in terms of the method of study used; and (2) the relationship that is assumed to exist between the traits of leaders and the group or situational context.

In terms of the first method of classifying trait studies, two major categories may be found: first, the impressionistic accounts and, second, the experimental studies employing forms of controlled observation. Both kinds of studies were alike, of course, in that they were guided by their use of this concept. Each author tended to conclude his work with a list of adjectives (or trait-names) of varying length and content. Charles Bird, for example, studying some twenty trait-analyses of leadership, found about seventy-nine traits mentioned altogether.

Typical of the early impressionistic analyses of leadership traits are the lists proposed by two military men, Munson and Miller. Miller maintained that the outstanding military leaders were typified by a personality structure manifesting self-control, assiduity, common sense, judgment, justice, enthusiasm, perserverance, tact, courage, faith, loyalty, and other traits. Among the general leadership traits mentioned by Munson were: personality, manner, use of language, tact, cheerfulness, courtesy, justice, and

Reprinted from *Studies in Leadership,* edited by Alvin W. Gouldner (1950), pp. 21–35 by permission of the author and Harper & Brothers.

discipline. E. S. Bogardus proposed five traits allegedly universal to leadership: imagination, foresight, flexibility, versatility, and inhibition.

Bertrand Russell, adding his list to the many already existing, commented: "To acquire the position of leader he (the individual) must excel in the qualities that confer authority: self-confidence, quick decision and skill in deciding the right measures." Robert Michels has suggested the following traits: force of will, relatively wide knowledge, Catonian strength of conviction, self-sufficiency, and others.

The *impressionistic* surveys of leadership traits were, in some respects, far surpassed by the more careful studies of Terman, Reaney, Nutting, Rohrbach, Bellingrath, Marion Brown Bennett, Jones, and T. L. McCuen. But they have been superseded mainly in the rigor of the investigational techniques by which the traits were isolated or determined. That is, they too assumed that leadership hinged on, and could be best described in terms of, the trait-qualities of individuals. Recently commenting on this, Lindesmith and Strauss have stated: "Leadership is commonly thought of in terms of leadership qualities. . . . In taking over this common-sense notion, social psychologists have been led to seek those traits of personality that are most usually associated with being a leader."

Thus, as Lindesmith and Strauss suggest, many of the trait analyses of leadership have apparently been influenced by current popular conceptions of leaders as being in some way unusual beings possessed of extraordinary powers alien to the common run of mankind. As such, they are objects capable of being transformed into the "magical helpers" sought by those whose need for security is resolved by finding some powerful authority upon whom they can become dependent. Moreover, these trait analyses also conform to the popular conceptions of leadership in that, by divorcing the leader from his group and institutional setting, they do not challenge the assumption that social crises may be met without institutional changes.

INADEQUACIES OF THE TRAIT APPROACH

The inadequacies of the above type of trait studies can be only briefly summarized here. Leaving aside questions concerning their investigational technique, the following points may be raised:

1. Those proposing trait lists usually do not suggest which of the traits are most important and which least. Not uncommonly, lists of more than ten traits are presented. In most such lists it seems very unlikely that each of the traits is equally important and deserves the same weighting. Bearing in mind that practical application of leadership studies (as, for example, in leadership selection or training) requires compromises due to time limitations and the number of candidates available, the failure to indicate the

rank order of importance of the traits makes it difficult to know *at what points* compromises may be made. It is only within very recent years that the work of trait-analysts, like Raymond Cattell, gives promise of coping with this problem.

2. It is evident, too, that some of the traits mentioned in a single list are not mutually exclusive. For example, Miller lists tact, judgment, and common sense as leadership traits. It would seem, ordinarily, that the first two would be included in the last.

3. Trait studies do not usually discriminate between traits facilitating *ascent* to leadership and those enabling it to be maintained. It seems to be assumed that all the traits which differentiate leaders from followers are functional to ongoing leadership. It appears entirely possible, however, that certain of the traits of leaders were necessary conditions for success in the *competition to become* a leader but are not needed by an *established* leadership.

4. Typically, most trait studies, and those of leadership are no exception, raise questions concerning the organization of behavior, the range of recurring behavior patterns manifested by individuals. They are largely descriptive. Usually they do not ask *how* these traits *develop,* or how the behavior *became* organized. Thus, in so many of the trait studies there is the tacit assumption that the leaders' traits existed *prior* to their ascendance to leadership. It is therefore inferred that the leaders' possession of these traits are to help explain how he became a leader.

Even in some of the trait studies which maintain that leadership traits are specific to the situation, that the situation makes them useful, it appears to be assumed that the individual *already possesses* the useful traits when he enters into leadership. The possibility that the reverse is true, namely, that it is the leadership position which fosters the *original* emergence of distinctive traits, is hardly ever systematically explored. In sum, one usually is not informed whether, and which, leadership traits exist before and which develop after leadership is assumed.

5. Finally, the study of the personalities of leaders, as of any other group of individuals, in terms of *traits* involves certain debatable assumptions regarding the nature of personality. It seems to be believed that the leader's personality can be, or is, described if all the traits by which it is composed are determined. Implicit is the notion that a personality is the sum of its component traits. This would seem, however, to ignore one of the fundamental properties of personality, its possession of *organization*. The same "trait" will function differently in personalities which are organized differently. To characterize the *component elements* of an entity such as personality is an insufficient description in that it omits consideration of the fact that these elements have varying *positions* or *arrangements*.

It is only when attention is paid to arrangement or position that organization, as such, can be brought into account.

Most trait studies, flowing from the empiricist tradition, have approached the study of personality atomistically, and with little regard for personality as an organized whole. Not being oriented to any systematic theory of personality, they have pursued the "facts" of personality only to find that empiricism can be just as treacherous a guide as the most speculative of theoretical systems. It is, in part, because of the lack of any theoretical guide lines that the trait studies of leadership have produced relatively little convergence. Some scholars, for example, speak of two, ten, nineteen, and some of thirty, traits of leadership. Charles Bird's analysis of trait studies of leadership found that only 5 percent of the traits mentioned were common to four or more investigations.

SITUATIONS AND GROUPS: THE SITUATIONIST CRITIQUE

As already indicated, traits studies may be subdivided according to the manner in which they relate traits to the leadership *situation*. In general, a twofold subdivision may be made: (1) those implying or stating that the traits of leaders are universal: in other words, that the traits of leaders do not depend upon the situation, but that leaders in any situation will possess the same traits; (2) the trait study which suggests that it is impossible to talk about leadership traits in general, but only about the traits manifested in concrete, particular situations. Leadership traits are conceived of as varying from situation to situation and group to group.

In order to understand the reasons which have fostered the emergence of the situational studies of traits, it is necessary to consider some of the implications of the proposition that leadership traits are universal and will not vary with the situation.

If this proposition were to be demonstrated, then several things should follow: (a) the traits or personal qualities which made an individual a leader in one group should also be useful for leadership in other groups; (b) a man who is a leader in one group should tend to be a leader in others.

That a leader is *involved in a network of relationships* with other individuals who, together with him, comprise a group, is a consideration the full implications of which elude these trait-analysts. No matter how spontaneous and informal the group, its members never engage in random, continually unpatterned activities. There is a certain degree of persistence or patterning in the activities which a group undertakes, be it bowling, playing bridge, engaging in warfare, or shoplifting. These persisting or habitual group-activities, among other things, set *limitations* on the kind of individuals who become group members and, no less so, upon the kind of individuals who come to lead the group.

If by nothing else, the traits of a group's leaders are limited by the traits of the individuals who comprise the universe from which leaders are drawn. Any group functions as an attracting, repelling, and selecting mechanism. Not all individuals would wish, nor could they if they so desired, to become members of any group. As obvious examples: modern trade unions practically always exclude employers from membership; Girl Scouts exclude boys; armies, those physically or mentally ill. Similarly, pacifists would not be *interested* in joining the National Guard, nor would political conservatives be interested in obtaining membership in radical parties.

Trait studies themselves inform us that psychological traits are not distributed uniformly through all social strata. The distribution of traits differs with age, education, occupation, and sex. From this it follows that members of particular groups will tend to possess certain traits both more and less than others. Since leaders tend to be members either of the group which they lead or of other limited groups, one may expect that the traits of leaders will vary with those of their group. Jenkins, in a recent summary of leadership studies, concludes that "Leaders tend to exhibit certain characteristics in common with the members of their group. Two of the more obvious of these characteristics are interests and social background." The probability seems great, therefore, that the leaders of some groups possess *some* traits different from the leaders of other groups, and that "leadership traits" are not universal. . . ."

Not only are the traits of leaders limited by the traits of the individuals from which leadership is drawn, but they are further limited by the character of the group's *specific* activities. Even one of the earlier studies, made by Caldwell and Wellman, found that while certain traits—physical prowess, for example—were influential in the selection of school *athletic* leaders, these traits were not characteristic of leaders in *other* school activities. While height may be helpful to basketball players, its absence did not deter three rather short men—Mussolini, Hitler, and Lenin—from assuming the leadership of nations. In this vein, Cecil Gibb writes: "There is no one leadership type of personality. One man might achieve leadership status because he has superior intellectual endowments which force him consistently upon the notice of others and make them dependent upon him. A second achieves leadership because he has a quiet helpful interest in fellow group-members and because what British psychiatrists call his 'contact' is good. Leadership resides not exclusively in the individual but in his functional relationship with other members of his group."

A. J. Murphy, emphasizing the relative fluidity of leadership traits, points out that the "self-confidence" of a *work* leader may disappear if his group is placed in a parlor situation. Or that a leader noted for his "dominance" may become "shy" when placed in a situation in which his *skills* are not useful. Thus not only must the *group* in which the leader operates be considered, but also the *situation* which the group encounters. Both of these elements seem to affect the character of leadership traits. Jenkins' first conclusion of his summary of leadership studies emphasizes this: "Leadership is specific to the particular situation under investigation. Who becomes a leader of a given group engaging in a particular activity and what the leadership characteristics are in the given case are a function of the specific situation including the measuring instruments employed."

SKILLS AND SITUATIONS: THE SITUATIONIST CRITIQUE CONTINUED

The interaction between skills and situations, noted by Murphy above, has recently received cogent amplification by the OSS assessment staff:

A member of an organization who cannot do what is expected of him is immediately confronted by the stress of self-criticism and of criticism, implicit or explicit, from his supervisor and from his co-workers. His self-confidence will diminish, and feelings of inferiority emerge; he is likely to become hypersensitive and defensive in his social relations, and blame others for his own shortcomings. . . . Thus, as soon as the strength of one component—in this case that of specific ability—drops below a certain minimum, other components are similarly affected. . . . Contrariwise, a man whose talents are exactly suited to the job assigned to him and who, therefore, attains or surpasses the level of social expectation for him, will be continually encouraged by signs of approval and of respect from his associates, and under these conditions, his energy and initiative, motivation, effective intelligence, emotional stability, and social relations are likely to reach their maximum.

The intricate relations between the psychological aspects or traits (skill, self-confidence, etc.) and the group aspects (respect, approval), so clearly described above, seem most likely to operate in the manner described *in a culture such as our own*. That is, in our culture great value is placed on *specialized skills* as the basis of legitimating occupancy of a great variety of roles, often including leadership roles. In consequence, the presence or absence of required *skills* may elicit a stronger group response in our society than it might in more traditional societies where skill was not such a primary basis of legitimation.

This suggests that skill may not be an open-sesame to leadership, *uni-*

versally facilitating ascent to or success in it. The situationists' emphasis on the role of skills may require trimming to more modest implications; in particular, limiting its operation to groups or societies outside the traditionalistic orbit. Formulated positively, the boundary conditions tacitly assumed by the situationists—and in terms of which their proposed interrelationship between situationally-functional skills and leadership appears probable—include a relatively high division of labor and degree of specialization, an emphasis on achievement rather than ascription of certain statuses, and the use of skills as a basis of achieving and legimating these statuses.

A second way in which the role of skills may be culturally bounded can be suggested. The OSS analysis of the *consequences* of skill-deficiencies or skill-competencies, their extraction of group deference, approval or respect, or their opposites, and their effects on the individual's traits (self-confidence, initiative, etc.) involve certain assumptions about *personality*.

Specifically, what must be assumed is that the individual has some motive or need for the high degree of responsiveness which he manifests to group judgments. The problem rests in the character of the motive or need. To find individuals responding to their groups, adapting, learning, modifying and being changed is not, in the light of modern psychology and sociology, in the least startling. Some degree of responsiveness and behavior modification must be accepted as "normal." But to find, or allege, individuals to be adaptable to the extent suggested by the situationists—that is, almost infinitely plastic—can be anticipated only under very limited psychological and, therefore, cultural conditions.

It may be hypothesized that the personality which would react as responsively or immediately to current group pressures is, perhaps, likely to manifest a weak or insecure ego and is in some measure, because of this, extremely dependent upon group judgments. Too, one might look for a heavy emotional investment in "success." Given these two psychological conditions, group judgments of individual worth may be swiftly responded to by the individual. Particularly so, if these judgments explicitly or implicitly involve assessments of the individual's "success," for it is with this that, in our culture, the individual's sense of worthiness is so intimately tied.

If such psychological conditions are pervasive, they must be presumed to be institutionally compelled. Possibly they emerge with the weakening of the stable traditional relations of family, neighborhood or church, and their substitution by the shifting, calculating ties of a market society. But the intent here is not to define the specific cultural boundaries yielding validity to the situationist propositions about the fluidity of traits, but only to suggest that these are *definable*.

To return to the situationist position:

"In practically every study reviewed," writes Jenkins, "leaders showed some superiority over the members of their group, in at least one of a wide variety of abilities. The only common factor appeared to be that leaders in a particular field tend to possess superior general or technical competence or knowledge in that area."

Thus distinctive situations make specifically different demands for skill, and individuals failing to possess these will be limited in their chances for leadership. It is in this context that William F. Whyte's comment . . . to the effect that street-corner gang leaders tend to initiate group activities in which they excel, may be placed.

The unique experiences of the OSS assessment staff underscore the role of the situation still further. Directed to provide the OSS with personnel capable of performing *secret* missions, the assessment staff therefore only had a *general idea* of the assignment each man was to undertake. Consequently the assessment men could rate candidates only "according to their conception of *all-round men in a given field of activity.*" (Our emphasis— A.W.G.) In attempting to explain why many of the men to whom they gave "high" ratings received "low" appraisals from the units to which they were assigned, the assessment staff writes: ". . . actually, the assessed man who went overseas was not called upon to deal fairly well with a multiplicity of rather general situations, but to deal very well with a limited number of specific situations . . . these men were appraised in the theater according to how effectively they performed a particular role in a particular location."

Though not intended to refer to leadership alone, these conclusions of the OSS staff strongly suggest the limitations which concrete situations place upon the utility of leadership traits. It was clearly not enough to know the candidate's *general field* of activity to successfully predict his performance; a man *generally* competent in a field often would be judged incompetent to handle the *specific situation* in which he found himself. It is significant, too, that the assessment staff's prediction about the performance of the candidates was much more successful for those who "undertook the missions originally proposed for them than it was in the case of men who were given entirely different missions on arriving overseas."

These, then, are some of the major lines of argument which those who consider, as Gibb states, that "leadership is relative always to the situation," have used in refutation of that branch of the trait school which held leadership qualities to be the same in all situations. By and large, the former school, characterizable as "situationists," have won the day. By now it is probably true that most social scientists would sympathize with A. H. Lloyd when he spoke even of *great* individual leadership as a "noble fiction." But uneasy rests the head that wears the crown of science.

UNIVERSAL TRAITS?

For even among the situationists themselves, one might say among the very situationists who have done some of the most original and distinguished thinking about leadership, certain incongruous notes are heard. The hypothesis that there are indeed *certain* traits found among all leaders occasionally peers out of the cracks of situationist paragraphs, jarring us out of our complacency. Even a field social-psychologist, such as J. F. Brown oriented to the determining role of the situation and its structure, has implied this. "It would be absurd," he writes, "to deny that two factors of a semibiological nature are important in leadership, intelligence and psychosexual appeal. Of these, probably the most important is intelligence."

It is significant, also, that the sociometrist, Helen H. Jennings, emphasizing as she does that leadership is the product of "interpersonal interaction and not of the attributes residing within persons," nevertheless concludes that while leadership roles differ greatly, certain *constant* characteristics of leaders were found in her own studies. Her comments seem to be of such crucial theoretical importance as to deserve extensive quotation:

In a population so large as that of the test-community, the varieties of leadership are manifold. Nevertheless, in personality a number of characteristics of leaders stand out as common attributes. *Each leader 'improves' from the point of view of the membership, through one method or the other, the social milieu. Each widens the social field for participation of others (and indirectly her own social space) by ingratiating them into activities, introducing new activities, and by fostering tolerance on the part of one member towards another. Each leader shows a feeling for when to censure and when to praise. . . . No leader is invariably a 'pleasant' person . . . instead each is definite in her stand and will fight for what she considers 'right' . . . each leader appears to succeed in controlling her own moods at least to the extent of not inflicting negative feelings of depression or anxiety upon others. Each appears to hold her own counsel and not to confide her personal worries except to a selected friend or two. . . . Each appears able to establish rapport quickly and effectively with a wide range of other personalities. . . . Each appears to possess to a greater or less degree unusual capacity to identify with others. . . .*

Gibb makes a similar comment: "There do seem to be, however, certain general characteristics of personality, the possession of which does not necessarily cause a man to have leadership status conferred upon him, but which does place him higher than he would otherwise be on the scale of choice in *any* group." (Our emphasis—A.W.G.)

The hypothesis that there are *some* traits common to all leaders is presently *unfashionable*. Recognition that this is so should serve as a warning signal, cautioning scientist and layman alike to "go slow." For without the utmost care we may too easily shrug aside the potentialities of this hypothesis. Several questions devolve about the problem:

1. Do social scientists today have any reliable evidence concerning allegedly universal leadership traits?

2. Whether or not such evidence exists, what reasons may be advanced for expecting that some traits common to all leaders might be found?

3. Finally, and this is the most crucial question of all, how is it that some traits have not been discovered which—while not universal— are at least common to leaders in more than one or two situations or groups? Jenkins' study found, for example, "wide variations in the characteristics of individuals who become leaders in *similar* situations, and even greater divergence in leadership behavior in different situations."

To consider the first question, is there any reliable evidence demonstrating the existence of traits common to all leaders? The answer is plainly no. Jenkins notes that a "number of studies suggest superiority of leaders over those in their groups in physique, age, education, and socio-economic background. . . ." He is perhaps enjoying an understatement when he adds: " . . . but the need for further research in this connection is evident."

INTELLIGENCE AS A LEADERSHIP TRAIT

"Psychosexual appeal" aside, Brown's reference to intelligence would seem a more formidable candidate for status as a universal trait. The work of Caldwell, Wellman, Partridge, Wetzel, Hollingworth, Fence, Carroll, and others has long suggested certain definite relationships between the leaders' intelligence and the average intelligence in their groups. These relationships appear to be twofold: (a) The leader tends to have an intelligence higher than the average in his group, and (b) there is a limit to the superiority of intelligence which a leader may possess. That is, superiority of intelligence beyond a certain degree, relative to the group, may prevent an individual from obtaining or holding onto leadership.

Regarding this last point, Murphy, Murphy, and Newcomb comment: "Children who are too superior in age and abilities are not accepted as leaders. For instance, children with intelligence quotients of 150 are more likely to be leaders in a group of children with intelligence quotients in the neighborhood of 130 to 140 than in a group of children with average intelligence."

The evidence is, however, by no means definitive. Perhaps the most which may be said is that lower than (group) average intelligence inhibits access to leadership, but higher than average intelligence is no guarantee of leadership. It should be emphasized, in passing, that those who would attribute to intelligence a role in leadership usually insist that the *specific level* of intelligence, either aiding or impeding leadership, is a function of the average of the group. So much of the evidence on this problem derives also from studies of children's groups that its applicability to adult situations is doubtful. Moreover, Krout relates, "The great men of the civilized world have been analyzed for us by competent psychologists on the basis of materials sufficient to determine brightness or intelligence. The results seem to show that 'great men,' including outstanding leaders in the public life of Europe and America, range all the way from dull normal to genius."

At this time there is no reliable evidence concerning the existence of universal leadership traits. Murphy, Murphy, and Newcomb suggest that "If there is such a thing as a psychology of leadership in the abstract, it will arise from studies in which behavior resemblances of leaders in varying life situations are investigated. . . ." In other words, the conduct of situationally oriented studies, far from impeding, may be the only basis for determining which of the traits of leaders are universal. This is a sound injunction, and deserves some amplification.

The crucial problem seems to be one of the *direction* in which leadership traits universal to all situations might be sought. It may well be that no universal traits have been found because those which might exist are very different from those conventionally anticipated, e.g., intelligence, superior height, etc. The mere study of leadership traits in different situations, and the comparison of these findings, however indispensable, will only *fortuitously* lead to the discovery of universal leadership traits unless *each* study is guided by theoretically rooted hypotheses.

The second question asked above now becomes relevant; on what grounds may we suspect the existence of universal traits? Why should any traits be *universal* to leadership? Whether traits are universal, or only specific to concrete situations, it is necessary to explain *why* they are manifested by the leadership and found useful to them.

Consideration of this problem may be opened by noting the popular formulation: "Leadership, or leadership traits, are relative to the situation." This means that a person's traits either develop out of his experience in playing a leadership role or that given types of leadership roles will attract individuals who already possess traits useful in the performance of the role. The diversity of leadership traits mentioned is presumed to be, in one of the two ways mentioned, a response to the diversity of the situation and the group.

Suppose, however, it were demonstrated that all human groups contained *some* elements in common, and that these could be spelled out. It should therefore be expected that there would be *some* leadership traits manifested commonly by all leaders. In short, there is no reason why leadership traits should constitute adaptations only to the *diversities* of groups; they should, too, involve adaptations to the *similarities* of groups. Thus some leadership traits should be unique, specific to concrete groups and situations, while *some* could be common to all leaders. . . .

Index of Names

(Names of contributors to this volume are capitalized.)